A HISTORY OF
VIOLENCE:
An Encyclopedia of
1400 Chicago Mob Murders
1st Edition

by

Dr. Wayne A. Johnson

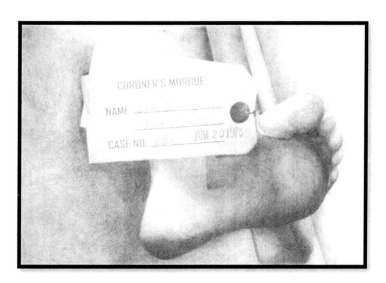

Dr. Wayne A. Johnson
Harper College
Chicago Police Department (retired)
Former Chief Investigator Chicago Crime Commission

Eddie O'Hare dead 1939

An LLR Book.

LLR

Litchfield Literary Books.

6845 Elm Street, McLean Va. 22101

(866) 248-7924

Infor@LitchfieldLiteraryBooks.Com

Visit our Web site: WWW. Litchfield Literary Books.Com

Contents

Acknowledgements-6

Caveat-7

About the Author-8

Chicago Outfit Bosses-9

Introduction-11

Chapter 1. Pre 1920s, Critical Events of the pre-1920s-20

Chapter 2. The 1920s, Critical Events of the 1920s-34

Chapter 3. The 1930s, Critical Events of the 1930s-127

Chapter 4. The 1940s, Critical Events of the 1940s-174

Chapter 5. The 1950s, Critical Events of the 1950s-196

Chapter 6. The 1960s, Critical Events of the 1960s-216

Chapter 7. The Critical Events of the 1970s-237

Chapter 8. The Critical Events of the 1980s-265

Chapter 9. The Critical Events of the 1990s-284

Chapter 10. The Critical Events of the new Millennium-288

The Outfit Street Crews-TOC Murder-290

Timeline-292

Photo Index-336

Bibliography-337

Internet Sources-339

Acknowledgements: I wish to sincerely thank the following persons for their help in preparing this book: Arthur J. Bilek, John Binder, Jeanette Callaway, Jackie Cooney, J.R. Davis, James Hubbard, Rich Lindberg, Allan May, Charito Romero, Gus Russo, Steve Simon, John W. Tuohy, Harper College Art Student Daniella Boyd (Cover Art) and many Law Enforcement personnel and Prosecutors who wish to remain anonymous.

This book is dedicated to the memory of my father Major Joseph L. Johnson
My inspiration in life
And
For my wife Donna and my sons Adam and Kevin
With Love and Gratitude

Caveat: This book in its first edition attempts to memorialize every murder at the hand of Chicago's Traditional Organized Crime factions i.e. Mob, Outfit or Syndicate or any individual associated with these insidious organizations. Working with newspaper articles, police reports, coroners reports and archives it is possible for mistakes to be made. Names, dates, locations and other data could be incorrect. If the reader comes across any mistakes, the author would appreciate being contacted so corrections may be announced on his website. Take note that sections marked as; *Police logs entered the case as follows:* are not edited and appear as they were scribed by police officials. If family members or friends of the people mentioned in this book would like to contribute additional information the author can be contacted. Crimes designated as Mob murders have acquired this status by a multitude of entities i.e. law enforcement, coroners' findings, prosecutors' offices, investigators, authors and the media. What we find here is that many of these crimes may not appear on every list. We can only assume that the common apathy and corrupt practices of the times contributed to this phenomenon. Everyday people of past generations take information regarding these crimes to the grave. My hope is that this books stirs emotions so strong that people step forward and offer up details of these crimes that may allow for a second edition of this book or even a solution to a long ago crime of the century. A portion of the proceeds from this book will be set aside in escrow and will be used to provide rewards for any information that leads to a case being solved.

Send information to:

HistoryofviolenceChicago@gmail.com

View our blogs at:

http://ahistoryofviolenceinchicago.blogspot.com/

http://drwaynejohnsonauthorcrimehistorian.blogspot.com/

SOLVED/ thefreedictionary.com defines "solved" as: **1.** To find a solution to.
2. To work out a correct solution to (a problem). While in a criminal context this word conjures up visions of great investigations, exciting arrests and successful criminal prosecutions. For the purposes of this book the cases deemed as **(solved)** may mean several things that include an investigation, arrest and prosecution, but may also mean a case that had been reversed on appeal, a not guilty verdict provided by a corrupt judge or jury or even an offender named by a source the author finds reliable.

About the Author

Dr. Wayne A. Johnson served as a member of the Chicago Police Department (retired) for 25 years with distinction. In his last assignment he supervised the Analytical Unit of the Intelligence Section, Organized Crime Division where he furthered his knowledge of The Chicago Mob.

Wayne's notable work with the Intelligence Section led him to his next appointment as Chief Investigator for the legendary Chicago Crime Commission, holding the position originally created by the much celebrated organized crime investigator, Virgil Peterson. During Wayne's five years at the helm as Chief Investigator he investigated and monitored The Chicago Mob.

The national notoriety Wayne received as the Crime Commissions investigator led to his recruitment as the first and only Superintendent of Police/Inspector General for the Town of Cicero, Illinois.

Mr. Johnson earned his Doctor of Education degree from Northern Illinois University, and Master of Science degree in Criminal-Social Justice from Lewis University in Romeoville, Illinois. He serves as an Associate Professor and Program Coordinator of Law Enforcement Programs at Harper College in Palatine, Illinois.

Wayne is also a nationally recognized investigative and educational consultant for law enforcement and the security industry and is widely considered to be one of the nation's leading authorities on Chicago Organized Crime.

Dr. Johnson has also lectured extensively on not only Organized Crime but also on Homicide Investigations, Criminal Profiling, Violence in the Workplace and Gang Crimes. He has been interviewed as an authority for numerous television specials on organized crime including the Biography Channel's in depth program on Mob Boss Anthony Accardo.

He has authored and co-authored articles in Law Enforcement and Education, most notably a Chicago Crime Commission ground breaking report on Organized Crime.

Professor Johnson's doctoral research "A Naturalistic Study of Homicide Investigation Expertise: Implications for Continuing Criminal Justice Education" is available through Bell and Howell Information Services-ProQuest Digital Dissertations at http://wwwlib.umi.com/dissertation/.

CHICAGO MOB/OUTFIT BOSSES 1910-1999

Southside

James "Big Jim/ Diamond Jim" Colosimo
1910-1919

Johnny "The Fox" Torrio
1920-1924

Al " Scarface" Capone
1925-1931

Frank "The Enforcer" Nitti
1932-1939

Paul " The Waiter" Ricca
1939-1944

Tony "The Big Tuna/Joe Batters" Accardo
1944-1956

Sam Giancana AKA: Momo Salvatore, Mooney, or Gilormo Giangono
1956- 1966

Sam "Teetz" Battaglia
1966

Felix "Milwaukee Phil" Alderisio
1967

Jackie Cerone
1968

Tony "The Big Tuna/Joe Batters" Accardo
1969

Fiore "FiFi" Bucierri
1969-1973

James "Turk" Turello
1973-1979

Joey "Doves" Aiuppa
1979-1986

Joe "Joe Negal" Feriola
1986-1989

Sam "Wings" Carlisi
1989-1992

John "No Nose" DiFronzo
1992-2011

Michael Sarno and Salvatore Cataudella
2011-????

Northside Gang Bosses
Charles Dion "Deanie" O'Banion
Hymie Weiss AKA: Earl Wajciechowski
Vincent "Schemer" Drucci AKA: DiAmbrosio
George "Bugs" Moran AKA: George Gage
Edward M. "Teddy" Newberry

Introduction

While leaving the courthouse at 26th and California in Chicago adrenaline coursed through my body causing palpitations. The discussion I just had over the phone with a federal inmate/informant revealed a chance to solve dozens of Mob killings and in doing so could lead to being the greatest Mob case the Cook County State's Attorney ever prosecuted.

This series of events started when my Commander in the Intelligence Section (Investigates and tracks the Chicago Outfit) of the Chicago Police Department assigned my partner and myself to work some old Mob murders with the Special Prosecutions Unit of the States Attorney's office. What I would learn over the next two years was there were a great many officials in law enforcement and government that did not want the boat rocked so to speak. My investigation became an exercise in futility and frustration and in the end I was not allowed to meet with or even contact the federal inmate/informant again.

At the local level we did push forward and in 1995 arrested Lenny Patrick, a prolific Mob hitman, for three killings, one of which occurred before I was born. In the end, even Lenny who killed many more than three people, beat us. For unexplained reasons the charges against him were dropped in 1996 and he lived to an old age and died a free man in suburban Chicago in 2006.

While we discuss organized crime in the mid-west with Chicago as its place of origin, I will reflect on events from the past. In doing this, we can talk about the realities of organized crime, what it is and what it is not, and how we should go about dealing with it in the future.

By Federal definition the Chicago Mob/Syndicate/OUTFIT is: An organized criminal enterprise which operates in Chicago and across the U. S., Locally, it has its roots in the prohibition era, it is a resilient and opportunistic criminal enterprise that is reflective and adaptive. It has learned from the mistakes of the past and views the future the same way any legitimate business may, using organizational and management principals to its own advantage. More than any time in the past, the OUTFIT will now work with other criminal organizations to turn a profit.

The one element that makes the OUTFIT the most allusive Traditional Organized Crime (TOC) entity to stifle, is its acceptance to American society, our political establishment and the pop culture that continues to romanticize TOC through misrepresentations i.e. the TV programs *The Sopranos* and *The Untouchables*. This coupled with misinformation by academics, politicians, law enforcement itself and the media makes public apathy an almost insurmountable obstacle in fighting TOC in America.

One myth we can dispelled right now is that: In the early days (1920s) TOC in Chicago was a collaborative venture run by the Torrio-Capone MOB. In reality conflict was the norm and many other gangs vied for a piece of the action in bootlegging and vice that included groups such as: the Unione Siciliana, Black Hand extortionists, the Gennas, the Aiellos, the Saltis-McErlane gang, the Marty Guilfoyle gang, the Druggan-Lake Valley gang, the Ralph Sheldon gang, Eddie Tancel in Cicero, the Westside O'Donnells, the Southside O'Donnells, the Touhy gang and the north side O'Banion-Weiss-Drucci-Moran gang. All of these gangs and their outlandish associates were in near constant conflict over territorial rights and boundaries.

What most people don't know is that in the early years of Prohibition many illicit partnerships formed between different gangs who were active in different rackets i.e. gambling, prostitution, robbery, burglary, kidnapping and bootlegging. But, what is most revealing is the fact that some of the strongest partnerships, such as the O'Banion partnership with the Torrio gang in breweries and casinos soured and was just one element that led to the bloody "Beer Wars" which left hundreds of hoodlums dead.

Chicago, like other large American cities saw TOC spring from street gangs that were sometimes formed for the purposes of disrupting union activities and even worked on behalf of warring newspapers in the early part of the 20th century.

Other myths include: The Chicago MOB-Syndicate- OUTFIT is Cosa Nostra or Italian Mafia. It is Not, Rocco Infelise the late former boss of the Taylor St. crew would carry out Mafia like rituals and tried to do things the "Old Way". His contemporaries would laugh at him behind his back for doing this.

Recent *Family Secrets* prosecutions did reveal more rituals, but I insist it was not the everyday protocol for a gang that put non-Italians in leadership roles. What was more common was that others would simply be told "you are one of us now" the meaning was implied.

Joey "The Clown" Lombardo

12

In 1989, Joe Lombardo, the charismatic OUTFIT advisor, stated during a detailed deposition that he never took part in any Mafia rituals that included bloodletting, oaths, burning paper, or using guns and daggers.

We must consider organized crime's effects on our major cities. The OUTFIT was developed and nurtured by ethnic groups of Irish, Jews, and Italians. Today's reality is that organized groups of Blacks, Puerto Ricans, Mexicans, Russians, Poles, Eastern Europeans, Asians, Drug Cartels, Motor Cycle Gangs, Street Gangs and South American Theft Groups are equally as troubling for Law Enforcement and now known as Non-Traditional Organized Crime (NTOC) according to the Chicago Crime Commission (CCC).

The closest Chicago TOC ever came to the Mafia was through the influence of the Unione Siciliana, groups such as Black Hand extortionist from Sicily, the northside Aiellos or the Terrible Gennas (an immigrant Taylor St. family, promoting alky cookers who fought for control of bootlegging in the area). Unione Siciliana was a benevolent organization of immigrant Sicilians that provided insurance, jobs and social services for its constituents. Although nationwide with tens of thousands of members, it was a little known organization until prohibition began and members began producing alcohol in their homes to increase their incomes. The group was originally from Sicily and lost members to killings at the hands of the north side gang and Capone. Another way Chicago organized crime mimic's the Mafia is in the terminology it uses to define itself. Terminology used by Mafia members in the East Coast Families (The Lucchese's, Gambino's etc.) are almost never used by members of the Chicago mob.

However, for rhetorical purposes I will provide some terminology to juxtapose Chicago terminology with traditional Mafia terminology as an example of what is common in east coast vernacular but, not heard in the environs of Chicago's TOC hangouts:

Mafia Terms:	Chicago Terms:
Famiglia-Borgata-Family	Crime Syndicate-Mob-OUTFIT
Crime Syndicate-Camorra-criminal society	Boss
Capo-Padrone	Advisor
Consigliere	Underboss
Sotto Capo/Underboss	Area Boss (overseer of geographic designations or crime specialties)
Caporegime/Captains	Area Underboss/Lieutenant
Capodecina-chief of ten	Crew Boss
Soldati-Soldiers or made guys	Members-Associates
Mafia-This thing of ours-Our thing	The Code of Silence
Omerta-the law of manliness or silence	Street Crew-Area Crew

The most common problem with tracking TOC is the ambiguity of terms and designations between members and associates. *An associate in organized crime is a person, a criminal, who is not a full-fledged member of the organization but does business with the organization either occasionally or exclusively and agrees to abide by the rules of the organization when conducting criminal business.*

Experts in the field that contributed to seminal CCC reports went on to estimate the number of associates in the Chicago OUTFIT at 700 to 1,200. This process is further complicated by federal authorities who insist on enacting east coast standards of the Mafia, mainly by using the ceremony of promoting a member to "Made" status. Again, as stated before these rituals have no place in the Chicago OUTFIT especially with members like Gus Alex, Murray Humphreys, Lenny Patrick and Frank Schweihs who have held positions of great significance but, are certainly not Sicilian or even Italian for that matter.

Until local and federal law enforcement steps up and supplies realistic definitions and descriptions for this level in the OUTFIT, it will be impossible to accurately determine the depth and breadth of TOC in Chicago. Since state and local law enforcement has deferred this responsibility to federal agencies, monitoring the activities of known TOC members will only be carried out as they relate to RICO cases and federal violations.

Most large city police departments have reassigned investigators who tracked mobsters for decades to other duties like street gangs and terrorism. Federal agents now focused on terrorism themselves seem only to pursue Mob cases when information is brought to them as in the case of the notorious "Family Secrets" case in Chicago. In that case the son of a Mob killer contacted federal agents and provided information which led to the investigation that resulted is several arrests and the solution of 18 murders occurring over several decades.

This was not the case in the late 60s and early 70s when Chicago Intelligence Detectives collaborated with Federal Agents and Prosecutors in a Federal Strike Force. Illustrated by a report from that era known as the "Top 300 Hoods in Chicago" this report provided names and details about individual mobsters and laid out a detailed organizational structure for the gang. This index was completed between (1974-5) by investigators (although no agency name appeared on the document) when resources and expertise was at a milestone in Chicago. Agency trust existed to a degree and cooperation was in vogue.

By Federal definition the Chicago Mob/Syndicate/OUTFIT is:

An organized criminal enterprise which operates in Chicago and across the U. S., Locally, it has its roots in the prohibition era, it is a resilient and opportunistic criminal enterprise that is reflective and adaptive. It has learned from the mistakes of the past and views the future the same way any legitimate business may, using organizational and management principals to its own advantage. More than any time in the past, the OUTFIT will now work with other criminal organizations to turn a profit.

Chicago TOC is considered a true crime syndicate in which all the gangs working in the local criminal rackets were courted by early mob boss John Torrio for the purpose of controlling all liquor distribution in the Chicago area during Prohibition.

It was Torrio that first hosted meetings that invited the leaders of these various rackets to consider merging in order to capitalize on the seemingly endless opportunities presented by prohibition. Many of the rackets did merge with the Capone organization, while others such as the Northside O'Banion-Weis-Drucci-Moran gang developed limited partnerships with the Southside gang. However, after a dispute over an Angelo Genna gambling debt at a Cicero joint-venture casino named "The Ship", the Northsiders felt betrayed in their business dealings with Torrio and fought to the bitter end, until they were either killed off or run out of Chicago. It was at that point that the Capone gang reigned supreme eventually becoming known as the Chicago OUTFIT.

A national organization was formalized by 1930 through John Torrio's genius and brought leaders from several large city TOC groups together in what was referred to as the "Commission".

The National Coalition of Gang Leaders known as the Commission would meet across the country as noted in Chicago (1928), Atlantic City (1929), Havana (1946), Appalachian, NY (1957), New Jersey, (1977), just to name a few that law enforcement learned of over the years. The Commission still exists today and facilitates TOC operations in the Mid-West, Las Vegas, Louisiana, Florida and California as well as outside the U.S., such as in the Caribbean.

What the two forms of TOC (Mafia - OUTFIT) do share are organizational attributes that not only allows them to exist, but adds to their success. They are developed from standards of conduct developed in Southern Italy. Concepts dealing with manliness/loyalty/silence "Omerta" and territory are central to their beliefs.

Abadinsky, probably the most prolific author of texts dealing with this topic, provides us with a concise list of what we consider shared traits among different types of Organized Crime groups i.e. TOC (Outfit, Mob) and NTOC, (Outlaw Motorcycle Gangs, Street Gangs and some ethnic organized crime groups), they are:

Nonideological (money-power)
Hierarchical (at least three levels)
Communication from top down (verbal)
Limited or exclusive membership (sponsor)
Use of violence and corruption
Exhibits a clear division of labor
Assignments based on skill
Carried out in an impersonal manner
Monopolistic i.e. gambling, vice, unions
Governed by strict rules and regulations
Perpetuates itself (reflective-adaptive)

My Kinda Town

Chicago was incorporated as a city in 1837 and adapted a political system fashioned after those in Boston and New York more commonly known as the Tammany Hall, Ward system of politics.

Members of what was known as the Tammany Organization sprang from the Society of Saint Tammany that formed in 1789 as a fraternal and patriotic society with chapters in several states and soon became the predominate political organization in New York. Tammany's leaders controlled high political appointments and elected officials on a local, state and federal levels.

Tammany Hall

Although originally known as nativist and Anti-Catholic, Tammany was a natural fit for immigrant Irish who spoke English, were willing to use their fists to bend the situation to their advantage. These Tammany characteristics became endemic to big city democratic organizations and their police departments and also extended out to the criminal element and as a result a close relationship was established between these political organizations and the street gangs that emerged in the growing ghettos of eastern cities. These New York street gangs (5 points, Bowery Boys, Cherry Hill), the precursors to TOC were quit effective in providing services for fees i.e. Punching $2, leg or arm broken $19, Murder $100. The political powers found great acceptance in plying these skills during election campaigns.

The stage was being set for the emergence of Chicago TOC and the next prominent myth of the day being: "TOC is an entity started and perpetuated by the Italian Mafia".

In reality, what has evolved into TOC in Chicago was facilitated first by Michael Cassius McDonald, who in 1873 was the gambling boss in Chicago, which was then a wide open town, run by gamblers, the liquor interests and brothel keepers, most of whom were Irish and politically active. The reality is that the first known appearance of any Mafia element was not in Chicago or New York at all, but rather in New Orleans in the 1870s.

Prosecutions in the wide ranging Family Secrets case in Chicago did reveal more rituals, but I insist it was not the everyday protocol for a gang that put non-Italians in leadership roles. What was more common was that others would simply be told "you are one of us now" the meaning was implied.

Mike McDonald

Membership in those early Mafia organizations was exclusively Sicilian and remained that way for decades.

Chicago's Ward system of government encouraged a decentralized political system allowing for Ward alderman (councilmen, healers, gray wolves) to develop fiefdoms and maintain absolute control over their kingdoms from selecting police captains to hiring workers for other ancillary city and county departments. Most employment involved fees paid directly to the ward alderman or committeeman. This authority used associations with mobsters to provide them with no-show jobs and muscle used during elections. The association with the gangs developed into a political unit known as the "West Block". This group of city alderman and state legislators would fight legislation that could improve law enforcement efforts against mobsters.

The Chicago Mob, unlike many Cosa Nostra/Mafia cities in the east, was a cooperative venture, but the Italians in fact soon became dominant. All important decisions are made at the executive level, where disputes are also resolved and contacts with outside organizations are controlled.

Mike McDonald, Chicago's gambling boss found himself with a foot in two arenas, gambling rackets and politics. Liquor played a significant role in McDonald's empire. His gambling activities were run from saloons and before the turn of the century there were 4,000 saloons in Chicago with a population of approx. 1,698,000 compared to approx. 5,000 taverns licensed currently with a population of 2,842,000. This indicated just how important liquor was to the mostly immigrant populace. The city leadership at the time also found it important to their existence with close to 20 percent of the city council members being in the liquor business.

It seemed that law enforcement around the turn of the century was concerned more with serving their political masters than the public or even the police chief. Most police activities surrounded union-anarchist movements, Clan Na Gael beliefs (Irish independence from England) and graft on behalf of the politician/gamblers who ran their wards from saloons across the city. McDonald was the first Chicago leader to establish a strong "Political Machine" later transforming into the Cook County Democratic Machine that was developed to perfection by Mayor Anton Cermak.

In the 19th century, Chicago's two largest immigrant groups were the Germans and the Irish. Although both European in origin, they were vastly separated by distinct cultural differences as well as the Irishmen's mastery over the English language. Not hobnailed by having to learn a new language, the Irish spoke English and easily glided into TOC, Law Enforcement and politics. Beginning in the 20th century with the emergence of Chicago TOC, 2 other prominent ethnic groups entered into it, those being Italians and Jews.

"Prohibition, in all its nobility and good intentions caused crime in America to skyrocket. Chicago and most other large American cities witnessed the rapid growth of common street gangs to large, complex criminal organizations".

The little publicized "Circulation War" which was a precursor to prohibition, pitted some of the most powerful publishers in the country against each other. In this war that ran from 1900 to approximately 1920 the newspaper executives controlling the battlefield incorporated the same sluggers, gangsters, racketeers and youth gangs as did the bootleggers, unions and vice mongers of the era. Harold Ickes a former political editor for the Chicago Record and Secretary of the Interior under FDR put it succinctly when he stated "After all, gangsterism which was a disgrace to this country for so long originated in Chicago where it grew out of the circulation war between Hearst and McCormick".

Chapter 1. Pre-1920s

From Chicago's inception as a city to the time of Prohibition, organized crime was carried out by dozens of racketeers, gangs or crews involved in different crimes ranging from thefts, gambling and vice to extortion via protective associations. Liquor interests and brothel keepers developed into a formidable political power that used dishonest Law Enforcement officers for their own means.

During the (American) civil war, Chicago's gambling/ political boss Mike McDonald a master gambler/politician used bounty hunters to help recruit men for various Union Army regiments. His gambling empire profited magnificently at the end of the war through the various gambling houses and brothels he owned as the city was flooded by returning soldiers eager for a good time. To secure a formal position of power he chose a gambler friend as a candidate for Mayor. Harvey Colvin easily won the office and McDonald reigned as the leader of the Democratic Machine until the turn of the century.

By the 1890s his power grew and allowed him to control politics and most rackets, anyone wishing to do such business in the city had to give "King Mike" and his machine a large portion of their profits.

In the late 1890s as he grew older and became weary, Mike's political mantle was assumed by a pair of eager first ward politicians, Michael "Hinky Dink" Kenna and John "Bathhouse" Coughlin. These men became political masters while the growing gambling interests were taken to a new level by Monte Tennes who in 1907 developed a nationwide wire service that provided timely racing information to the entire country by telegraph wires, locally he controlled several hundred handbooks and most gambling on the Northside. He protected them from police raids by graft and required anyone who wanted to enter the business to apply through him. However, when he tried to wrestle control of gambling in the loop from Tom McGinnis a bombing war transpired. These territorial concerns would continue for decades and Tennes would survive long enough to collaborate with the Chicago Mob that grew out of the infamous first ward until he became subordinate to them for his own survival.

Monte Tennes

Hink and Bath as they were known, found themselves deeply involved in gambling and crime while mastering a political organization. Their associations and importance to mayoral candidates was unquestioned. Their skillful use of street gangs in political functions fell right in line with their east coast Tammany Hall counterparts.

They financed their political war chest with the Annual First Ward Democratic Ball that brought the two 25 thousand dollars yearly and saw politicians, police officials, and vice peddlers come together for the event. It grew so large that it was held in an armory and so outrageous that in 1910 the Federated Counsel of Churches and the Catholic Church denounced it and demanded it stop. The groups also asked for the formation of a municipal vice commission. The commission that emerged was funded by the City Council and released its first report by 1911 detailing vice conditions in the city.

Michael "Hinky Dink" Kenna and John "Bathhouse" Coughlin.

In 1897, shortly after the two skillfully orchestrated the nomination of democratic candidate Carter Harrison Jr. for Mayor, New York's Tammany Boss Richard Croker recruited Kenna to assist in a mayoral campaign in New York. He did and that candidate won by a large margin.

Over the next several years the pair remained the preeminent political force in Chicago, until Mayor Harrison broke with them and enacted some reform in the city. This caused the men to try and align themselves with a Republican candidate for Mayor by the name of William "Big Bill" "Bill the Builder" Thompson. This man ran as a reformer, but within months of his 1915 election broke every campaign promise he ever made and in a study (2000) from the University of Illinois at Chicago was considered the worst Chicago Mayor of all time.

Mayor William "Big Bill" Thompson

It was during this stretch that Hink, Bath and Tennes found out what the future of TOC in Chicago's first ward would be. Their power and influence was reduced significantly under the Republican mayor, with which they had little standing. One of their precinct captains, who garnered much of the first ward's Italian vote, emerged as a growing force and took control over the red light district known as the "Levee". This man was James "Big Jim" or "Diamond Jim" Colosimo. Colosimo after coming from Italy via New York as a child in 1872 grew up in the district developing work skills and criminal skills to include: pickpocket, pimp, white slaver and ultimately brothel keeper. All while on the city payroll as a street cleaner and later a foreman. He eventually formed the sweeps into a social club that later became a labor union, a precursor to one of the many labor unions that provide city services to this day.

James "Big Jim" or "Diamond Jim" Colosimo

Big Jim also ran Colosimo's Café which opened in 1897 and entertained luminaries from society, entertainment, politics and Law Enforcement. His success made him the target of Black Hand (La Mano Negro) extortionists. (Black Handers were immigrant Sicilian/Italians who would target successful Italian businessmen and threaten harm to the men or their families by use of gun or bomb. Notes were written that would be marked with an outline of a hand and at shootings it was a Blackhand symbol to toss a gun used, at the corpse of their victim). In response to this, Colosimo employed the help of a New York tough named Johnny "The Fox" Torrio of the "Five Points gang" and an associate of Frankie Yale AKA: Uale or Ioele. Yale was the National Head of the Unione Siciliana the fraternal organization for immigrant Sicilians with a Chicago chapter that started in 1895. Torrio is said to have been related (never proven) to Colosimo or his wife and took up the task of protecting the vice kingpin.

It was reported that he was a business associate of Big Jim and was lured to Chicago in 1909 to work for him. One of Torrio's first tasks was to deal with the Blackhand extortionists who had threatened his boss. It was shortly after this problem was eradicated that Colosimo gave Torrio his own place in Burnham, IL. Shortly thereafter Colosimo purchased the Arrowhead Inn in Burnham and became a competitor to his own subordinate. This put a great deal of strain on the relationship.

The Turn of the Century

By this time Torrio took up the task of running most of Colosimo's operations, which allowed Big Jim to spend time with his second wife Victoria Moresco who he married in 1902. They would attend the opera on a regular basis.

During his tenure Colosimo imported more than 600 young women for sale in the flesh trade by 1909. This led to a scrape with the federal authorities over white slavery allegations (Mann Act, 1910), which went away when the complainant was murdered. Later the decision by city leaders to shut down the Levee (1912) in response to public outrage caused Torrio to expand into several suburbs of Chicago. The roadside brothels and gambling establishments known as "roadhouses", along with other TOC interests were scattered throughout the suburbs of southern Cook County with the bribing of public officials and residents in Burnham, Stickney, Cicero, Posen, Burr Oaks, Blue Island, Steger and Chicago Heights. Torrio then opened the "Four Deuces" a block from Colosimo's and set up his headquarters there along with a saloon, brothel and gambling house. Business was good and John Torrio was a shrewd manager making Jim Colosimo very rich as he expanded his holdings to 35 houses.

Critical Events of the pre-1920s:

On **July 6, 1900** Harry Bush was stabbed to death at Armour Ave. and 29th St. over Circulation War issues. The attacker Wm. Armstead was convicted and sentenced to a life term in prison **(solved)**.

On **March 8, 1901** Morris F. Clark was shot to death at 35th and Cottage Grove Ave. by Lawrence Finn who was aided by Jack Daley AKA: Chicago Jack. The men worked for rival newspapers and this was an example of the violence surrounding the Circulation War. Both men were acquitted at trial **(solved)**.

On **September 28, 1901** William B. Craig was shot to death at Wells and Kinzie Sts. by Joseph Greenburg. The men worked in the newspaper business and this killing was a result of the Circulation War. The defendant was convicted of Manslaughter **(solved)**.

On **November 12, 1905** Raia Biaggis 37 yrs. was shot to death in front of his store at 100 Milton Ave. by a gang of men identified as George Fiorenzo, Vito Cape (or Capone) and Colegro Lucicero who were detained and eventually released. George Maggio, Callegro Montalbano, Pietro Merio and Michael Armato were also arrested for the crime and indicted. Armato was acquitted at trial and the outcome of the others is unknown although officials at the time classified the crime as a gang killing, possibly Blackhand related **(solved)**.

On **November 30, 1906** Richard Thorus 27 yrs. was shot on the street at 4500 S. Halsted St. during a dispute related to the circulation wars and the associated labor racketeering. He was taken to St. Bernard's Hospital where he died on December 3, 1906. James Ragen was charged with the shooting and acquitted after a trial **(solved)**.

In **1911** Federal authorities raided a whorehouse in Bridgeport, Connecticut and interviewed an unidentified prostitute that claimed she was transported there against her will from Chicago by John Torrio and Maurice Van Bever both working for Jim Colosimo. The girl agreed to testify against the men and was kept in a local jail for her protection. Chicago prosecutors were notified and began to prepare an indictment. Torrio was tipped to this situation by his informants in the police department and notified his associate on the east coast, Frankie Yale. Yale arranged for two of his men to go to the jail and pose as federal agents and remove the girl for her protection. The following day the girl was found in a Bridgeport cemetery, dead with twelve bullet wounds. The jailers identified the two bogus agents as members of the James Street Gang that Torrio once led although in is not known if they were ever apprehended and charged. Torrio and Colosimo were questioned at the federal building in Chicago and later released.

Frankie Yale

On **March 23, 1911** Vincent Altman 32 yrs. was shot and killed in the Briggs House barroom by Maurice "Mossie" Enright AKA: Moss of 1110 W. Garfield Boulevard, Thomas Kearney a prominent labor leader, Sean O'Donnell and Jos. Galvin. The victim Altman was a former police officer who was dismissed in 1906 on brutality charges and became a labor slugger and bomber opposing Enright, one of the most powerful labor racketeers of the time. Enright and Kearney were eventually arrested and Enright was convicted of the crime and sentenced to life in prison. He would use his political influence to be pardoned of the crime after serving only two years in prison. Union issues and the "Circulation Wars" provided a motive for this murder **(solved).**

On **May 22, 1911** William "Dutch" Gentleman 28 yrs. was shot and killed by Maurice "Mossie" Enright AKA: Moss and Chas. McAndrews in Pat O'Mally's saloon at 166 N. State Street. Enright claimed self-defense. He was not charged in this murder while McAndrews was, but after being indicted was released and the charges dropped. Union issues and the "Circulation Wars" provided a motive for this murder **(Solved).**

Sometime in **1911** James Bukucci disappeared and was presumed murdered. He was a victim of Black Hand extortionist and was instructed to contact Bruno Roti who was connected to the Colosimo Gang. Roti was arrested after Bukucci's home was blown up, but when it came to the trial Bukucci was missing and never seen again.

On **November 22, 1911** Pasquale Damico, Francisco Denello and Stefano Denello were shot at a railroad crossing at 2047 Archer Road. Two of the men were dead on the scene and the third died later at a hospital. These are the three Black Hand extortionists that were trying to victimize Big Jim Colosimo until John Torrio set them up and shot them although he was never charged.

On **June 15, 1912** Frank Witt 27 yrs. was shot to death by Edward and Chas. Barrett and Arthur Friedman during a riot related to the Circulation Wars and associated Union racketeering. The civil unrest occurred at 5ᵗʰ Ave. and Washington St. The accused were acquitted at trial **(solved).**

Chas. Fischetti

On **August 8, 1912** George Hehr 25 yrs. was shot to death by Edw. Barrett, James Ruggio, John Howard, Thos. Delahanty, Wm. Masterson, Harry Wilson and John Rioza. The incidents occurred during civil unrest related to the circulation wars and the associated union racketeering. The incident occurred at Adams and DesPlaines Sts. The perpetrators were taken in front of a Grand Jury who returned a no bill and no charges were placed **(solved)**.

On **January 20, 1913** Patrolman Peter M. Hart was shot to death in a struggle over his weapon while trying to arrest Robert Webb, a member of the Perry Auto Gang. During his questioning Webb placed blame on an associate he knew as "Dago Mike" Cassella, the owner of the building he lived in and a self-admitted black hander. However, the police built their case against Webb and he was convicted and sentenced to Life in prison **(solved)**.

On **April 7, 1914** Isaac Henagow was shot to death in Roy Jone's saloon at 21st St. and Wabash Ave. by James "Duffy the Goat" Franche a member of Jim Colosimo's gang. The victim was suspected of being the informant that allowed the Moral's Squad to set up Harry Cullett, another Colosimo operative, in a bribery case which was later dismissed by a questionable judge. Franche was charged with this murder, found guilty and sentenced to hang. However, he was awarded a new trial on technicalities and found not guilty at trial **(Solved)**.

On **June 15, 1914** Henry Williams 39 yrs. was shot to death at 19th and Federal Sts. by Labor Racketeer Mike Carrozzo. The assailant fled the scene and was later apprehended and exonerated for the crime **(solved)**.

On **July 16, 1914** Detective Sergeant Stanly J. Birns was shot dead at 67 E. 22nd St. while he and other members of Second Deputy Superintendent Funkhauser's squad led by Fred Amart came across men from the city's morals squad lead by Inspector W.C. Dannenberg after a raid of the huge Levee brothel called the Turf on 22nd Street near State. During the raid a crowd of hecklers including Johnny Torrio and Roxy Vanille his cousin were harassing and targeting the raiders. At least 2 versions of the events have been reported over the years: One describes the victim as backing up other officers in a gun battle with gangsters (Vanille the shooter) where the victim is killed and 3 other officers are wounded while the gangsters escape albeit wounded. In the second version it has been reported that the victim was killed during a shootout between two police squads and a case of mistaken identification. By July 23rd this incident resulted in arrests, vice lords Jackie Adler and Maurice Van Bever are taken into custody by the State's Attorneys Office for conspiring to kill the police raiders and the outcome of that investigation is unknown. State's Attorney Hoyne seemed to sort out the conspiracy of gangsters who intended to assault members of the Moral's Squad and identified Torrio and Vanille for their roles, although the outcome of the criminal case is not known. What is known is this event led to the closing of several establishments and the downfall of the Levee altogether. Reports of John Torrio killing Inspector W.C. Dannenberg in 1914 cannot be substantiated and seem to be urban legend.

On **September 28, 1914** Joseph D'Andrea 36yrs. was shot to death at Halsted and Harrison Sts. over a dispute involving construction contracts. He was gunned down by an assassin wielding a shotgun as he left his union hall.

In **May of 1915** it was reported that Mrs. Antonio Augustino was found shot in the head and abdomen in her home. She died the next day at St. James Hospital. Her husband was a labor racketeer for the Chicago Mob and controlled labor locals in Joliet, Illinois. He claimed his wife committed suicide while deranged.

On **October 15, 1915** Nicholas Cozzo 44 yrs. was beaten to death and his throat cut at the 2300 blk of Lake St. by Tony Cifaldo on the orders of " Dago Mike" Carrozzo for a $500 debt the victim refused to pay. The killer was arrested, tried, convicted and sentenced to prison for the crime **(solved).** *Police logs entered the case as follows:* Cozzo, Nicholas - Age 44 - Stabbed and beaten to death with wrench on Lake Front between 23rd & 24th Sts., 10/21/15 Tony Cifaldo brought back from Detroit, Mich, and on 11/16/15 held to G.J. by Coroner who also recommended arrest of John Cifaldo, 4th Pct. 3/20/16 Cifaldo sentenced to Joliet Pen by Judge Turney.

On **February 21, 1916** Frank Lombardi was killed in his saloon at 1120 W. Taylor St. by three gunmen. Lombardi a successful area businessman had the audacity to back Irish 19th ward Alderman Johnny Powers against his countryman Anthony D'Andrea in a heated aldermanic race. The campaign became very violent with threats, bombings and shootings on both sides. D'Andrea was a well- educated labor racketeer who held great sway with the Unione Siciliana and sought political office to legitimize his money making ventures. He was also considered by some a Mafioso leader within a group that became central to the upcoming bootlegging industry.

Johnny Powers

On **March 1, 1916** Sam Moleno 31 yrs. was shot to death while walking down the street with Paul Toreno at Milton Ave. and Elm St. The assailant used a sawed off shot gun and escaped on foot. Authorities at the time ruled the killing a Blackhand murder.

On **May 4, 1916** Antonio Militello 49 yrs. was shot to death at the alley north of Elm St. between Milton and Cambridge Aves. The assailant used a double-barrel sawed off shotgun and escaped on foot. Authorities at the time ruled the killing a Blackhand murder.

On **May 10, 1916** Joseph P. Cooney 44 yrs. was shot to death in the Hod Carriers Hall at Green and Harrison Sts. Authorities considered the victim an extortionist and described his occupation as a Machinist. William Rooney was held to a Grand Jury in the murder, but was acquitted. The case appears to be the result of labor racketeering **(Solved).**

On **June 14, 1916** Oak Park Police Officer Herman J. Malow Jr. was shot and killed by gangster Frankie McErlane while he approached a disturbance on the street at Washington and Cuyler in the western suburb. Four suspects were identified including McErlane who was paroled the previous March of that year after serving time for auto theft. One suspect was convicted and hanged while McErlane was convicted and sentenced to prison where he escaped in 1918. He was recaptured and served a total of 3 years for the murder. He went on to have a prolific career as a leader of the Saltis McErlane gang and killed dozens of people before dying of natural causes in 1932 **(solved).**

Frankie McErlane

On **November 23, 1916** Joe "Dandy Joe" Hagarty was shot to death in the Burnham Inn in Burnham, IL. This town was in southern Cook County and was one of John Torrio's first forays outside of Chicago. Torrio owned most of the roadhouses in the area and the Mayor Johnny Patton worked for Torrio. The victim owned a nearby cigar store and was killed during a dispute with gangsters. The case remains unsolved.

In **1917** future Mob boss of the south suburbs Frank LaPorte reportedly killed a man in Chicago Heights. While he was only a teenager at the time he showed his mettle and immediately entered vice and bootlegging operations in the south suburbs. Years later he would take control of this territory upon the exit of Al Capone.

On **March 20, 1917** Rosario Manzello 65 yrs. was found dead with his throat cut in his residence at 1214 Larrabee St. Authorities at the time ruled the murder to be Blackhand related although no arrests were made.

On **April 24, 1917** Giovanni Mateleano 36 yrs. an alleged Blackhand extortionist was shot to death by Joe Christino whom was the target of Blackhand. Christino was exonerated of the crime (**Solved**).

On **April 18, 1918** Rosario Cutroma 28 yrs. was shot to death in the rear of 872 Milton Ave. The murder was ruled Blackhand although no arrests were made.

On **January 4, 1919** Frank Poroino was murdered by unknown gangsters.

On **January 12, 1919** Joseph Introviaia AKA: Guissippi Latravara was murdered by unknown gangsters.

On **January 19, 1919** Charles Stillwell AKA: Chancelor Stillwell was murdered by unknown gangsters.

January 19, 1919 Jimmy Cherin AKA: The Peacock was found murdered on a country road southwest of Chicago in Stickney, IL. A police investigation found gangster Thomas "Terrible Tommy" O'Connor responsible for the slaying. O'Connor was hunted for the crime and killed a Chicago Police Sergeant during the manhunt in 1921 and was later arrested and convicted before escaping (**Solved**).

On **January 21, 1919** Tony DeBrouse and Hanes Cheren were murdered by unknown gangsters.

On **February 20, 1919** Luigi Cascio was murdered by unknown gangsters.

On **February 28, 1919** Garnetta Ellis was murdered. This 6 year old was reported to be the innocent victim of a bombing perpetrated by gangsters.

On **March 5, 1919** Frank Gento was murdered by unknown gangsters.

On **March 6, 1919** Guitano Lopresti was murdered by unknown gangsters.

On **April 5, 1919** Fred Woeifel was murdered by unknown gangsters.

On **April 25, 1919** John Altobelli was murdered by unknown gangsters.

On **May 11, 1919** William Marshan AKA: Marchand was murdered. Terrance Drugen and Harold Toomey were charged in the case that was later dismissed by Judge Sabath on July 26, 1920 **(solved)**.

On **May 12, 1919** Moses Flanigan AKA: Thomas Mulroney was murdered by unknown gangsters.

On **May 22, 1919** Vincenzo Rieno AKA: Jim Arine and Giavano Russo AKA: John Russo were murdered by unknown gangsters.

On **June 5, 1919** Joseph L. Doyle 34 yrs. was shot to death in an auto and dumped on the street at Potomac and Cicero Sts. Authorities at the time ruled the murder a gangland "Hit", however no arrests were made.

On **July 15, 1919** Giuseppe A. Saliana was murdered by unknown gangsters.

On **July 28, 1919** Patrolman John W. Simpson was shot and later died from his injuries. He was found outside the 31st Street Police Station at 31st and Wabash. Simpson was the first black police officer to die in the line of duty in Chicago. The details are vague to say the least, but it was related to several days of race riots that began at Chicago's segregated beaches on the Southside. The group most responsible for the death and destruction during the riots was a gang known as Regan's Colts. This Irish gang became part of the Capone organization at the onset of Prohibition.

On **August 1, 1919** Frank A. Surianello was murdered by unknown gangsters.

On **September 1, 1919** Peter Gentleman was killed in a dispute over profits by Martin "Trigger Happy" Guilfoyle. Guilfoyle managed to co-exist with the other gangs in his business that was headquartered at Kedzie and Chicago Aves. His northwest side bootlegging gang made millions of dollars a year in beer traffic. Guilfoyle would become an associate of the Torrio/Capone gang, but was never arrested for this crime **(Solved)**.

On **September 7, 1919** Rosario Cacciatore was murdered by unknown gangsters.

On **September 8, 1919** John Gagliardo and Charles Ramondi were murdered by unknown gangsters.

On **October 15, 1919** an unnamed security guard was killed by Charles Gloriana and Carl Moretti of the Gloriana gang during a payroll heist. After being indicted the case was stricken from the court docket and the men walked free. The Gloriana gang provided many members to the Chicago Mob when prohibition took effect **(Solved).**

On **November 17, 1919** Joseph McArdle was murdered and Gastano Esposito AKA: Gaitana was arrested and indicted. He was tried before Judge Pam and acquitted **(solved).**

On **November 19, 1919** Balasario Aborino was murdered by unknown gangsters.

On **December 10, 1919** Rocco Mossow was murdered by unknown gangsters.

On **December 20, 1919** Charles Crapa 48 yrs. was shot to death at 6634 24th Pl. authorities at the time ruled the murder to be a Blackhand murder although no arrests were made.

Al "Scarface" Capone

Approx. number of Chicago TOC related murders pre 1920s: 57
Approx. number of Chicago TOC related murders pre 1920s
solved: 21
Approx. number of Chicago TOC related murders of Police Officers: 4

Chapter 2. The 1920s

On January 17, 1920 the Volstead Act (Prohibition) takes affect after ratification by more than 36 states in the union. It just happens to land on Al Capone's 21st birthday. When it emerged and Big Jim Colosimo resisted Torrio and Capone's interests in capitalizing on the prohibition situation, he was murdered in the vestibule of his café at 2126 S. Wabash.

Politically as the decade began, Bill Thompson the powerful Mayor ran Chicago promising to keep it an open town despite Prohibition laws that took effect. He knew how to appeal to ethnic groups and would scorn one while talking to the other. He would use inflammatory rhetoric wherever he went and would speak out against foreign leaders if it pleased his audience. He aligned himself quickly with the Torrio-Capone syndicate and received a great deal of financial support from them.

In TOC, Torrio, being the skilled manager and diplomat, immediately assumed control over Colosimo's first ward Italian syndicate. He improved his political concerns and even befriended the Governor of Illinois Len Small. But, Johnny "The Fox" was only beginning. He soon began collaborating with other criminal organizations without ethnic bias, attempting to bring them under the banner of the Torrio-Capone Crime Syndicate. This did not sit well with some of the groups especially north side gang leaders Charles Dion "Deanie" O'Banion, Hymie Weiss AKA: Earl Wajciechowski and George "Bugs" Moran AKA: George Gage and Joe Aiello. What occurred over the next several years was the formation of a Criminal empire to which modern America had never seen.

John Torrio began a dialogue with other criminal organizations to extol the virtues of bootlegging and the enormous profits that may be shared in his collaborative vision, trying to sway these groups into leaving their other criminal enterprises and concentrating on the opportunity at hand. At the time Torrio and other gang leaders had acquired controlling interests in several local distilleries and breweries. The groups he was attempting to recruit included: the O'Banion-Weiss-Drucci-Moran Gang, the Circus Gang, the Westside Klondike O'Donnell Gang, the Druggan-Lake-Valley Gang, the Guilfoyle's, the Touhy Gang, the Aiello's, the Genna's, the Saltis-McErlane Gang, the Ralph Sheldon Gang, and the Southside Spike O'Donnell Gang.

During the first years of Prohibition relative peace existed between the numerous bootlegging gangs. Torrio even partnered with O'Banion in a gambling casino venture in west suburban Cicero called "The Ship".

What Torrio accomplished was a division of bootlegging territories (see Map) with his gang controlling most of the south and south-west side of the city and suburbs extending all the way to Calumet City and Burnham on the south and Stickney and Cicero to the west.

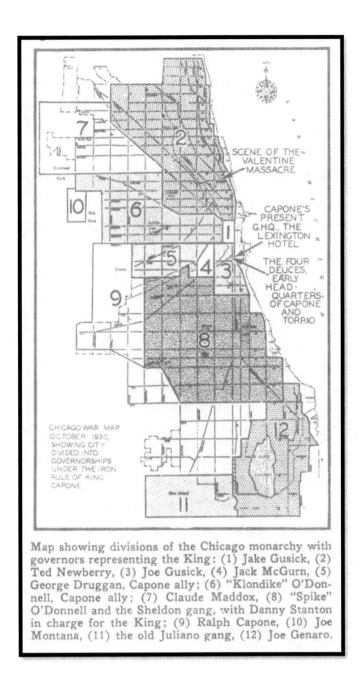

Map showing divisions of the Chicago monarchy with governors representing the King: (1) Jake Gusick, (2) Ted Newberry, (3) Joe Gusick, (4) Jack McGurn, (5) George Druggan, Capone ally; (6) "Klondike" O'Donnell, Capone ally; (7) Claude Maddox, (8) "Spike" O'Donnell and the Sheldon gang, with Danny Stanton in charge for the King; (9) Ralph Capone, (10) Joe Montana, (11) the old Juliano gang, (12) Joe Genaro.

Bootlegging territory map-NP (Gem of the Prairie)

What existed in the area was a loose confederation of 8 gangs that controlled speakeasies which were provided with Torrio beer from his breweries. Outside of the Torrio-Capone syndicate was a territory run by the Saltis-McErlane gang which supplied their speakeasies with beer from their own breweries. One group left out of this division was the Southside O'Donnells led by brother Spike. They are not to be confused with the Westside O'Donnells led by brother Klondike and no relation to the other O'Donnell clan. On the Southside Spike O'Donnell and his gang were playing catch up after Spike was released from prison in 1923 after serving time for bank robbery. At this time he began to muscle in on the lucrative bootlegging business. At first he began to take Torrio customers by selling to saloon owners at a better price than Torrio, but Torrio responded and dropped his prices to a level that O'Donnell could not match. He also moved in on the Saltis-McErlane and the Ralph Sheldon gang's customers using the same tactics. While these gangs co-existed they despised each other, but came together to repel the Southside O'Donnells.

This is when the threatening started and the "Beer Wars" actually began with the killing of Jerry O'Connor a Southside O'Donnell gunman in 1923. However, this warning to Spike went unheeded and within days two more O'Donnell gunmen died. What happened then was a crackdown by police albeit temporary.

On the TOC front, the bootlegging syndicate first crafted by Torrio entered into a conflict or a free for all with other bootleggers lasting for four years. This conflict was precipitated by police raids under reformers Mayor Wm. Dever and Chief Morgan Collins. This police action put payoffs and other agreements in disarray and the bootleggers developed an "every man for himself" attitude. During this conflict the Southside Saltis and McErlane gang moved against their adversaries introducing the Thompson submachine gun into the mob arsenal and the term "take em for a ride" was first coined. On September 25, 1925 the gang attempted to kill Spike O'Donnell while he was standing on the corner of 63rd and Western. O'Donnell survived the attack, but Ralph Sheldon was later wounded while standing in front of a Westside Hotel, but he too survived the attack. These events on the south and west sides of Chicago and the surrounding suburbs saw wholesale violence as never before.

The Chicago Crime Commission recorded 261 TOC murders between 1926 and 1929 with very few being solved and culminating in the St. Valentine's Day Massacre. What resulted was a dominant TOC empire run by Capone with very little resistance from the Northsiders and other independent gangs whose limited territories were drawn by Capone and liquor ran freely in Chicago.

During the formation of this huge bootlegging syndicate Big Bill Thompson's tenure was interrupted in 1923 with the election of a true reform Mayor, William Dever. The efforts of Mayor Dever and his hand-picked Police Chief Morgan Collins were beginning to take hold. Federal prosecutors took over some cases from the corrupted county prosecutor's office. Shortly after a failed assassination attempt took Torrio out of the picture and elevated Al Capone to power. Now the heat was on Capone who was forced to move his headquarters out of Chicago and into the neighboring Town of Cicero in the Hawthorne Inn at 4833 W. 22nd St. This location is where the Mob would open their first gambling den in a Town which was essentially run by the Mob.

By September of 1923 back in Chicago, Police Chief Morgan Collins under the orders of newly elected Mayor William Dever closed down 4,000 saloons and 1,400 speakeasies. This action was within 150 days of Dever's inauguration.

Mayor William Dever

This was the beginning of the end for the bootlegging cartel John Torrio orchestrated with the introduction of Prohibition. What resulted were a breakdown of the protection systems and a fragmentation of the cartel that led to open warfare. Shortly after his rise to the top, Capone tried to stifle the violence that included several attempts on his life by Northside gunman including an ambush at 55th and State on January 10, 1925. He carried out at least two meetings in 1926 with other gang leaders in the Loop, as Torrio had previously attempted in 1923. He had limited success after a meeting in the Morrison Hotel on October 21, 1926 when he was unable to develop a truce with Northside gang leader Vincent "Schemer" Drucci AKA: DiAmbrosio only ten days after the gangs previous leader, Hymie Weiss AKA: Earl Wajciechowski, was gunned down in the street and two years after the death of the gangs founder Dean O'Banion. The sticking point it seemed, was the demand from Drucci (to Capone) to turn over the men that had killed his (Drucci's) comrades. "I wouldn't do that to a dirty yellow dog" Capone said of the demand.

Dion O'Banion

During research on this topic a fascinating article that appeared in a *Chicago newspaper* brings another element of the day forth. That element is the alleged political involvement in bootlegging that perpetuated the violence as presented by a police informant to the newspaper. It is presented here verbatim: *The Chicago Evening American* circa: 1927

POLICEMAN'S INSIDE VERSION OF BEER FEUD WARFARE IN CHICAGO
The beer runners' feud, in which three men have lost their lives in little more than a week, is the result of the injection of political influences and graft into Chicago bootlegging. This was the statement of the Chicago Evening American today by a member of the police force, whose knowledge of conditions is second to none. Two well-known Democratic leaders were named as the leaders of the politicians who he said have precipitated the feud by a policy of covetousness and extortion. Both are prominent personages in the administration of the county government. "The situation is this" The Chicago Evening American's informant stated: "Of the saloons in Chicago, practically 90 per cent are selling real beer. In Chicago and the immediate vicinity are breweries, backed by Chicago politicians.

INDEPENDENTS WERE FIRST.
"Now there are also a number of independent beer-running gangs. These, in fact were in the field before the political breweries began operating. And of course each gang had its regular customers. "Well, now along comes a representative of Mr. X or Mr. Z our county-official-bootleggers, and drops into a saloon which has been a regular customer of an independent gang. The saloonkeeper is buttonholed over a corner, and---- "Mr. X suggests that you buy in the future from such-and-such a brewery, represented by such-and-such a gang of beer-runners," says the agent.

THREAT TO JAIL.

"Perhaps the saloonkeeper demurs. In that case the agent whispers: Mr. X has a lot of influence with the police. A word from him and your place will be raided and you'll probably go to jail. Think it over." "Of course the saloonkeeper 'thinks it over.' He arrives at the only possible conclusion. The political brewery gets his next order. "Now what happens? The gang he has been buying from discovers that it has lost a customer. A gangster or several of them, visit him, and suggest that for the sake of his wife and children, he purchase his beer from the gang and tell his political friends to go to Jericho.

PLIGHT OF DEALERS.

The saloon keeper is now between the devil and the deep sea. Either he must go to jail or to the cemetery. What to do? "He does the logical thing. He informs his politician-master of the gangsters' threat. Now then, let's suppose that the independents are the O'Donnell gang, and the politician is faced with the problem of 'backing' them if he is to retain his trade. What does he do? "Why, he hires another gang, just for the sake of an example, let's suppose it's the Torrio gang, and arranges to have his customers 'protected.' "There can only be one outcome, a fight. At first it's a matter of business, pure and simple. Torrio's *crew* fight because they're paid to fight. "They have no animosity toward the O'Donnell gang, of course, is bitter, but it's impersonal with them, too. "But sooner or later someone gets killed. And what happens? "The aspect of the whole situation changes. Bill Jones has been killed by Sam Smith. All right, GET SAM SMITH! "Sam Smith is 'got' by Hank White. And so it goes. It's a feud.

GREED BLAMED.

"The whole trouble is that Mr. X and Mr. Z were, and are, too greedy. They can't leave the independents' customers alone. "If they worked hard enough and long enough, the police probably could ferret Mr. X and Mr. Z out. What an explosion there would be if that ever happened! "But now, as things are, they're safe, both of them. And there they sit in their offices, reading in the newspapers about the deaths of their victims. Ghastly, isn't it, when you consider it that way?"
THE END!

In 1921 Lennington Small, a Republican from Kankakee was elected Governor of the State of Illinois. Reportedly he was considered the most corrupt Illinois Governor in history and considered the worst Governor in American History according to a Tribune article. Shortly after his election he was indicted for converting state funds for his own use while State Treasurer. Refusing to surrender to authorities for three weeks he used National Guard troops to protect him from arrest. After a six week trial in 1922 a jury found him not guilty, he paid back $650,000 after a civil suit was filed and went on to win re-election. He served from 1921 to 1929 when he was finally defeated. He developed a working relationship with Mobsters in Chicago. Small would prove useful at the time when he would pardon gangsters (estimated at 1,000) at Torrio's request.

Gov. Len Small

In Little Italy immigrant Italians under the auspices of the Unione Siciliana developed home distilleries and began the chore of cooking alcohol in their bathtubs. Thus, the term was coined "Bathtub Gin". While the Unione's national leader Frankie Yale AKA: Uale or Ioele was developing offshore contacts for the delivery of whiskey, with the Torrio/Capone syndicate as his best customer.

As yet we try to dispel a popular myth of the time, that being the alleged life-long association of Frank Nitti and Al Capone from their early days in New York. In reality it was through the efforts of illicit banker and fence Alex Louis Greenberg that the men met in Chicago. Greenberg was responsible for introducing his business partner Frank Nitti AKA: Francesco Nitto, Ralph Nitto, Frank Raddo and Frank Sasso to Al Capone in 1923. Nitti would rise through the ranks and lead the gang upon Capone's incarceration.

In the 1927 election, the Voters made it clear to the rest of the country, that their liquor was more important to them than reform and Thompson running on a platform promising the immigrant population to let the liquor flow again, was swept back into office that year. Capone once again moved his headquarters back to Chicago while maintaining control over Cicero.

While the depression of 1929 cut deeply into profits generated by bootlegging and gambling, Capone recognized a need to diversify his interests to keep the organization intact. Until this time labor racketeering had existed, but had not been a focal point to TOC leaders. But, recognizing the probability of a repeal of the Volstead Act, new sources of income were needed.

Realizing the end of Prohibition was inevitable Capone directed his men to look for new sources of revenue. The new activities began on a grand scale and included: extortion of butchers, fish stores, construction industry, garages, bakeries, laundries, beauty parlors, dry cleaners, theaters, sports arenas, and bootblacks. By the end of the decade 91 unions and business associations fell under TOC control.

Critical Events of the 1920s:

On **February 2, 1920** Maurice "Mossie" Enright AKA: Moss was gunned down at the curb of his palatial home at 1110 W. Garfield Boulevard. Mossie was a fabled killer and labor racketeer at the turn of the century when labor issues were a primary concern of politicians and police in the growing industrial giant Chicago was becoming. Mossie and his former protégé Tim Murphy were fighting over control of the Street Cleaners and Gas Workers Unions. Four men were identified and charged: James Vinci, Michael Corrozza AKA: Carozza, Vincenzo Comano AKA: Cosmano and Timothy Murphy. The investigation revealed that Corrozza had threatened to kill Enright earlier in the year and Enright retaliated and shot at Corrozzo and an associate in the Vestibule Café. The men identified for the murder were indicted, but only one was convicted and sent to prison on and that was Jimmy Vinci of the "Violent Vinci's" who was the only one to confess to the crime and cooperate with police. He was sentenced to 25 years, but his conviction was reversed by the Supreme Court while the others' cases were dismissed. A second trial led to his acquittal. Corozza who controlled the city's street sweepers would go on to be installed as the head of the Hod Carrier's Union by the Torrio-Capone Mob. Bruno "The Bomber" Roti Sr. was also picked up and questioned regarding this killing. Police believed Roti disposed of the shotgun used in the killing, but he was never charged. Issues in the Street Cleaners Union and the "Circulation Wars" provided two possible motives for this murder **(solved)**.

On **February 13, 1920** Bernard J. Reilly 28 yrs. was killed at 4017 Irving Park Blvd. by Thomas F. Jakubow who was convicted of the crime and sentenced to 25 years in prison **(solved)**. *Police logs entered the case as follows:* February 9, 1920 O'Reilly, Bernard - Age 28 - Shot and fatally wounded 2/9/20 while working as a Non-union hod-carrier at 4017 Irving Park Blvd., by Thomas Jakuborosky, a union official, who was held by the Coroner 2/14/20. 26 Pct. 6/30/20 - 25 years in Joliet Pen – Barrett.

On **March 17, 1920** Joseph Hurley 27 yrs. was killed at 35th and Wallace Sts. Joseph Carville was arrested and tried. He was found not guilty by Judge Barret **(solved)**. *Police logs entered the case as follows:* March 17, 1920 Hurley, Joseph - Age 27 - Shot to death in saloon at 35th and Wallace Sts. and dragged into vacant lot rear of 544 W. 35 St. On 4/1 Joseph Carville was indicted for murder and John Callaghan and John Cronin were indicted as accessories. 15 Pct.

6/30/20 - Carville acquitted - Barrett - 7/1/20 Callaghan - Nolle Prossed###. 7/14/20 Cronin Nolled - Kersten.

On **April 23, 1920** Edward J. Coleman was murdered by unknown gangsters.

On **May 5, 1920** Robert J. Hopkins was murdered by unknown gangsters.

On **May 10, 1920** Joseph Beneditto was murdered by unknown gangsters.

On **May 11, 1920** Big Jim Colosimo was killed in the vestibule of his Café by either Frankie Yale AKA: Uale or Ioele or Al Capone or a number of their killers, although Capone allegedly admitted to a reporter that he committed the crime years later. Police immediately located over a dozen gunman and relatives of Big Jim's ex-wife. They were grilled for hours and then released. During the investigation an informant told police that Torrio paid Yale $10,000 dollars for the hit. Chicago detectives learned that Yale was in Chicago at the time, but were unable to locate him before he fled. They made a request to New York detectives to pick Yale up and hold him. Yale was located in late May and Chicago detectives traveled by train to New York with a porter who saw the gunman. However, the witness became so afraid she was unable to identify Yale in a line up. Yale was grilled for several hours and released when he admitted nothing. The case remains unsolved.

Jim Colosimo dead

On **May 17, 1920** John Kikulski was murdered by unknown gangsters.

On **June 13, 1920** Paul G. Torina was murdered by unknown gangsters.

On **June 17, 1920** Patrick Ryan AKA: Paddy the Bear a gang leader in the Valley District was murdered in his Valley Saloon. It was later reported that Walter Quinlan a collector for the Westside O'Donnells was the killer and he was killed in 1926 by John "Paddy the Fox" Ryan a member of the Ralph Sheldon gang and son of this victim.

On **June 21, 1920** Nick Valente was murdered by unknown gangsters.

On **June 24, 1920** Ethel O. Roberts was murdered. It was reported that she was the victim of a bombing by gangsters.

On **August 13, 1920** Frank Gebbia was murdered by unknown gangsters.

On **August 23, 1920** Detective Sergeant William E. Hennessy and Detective Sergeant James A. Mulcahy were shot and killed while investigating organized crime activities in the Pekin Theatre Building at 2700 S. State St. During the investigation Sgt. Mulcahy was accosted by Hirche Miller a whiskey runner, former boxer and Municipal Court Bailiff and Samuel J. Morton. When Sgt. Hennessy came to his partner's aid, Miller drew a pistol and shot both officers. They were eventually captured, tried and acquitted for the crime by a corrupt criminal justice system **(solved)**.

On **August 29, 1920** Joseph Galldio was murdered by unknown gangsters.

On **September 1, 1920** Fred Russo was murdered by unknown gangsters.

On **November 1, 1920** Louis Porrovicchio was murdered by unknown gangsters.

On **November 2, 1920** George Stevenson was murdered by unknown gangsters.

On **November 3, 1920** Edward Carney of 4225 S. Wells St. was shot by Robert Rutshaw at 42nd Pl. and Princeton Ave. A coroner's jury returned a verdict of justifiable homicide and Rutshaw was released. Rutshaw would be murdered by unknown gangsters in 1928.

On **November 9, 1920** Anthony Bentivegna was murdered by unknown gangsters.

On **November 10, 1920** Eugene McSweeney was killed. James Daly was arrested, tried and found not guilty of the crime on February 9, 1921**(Solved).**

On **November 12, 1920** John W. Harris was murdered by unknown gangsters.

On **November 18, 1920** Patrolman Joseph L. Pijanowski died at St. Anthony Hospital from gunshot wounds he received on November 14th. The Officer was assigned to bodyguard William Held a former city alderman, a clerk in the police court and a suspect in illegal liquor deals. The men were in front of Held's residence at 2544 S. Kedvale. There men approached and one drew a weapon and shot the Officer and Held. After an extensive investigation Raymond Knight, Albert Willer and Henry Schmidt were charged with the crime. While charges against Schmidt were dropped, Knight and Willer received life sentences at the Illinois State Penitentiary in Joliet, Illinois **(solved)**.

On **November 28, 1920** William J. Tynan 33 yrs. was shot and killed at 3076 Lock St. Joseph Carville was indicted, but the charges against him were dismissed **(solved)**. *Police logs entered the case as follows:* November 26, 1920 Tynan, Wm. - Age 33 - Fatally shot 11/26/20 in rear of saloon 3076 Lock St., by a man whom he identified as Joseph Carville, who was arrested and on 11/30/20 held by the Coroner. 15 Pct. 3/14/21 - s/o – Wilson.

On **December 14, 1920** Vincent Salano was murdered by unknown gangsters.

On **December 15, 1920** Fred DeVita was murdered by unknown gangsters.

On **January 17, 1921** Mike DeRosa was murdered by unknown gangsters.

On **January 18, 1921** Leonardo DiMarco of 1333 Clybourn Ave. and Armond Boquist were murdered by unknown gangsters at Larrabee and Rush Sts.

On **February 22, 1921** Northside Gang Boss Charles Dion "Deanie" O'Banion gets into a tiff with John Duffy of Philadelphia in front of John Torrio's "Four Deuces" on Wabash Ave. O'Banion is suspected of shooting Duffy whose body is found on the side of the road near Joliet, Illinois. He was never charged and the case remains open.

On **February 26, 1921** Gaetano "Guy" Esposito was kidnapped driven to Columbus Hospital at Lytle and Gilpin streets shot and dumped on the street. He was just one of the prominent Italian men that backed Johnny Powers in the aldermanic election against Anthony D'Andrea. Salvatore "Samoots" Amatuna, Frank "Don Chick" Gambino and "Two Gun Johnny" Gardino were the Genna gunmen (The Genna's backed D'Andrea) assigned to enact revenge for those who betrayed the D'Andrea campaign although they were never charged and the case remains unsolved.

On **March 6, 1921** Dinutris Marabito was murdered by unknown gangsters.

On **March 8, 1921** Paul Labriola 38 yrs. was shot near his home at 843 W. Congress. He a bailiff and supported 19th ward Alderman John Powers over Anthony D'Andrea. Genna gangsters Salvatore "Samoots" Amatuna, Frank "Don Chick" Gambino and "Two Gun Johnny" Gardino were the shooters. Amatuna and Gambino were arrested, but the charges were later dismissed after which Angelo Genna was charged in the killing, but found not guilty **(Solved)**. *Police logs entered the case as follows:* March 8, 1921 Labriola, Paul - Age 38 - Shot to death in Congress St., about 45 feet east of Halsted St., by some unknown person or persons. (19th Ward political feud). Frank Gambino, Sam Amatuna, and Angelo Genna arrested and indicted. 21 Pct. 5/9/21 - Amatuna and Gambino cases s/o - David. 10/7/21 Genna acquitted - Caverly.

On **March 8, 1921** Harry Raimondi is killed in his cigar store at 910 Garibaldi Place. He supported 19th Ward Alderman John Powers over Anthony D'Andrea.

On **March 10, 1921** William Weltenstein was murdered by unknown gangsters.

On **March 23, 1921** Detective Sergeant Patrick J. O'Neill was shot five times and killed at the hand of gangster Thomas "Terrible Tommy" O'Connor. O'Connor a well-known hoodlum of the day was wanted for the murder of an associate Jimmy "The Peacock" Cherin. Acting on information that the wanted suspect was holed up at his brother in-laws residence at 6415 S. Washtenaw the squad of 5 detectives surrounded the home, the good sergeant was at the rear door when O'Connor emerged and the Sergeant was shot to death. The killer escaped and was later arrested in St. Paul, MN. He was returned to Chicago convicted of the killing and sentenced to hang. However, O'Connor escaped from the old Cook County Jail at State and Hubbard Sts. and would stay on the lamb until his death in 1951 **(solved)**.

On **April 8, 1921** Sam Caruso was murdered by unknown gangsters.

On **April 10, 1921** Michael Danoras was murdered by unknown gangsters.

On **April 18, 1921** Pasquale Bavagonti was murdered by unknown gangsters.

On **April 20, 1921** Antonio Salfornis was murdered, gangster Tomassino DeMeo was wanted for the killing although it is not known if he was brought to justice.

On **April 30, 1921** John J. Mahoney 30 yrs. of 3625 S. Wells St. was shot by unknown gangsters in the rear of 1814 S. Peoria St.

On **May 12, 1921** Anthony D'Andrea prominent labor racketeer, Unione Siciliana leader and political hopeful succumbed from shotgun wounds he received from unknown gangsters the previous day while entering his home at 902 S. Ashland. Apparently he alienated powerful forces during his violent run for office that cost him his life.

On **May 26, 1921** Michael Licari AKA: Lucari 36 yrs. was shot to death by unknown gangsters in front of 153 W. 37th St. He was a gunman for Anthony D'Andrea and thought moving out of the 19th ward would extend his life, it did not, retribution against D'Andrea et. al. continued.

On **June 9, 1921** Thomas A. Skriven a yellow cab chauffer was murdered by gangsters. The killing was reportedly the result of union conflicts referred to as the "Cab Wars". One of those charged Max Podolski was a business agent for the Poultry Handlers Union and a close associate of Joey Glimco who would become the head of the Cab Drivers local. Philip Fox, Morris R. Steiben, John Soveika, James Mogley, Max Podolski and Charles Goldstein were indicted and tried for the killing. Only Fox and Steiben were found guilty and sentenced to life in prison, while the others were acquitted. Podolski was able to have his arrest record destroyed at the same time as Glimco through corrupt police officials **(solved)**.

Joey Glimco

On **June 22, 1921** Carmente Basile AKA: Clemento Basito, Bharemenda 26 yrs. was shot to death in front of 625 S. Morgan. Patsy Panico, Frank Danno, Andrew Foticati AKA: Fatealo, James Esposito and James Staminato were arrested and tried. All the accused were found not guilty. Authorities at the time considered the case Prohibition related **(solved)**. *Police logs entered the case as follows:* June 21, 1921 Basito, or Basile, Bharemenda or Clemento - Age 26 - Shot to death in front of 625 So. Morgan St. during a quarrel after an Italian Afinger game.@ On 6/24 Patsy Panics, Frank Donno, Jim Esposito, Andrew Fatealo and Jim Stamanato were held by the Coroner. 17 Pct. 11/30/21 all 5 were acquitted – Fitch.

On **June 23, 1921** Antonio Marschese was murdered by unknown gangsters.

On **June 26, 1921** Joseph Lapisa AKA: Lastasia was shot to death by associates in his own car. He was a bodyguard for Anthony D'Andrea and on the day of his killing he left his neighborhood and traveled to the Northside Little Sicily area to post signs for an Italian fundraising picnic. While traveling along Oak St. his compatriots shot him and fled as the vehicle came to rest at Cambridge Ave. It is not know if any of the men were ever brought to justice.

On **July 19, 1921** Nick Torino was murdered by unknown gangsters.

On **July 22, 1921** Andrew Orlando AKA: Andrea Ortolano 28 yrs. was shot by associates in his own car at 103rd and Peoria Sts. who escaped in another auto, the case remains unsolved. The victim a bootlegger, sometime barber was a close friend of Anthony D'Andrea, the political retribution continued.

On **July 23, 1921** John "Two Gun Johnny" Gardino AKA: Gaudino was shot to death in front of 947 W. Polk St. He was a gunman for D'Andrea and swore vengeance on his Boss's killers, which probably was not a good idea at the time.

On **August 10, 1921** Vitoale or Vitola Pietro 33 yrs. a Blackhand Extortionist was shot to death in the rear of 907 S. Racine by John Rizzo his brother-in-law whom he targeted with a Blackhand letter. Rizzo was exonerated for the shooting **(solved)**.

On **August 14, 1921** Vincenzo "Joseph or James" Sinacola 46 yrs. was gunned down in a drive by shooting while sitting in front of his home and in front of his wife and children, a new low for the gangster element. He had been wounded weeks earlier in an attempt on his life. Sinacola was a foreman for Joe Lapisa and after Lapisa's death took over his business and supported the Lapisa family. He also heeded the call from a local priest to stop the killing and cooperate with the police which he did. The cooperation more than anything else is probably what cost him his life.

On **August 26, 1921** Dominic Gutillo a retired grocer and supporter for Johnny Powers was killed after he moved to the Little Sicily neighborhood. This was one of the last three murders attributed to the D'Andrea political feud, but others would soon emerge.

On **September 7, 1921** Michael Henry was murdered by unknown gangsters.

On **October 6, 1921** Joseph Marino a D'Andrea gunman was killed by unknown gangsters.

On **November 24, 1921** Nicola Adamo AKA: Nickolas Adams a supporter of Johnny Powers was killed by unknown gangsters, possibly the last in the 19th ward feud.

On **November 29, 1921** Malate Milici was murdered by unknown gangsters.

On **December 31, 1921** Guisepe Gangidno was murdered by unknown gangsters.

On **January 5, 1922** Tony Sino succumbed to a gunshot wound he received on October 24, 1921 from Police Officer Patrick Alcock at 742 S. Robey St. Sino an alleged Blackhand Extortionist drew a gun on the police officer who was there to arrest Sino when he attempted to collect money after making a Blackhand threat, the officer was exonerated in the shooting **(solved)**.

In **1922** Adolph George and George Gast-Donat were murdered in a Loop saloon. Thomas Kearney a corrupt union official was indicted for perjury regarding this case that reportedly involved labor racketeering the outcome of the cases are unknown.

On **February 5, 1922** Mike Maro was murdered by unknown gangsters.

On **February 14, 1922** Peter Cannella was murdered by unknown gangsters.

On **February 17, 1922** John Gurrieri 37 yrs. of 2607 Wentworth Ave. was murdered by unknown gangsters in an alley near 23rd and Princeton Ave. The police questioned Paul De Francisco in the killing as he testified for the victim's wife in a divorce proceeding. It is not known if charges were brought against him and the case went unsolved.

On **February 18, 1922** Antonio Vaccorilla was murdered by unknown gangsters.

On **February 20, 1922** Dominick Coffaro was murdered by unknown gangsters.

On **February 22, 1922** Michael Blanza and Frank Piotrowski were murdered in a tavern by Pete Fricano. At trial the defense stated that the accused was only protecting himself and the case was self-defense. The outcome of the trial is not known. Fricano would be murdered himself in 1940 **(solved).**

On **March 6, 1922** Anacleto Benedetti was shot by unknown gangsters on the corner of Division and Sedgwick Sts. The coroner's jury recommended the apprehension of Leo Galligani and the release of Frank Salerno the brother of Sam Salerno (killed in 1927) however, the outcome of the investigation is unknown.

On **March 11, 1922** Nicolo "Nick" Maggio 38 yrs. of 2246 Wentworth Ave. was shot by unknown gangsters near his home as he walked to work. Police suspected Blackhand extortionist in the killing and told the press that the victim knew who shot him. He was a friend of the Genna brothers when he was killed.

On **March 16, 1922** Paul Notte AKA: John Notti 32 yrs. of 3134 S. Wells St. was shot by unknown gangsters near his tavern at 244 W. 31st St. The victim a local merchant in Little Italy was murdered and Angelo Genna was held in the killing after a bedside identification, but was released when the case was dropped over problems with the identification **(Solved).** *Police logs entered the case as follows:* March 16, 1922 Notte, Paul - Age 32 - Fatally shot in front of 244 W. 31 St. by another Italian whom he identified as Angelo Genna, who, on 3/17/22, was held by the Coroner. 2 Dist. 6/22/22 Nolle Prossed. - Fisher.

On **March 20, 1922** Sam Buba 32 yrs. was shot to death at 7731 Dobson Ave. by Vito Ferro. Buba was in the process of extorting Blackhand money from Ferro.

Ferro was exonerated in the killing **(solved)**.

On **March 28, 1922** Steve Moggio was murdered by unknown gangsters.

On **April 3, 1922** Louis Cutia was murdered by unknown gangsters.

On **April 9, 1922** Abe Rubin 42 yrs. was murdered in a saloon at 2059 W. Division. Louis Roma, William Cohen, William Friedman, David Edelman and Max Miller were all arrested and charged in the killing. Miller and Edelman were found not guilty, while the charges on the other men were dropped **(Solved)**. *Police logs entered the case as follows:* April 9, 1922 Rubin, Abe - Age 42 - Shot to death in saloon at 2059 Division St., by one of several men who entered and began firing. On 4/14/22 Max Miller, Wm. Cohen, David Edelman and Wm. Freedman were held by the Coroner who also recommended arrest of one Louis Romano. On 4/10/22 Chas. Hadesman, Edward Newman, Max Eisen, and Harry Goldstein also were arrested and on 4/14/ Exonerated by the Coroner and cases nolle prossed by Judge Prindiville 4/18/22. 23 Dist. 6/23/22 Max Miller and Edelman acquitted - Caverly. 6/20/23 - Cohen, Freedman, Romano - Nolled - Kersten.

On **April 10, 1922** David Friedman was murdered by unknown gangsters.

On **April 16, 1922** Samuel Bianco was murdered by unknown gangsters.

On **April 27, 1922** Peter Tomasello was murdered by unknown gangsters.

On **April 29, 1922** Pasquale Parcelli was murdered by unknown gangsters.

On **May 2, 1922** Ignatzio Landando was murdered by unknown gangsters.

On **May 10, 1922** Patrolman Thomas J. Clark 27 yrs. was murdered at 22nd and Jefferson Sts. while trying to question three suspicious men for the bombing of a factory. Timothy Murphy, Fred Mader, Con Shea, Isadore Braverman, Daniel McCarthy, Jerry Horan, Tom Hogan and Robert McCloud were arrested and indicted for the killing, but all charges were later dropped. The men were all known bombers at the time and were involved in Labor Racketeering **(Solved)**. *Police logs entered the case as follows:* May 10, 1922 Clark, Thomas J. - Age 27 - Patrolman, 16th Dist. Shot to death at 22nd & Jefferson Sts., when about to question three suspicious men in an old Ford auto, at 12:05 A.M. Clark was detailed in the vicinity of a factory which had previously been bombed and is believed to have been killed by the same three men who a half hour later killed Off. Terrance Lyons of the West Park Police. Verdict of Coroner: "Killed by Unknown Persons." (See Lyons Case) 16th Dist.

Also on **May 10, 1922** Patrolman Terrence Lyons 30 yrs. was murdered at 1726 W. Jackson Blvd. when he and two other officers tried to detain a car with suspicious occupants. Timothy Murphy, Fred Mader, Con Shea, Daniel

McCarthy, John Miller, Margaret Hoffet, Charles Duschkowski and Stanley Byloch were arrested and indicted for the killing and Duschowski was sentenced to 25 years in prison for this crime. All the suspects were involved in Labor Racketeering **(Solved)**. *Police logs entered the case as follows:* May 10, 1922 Lyons, Terrance - Age 30 - West Park Police Officer. Shot to death in front of 1726 Jackson Blvd., while in an auto with two brother officers, when they attempted to halt three men in an old Ford auto at 12:30A.M. These men believed to be same who a half hour earlier killed Patrolman Thos. J. Clark at 22nd & Jefferson Sts., to escape questioning. The following men were indicted by the May 1922 G.J.: Timothy Murphy, Fred Mader, Cornelius Shea, Isadore Braverman, Daniel McCarthy, Jerry Horan and Robt. McCloud. On 5/24/22 all these were Nolle Prossed by Judge Scanlan and new indictments returned against: Timothy D. Murphy - 8/19/22 - Nolled - Taylor; Cornelius Shea - 8/2/22 - Nolled - Taylor; Fred Mader - 11/25/22 - Acq. - Hebel.; Daniel McCarthy - 11/25/22 - Acq. - Hebel. Johne Miller - 14 yrs. Joliet Pen. - Hebel; Margaret Hoffert - 9/9/22 - s/o - Kavanaugh. Chas. Duschkowski (see on left) - 10/10/23 - s/o - Hurley; Stanley Bylook - 10/10/23 - s/o - Hurley. 1/5/23 Duschkowski arrested in SanDiego, Cal. brought back and turned over to Sheriff. 5/26/23 - 25 yrs. Joliet Pen. - Hebel. 20 Dist.

Big Tim Murphy

On **May 13, 1922** Vito DeGeorgio and James Locasio were murdered by unknown gangsters.

On **June 6, 1922** Antonio Albinanti was murdered by unknown gangsters.

On **July 2, 1922** T. R. Petrotla was murdered by unknown gangsters.

On **July 4, 1922** John Talarico 40 yrs. was shot to death at 92nd St. and Harper Ave. by his cousin Michael Carelli. Talarico was in the process of extorting

Blackhand money from Carelli. Carelli was exonerated in the killing **(solved)**.

On **August 1, 1922** Angelo Damco was murdered by unknown gangsters.

On **August 5, 1922** John Patti was murdered by unknown gangsters.

On **August 21, 1922** James Colabria was murdered by unknown gangsters.

On **August 30, 1922** Albert Schulz was murdered by unknown gangsters.

On **October 7, 1922** George W. Heller 40 yrs. was murdered behind 923 W. Madison. William McDermott, William J. Dillon and John Connors were all held, but a grand jury handed down a no bill on the case **(Solved)**. *Police logs entered the case as follows:* October 17, 1922 Heller, Ges. W. - Age 40 - Found shot to death in alley rear of 923 W. Madison St. Result of quarrel among booze runners. 10/9/22 Wm. Dillon was held by the Coroner as accessory and arrest of John Connors recommended. On 10/10/22 Wm. McDermott arrested for the murder and John Connors as accessory and both turned over to the Sheriff. Oct. 1922 No Bills on all 3. 19 Dist.

On **October 8, 1922** Vito Amaro 26 yrs. was shot to death at 25ᵗʰ Pl. and Lowe Ave. The case was reported as a Blackhand murder and went unsolved.

On **October 26, 1922** Vito Delise was murdered by unknown gangsters.

On **November 4, 1922** Vito Fondanette was murdered by unknown gangsters.

On **November 5, 1922** Giovani Scalzetti AKA: John Scully 60 yrs. was shot in the gangway between 1424 and 1426 Spruce St. The murder was determined to be gang related and was carried out as a drive by shooting.

On **November 6, 1922** Charles P. Brennan was murdered by unknown gangsters.

On **November 24, 1922** Dominico Granno was murdered by unknown gangsters.

On **December 1, 1922** Fred J. Ragan was shot by Emil Franke at the Waiter's Club at 500 S. State St. Franke was arrested for the killing, but found not guilty at trial. The victim was a member of the Waiters Union Local #7 and recently ran for a concessions post and lost, later demanding a new election which he won. This case was another example of union racketeering that was sweeping the nation **(Solved)**.

On **December 6, 1922** Giuseppe Albergo was murdered with an ax when he tried to prevent his wife from giving money to Rocco Maggio. Maggio was wanted for this crime and was considered a terrorist in the Italian Community. The outcome of this investigation is unknown.

On **December 8, 1922** Guiseppe Maggio was murdered by unknown gangsters.

On **December 18, 1922** Rosario DeMarco was murdered by unknown gangsters.

On **January 8, 1923** Angelo DeMora was murdered by unknown gangsters. He was the stepfather of "Machine Gun" Jack McGurn AKA: James or Vincenzo Gibaldi.

On **January 14, 1923** Joseph Cichy was murdered by unknown gangsters.

On **January 27, 1923** Peter Sciangula was murdered by unknown gangsters.

On **January 28, 1923** John Granita was murdered by unknown gangsters.

On **February 18, 1923** Steve Kelliher was killed in Al Tearney's Café by Daniel "Dapper Dan" McCarthy. Kelliher was President of the Theater Janitors Union and was a seasoned labor racketeer who was convicted in 1899 of attempted murder of a police officer. McCarthy too, was a long time labor thug who was involved in the killing of 2 police officers and walked free. It is not known if he was ever brought to justice in this killing.

On **February 26, 1923** William J. Kinsella 23 yrs. was murdered at 3420 Roosevelt Rd. Albert B. Green was arrested and found not guilty in front of Judge Williams on January 30, 1924 **(Solved)**. *Police logs entered the case as follows:* February 26, 1923 Kinsella, Wm. - Age 23 - Shot to death at 3420 Roosevelt Rd. during a meeting of the Butchers? Union , by Albert Green, who, on 3/3/23, was held by the Coroner. 21 Dist. 1/30/24 - Acquitted - Williams.

On **February 26, 1923** Paul Radin 14 yrs. was murdered at 3420 Roosevelt Rd. Albert B. Green was arrested and found not guilty in front of Judge Williams on December 22, 1923 **(Solved)**. *Police logs entered the case as follows:* February 28, 1923 Radin, Paul - Age 14 - Fatally shot 2/26/23 at 3420 Roosevelt Rd., while entering the Butcher's Union meeting, by a stray bullet fired by Albert Green, who was shooting at Wm. Kinsella whom he killed. On 3/3/23 Green was held by the Coroner. 21 Dist. 12/22/23 - Acquitted - Williams.

On **March 23, 1923** Frederico Amadio was murdered by unknown gangsters.

On **April 9, 1923** Stanley O. King was murdered by unknown gangsters. It was reported that the he was an innocent victim of a bombing by gangsters.

On **April 10, 1923** Cassino Polumbo was murdered by unknown gangsters.

On **April 21, 1923** Luigi Rocchette was murdered by unknown gangsters.

On **May 8, 1923** Joe Howard AKA: "Ragtime" 28 yrs. a local con man, bootlegger and hijacker was killed at Heinie Jacobs' tavern at 2300 S. Wabash near the infamous Four Deuces. At least two versions of the incident were reported: in the first Howard made the mistake of slapping Jake Guzik the financial genius behind the Torrio gang. In a rage, Al Capone the gang's muscle at the time promptly put 6 bullets into Howard in defense of the diminutive Guzik. In the second, Capone was enacting revenge for Howard hijacking Torrio liquor the day before. The crime was witnessed by David Runelsbeck, George Bilton, Tony Bagnola, Clifford Eaton and Jacobs himself. When the police arrived Capone was gone and none of the patrons saw anything. Capone laid low for a few weeks and then walked into the Police Station and asked if anyone was looking for him. He was told no and left. *Police logs entered the case as follows:* May 8, 1924 Howard, Joseph - Age 28 - Shot to death in soft drink saloon at 2300 So. Wabash Ave., by one of two men who escaped. Messages sent out for arrest of Al Brown, alias Alphonse Capone. 2nd Dist.

On **May 20, 1923** Guiseppe Tropea was murdered by unknown gangsters.

On **May 29, 1923** Charles Gullo 49 yrs. of 241 Alexander St. was shot by unknown gangsters as he left his home for work at 217 Alexander St. The two men who shot the victim ten times were seen by the victim's wife as they fled. After firing the shots the men threw their revolvers at the victim, a sign of Blackhand extortionists.

On **June 4, 1923** Rose Santorsala AKA: Blackhand Rose 37 yrs. was shot to death in her home at 416 N. Racine Ave. The case was reported as Prohibition related and went unsolved.

On **June 6, 1923** Francis Sexton 25 yrs. was murdered at 2003 W. Division. John H. Rose and Max Raifman were arrested. The charges against Rose were dropped, while Raifman was found not guilty in front of Judge Wells on April 20, 1924 **(Solved)**. *Police logs entered the case as follows:* June 6, 1923 Sexton, Frank - Age 25 - Shot to death during affray between taxicab drivers in front of 2003 W. Division St. On 7/2/23 John Rose and Max Raifman were held by the Coroner and Emanuel Goldstein who had also been arrested was exonerated. 23 Dist. 4/30/24 Raifman acquitted - Wells. 4/30/24 Rose - cause abated a/c dead - Wells. Rose was killed on 4/21/24 outside of Judge Wells Court Room by Frank Sexton Senior.

On **June 29, 1923** George Cherowkac AKA: George Charkus 44 yrs. and Omastosios "Thomas" Visvardis 35 yrs. were shot at 740 S. Halsted St. George Garines, Dennis Kipriotis, Sam Vithoulkas and Angelo Barbas were arrested for the killing and convicted. Reports indicated at the time that the motive was a war over illicit liquor and gambling operations in the area. However, the men were all released by the Supreme Court at a later date **(Solved)**. *Police logs entered* *the case as follows:* June 29, 1923 Cherowkac, Ges. - Age 44 - Shot to death (with Omastosios Visvaidis) at 740 So. Halsted St. On 7/23/23 Ges. Garines, Sam Vithoulkas, and Deunis Kypriotis were held by the Coroner who also recommended the arrest of George Barbac.16 dist. 11/21/23 Ges. (Angola) Barbas arrested and turned over to the sheriff. 12/22/23 all four to Joliet Pen for life - Lewis. 10/10/24 - charge s/o on each - Lewis. 11/18/24 Barbas NP - a/c dead - Lindsay. 3/11/26 - Vithoulkas & Kyriotis s/o - Rush. Barbas, who was out of a writ of supersedeas, was murdered on Nov. 7 -?24. *Police logs entered the case as follows:* June 29, 1923 Visvaidis, Omastasios - Age 35 - Shot to death (with Geo. Cheroukas) at 740 So. Halsted St. On 7/23/23 Ges. Garmes, Sam Vithoulkas and Dennis Kypriotis were held by the Coroner who also recommended the arrest of Ges. Barbos. 16 Dist. 11/21/21 Ges. Barbas arrested and turned over to the Sheriff. 12/22/32 all four to Joliet Pen. for life. - Lewis. 3/10/24 (1) charge s/o - on each - Lewis. 12/20/24 all four sentences reversed by Supreme Court - Hopkins. 1/30/26 - Vithoulkas Nolle Prossed - Kypriotis Acquitted - Ruch.

On **July 1, 1923** Lucia Tricla was murdered by unknown gangsters.

On **July 2, 1923** Alvin "Red Buck" Jones was killed in a shootout at 107th St. near Archer Rd. Police informed the press that the incident seemed to be two groups of gangsters trying to carry out a hijacking and/or kidnapping. Harvey Wellmen and William Stevens were also wounded in the fracas, while the rest of the participants some of whom were also wounded fled the scene. Jones was a known bootlegger. The outcome of the case is unknown.

On **July 4, 1923** John Czarnik was murdered by unknown gangsters.

On **July 5, 1923** Procopis Palazzallo was murdered by unknown gangsters.

On **July 9, 1923** Joseph Chiarelli was murdered by unknown gangsters.

On **July 18, 1923** Gerome Gambino was murdered by unknown gangsters.

On **July 25, 1923** Joseph Costello was murdered by unknown gangsters.

On **August 10, 1923** Mike Lorchar was murdered by unknown gangsters.

On **August 21, 1923** Bias Jefferson was murdered by unknown gangsters.

On **August 25, 1923** Sam Geroci was murdered by unknown gangsters.

On **August 29, 1923** Nicola Mastro 24 yrs. was murdered at 1245 Ohio St. Rocco Marchesi was arrested for the crime, but a No Bill was passed by the Grand Jury **(Solved)**. *Police logs entered the case as follows:* August 29, 1923 Mastro, Nick - Age 24 - Shot to death at 1245 Ohio St., during an argument by Rocco Marchesi (or Marchieche) whose arrest was recommended by the Coroner

8/30/23. 22 Dist. Nov. 1923 No Bill. On 10/15/23 Marchesi surrendered in Judge Steffan?s Court and gave $5000.00 bond.

On **September 3, 1923** Vincenzo Vitale was murdered by unknown gangsters.

On **September 5, 1923** Thomas Raymond AKA: John Gall was murdered by unknown gangsters.

On **September 7, 1923** Jeremiah "Jerry" O'Connor 24 yrs. a slugger for the Westside O'Donnells was murdered in a saloon at 5358 S. Lincoln St. Several men were arrested, but the charges were dropped against all of them. It was this killing that the press labeled as the first in the bootleg war (Beer Wars). Reform Mayor Dever used this killing as an example of what was going on in the streets and vowed to close off the liquor business in the city. It was also revealed by the press regarding this case, that there was deep involvement of police officers in the liquor business in Chicago **(Solved)**.   *Police logs entered the case as follows:* September 7, 1923 O'Connor, Jerry - Age 24 - Shot to death in soft-drink parlor at 5358 So. Lincoln St., by one of six men. On 9/12/23 Daniel McFall was arrested by Judge Caverly, and indicted. On 9/24/23 Wm. Dickran was arrested and on 11/11/23 indicted. On 9/24/23 Joseph Larson, Walter O'Donnell and Joseph Mucher also were arrested and on 10/11/23 cases nolle prossed by Judge O'Connell. 13 Dist. 1/10/24 - McFall acquitted - Wells. 2/16/24 Ralph Sheldon arrested - turned over to the Sheriff - brought before Judge Caverly and turned out when witnesses failed to identify him.

On **September 10, 1923** Ernest Yearn was murdered by unknown gangsters.

On **September 13, 1923** Sam Algozeno was murdered by unknown gangsters.

George Meegan

On **September 17, 1923** George "Sport" Bucher 26 yrs. and George "Georgie" Meegan 21 yrs. both sluggers for the Westside O'Donnells were shot by gangsters from a passing auto at Laflin and Garfield Blvd. in what the press has labeled as the "Beer Wars". Again Daniel McFall a gunman for the Saltis-McErlane gang was arrested for the killing, but not indicted, McErlane was also a suspect, but never charged **(Solved)**. *Police logs entered the case as follows:* September 17, 1923 Bucher, George - Age 26 - While riding in a Ford auto in Laflin St., between north and south drives of Garfield Blvd., with Ges. Meegan, both men were shot to death by two of three men who ranged alongside in a stolen automobile. No arrests in this case. See Meegan Case. 11 Dist. *Police logs entered the case as follows:* September 17, 1923 Meegan, George - Age 21 - While riding in a Ford auto in Laflin St. between north and south drives of Garfield Blvd., with George Bucher, both men were shot to death by two of three men who ranged alongside in another automobile. On 10/25/23 Frank McErlane was arrested and indicted. Daniel McFall (who was arrested 4/2/23 following Jerry O'Connor murder) was also indicted in this case. One Thomas Hoban was arrested in and brought back from Crown Point, Ind. And indicted. This latter arrest was handled entirely by the Sheriff's office. 11 Dist. 4/10/24 - McErlane - McFall and Hoban cases Nolle Prossed - Rush.

Chief Morgan Collins

On **September 28, 1923** Anthony Forti was murdered by unknown gangsters.

On **October 11, 1923** Anastasia Plaznetia was murdered by unknown gangsters.

On **October 27, 1923** Patrolman Lawrence C. Hartnett Jr. 28 yrs. was shot to death and Sgt. Stephen Barry was wounded while conducting a bootlegging raid at 914 W. Polk St. in the Italian quarter. The location of the raid was the residence of the Montana Family. It was common at the time for immigrant families in the Italian Quarter to be in the employ of the Genna gang in operating stills in their homes. While all family members were arrested it was Joseph Montana Jr. who was arrested for the killing. The entire family was acquitted of the charges against them **(Solved)**. *Police logs entered the case as follows:* October 27, 1923 Harnett, Lawrence C. - Patrolman - Age 28 - Shot to death in passageway of 914 W. Polk St. by Joseph Montana Jr., when he, accompanied by Sergt. Stephen Barry and Patrolman F. Fuerst went to investigate a moonshine plant. Barry was wounded. On 12/14/23 the Coroner held Joseph Montana Jr. to the Grand Jury. The November G.J. indicted the whole Montana family as follows: Joseph Jr. - 4/24/24 - Acquitted - Lindsay Joseph Sr. - 4/24/24 - Acquitted - Lindsay John 4/24/24 - Acquitted- Lindsay. Madelina 4/24/24 - Acquitted - Lindsay Rosena - 4/24/24 - Acquitted - Lindsay

On **November 3, 1923** Vincenzo Albanese was murdered by unknown gangsters.

On **November 5, 1923** Mike Izzo was murdered by unknown gangsters.

On **November 7, 1923** Frank DiMarco was murdered by unknown gangsters.

On **November 10, 1923** Peter Mangles and Robert Menga were murdered by unknown gangsters.

On **November 13, 1923** Martin DeVries was shot by Robert Sullivan at a union conference at 220 S. Ashland Ave. The victim was a business agent of local 734 Teamsters and Sullivan was a common teamster who ran a soft drink parlor at State and Rush Sts. The outcome of the case is unknown.

On **November 21, 1923** Attorney Lewis A. Hauschild was shot in a fishing shack at Lake Marie in Lake Co., IL. He was taken to a hospital by Donald Lagerstrom where he died. The only witness claimed that the shooting was accidental. But, examining physicians claim the story did not add up. The murder was thought to involve the theft of $1,000,000 in securities from the Werner Bros. Safe Deposit Co. Authorities were searching for Charles Brown a safe blower and Ralph Sheldon a gang leader in this case. It is not known if anyone was ever brought to justice for the killing.

On **November 25, 1923** Freeman L. Tracy 24 yrs. of 1317 E. 53rd St. was shot by unknown gangsters and thrown from an auto where he was found.

On **December 1, 1923** Morrie Keane was found murdered on Joliet Rd. He was identified as a known independent beer runner. Frank McErlane a gang leader was identified as the killer, but was eventually released by the State's Attorneys Office **(solved).**

On **December 2, 1923** Mike Diovardi was murdered by unknown gangsters.

On **December 3, 1923** Adolph Skoff 21 yrs. was murdered in a roadhouse in Lyons, Illinois. Harry Heywood and Gene Stafanini were charged with the killing, Stafanini was found not guilty and Heywood was found guilty and sentenced to life in prison **(Solved)**. *Police logs entered the case as follows:* December 3, 1923 Skoff, Adolph - Age 21 - Died at St. Anne's Hospital from a gunshot wound received the same day at a roadhouse in Lyons, Ill. Assailant is unknown. 24 Dist. 12/4/23 Harry Haywood and Eugene Stepinini were arrested and turned over to Cicero, Ill. 2/1/24 - Stepinini acquitted - ???. 2/18/24 - Haywood to Joliet Pen. - Lindsay.

On **December 6, 1923** Dominick Armato was murdered by unknown gangsters.

On **December 7, 1923** Henry Bing 49 yrs. and Leopold P. Guth were murdered by John Sheehy who was killed on that day by Patrolman John T. O'Malley, patrolman Wm. O'Malley was wounded **(Solved)**. *Police logs entered the case as follows:* December 7, 1923 Bing, Henry - Age 49 - Shot to death in the Rendezvous Café, 626 Diversey Parkway, by John Sheehy, alias George Thomas, who also killed the steward, Leopold Guth and wounded Patrolman Wm. O'Malley. Sheehy was shot to death by Patrolman John T. O'Malley. 3rd Dist. On 12/7/23 Margaret Collins and Annie Gests were arrested as accessories after the fact. The latter two were not mentioned in the Coroners Verdict and on 12/10/23 were discharged by Judge Eberhardt.

On **December 15, 1923** Sam Belcastro was murdered by unknown gangsters.

On **December 26, 1923** Fred Guerrieri was murdered by unknown gangsters.

On **January 7, 1924** John A. Gilmore was murdered by unknown gangsters.

On **January 9, 1924** Vito Partipilo 40 yrs. was murdered at 1016 S. Morgan. Frank Spinelli, Peter Morgese and Munziati Mortilalto were arrested, but the results of the trial are not known **(Solved)**. *Police logs entered the case as follows:* January 9, 1924 Partipillo, Vito - Age 40 - Shot to death in front of 1016 So. Morgan St. Believed to be result of quarrel with Francisco Spinella, Nunciate Martillotto, and Pietro Morgese over use of horse and wagon without his consent. On 2/7/24 the arrest of the three men was recommended by the Coroner. 16 Dist.

On **January 10, 1924** Ferdinand Tatge 57 yrs. of Northfield, Township was shot by unknown gangsters. The victim was a wealthy farmer in Northbrook and Wheeling IL. and was found frozen by neighbors on his property in Northbrook with bullet wounds in his back. In 1936 police were provided with an anonymous letter naming three brothers as the killers, they were Henry Dehne of Long Grove, IL, Fred of Glenview, IL and Willie of Wheeling, IL. They were reported to be bank robbers, train robbers, truck hijackers and killed during these pursuits. They reportedly fled the area after the killing. It is not known how deeply these leads were pursued by authorities.

On **January 20, 1924** John Puccio was murdered by unknown gangsters.

On **February 2, 1924** John Noonan AKA: Wm. Newman 40 yrs. was murdered at 1600 W. Van Buren. Anthony Kissane was arrested and found not guilty at trial **(Solved)**. *Police logs entered the case as follows:* February 2, 1924 Noonan, John, alias Wm. Newman - Age 40 - Shot to death in the Ashland Auditorium, 1600 W. Van Buren, while attending a Chauffeur & Teamster's Dance, by one Anthony Kissane, who was held by the Coroner on 2/21/24. 4/30/24 - Acquitted - Lewis.

On **February 7, 1924** Ignazio Pieilli was murdered by unknown gangsters.

On **February 11, 1924** Leo Gistenson 28 yrs. and Israel Rappaport AKA: Rappart were murdered. Jack Cherbo, James Mogle, Dave Ostram, James Foley, Sidney Mogley and MOB labor racketeer/Capone gunman Danny Stanton were arrested and found not guilty of the killings in front of Judge Lindsey on July 29, 1924 **(Solved)**. *Police logs entered the case as follows:* February 11, 1924 Gistenson, Leo - Age 28 - Shot, 2/9/24, in Checker Cab Garage, 4642 W. Madison St., by several men who drove up in a large auto, and after firing a fusillade escaped. Israel Rappart was shot to death at the time. On 2/11/24 the Coroner recommended the arrest of John Foley, Daniel Stanton, James Mogley, Dave Ostren, John Cherbo, and Sid Gordon, alias Sidney Mogley. 24th Dist. On 2/19/24 five of the men surrendered. John Foley - 7/29/24 - Acquitted - Lindsay. Daniel Stanton - 7/29/24 - Acquitted - Lindsay. James Mogley - 7/29/24 - Acquitted - Lindsay. Dave Ostron - 7/29/24 - Acquitted - Lindsay. John Cherbo - 7/29/24 - Acquitted - Lindsay. Sidney Mogley - 7/29/24 - Acquitted - Lindsay.

Daniel Stanton

On **February 22, 1924** Leah Belle Exley 22 yrs. was murdered by John Duffy AKA: John Dougherty her common law husband, however, Duffy was murdered the following day by unknown assailant(s) before he could be brought to justice **(Solved)**. *Police logs entered the case as follows:* February 22, 1924 Exley, alias Mrs. John Duffy, Maybelle - Age 22 - Shot to death in her home, 1216 Carmen Ave., supposedly by her common-law husband, John Duffy, alias Daughterty. On 2/26/24 Wm. Eugelke, who is alleged to have witnessed the murder, was arrested and indicted by the March Grand Jury as an accessory 33 Dist. 11/7/24 - Eugleke - Nolle Prossed - Lindsay.

On **March 2, 1924** Joseph Rito was murdered by unknown gangsters.

On **March 5, 1924** William P. Calaghan was murdered by unknown gangsters.

On **March 6, 1924** Joseph Tuleo was murdered by unknown gangsters.

On **March 21, 1924** John H. Rose 35 yrs. was murdered in the County building. Patrick Sexton was arrested and found not guilty at trial **(Solved)**. *Police logs entered the case as follows:* March 21, 1924 Rose, John H. - Age 35 - Supt., Checker Cab Co. - Shot to death at north end of 11th floor corridor of the County Building, just after coming out of Judge Wells' Court where he appeared as a defendant in the murder of Frank Sexton on 6/6/23. He was shot by Patrick Sexton, father of Frank, after he had obtained the eleventh continuance of his case. On 4/22/24 Sexton was held by the Coroner for Manslaughter. 1st Dist. 2/10/25 - Acquitted - Brothers.

On **March 22, 1924** Philip Mazzio was murdered by unknown gangsters.

On **April 1, 1924** during yet another raucous primary election in Cicero, Capone gangsters raided the offices of Democratic reformers, beat and threatened their members and kidnapped their precinct workers. Outraged by these reports Cook County Judge Edmund Jarecki ordered 120 Chicago police officers to be sworn in as County Sheriffs and to restore order in Cicero. As the police moved into the town they engaged several gangsters in a gun battle near Cicero and 22nd St. (later named Cermak after the murdered Mayor). During the exchange Salvatore "Frank" Capone the older brother of the gang chief was mortally wounded and died later that day. Northside gangster Charles Dion "Deanie" O'Banion provided 3,000 roses from his florist shop for the funeral **(solved)**.

On **April 2, 1924** Philip Smith 26 yrs. of 3818 Washington Blvd. was shot by unknown gangsters. The victim was with a group of other Yellow Cab Drivers and became involved in a brawl at the infamous Tancl's Café at 4801 Ogden Ave. Cicero, IL., when shots were fired and the victim was struck while seated in his auto in front of the café. The owner of the Café, Edward Tancl was killed during a dispute with members of the Klondike O'Donnell Gang in November of 1924.

On **April 17, 1924** during the struggle to maintain control over their vast suburban interests, Capone men Jimmy Emery and Dominic Roberto took over Chicago Heights. Their gunman Martino, Lamberta and Piazza killed Chicago Heights Boss Antonine "Tony" Sanfilippo who resisted.

On **April 28, 1924** Samuel S. Bills 37 yrs. of 4256 S. Richmond St. and Robert Johnson AKA: Devere 43 yrs. of 801 Bradley Pl. were shot by unknown gangsters during a dispute at the Electrical Workers Union at 1507 Ogden Ave. There were many witnesses to the killing and it is not known what the outcome of the investigation was.

On **May 4, 1924** William Sedlacek was murdered by unknown gangsters.

On **May 4, 1924** Thaddeus S. Fancher was shot by Frank McErlane in a bar on Cedar Lake Rd. in Crown Point, Indiana. The victim was an attorney who was in the bar for a drink. Two stories were put forth on how this killing happened: One was that a large group of people were drinking with McErlane, a brawl started and Fancher was shot. The second stated that gang boss McErlane was there drinking heavily with John O'Rielly and Alex McCabe, when they challenged him to prove his skill with a gun. He pulled out his pistol and shot Fancher in the head at the end of the bar. McErlane escaped while his companions were arrested tried and convicted. O'Rielly was sentenced to life in prison while McCabe was eventually released and McErlane was tried, but not convicted of the crime **(solved)**.

On **June 5, 1924** Joseph Roberts was murdered by unknown gangsters.

On **June 7, 1924** Attillio Mancini was murdered by unknown gangsters.

On **June 19, 1924** George T. Swan of 2706 Michigan Ave. was murdered. It was reported that he was an innocent victim of a bomb placed by gangsters in the Saloon of Pat O'Malley at 742 S. Dearborn.

On **June 24, 1924** Peter Chiarelli was murdered by unknown gangsters.

On **June 26, 1924** James P. McFarland 34 yrs. of 1627 W. Madison St. was shot by Frank E. Carpenter of 533 S. Aberdeen St. in a saloon at 1809 W. Madison St. Carpenter was released by the coroner's jury after he stated that the victim was attempting to rob the saloon. Carpenter was killed in 1928 **(solved).**

On **July 4, 1924** Alfred D. Deckman 25 yrs. of 2048 W. Monroe St. was shot to death after a traffic altercation, while seated in his car on Garfield Blvd. near Western Ave. and his companion Earl Cooper was beaten. Walter O'Donnell 25 yrs. of 8253 S. Laflin St. the brother of Gang leader Spike O'Donnell was taken into custody near the scene. Others arrested were George Primm, Walter Mallory, Hugh Shanley, Frank Fisher and Charles Fitzpatrick a former South Park policeman. All the defendants were released by a coroner's jury **(solved).**

Spike O'Donnell

On **July 5, 1924** Charles Salomana 37 yrs. of 907 Sedgwick St. was shot by unknown gangsters on Locust St. near Townsend St. Investigators at the time suspected Blackhand extortionists in the killing.

On **July 26, 1924** Fred Ziegler was murdered. James Dougherty was identified as the offender, but it is not known if he was ever apprehended.

On **July 30, 1924** Samuel Roccardo was murdered by unknown gangsters.

In **August of 1924** Frank Lamaccia was murdered by Rocco Maggio who was considered a terrorist in the Italian Community. Maggio was arrested in 1925 in the company of a woman whose husband was killed by Maggio in 1922. Maggio was convicted and sentenced to life in prison but released in 1926 when the Illinois Supreme Court reversed the finding **(solved)**.

On **August 8, 1924** George Mustakis 33 yrs. of 500 S. Halsted St. was shot by unknown gangsters in front of 627 Blue Island Ave.

On **August 10, 1924** Vincenzo DeCaro was murdered by unknown gangsters.

On **August 13, 1924** Michael Laricchia was murdered by unknown gangsters.

On **August 28, 1924** Salvatore Falzone was murdered by unknown gangsters.

On **August 29, 1924** Frank Marotta 26 yrs. of 462 W. Division St. was shot by unknown gangsters as he left his home. Police suspected Blackhand extortionists at the time.

On **September 8, 1924** Jack Graziana 50 yrs. of Taylor and Throop Sts. was shot by unknown gangsters on the northwest corner of Taylor and May Sts. It was reported to involve Blackhand extortionists at the time.

On **September 24, 1924** Samuel Goldfarb 37 yrs. was murdered at 3420 Roosevelt Rd. Henry Lipkins was arrested and found not guilty at trial **(Solved)**. ***Police logs entered the case as follows:*** September 24, 1924 Goldfarb, Sam - Age 37 - Fatally shot 9/22/24 in Liberty Hall, 3420 Roosevelt Rd., during an argument at a meeting of the Baker's Union, by one Harry Lipkin, who was held by the Coroner 9/25/24. 21 Dist. 12/16/24 - Acquitted - Lindsay.

On **September 25, 1924** Patrolman David L. Boitano 41 yrs. of 6201 Glenwood Ave. was shot and killed at the corner of Elm and Townsend (now Larrabee and Chicago) known as Death Corner in the Little Sicily neighborhood on the northside of Chicago. The officer had spent over a decade pursuing Black Hand extortionists of the Sicilian Mafia. On this day the officer left his home in the evening in pursuit of Black Handers when he was approached by a man running toward him firing a gun. The officer returned fire as he fell, but the assailant ran off. Four years later information identified Carlo Aiello of the infamous Aiello gang as the killer. It is not known if the killer was ever brought to justice.

On **September 30, 1924** Dominick Busta 42 yrs. of 425 S. Campbell Ave. was shot by three unknown gangsters as he walked down the street at Van Buren St. near Racine Ave. It was reported to involve Blackhand extortionists at the time.

On **October 3, 1924** Carmela G. Bartucci was murdered by unknown gangsters.

On **October 5, 1924** Philip "Humdinger" Corrigan was murdered. He was a hoodlum in the Klondike O'Donnell gang and was caught trying to burn down Ed Tancl's Hawthorne Park Inn at 48th and Ogden in August of 1924. Apparently

Tancl took exception to the act and Corrigan was found shot in the head months later.

On **October 19, 1924** Bruno Martine AKA: Mike Searfi was murdered by unknown gangsters.

On **November 4, 1924** Anthony Kissane and John Mackey AKA: McCay were killed in a union related gun battle. Claude "Screwy" Maddox AKA: John E. Moore was identified as the killer but, escaped injury in the incident and was not brought to justice.

DeGrazia, Campagna, Maddox

On **November 7, 1924** Angelo Barbas was murdered. He was out of jail on a writ of supersedeas for the killing of Cherowkac, Geo. AKA: George Charkus and Omastosios "Thomas" Visvardis in June of 1923.

On **November 10, 1924** Salvatore DeLaurentis 38 yrs. of 700 S. Laflin was shotgunned by unknown gangsters in front of his home. The victim reportedly shot Frank Trombetta at 1955 W. Harrison St. on June 20th in a dispute over a lease and his wife claimed he was killed by two nephews of Trombetta while the police laid blame on Blackhand extortionists.

On **November 10, 1924** Charles Dean "Deanie" O'Banion 31 yrs. was gunned down in his north side Flower shop at 738 N. State St. At about 11:30 am three men entered the shop while orders were being prepared. While one of the men shook hands with the affable Irishman the others shot him in what would become known as the "Handshake Murder". Frankie Yale AKA: Uale or Ioele, Mike "The Devil" "Il Diavolo" Genna, Angelo Genna, John Scalise and Albert Anselmi were all suspected, but it was Torrio or Angelo Genna who was responsible. It was also reported that John Torrio was the first to import killers to carry out such assignments and the other gangs followed suit shortly thereafter. It seems that things had changed with the O'Banion's becoming the first gang to hijack shipments of alcohol from other peddlers. One issue was the dispute between

Torrio and O'Banion over the markers of Angelo Genna held by the "Ship" a casino in Cicero, IL. that was co-owned for a time by Torrio and O'Banion. And finally the setup of John Torrio who was arrested during a police raid at the Seiben Brewery during a negotiation with O'Banion to purchase his share of the business. ***Police logs entered the case as follows:*** November 10, 1924 O'Banion, Dion - Age 31 - Shot to death at 11:45 A.M., in his floral shop, 738 N. State St., by three unidentified men, who escaped in an automobile. 28 Dist.

John Scalise and Albert Anselmi

On **November 20, 1924** Tony Mancuso 33 yrs. of 925 S. Loomis St. was shot by unknown gangsters in the alley behind 2832 Princeton Ave. At the time police suspected involvement by Blackhand extortionists.

On **November 23, 1924** Leo Klimas and Edward Tancl of 193 Longcomon Rd., Riverside, IL. (the rough and tumble former prize fighter) were gunned down in his Cicero saloon the Hawthorne Park Inn at Ogden and 48th Ct. Their assailants Myles O'Donnell and James Dougherty were arrested and tried for the killings, but were found not guilty. This was the last chapter in the battle between Tancl and his adversary Klondike O'Donnell. It was later reported that the case was prosecuted by Assistant State's Attorney William H. McSwiggin who died in a drive-by shooting with Doherty and another in 1926 **(Solved)**.

On **November 29, 1924** Walter Langille 35 yrs. of 3457 Flournoy St. was shot by four unknown gangsters at the northeast corner of Robey St. and Ogden Ave. It was reported that the victim knew who shot him, but would not tell authorities.

On **December 6, 1924** Michael Pernice was murdered by unknown gangsters.

On **December 11, 1924** Omar Finch was murdered. Edward M. "Teddy" Newberry of the northside Moran gang was arrested and Reggy Moran and Eugene McLaughlin were wanted in connection with the crime. The charges against Newberry were ultimately dropped and Morgan and McLaughlin were not indicted **(Solved)**.

Ted Newberry

On **December 16, 1924** Harry D. Johnson 31 yrs. 7618 S. Marshfield Ave. was beaten and shot by unknown gangsters at 54th Place near Wallace under a railroad viaduct.

On **December 19, 1924** Nick Ranieri 40 yrs. of 820 N. Oakley was shot to death in front of his butcher shop at Western and Grenshaw by unknown gangsters who lured him outside and then shot him. This was a short time after another butcher shop at Laflin and Spruce Sts. was bombed.

On **December 21, 1924** John Pusateri 23 yrs. of 1738 W. Erie St. was shot by unknown gangsters as he exited his Ford automobile in front of 1849 Grand Ave. It was reported that Blackhand extortionists were suspected of involvement at the time.

On January 24, 1925 John Torrio was shot as he entered the vestibule of his apartment building at 7011 S. Clyde. This was part of the intrigue surrounding events that included the Genna gambling debt, the Seiben raid and then the murder of Northside gang Boss Charles Dion "Deanie" O'Banion. Hymie Weiss AKA: Earl Wajciechowski, George "Bugs" Moran AKA: George Gage and Vincent "Schemer" Drucci AKA: DiAmbrosio carried out the shooting, but were never charged. At the time Torrio was out on bond waiting to serve his jail term. He survived the attack and spent weeks recovering before beginning his sentence in DuPage County. Afterward he took a European vacation; he then retired to

Brooklyn with a fortune. He turned the gang and all of its holdings over to Al Capone.

On **January 26, 1925** Raffela Amores 38 yrs. of Melrose Park, IL. was murdered in his soft drink parlor at 2100 Lake St. by unknown gangsters.

On **February 2, 1925** Mike DeMilio 44 yrs. of 3424 w. Flournoy St. was shot to death at the northwest corner of Curtis and Grand Ave. by unknown gangsters. The victim was a Deputy Sheriff and owner of a private watchman service. He was also an alleged bomber and extortionist when he was killed.

On **February 2, 1925** Gabriel Serpio 34 yrs. of 908 W. Taylor St. was shot to death on his rear porch by unknown gangsters.

On **February 9, 1925** Harry Filice 34 yrs. of 2873 East 91st. St. was shot to death in the kitchen of his home by unknown gangsters. He told his wife of an altercation a few days before the killing, but gave no details.

On **February 9, 1925** Anthony Dominick 24 yrs. of 814 S. Loomis St. is shot in front of 736 S. Loomis St. by two unknown gangsters and dies eight days later in Cabrini Hospital. A police investigation revealed that the victim had done time for assaulting a woman in the past and on the day of the shooting he was approached by two men who exited a car and argued with him before shooting him and fleeing.

On **February 10, 1925** Lozzero Clemente of 1307 23rd Ave. Melrose Park was shot to death in the backyard of his home by unknown gangsters. It was reported that the victim had gambling debts prior to his murder and Blackhand extortionists were also suspected.

On **March 3, 1925** Thomas J. Gaughan 44 yrs. of 1123 Chatham Court and Peter Hayden 47 yrs. of 656 Elm St. are both shot to death at 873 Larrabee Street by unknown gangsters. Police suspected that Gaughan who wore a warden's badge of the Forest Preserve along with Hayden would go to the Italians in the neighborhood who made wine and shake them down leading to the killing.

On **March 9, 1925** Favo Randazzo AKA: Faro 44yrs. of 909 N. Franklin St. was shot to death in front of 870 N. Franklin by unknown gangsters.

On **March 15, 1925** Louis A. Cella Jr. 27 yrs. was murdered at 753 N. Clark St. Tom Edwards was arrested, but a no bill was passed by the grand jury and he walked free **(Solved)**. *Police logs entered the case as follows:* March 15, 1925 Cella, Louis - Age 27 - Fatally shot at 3:58 A.M., in front of 753½ N. Clark St., during an argument with Tom Edwards, who was held by the Coroner on 3/16/25. Both had been drinking. 28 Dist. March 1925 No bill.

On **March 22, 1925** David J. Phillips 22, of 457 N. Harding Ave. was killed by a group of men that included Mob luminaries Thomas McElligott and Fred T. "Juke Box" Smith 21 yrs. of 3051 W. Fifth Ave. Eight arrests were made and Smith, McElligott and the others were tried for the murder; James J. O'Callahan was identified as the shooter but remained a fugitive. The others were acquitted in 1930. Smith would rise to become a leader in the IBT Jukebox Division Local 134, where he would obtain his moniker **(solved)**.

"Michael 'Bubs' Quinlan, south side gangster . . . rival of Saltis."

Chicago Sunday Tribune

Bubbs Quinlan

On **April 3, 1925** Walter Quinlan 28 yrs. was murdered in Joe Sindelar's Saloon at 1700 S. Loomis St. John "Paddy the Fox" Ryan 28 yrs. was wanted for the killing and was arrested in a sheet metal shop at 3614 W. Harrison St. It turns out that Quinlan killed Ryan's Father Paddy the Bear in 1920 and young Ryan swore vengeance while working in the Ralph Sheldon gang. The outcome of the investigation is not known. It was later reported that Quinlan was commissioned by the Westside O'Donnell gang to do the collecting from their liquor customers with the help of William "Rags" McCue who would do the actual collecting that Quinlan would track. Apparently when the books did not jibe Quinlan had no explanation and McCue was suspected in the killing **(solved)**. ***Police logs entered the case as follows:*** April 3, 1925 Quinlan, Walter - Age 28 - Shot to death at 4 PM, in a soft-drink parlor at 1700 So. Loomis St., by John P. "Paddy" Ryan, who escaped. On 4/10/26 his arrest was recommended by the Coroner. 4/5/26 Wm. "Rags" McCue and Sam Richer were booked as accessories. On 4/17/26 McCue was found murdered in a ditch near Hinsdale, Ill. 6/10/26 Richer case nolle prossed in Mun. Ct. - Judge S. Trude. 11/17/26 John F. Ryan, alias "The Fox" arrested and turned over to the Sheriff. Nov. 1926 No bill on Ryan.

On **April 4, 1925** Joseph Montana 37 yrs. was murdered at 1123 S. Peoria by unknown gangsters. ***Police logs entered the case as follows:*** April 4, 1925 Montana, Joseph - Age 37 - Fatally shot 9:50 PM, 4/1/25, in the gangway of 1123 So. Peoria St., when about to enter his home, by unknown gangsters.

On **April 7, 1925** Joseph Larson 36 yrs. of 3217 W. Ohio St. was shot to death in the rear of 511 North Halsted by unknown gangsters.

On **April 15, 1925** Guiseppe Giordano 28 yrs. of 1631 W. North Ave. was shot to death on the street on Central Park Ave. just south of Evergreen St. by unknown gangsters.

On **April 17, 1925** Joseph Tuminello 32 yrs. of 632 S. May St. was shot to death in front of his home by unknown Blackhand extortionists.

On **April 29, 1925** Louis Cama 42 yrs. of 609 Forquer St. was shot by unknown gangsters at the front of his bakery/residence possibly by Blackhand extortionists.

On **May 12, 1925** Joseph Saitta 40yrs. of 1737 N. Lockwood was shot to death in the alley between Latrobe and Lockwood Sts. about 75 feet north of Wabansia Ave. by unknown gangsters.

On **May 19, 1925** George Garines 24yrs. of 4332 S. Michigan Ave. was shot to death by unknown gangsters traveling in a large black auto in front of 4332 S. Michigan.

On **May 25, 1925** Frank DeAngelo 41yrs. of 1133 S. Lincoln St. was shot to death near Grenshaw and Cypress Sts. by unknown gangsters.

On **May 25, 1925** John Ciapetta 54yrs. of 1541 S. Vincennes Ave. was shot to death in front of 82 E. 16th St., Chicago Heights, IL. by unknown gangsters.

Genna Family

On **May 26, 1925** Angelo Genna 27 yrs. President of Unione Siciliana and the youngest brother of Taylor Streets' "Terrible Gennas" (Pete, Tony, Jim, Mike and Sam) was gunned down by either Capone gunman or Northside killers while driving his car on north Ogden Ave. near Hudson Ave. The Gennas developed a bootlegging empire that enlisted the help of hundreds of immigrant families in the Little Italy neighborhood that supported themselves' by cooking rotgut alcohol in the bath tubs of their flats. The Gennas also put themselves in the unenviable position of warring with the Capone organization over control of the Unione Siciliana and the O'Banion Gang who were furious over Angelo's $30,000 debt at the "Ship" casino in Cicero (a gambling joint in which the Torrio/Capone and the O'Banion gang were partners for a time). Another factor was the northside gang's territory bordered the Gennas'. The Northsiders were not pleased when the Gennas expanded beyond their agreed territories. The Gennas were also held partially accountable for the murder of Deanie O'Banion (Capone killers Anselmi and Scalise started out working first for the Genna's and were suspected in the O'Banion killing) and Angelo's killing may have been in retaliation and orchestrated by northside gang boss Hymie Weiss AKA: Earl Wajciechowski, reportedly Schemer Drucci or Bugs Moran were the shooters in this killing, but never charged. ***Police logs entered the case as follows:*** May 26, 1925 Genna, Angelo - Age 27 - Shot to death at 9:30 AM, while riding south in Ogden Ave., near Hudson Ave., by four men, with shotguns, who drove alongside of him in another automobile. His assailants escaped. 29 Dist.

Hymie Weiss

On **June 9, 1925** Walter A. O'Donnell 25yrs. of 8253 S. Laflin St. was shot to death in the Capitol Inn at 95th and Western Aves. by unknown gangsters.

On **June 13, 1925** Patrolmen Charles B. Walsh 30 yrs. and Harold F. Olson were murdered and Sergeant Michael Conway was seriously wounded during a high speed chase with Genna/Capone killers Albert Anselmi and John Scalise at 59th and Western. The men were accompanied by gangsters Salvatore "Samoots" Amatuna who escaped on foot and Mike "The Devil" "Il Diavolo" Genna 28 yrs. who was killed during the incident by Patrolman William Sweeney. The men were charged with the killings. The defense of these two prolific killers by Mob bosses was the subject of a massive fund raising effort in the Italian quarter and led to several killings of businessmen less than enthusiastic about making such contributions. The killers were found guilty and sentenced to prison. Subsequent retrials resulted in their acquittal on June 26, 1926. Public outrage was felt when the reasoning for the acquittal was that the officers had no warrant or known probable cause to give chase and therefore the mobsters were not guilty of murder. At this point in time it seemed that the whole criminal justice system was corrupt **(Solved)**. *Police logs entered the case as follows:* June 13, 1925 Genna, Michael - Age 28 - Shot to death at 9:20 AM, in the rear of 5941 Artesian Ave., by Patrolman Wm. Sweeney of DB Squad 8-C, two of which were killed by Genna, Albert Anselino and John Scalice whom the squad attempted to arrest. 11A Dist. June 13, 1925 Walsh, Charles B. - Patrolman - Age 30 - Shot to death at 9:20 AM, in front of 5940 Western Ave., together with Patrolman Harold Olson, both DB Squad 8-C by Michael Genna, Albert Anslino and John Scalise, who were resisting arrest. Genna was killed by Officer Wm. Sweeney. Anselmi and

Scalise were captured and on 6/15/25 turned over to the Sheriff on indictment. 11-A Dist. 3/8/26 - both men acquitted - Brothers.

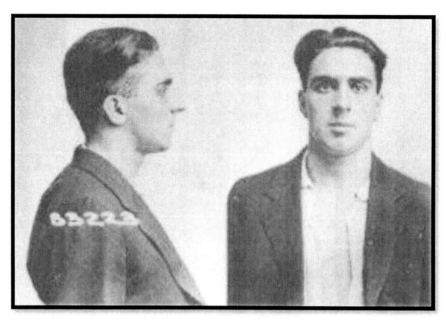

Schemer Drucci

On **June 27, 1925** Otto Corra 19 yrs. was murdered at 508 N. Green St. Joseph Lonero was wanted for the killing but, it is not known if he was ever brought to justice **(Solved)**. *Police logs entered the case as follows:* June 27, 1925 Carrao, Otto - Age 19 - Fatally shot 7 PM, 6/25/25 in vacant lot at 508 N. Green St., during an argument by Joseph Lonero, who escaped. 22 Dist.

On **July 6, 1925** Joseph Lasorelli 30 yrs. of 462 N. Curtis St. was shot by unknown gangsters in front of 1208 Frontier St.

On **July 8, 1925** Anthony "The Gent" Genna 30 yrs. of 5556 S. Sawyer Ave. was shot at 1057 Grand Ave. Tony was set up by Joseph Nerona AKA: Guiseppe Nerone, Caveliero, Tony Spano. One report claims that Schemer Drucci was the shooter in this killing. Charles Cuttila was arrested for possible involvement, but later released by police. Shortly thereafter, Jim Genna went into hiding while Sam and Pete Genna fled to Italy basically leaving the territory up for grabs and their associates scrambling to keep the operation going and staying alive. It was later reported that the victim told police on his deathbed who was responsible for his condition by saying "The Cavalier put me on the spot". Nerone fled to Chicago Heights and tried to set up alkie cooking operations there that caused several killings until he was lured back to Chicago and killed **(Solved)**. *Police logs entered the case as follows:* July 8, 1925 Genna, Tony - Age 30 - Fatally shot at 10:36 AM, at the S.E. corner of Curtis St. and Grand Ave., by one of two unknown men, one of whom approached and shook hands with him as the other crossed the street and shot him. 22 Dist. 7/8/25 Chas. Cuttila was arrested and on 7/21/25 Discharged by Judge Richardson.

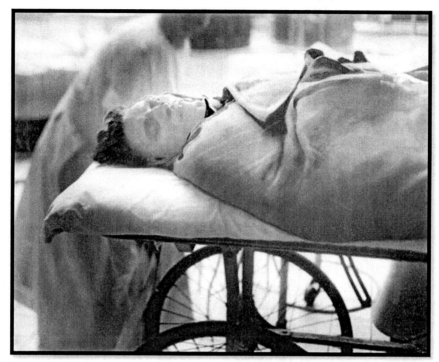

Tony Genna dead

On **July 14, 1925** Savario "Sam" Lavenuto 33 yrs. of 807 S. Racine Ave. was shot by unknown gangsters in front of his residence for trying to be an independent bootlegger.

On **July 14, 1925** Vincenzo "James" Russo was shot by unknown gangsters for trying to be an independent bootlegger.

On **July 15, 1925** Anthony Campagna 34yrs. of 1114 W. Congress St. was shot to death while sitting in an auto in front of 6243 S. Morgan St. by unknown gangsters.

On **July 16, 1925** Louis I. Sniderman 27yrs. of 822 Wabash Ave. was shot to death at Webster and Sedgwick Sts. by unknown gangsters.

On **July 18, 1925** Joseph Granata 27 yrs. of 2040 W. 68th St. and James Vinci 31 yrs. shot and killed each other on the northeast corner of 29th and Wells Sts. **(solved)**. *Police logs entered the case as follows:* July 18, 1925 Vinci, James - Age 31 - Shot to death at 10:29 PM, at the N.E. corner of 29th and Wells Sts., during an argument over a bond forfeiture, by Joseph Granata who himself was killed by Vinci and a third unknown man. 2nd Dist.

On **July 23, 1925** George Karl Jr. AKA: Big Bates 28 yrs. of 5214 Kimbark Ave. was shot to death and found in a prairie at 80th St. and Austin Ave. He was killed by unknown gangsters.

On **August 7, 1925** Carmen Tedesco 41 yrs. of 827 Sholto St. was found stabbed to death by unknown gangsters in the rear of his soft drink parlor at 716 W. Harrison St.

On **August 8, 1925** Joseph DiMarco 19 yrs. of 837 Garibaldi Pl. was stabbed by unknown gangsters in the hallway of 912 Garibaldi Pl.

On **August 17, 1925** Felix Scalto AKA: Scalzo 21 yrs. of 1116 Hamilton Ave. was shot to death while seated in an auto in front of 816 Forquer St. by an unknown gangster.

On **August 17, 1925** John Ignosso 43 yrs. of 900 Townsend St. was shot by unknown gangsters in front of his home.

On **August 23, 1925** Frank Spino AKA: Spina 39 yrs. of 2210 W. Ohio St., Joseph Vecchio 32 yrs. of 2146 W. Warren Ave. and Joseph Preiti AKA: Praiti, Reiti 29 yrs. of 2126 W. Warren Ave. were all shot to death at Rockwell and Huron Sts. by an unknown gangster with one victim dying the following day. Preiti was a know blackhander. Ralph Comiglio and Anthony Casahsis were arrested 8/23/25; Frank Cresto and Nick Cosentino were arrested on 10/1/25. All the charges were eventually dropped **(Solved).**

On **August 28, 1925** Harry Berman and Irving Schlig were killed by unknown gangsters for trying to be independent bootleggers.

On **September 3, 1925** William Dickman 34yrs. was shot to death in the vicinity of 52nd and Troy Sts. and then dumped from an auto at 5212 S. Troy by unknown gangsters. It was later reported that he was killed by his own Saltis McErlane gang for exchanging greetings on the street with rival Spike O'Donnell, but the case remains open.

On **September 7, 1925** Joseph Agate 26 yrs. of 9147 W. Harrison St. was shot on September 5th in front of 2208 W. Polk St. by unknown gangsters.

On **September 10, 1925** Nick Malella 27yrs. of 1022 S. Sangamon St. was stabbed and slashed to death by two unknown gangsters who entered his bedroom to attack him.

On **September 11, 1925** Howard Berkovitz was shot in the poolroom at 1702 W. Roosevelt Rd. by Robert Stamm. The case involved the Yellow Cab Co. and the outcome of the trial is unknown. Stamm was murdered in 1934.

On **September 14, 1925** Frank Izarella 26yrs. of 817 Cambridge Ave. was shot to death by unknown gangsters in the hallway of his residence.

On **September 15, 1925** Manuel Lozano 27 yrs. of the C. R. I. & P. Railroad Camp, 123rd St. and Blue Island was beaten to death suffering severe head trauma at 120th St. and Ashland Ave. in Burr Oak, Illinois by unknown gangsters.

On **September 27, 1925** Aniello Taddeo was gunned down in front of his restaurant. He was bootlegging boss for Salvatore "Samoots" Amatuna in Melrose Park IL. and helped move a portion of the city operation out west to avoid the police raids by reform Mayor Dever. Seeking justice for the murder of his friend, James Campanille was killed in almost the same spot a short time later in January 1926.

Samoots Amatuna

On **October 3, 1925** Charles Kelly and Thomas Hart were killed by machine gun fire into the headquarters of the Ralph Sheldon gang at the Ragen Athletic Club at 5142 S. Halsted, marking the first death by a Thompson sub-machinegun or "Tommy Gun" as it became known. It was determined by police that Charles Kelly was not a gangster and only happened to be walking down the street when he was cut down. It was reported that members of the Saltis McErlane gang were responsible, but never charged.

On **October 4, 1925** John Ambrosini 21 yrs. of 11626 Front Ave. was stabbed to death by unknown gangsters at 115th and Watt Ave.

On **October 10, 1925** Frank Beto 28 yrs. was shot by unknown gangsters at 928 S. Robey St.

On **October 12, 1925** Edward Lottjak 27 yrs. was shot to death and left in a ditch at 83rd St. and State Road in Stickney, IL. by unknown gangsters.

On **October 13, 1925** John Russo 32 yrs. of 217 S. Robey St. was shot to death while sitting in his auto in his backyard by unknown gangsters.

On **October 18, 1925** Christopher Murray 30 yrs. of 2943 S. Halsted St. was shot to death in front of his residence during an altercation with an unknown gangster.

On **October 20, 1925** Rosario Giorvano AKA: Giordano 31 yrs. of 3219 Chicago Road, Chicago Heights, IL. was shot to death in the Moonlight Inn on Lincoln Highway and State St. in Bloom Township by unknown gangsters.

On **October 21, 1925** Pasquale Polizzetto 38 yrs. of 132 E. 24ᵗʰ St., Chicago Heights, IL. was shot to death in front of 97 E. 25ᵗʰ St., Chicago Heights, IL. by unknown gangsters.

On **October 22, 1925** Ralph Bernardo 32 yrs. of 904 Forquer St. was stabbed to death by unknown gangsters.

On **October 30, 1925** Clement Valentine 40 yrs. of 1145 Washington Blvd. was stabbed by unknown gangsters.

On **November 2, 1925** Frank Canale 35 yrs. of 1473 Larrabee St. was shot to death in front of 561 Veeder St. by unknown gangsters.

On **November 9, 1925** Patrolman Frederick M. Schmitz was killed by a dynamite bomb placed at the basement window of his residence 5233 W. Van Buren St., while he worked on his furnace in the basement of his home. The investigation revealed that this attack was probably a case of mistaken identity in that the victim's next door neighbor was Captain Ira McDowell who had driven gamblers and bootleggers from his district and was assumed to be a target of gangsters in Chicago.

On **November 13, 1925** Salvatore "Samoots" Amatuna 27 yrs. of 1209 W. Roosevelt Rd. was gunned down by Vincent "Schemer" Drucci AKA: DiAmbrosio in Isidore Paul's barber shop at 804 Roosevelt Road just before his wedding was to take place. Samoots was the current President of the Unione Siciliana and had a confrontational relationship with the "Terrible Gennas" and possibly the Capone gang. He preceded Angelo Genna at the Unione and was to wed Mike Merlo's niece Rose Pecoraro. He also led the effort to secure a defense fund for cop killers Scalise and Anselmi which led to intimidations and Bloodshed for those who resisted. It was Antonio "Tony" Lombardo who would replace him at the Unione at the pleasure of Capone. A short time later, Lombardo opens membership to non-Sicilians and changes the group's name to Italo-American National Union, which infuriates the Sicilian membership. It was later reported that Amatuna would occasionally participate in the enterprises of the O'Banion gang which is not widely known. ***Police logs entered the case as follows:*** November 13, 1925 Amutina, or Amatuna, Sam, alias "Samoots" - Age 27 - Fatally shot 6:50 P.M., 11/10/25, in a barber shop at 804 W. Roosevelt Rd., by two unknown men who escaped. 16th Dist.

On **November 13, 1925** Marco Inburgia 72 yrs. of 2738 W. Chicago Ave. was shot to death in front of 451 W. Oak St. by an unknown gangster.

On **November 15, 1925** Placide DiVarco 21 yrs. of 1107 Townsend St. was shot in front of 1011 Sedgwick St. Tom Damiano and a second offender known as John Abbananti AKA: "Little Johnny" were wanted for the killing, but it is not known if they were ever brought to justice **(Solved)**. *Police logs entered the case as follows:* November 15, 1925 Davarco, Joseph - Age 21 - Shot to death at 8:17 AM, in front of 1011 Sedgewick St., by Thomas Domiano, whose "girl" he was escorting. Domaino, accompanied by one "Little Johnny" alias John Abbananti, escaped in an automobile. On 11/16/25 the arrest of the two men was recommended by the Coroner. 28th Dist.

On **November 18, 1925** Edward C. Zine AKA: Zion was gunned down. He was a Westside alky distributor and loyal henchman for Salvatore "Samoots" Amatuna and was killed approximately a week after his boss. He was returning from paying his respects for Samoots.

On **November 20, 1925** Mariano Muscarello 32 yrs. of 1116 Larrabee St. was shot to death at 1148 Larrabee St. by unknown gangsters.

On **November 20, 1925** Michael Vinci 25 yrs. of 3115 Shields Ave. was shot at 31st and Dearborn Sts. Joseph Annoreno AKA: Joe "Peppy" Genero was charged with the killing and found not guilty **(Solved)**. *Police logs entered the case as follows:* November 20, 1925 Vinci, Mike - Age 25 - Shot to death at 12:30 AM, at 31st and Dearborn Sts., and before he died he accused Joe Genero, alias Annoreno as his assailant. Genero was arrested and on 12/2/25 was held by the Coroner. It was at this inquest that Sam Vinci, brother of deceased, shot and killed John Minatti, a witness. 2nd Dist.

On **November 21, 1925** John Minetti was murdered. Sam Vinci was charged in the killing and sentenced to 26 years in prison after being found guilty. The killer stated at the inquest of his brother that: John killed my brother Mike and I thought the jury was going to set him free **(Solved)**.

On **November 21, 1925** Abraham "Bummy" Golstine AKA: Goldstein 22 yrs. of 1158 Hastings St. was shot to death in front of 1400 Blue Island Ave. by unknown gangsters. He like Ed Zine was a Westside alky distributor and loyal henchman for Salvatore "Samoots" Amatuna and like Eddie was dead within two weeks of Samoot's murder. It was later reported that he was one of the assassins of Amatuna but was never charged.

On **December 13, 1925** Frank Alonzi 27 yrs. of 1423 Sedgwick St. was a known moonshiner and was shot to death in his home by unknown gangsters.

On **December 13, 1925** Charles Williams 28 yrs. was found shot to death at 121st and Ashland Aves. in a prairie in Burr Oak, IL. by unknown gangsters.

On **December 13, 1925** Officer Edward Pflaume was shot and killed as he and other officers attempted to arrest two men suspected of committing two robberies earlier in the day. The suspects opened fire on the officers, killing Officer Pflaume and wounding a second officer. One of the suspects Jimmy Johnstone was killed and the other was wounded as he attempted to flee. The wounded suspect, William "Three-Fingered Jack" White, one of Al Capone's top lieutenants, was convicted of Officer Pflaume's murder and sentenced to life on January 21, 1927. In February 1929, he won a reversal in the Supreme Court which held that it had not been proved that Officer Pflaume and the other officers had the right to arrest him. At his new trial he was again found guilty of Officer Pflaume's murder but was only sentenced to 14 years in prison on March 14, 1931. On May 23, 1932 the Supreme Court reversed the conviction altogether. On January 23, 1934, White was shot and killed by rival gangsters in Chicago **(Solved)**.

On **December 21, 1925** Frank Gibbi 38 yrs. of 937 Larrabee St. was killed by unknown gangsters in the alley behind 1226 Sinnot Pl.

On **December 22, 1925** Edwin A. Harmening 25 yrs. a Highway Deputy Sheriff of 711 W. 65th St. and Joseph B. Brook AKA: Joseph Michael Brook 25 yrs. of 721 76th St. were both shot to death and found in Brook's Studebaker auto in Marquette Park at 70th St. and California Ave. They were killed by unknown gangsters. It was reported that the men had been hijacking beer trucks for Brook's tavern and when they took a truck belonging to the Saltis McErlane gang they were set up and killed, the case remains open.

On **December 29, 1925** James Lenti 40 yrs. of 7731 Greenwood Ave. was shot by unknown gangsters in the basement of his home.

On **December 31, 1925** Bernardo Gentile 40 yrs. of 5877 Archer Ave. was shot by unknown gangsters in a coal yard at that location.

On **January 7, 1926** James Campanile was killed by unknown gangsters at almost the same spot as his close friend Aniello Taddeo some three months earlier. He intended to seek revenge for his friend, but did not live long enough to do that.

On **January 7, 1926** James O'Brien 30 yrs. was shot to death by unknown gangsters and found at 21st Ave. and North Ave. in Melrose Park, IL.

On **January 10, 1926** Henry Spingola 28 yrs. of 417 S. Taylor Ave. Oak Park, IL. a well thought of businessman and Unione Siciliana member was shot to death after attending a card game at Amata's restaurant at 914 S. Halsted St. Henry donated $10,000 for the defense fund of Genna/Capone Gunman Anselmi and Scalise for their first trial in the killing of two police officers. Later before the second trial was to begin he would only donate another $2,000, rejecting a bid for more money. Apparently that did not sit well with the Capone gang and

Orazio Tropea (their collector) arranged for the murder of Spingola. ***Police logs entered the case as follows:*** January 10, 1926 Spingola, Henry – Age 26 – Shot to death at 9:00 P.M. at the wheel of his auto, just after leaving a restaurant at 914 So. Halsted St., by four unknown men who apparently waited for him in an auto across the street. His assailants escaped. Spinola was a brother-in-law of the Gennas. 16th Dist.

On **January 16, 1926** Harry Schneider 58 yrs. of 924 S. Robey St. was shot to death on the front porch of his residence by unknown gangsters.

On **January 19, 1926** Edward Ryan 51 yrs. of 10 Cedar St. was shot to death in front of 1100 Townsend St. by unknown gangsters.

On **January 27, 1926** Augustino Morici 36 yrs. 925 Lakeside Pl. and Antonio Moreci 50 yrs. also of 925 Lakeside Pl. were shot by unknown gangsters. The men were very successful grocers and macaroni manufacturers with offices at 662 W. Washington. Augustino and Antonio also provided ingredients for the Genna alky cooking operations. During the trial of Angelo Genna in the Labriola murder Augustino testified as a character witness for the accused, but when the pair refused the demands of the Anselmi and Scalise defense fund they were shot to death as they drove north on Ogden Avenue at Wisconsin St. on their way home. Antonio died two days after his brother.

On **January 31, 1926** Isaac Stein AKA: Harry, Teddy 24 yrs. was murdered at 2153 13th St. Louis "Big" Smith was arrested for the killing while Lizzie Cohen was held as an accessory and a third party only known as Herb was wanted. An indictment was passed on Smith, but he was killed before the trial **(Solved)**. ***Police logs entered the case as follows:*** January 31, 1926 Stein, Harry "Teddy" – Age 24 – Fatally shot 5:50 PM, in the passageway of 2153 13th St., and died at 8:13 PM, accusing Louis Smith, alleging they had quarreled over the use of a Paige auto they had purchased jointly. On 2/4/26 Smith was held by the Coroner as was Lizzie Cohen as an accessory. 17th Dist. Feb. 1926 No Bill on Cohen. 8/10/26 Smith was murdered in front of 1520 So. Avers Ave. 3/13/26 cause abated a/c dead.

On **February 6, 1926** Charles Pope AKA: Pepe 33 yrs. of 2905 Princeton Ave. was shot to death at 28th and Stewart Ave. by unknown gangsters.

On **February 15, 1926** Clarence W. Glynn AKA: Glenn 33 yrs. was murdered at 2802 W. 38th St. Virgil Litzinger was arrested and tried for the killing only to be acquitted at trial **(Solved)**. ***Police logs entered the case as follows:*** February 15, 1926 Glenn or Glynn, Clarence - Age 33 - Shot to death at 3:30 PM, in his saloon at 2801 W. 38th St., by Virgil Litzinger, who escaped. The murder, preceded by threats, was due to jealousy in business. On 2/15/26 the Coroner recommended Litzinger's arrest. 15 Dist. 11/21/28 Litzinger surrendered to U.S. Auth. and was indicted by Nov. 1928 grand jury. 3/22/29 - Acquitted - McGoorty.

On **February 15, 1926** Orazio "the Scourge" Tropea 35 yrs. of 522 S. Halsted St. was shotgunned to death in the intersection of Taylor and Halsted after he swore at a green vehicle that almost hit him as he exited a trolley car. The Scourge as he was known was one of the point men in collecting funds for the Anselmi/Scalise defense fund. He was suspected of funneling as much as $20,000 into his own accounts and that angered gang leaders. It was later reported that a group of avenger's from the Italian quarter not associated with the gang life were responsible for this and other gang slayings.

On **February 17, 1926** Alberto Speciale 34 yrs. of Milwaukee, WI. was shot by unknown gangsters at Lyon and Jackson Sts., Milwaukee, WI. It was reported that Speciale was involved in the illicit liquor business and refused overtures to join the Chicago "Alcohol Society" run by Chicago mobsters.

On **February 20, 1926** Vito Bascone AKA: Basccno a Genna man and close associate of Orazio Tropea was killed in Stickney, Illinois. During 1926, a full assault commenced on the remaining members of the Genna organization. It was later reported that this killing was carried out by a group of vigilantes from the Italian quarter.

On **February 23, 1926** Edward/Ecola "The Eagle" Baldelli 23 yrs. was found murdered behind 411 N. Curtis St., he was a driver for Orazio Tropea and "Machine Gun" Jack McGurn AKA: James or Vincenzo Gibaldi was suspected. The Genna gangster was found shot to death in the rear alley of 411 N. Curtis St. He was apparently killed elsewhere and dumped at that location. McGurn was never charged in the killing, but it was later reported that this killing was carried out by a group of vigilantes from the Italian quarter. ***Police logs entered the case as follows:*** February 23, 1926 Baldelli, Edward - Age 23 - Found shot to death at 11:25 P.M., in the alley rear of 411 N. Curtis St., by watchman. The body was apparently brought to and deposited at that place by the unknown murderers in an auto. 22nd Dist.

On **March 2, 1926** David P. Feeley 41 yrs. of 7 E. 23rd St. was shot to death at 18th St. and Clark by two unknown gangsters. It was reported that the victim was a member of the Saltis McErlane gang and died for talking with Spike O'Donnell, the case remains open.

On **March 6, 1926** Joseph "Little Joe" Calabrese the Genna gang's collector and enforcer was riding with several men in a car heading to Cicero when at 22nd and Keeler a car pulled alongside and peppered their car with shotgun pellets killing Little Joe.

On **March 6, 1926** Francis Patrick Lawrence 30 yrs. of 7216 S. Yale a soft drink parlor proprietor was shot to death in the parlor at 2011 W. 63rd St. by unknown gangsters. He was left by two men in the doorway of Auburn Park Hospital. It was reported that he turned down the Saltis McErlane gang who wanted to sell him beer.

On **March 11, 1926** Harold Flynn 30yrs. of 4309 Wilcox St. was shot to death in the 27th Ward Republican Boosters Club at 1454 W. Madison St. by unknown gangsters.

On **March 15, 1926** Daniel Cerone was murdered. The victim was believed to be the Cousin of future Mob Boss "Jackie the Lackey" Cerone who rose to prominence in Chicago under the leadership of Joey Aiuppa.

On **March 17, 1926** Joseph Staliga 50 yrs. of Racine, Wisconsin a proprietor of a soft drink parlor and Effrey Marks 37 yrs. of 4932 Forrestville Ave. were both shot to death by unknown gangsters in Staliga's soft drink parlor at 4631 W. 12th Pl. in Cicero, IL.

On **March 23, 1926** George J. Dietrich 38 yrs. of 7 S. Central Park was shot to death by unknown gangsters in the soft drink parlor at 1657 W. Lake St.

On **April 1, 1926** Fred Boeseneiler AKA: Andre Anderson was murdered. Leo Mongoven was arrested, tried and found not guilty **(Solved)**. At this time the CCC notes that since January there were 27 gangland killings and none led to convictions.

On **April 10, 1926** Walter Johnson AKA: Johnston 26 yrs. of 5137 S. Troy was shot in the head by unknown gangsters and found along Ridgeland Ave. near 94th St. in Worth Township. It was reported that Johnson was not in the liquor business, but was a friend of gangster Ralph Sheldon and the Saltis McErlane gang deemed that a reason to die. Later reports stated that the victim was a precinct worker for State's Attorney Crowe and his death may have been related to an election.

On **April 10, 1926** Francisco DeLamentis AKA: DeLaurentis 29 yrs. of 2438 W. Harrison St. and Jacomino Tuccillo 33 yrs. of 3716 W. Harrison St. were found shot to death by unknown gangsters in Tuccillo's auto in front of 6553 S. Rockwell St. which happened to be the residence of gangster Ralph Sheldon. It was reported that the men were selling alcohol and approached a customer of the Saltis McErlane gang.

On **April 14, 1926** Santo Ilacqua AKA: Calabresi 37 yrs. of 2253 Wentworth Ave. was shot to death by unknown gangsters and dumped along 22nd St. between 3rd and 4th Aves. in Broadview, IL.

On **April 16, 1926** Gioachino Cuilla AKA: Ciulla 22 yrs. of 448 Rush St. was shot to death by unknown gangsters in the rear of 1007 Townsend St., two girls and one man were seen leaving about that time.

On **April 17, 1926** William "Rags" McCue was found murdered in a ditch near Hinsdale, IL. On April 3rd 1925 he along with Sam Richer were booked as accessories in the murder of Walter Quinlan at 1700 S. Loomis. It was later reported that McCue worked for Quinlan as a collector for the Westside O'Donnell gang and after he helped dispose of Quinlan he continued to make collections on his own that the gang never saw. Apparently they took exception to the practice.

On **April 19, 1926** William Byrne 34 yrs. of 2452 Grace St. was shot to death by unknown gangsters and found on Niles Center Road near Dempster St. in Niles Center, Il.

On April 23, 1926 Westside O'Donnell gang member James "Fur" Sammons was wounded inside the beauty shop of his girlfriend Pearl Hruby when machine gun fire pierced the windows at 2208 S. Austin. He was a lead member of the Westside O'Donnell gang and thus was a target of the Capone organization.

On **April 27, 1926** Lena Chepulis 28 yrs. of 4458 S. Honore was shot to death by unknown gangsters in the soft drink parlor she ran with her husband at that same location when the men attacked her husband.

On **April 27, 1926** Assistant Cook County State's Attorney William H. McSwiggin, James J. Doherty and Thomas "Red" Duffy were gunned down by Willie Heeney and other Capone gunman in front of Madigan's saloon at 5613 W. Roosevelt Rd. Cicero, IL. After the shooting McSwiggin was taken to William O'Donnell's home at 122 S. Parkside Ave. Doherty and Duffy were known gunman for Klondike O'Donnell and Doherty was actually prosecuted by McSwiggin in 1924 for the murder of Ed Tancl and Leo Klimas for which Doherty was acquitted. Some accounts claim that Capone was present in one of the assailant's cars. One of the Capone gunmen Carl Torraco AKA: Charlie Carr had additional duties of supplying guns for the gang. He would provide them for killings and then discard them. On this occasion it is reported that he purchased the Thompson machine guns from a hardware merchant named Alex Korecek. While no one was ever charged with the killings, it was thought to have been a result of the Westside O'Donnells expanding their bootlegging activities into areas of their competitors, although the scene of the murder on Roosevelt Rd. was within their territory. McSwiggin was apparently unaware of the expansion and was only along for the ride. Later reports reveal that police suspected one of the O'Donnells and Fur Sammons who were in fact at the scene of the shooting and were the intended targets.

After the killing of the State's Attorney the heat was turned up on Capone. He decided to cool his heels in Hot Springs, Arkansas a favorite spot for vacationing hoods at the time. However, while driving through the mountains in Hot Springs his car was sprayed with machine gun fire and Capone narrowly escaped injury.

Atty Bill McSwiggin dead

On **April 27, 1926** Salvatore Policano AKA: Polizano 35 yrs. a bartender, was shot to death by unknown gangsters at Elm and Townsend Sts.

On **May 7, 1926** Antonio Victor DeFrank 27 yrs. of 301 E. 17th St. was shot to death by unknown gangsters and found slumped over the wheel of his Paige auto on State St. and 34th St. in Bloom Township.

On **May 17, 1926** Thomas Dire 27 yrs. was murdered at 306 E. 43rd St. James McDonough was wanted for the killing along with Alma Wheeler as an accessory **(Solved).** *Police logs entered the case as follows:* May 17, 1926 Dire, Thomas - Age 27 - Shot to death at 8:15 PM, in front of 306 E. 43rd St., by a man who drove up in an auto containing a woman passenger, got out and exchanged shots with him. On 6/16/26 the Coroner recommended the arrest of James McDonough and Alma Wheeler. 3 Dist. 12/3/31 McDonough arrested in Los Angeles, Calif. but State Att. Decided he could not be convicted because one principal witness could not be found and another changed his story. Los Angeles notified to release him.

On **May 21, 1926** Frank Cremaldi was taken for a ride, shot in the head five times and killed. He was a Genna alky cooker and later a Capone bootlegger, Hymie Weiss was suspected but never charged.

On **June 2, 1926** Geralanes Lamberto AKA: Lamberta 41 yrs. of 1540 Thorn St. and Crystal W. Barrier of 1639 Oak St. both of Chicago Heights were shot to death by unknown gangsters in front of the Derby Inn at 175th and Halsted St. in Thornton Township. Lamberta was suspected in the killing of Tony Sanfilippo in 1924 and fell into disfavor of his Mob bosses Jimmy Emery and Dominic Roberto.

On **June 7, 1926** James E. Sexton 24 yrs. of 1625 Washburne Ave. was shot to death by unknown gangsters and found on Wolf Rd. south of Roosevelt Rd.

On **June 18, 1926** Patrolman Michael A. Madigan succumbed to injuries he received on June 5th when he was shot by a known bootlegger. The killer James Beninato ran a soft drink parlor at 2724 S. Union and was suspected of selling alcohol from the premises. When Officer Madigan went to search a cabinet Beninato drew a pistol and shot him in the head. The victim's partner Officer Michael Connaughton fired at the assailant but he survived his wounds. Like so many cop killers before him, Beninato was acquitted of the killing **(solved)**.

On **June 23, 1926** Charles Carrao AKA: Corrao 35 yrs. of 1635 N. Austin Blvd. was shot to death by unknown gangsters at 1121 W. Grand Ave. He was on parole and awaiting trial for Malicious Mischief along with Phillip Vinci and Emmet Flood at the time of his death.

On **July 4, 1926** Carl Cafforello 22 yrs. of 816 N. California Ave. was shot to death by unknown gangsters at May and Erie Sts.
On **July 7, 1926** Louis Barbogallo 31 yrs. of 2022 Augusta St. was shot to death by unknown gangsters and found at Oak Park Ave. and 43rd Ave. in Stickney, IL.

On **July 13, 1926** Joseph Cicore AKA: Ciccone, Bicone 37 yrs. of 3139 Flournoy St. was shot to death by unknown gangsters in front of his home.

On **July 14, 1926** Jules Portuguese a Capone operative was killed and his body dumped near Niles, IL. The car used was found near Cicero Ave. and Irving Park Rd. He was awaiting trial for a $300.000 diamond robbery in which his two accomplices escaped. He did not talk, but allegedly tried to squeeze the men to help pay his $1,100 legal fee. Police suspected the accomplices to be Louis "Big" Smith and Sam "The Greener" Jacobson. When last seen he was in his father's car heading to meet a man named O'Donnell in Cicero, IL. Myles O'Donnell was sought for the crime, but the outcome is unknown.

On **July 21, 1926** Ben Russo AKA: Berdardino 35 yrs. of 441 W. Oak St. was shot by unknown gangsters as he entered his home.

On **July 22, 1926** Philip Piazza AKA: Fillippo Piaza 44 yrs. of 140 E. 16th St. Chicago Heights, IL. was reportedly shot to death by Guiseppe Nerone outside of his address. Nerone fled Chicago after he killed Tony Genna and tried to form a partnership with Piaza, the owner of the Milano Cafe. Piaza was suspected in the killing of Tony Sanfilippo in 1924 and fell into disfavor with his Mob bosses Jimmy Emery and Dominic Roberto who were also suspected in the killing.

On **July 23, 1926** Frank Conlon AKA: John 23 yrs. of 7037 S. Green St. was shot to death by unknown gangsters in the rear of a tavern at 6154 S. Ashland Ave. Police suspected that this murder occurred while Capone ally Ralph Sheldon and his men were attempting to kill Vincent McErlane (brother of Frank McErlane who was in jail) of the Saltis-McErlane gang. Police later learned that John "Mitters" Foley of the Ralph Sheldon gang was the shooter, but it is unknown if he was ever prosecuted.

On **August 3, 1926** the body of Tony Cuiringione AKA: Tommie Rossi, Rosa 36 yrs. of 9234 Saginaw Ave. was found beaten to death by unknown gangsters who weighted the body and dumped it into a cistern at 95th St. and 100th Ave. in Palos Park, IL. The subject was a missing driver for the Capone gang and was thought to have been murdered by Weiss and Drucci.

On **August 3, 1926** Guiseppe Salvo AKA: Joseph Salvo 27 yrs. of 342 E. 14th St. Chicago Heights, IL. was shot to death by friends of Philip Piaza because of his partnership with Guiseppe Nerone who killed Piaza. Nerone fled Chicago after he killed Tony Genna and later was killed when he was lured back to Chicago.

On **August 6, 1926** John "Mitters" Foley 28 yrs. was murdered 65th and Richmond Sts. Joe Saltis, Frank Koncil, Edward Herbert, John O'Berta and a subject only known as Darrow were arrested for the killing. Mitters was wounded in February of this same year and survived for a short period of time. Saltis and Koncil were found not guilty while the charges were dropped against the others **(Solved)**. *Police logs entered the case as follows:* August 6, 1926 Foley, John "Mitters" - Age 28 - Killed with shotguns at 2:35 PM, at the NW corner of 65th and Richmond Sts., by three men, who were in an automobile, and whom he evidently recognized, having leaped from his auto and attempted to escape. On 8/24/26 Joe Saltis and Frank Koncil were arrested and brought back from Merrill, Wis. On 9/23/26 John Alberta, alias O'Berta, was arrested and on 9/29/26 Edw. Herbert was arrested. All four were turned over to the Sheriff. 11A Dist. 11/9/26 Saltis and Koncil acquitted - Miller. 11/15/26 Herbert and Alberta cases stricken off - Miller. One Darrow also indicted Aug. 1926 - 1/10/27 -s/o - Miller. 11/19/28 abated a/c dead having been killed 10/28/28 by Off. Thos. Curtin.

John Mitters Foley

In **1926** Ray Long and Paul Hartgenbusch disappeared and were presumed dead at the hands of the Saltis-McErlane gang. The two men were mechanics who worked on a car used by Saltis in the John Foley murder. The men were able to link the car to Saltis and were going to testify against the gang chief when they disappeared.

On **August 8, 1926** Joseph Catanda AKA: Guiseppe 39 yrs. of 1441 Wallace St. was shot to death by Guiseppe Nerone in his home. Nerone was avenging the murder of Joseph Salvo. Nerone fled Chicago after he killed Tony Genna but was killed himself after being lured back to Chicago.

On August 10, 1926 in retaliation for the murder of Cuiringlone and the shooting of Johnnie Torrio northside gangsters Hymie Weiss AKA: Earl Wajciechowski and Vincent "Schemer" Drucci AKA: DiAmbrosio were ambushed in broad daylight in front of the old Standard Oil building at 9th Street and Michigan Avenue. Both men escaped injury, but would be dead by year's end. Drucci was captured by police with gun in hand and was charged only with possession, James Garden of 6907 Aberdeen St. was the only person (a passerby) wounded in the fray and wisely choose not to press charges.

On **August 10, 1926** Louis "Big" Smith 35 yrs. of 721 Oakwood Blvd. was shot to death by unknown gangsters at 1520 S. Avers. Smith was arrested for the killing of Isaac Stein AKA: Harry, Teddy in January, but the outcome is unknown.

On **August 20, 1926** Joseph Nerona AKA: Guiseppe Nerone, Caveliero, Tony Spano 35 yrs. who resided in the Thomas Hotel in Chicago Heights, IL. was shot to death in front of 456 W. Division St. by gangsters Tony Aiello, Patsy Arnodo and an unknown male. However, the charges were dropped against Aiello and Arnodo after their indictment. It was later reported that Nerona was the killer of Tony Genna and fled the city for a while setting up shop in Chicago Heights causing several murders there **(Solved)**. *Police logs entered the case as follows:* August 20, 1926 Narone, Joseph, alias Tony Spano - Age 35 - Shot to death at 8:30 AM, in front of 456 W. Division St., by two men, one of whom was identified as Tony Aiello, by a 9 yr. old boy witness. On 8/21/26 the coroner recommended the arrest of Aiello and the other unknown man. 29 Dist. 12/16/26 Aiello arrested and indicted. 3/28/27 - Aiello case s/o - J. Sullivan

Tony Aiello

On **August 21, 1926** Harold Cantrell 23 yrs. of 2663 E. 75th St. was shot by Daniel Lynch in a taxi in front of 224 E. 42nd St. Lynch a city employee for the Water Department was arrested, but it is not known if he was convicted for this crime. In 1930 he killed a police officer and was not convicted for that crime either. Lynch would be killed in 1933 **(Solved)**.

On **August 23, 1926** Joe Delbuors AKA: Delbuona, Michael Blando 34 yrs. of 1021 S. Halsted St. was shot to death by unknown gangsters and found in the front seat of his auto in front of Emmett Hall at Taylor and Ogden Aves.

On **August 29, 1926** Frank Cappello 28 yrs. of 200 E. 16th St. Chicago Heights, IL. was shot and killed by unknown gangsters at State and 26th St. in Bloom Township.

On **September 2, 1926** Tony DeStefano AKA: DiStefano 32 yrs. who resided in the Victoria Hotel in Chicago Heights, IL. was strangled to death by unknown gangsters and found along Joe Orr Road west of Cottage Grove Ave.

On **September 10, 1926** Joan Andreadis 42 yrs. of 1601 Halsted St. was shot to death by unknown gangsters in the kitchen of the C. H. Lunch Room at 80 East 16th St. Chicago Heights, IL.

On **September 18, 1926** William Girard 55 Yrs. was murdered 1834 S. Dearborn St. Sam Giancana AKA: Momo Salvatore, Mooney, or Gilormo Giangono was indicted for the murder of the barber, however the only witness Alexander Burba was killed on April 8, 1927 and the case against Momo was dropped **(Solved)**. *Police logs entered the case as follows:* September 18, 1926 Girard, Wm. G. - Age 55 - Died from gunshot wounds received at 3:15 AM, 9/13/26, in a cigar store at 1834 Dearborn St., while resisting holdup men. On 9/26/26 James Pape, Dugo Ricco and Sam Giancana were arrested and indicted. 1A Dist. 4/28/27 - all three cases s/o - Brothers.

Sam Giancana

On September 26, 1926 the northside gangsters under the direction of Hymie Weiss AKA: Earl Wajciechowski, Vincent "Schemer" Drucci AKA: DiAmbrosio and Bugs Moran carried out their most brazen attempt to kill Capone to date when several car-loads of gunman drove to the Hawthorne Hotel in Cicero and shot up the establishment, firing some 5,000 rounds with Capone inside. No gangsters were hurt during the melee and miraculously no one was killed.

On **September 22, 1926** Ignazio Mingare 33 yrs. of 3002 S. Wells, a merchant was shot to death by unknown gangsters using a shotgun from a passing car at 31st and Wells Aves. This crime was categorized as a Blackhand killing.

On **September 27, 1926** Joseph Chivetta 41 yrs. of 906 Cambridge Ave. was shot by unknown gangsters and found in an alley behind 852 Milton St.

In early October of 1926 Capone arranged for a meeting with Weiss in a downtown hotel. The purpose was to end the gang war so both antagonists could move on and continue to make money. Tony Lombardo the head of the Unione Siciliana and a trusted Capone aid mediated. Both sides wanted peace but, Weiss insisted on the surrender of either Mops Volpe & Frank Clementi (shooters in the Standard Oil shooting) or Anselmi & Scalise (suspected killers of O'Banion). Capone would not betray any of his men and Weiss stormed out, Capone then knew what had to be done.

On **October 11, 1926** Hymie Weiss 35 yrs. AKA: Earl Wajciechowski, Earl J. Weiss and Patrick Murray 36 yrs. were murdered while W. W. O'Brien, Samuel Peller (armed with revolver) and Ben Jacobs (armed with revolver) were wounded at 742 N. State St. Weiss the successor to the north side gang of Dion O'Banion and his men may have been betrayed by two of their own men Samuel Peller and Ben Jacobs who were present (held to grand jury) and may have been operating at the behest of Tony Accardo and "Tough Tony" Capezio. The killing happened in front of the flower shop at 740 N. State Street where Dion O'Banion was murdered. While responding to the incident police found a jammed machinegun, a revolver, a shot gun, the stock of a machinegun and two abandon autos nearby and the subsequent investigation discovered an additional snipers nest down the street that was not used during the attack. This put Vincent "Schemer" Drucci AKA: DiAmbrosio and George "Bugs" Moran AKA: George Gage in direct charge of the north side operation. No one was ever tried for the killings. *Police logs entered the case as follows:* October 11, 1926 Weiss, Earl J. - "Hymie" - Age 35 - Shot to death at 4:00 PM, in front of 742 N. State St., together with Patrick Murray, another bootlegger as they were walking along with Attorney W.W. O'Brien, who also was wounded, by some unknown person or persons who fired a machine gun from a second floor window across the street. On 10/21/26 Samuel Peller and Ben Jacobs, Weiss' body guards, who also were wounded, were held by the Coroner because they "were present and armed and had fore knowledge of the shooting. 28th Dist.

On **October 17, 1926** John D'Anna 31 yrs. of Linden and Wilcox in Bellwood, IL. was shot to death by unknown gangsters on Grand Ave. near Manheim Road in Franklin Park, IL.

On **October 21, 1926** James C. Williams 28 yrs. was murdered at 2742 W. 22nd Pl. Lee McEvan, Charles Heurer and Dave Anderson were apprehended for the crime. The men all from St. Louis were released for lack of evidence. One can only assumed the killers were part of the contract employees of Capone known as the "American Boys' and the victim was associated with the northside gang **(Solved)**. *Police logs entered the case as follows:* October 21, 1926 Williams, James E. - Age 28 - Found shot to death at 5:30 AM, in the rear alley of 2742 W. 22nd Pl., the Coroner's Verdict showing that he had been shot "while riding in a Hupmobile Sedan" (place not mentioned) and the arrest of Lee McEwan, John Heuer, alias Dave Anderson, alias Ed Barcume, and Charles

Heuer was recommended. All three are St. Louis gangsters. 17 Dist. 2/24/27 John Heuer and Dave Anderson brought back from St. Louis and turned over to the Sheriff. 6/7/27 Anderson & J. Heuer s/o - Hopkins.

On October 21, 1926 after a peace meeting in the Sherman/Morrison Hotel arranged by "Dingbat" O'Berta, Schemer Drucci agreed to a peace accord, it lasted for about seven months until Capone learned of Northside gangster Joe Aiello's attempt to have him poisoned at one of his favorite restaurants, Esposito's.

Joe Aiello

On **November 16, 1926** Edward Dunn 55 yrs. was murdered at Richmond and Fillmore Sts. He was reportedly a colored man organizing colored janitors into a union. Albert Cress, Thomas H. Conover and Michael Sexton were charged with the killing and found not guilty **(Solved)**. *Police logs entered the case as follows:* November 16, 1926 Dunn, Edward, Age 55 - Colored - Union Organizer of colored janitors. Shot to death at 5:46 PM, at the S.E. corner of Richmond and Fillmore Sts., by three men in an automobile with whom he was talking. The killers, Albert Cress, Michael Sexton, and Thomas Conners, members and officers of regular flat janitors' unions were immediately placed under arrest by a bureau squad which witnessed the murder and on 11/19/26 were held by the Coroner. 17 Dist. 3/24/27 - Sexton acquitted - Miller. 4/19/27 - Cress and Conners both acquitted - Miller

On **November 18, 1926** George Martini 31 yrs. was murdered at 2917 Lexington St. James Rose and Frank Rango were wanted for the killing **(Solved)**. *Police logs entered the case as follows:* November 18, 1926 Martini, George – Age 31 – Found shot to death at 10:20 PM, seated in his Ford auto in rear of 2917 Lexington St. Murdered by some unknown person or persons whose arrest was recommended by the Coroner 1/20/26. 17 Dist. On 11/18/26 James Rose and Frank Rango, barber union officials, were booked for murder, but were exonerated by the Coroner and on 12/3/26 discharged by Judge Eberhardt

On **November 20, 1926** William Raggio 28 yrs. of 717 W. 61st Pl. was shot to death by unknown gangsters at 56th St. near Keating Ave. It was reported that he was killed by his Saltis McErlane associates for talking on the street with rival Ralph Sheldon, the case remains open.

On **November 26, 1926** James Gusdagno 27 yrs. of 825 S. Hermitage Ave. was shot by unknown gangsters at Polk and Marshfield Aves.

On **November 28, 1926** Theodore J. Anton the owner of the hotel and smoke shop that Capone now called home, was murdered, Capone is suspected of killing him in a drunken rage, but never charged.

Theodore Anton dead

On **December 9, 1926** Joseph Albergo 27 yrs. of 444 N. Sangamon was shot to death by unknown gangsters at Curtis and Ohio Sts. Police suspected Blackhand extortionists in this murder.

On **December 11, 1926** Charles Tremblay AKA: Chick Moran 28 yrs. was murdered by unknown gangsters and found at 26th and State St. in Bloom Township. The body had been soaked in gasoline and badly burned.

On **December 12, 1926** Joseph Wokrol 47 yrs. was murdered at Kilbourne and Adams Sts. He was the President of Checker Cab Co. and was embroiled in a dispute known as the "Cab Wars". Eugene "Red" McLaughlin and Robert "Firsco Dutch" Schmitt were charged with the killing, the charges against McLaughlin were dropped and Schmitt was found not guilty **(Solved)**. *Police logs entered the case as follows:* December 12, 1926 Wokral, Joseph - Age 47 - Fatally shot

9AM, 12/9/26 at the S.W. corner of Kilbourne Ave. and Adams St., by two men in a Cadillac auto, one of whom he recognized as Eugene McLaughlin, well known stickup and labor slugger. McLaughlin and one Robt. Schmidt, alias Harry Brown, alias "Frisco Dutch" are wanted. 21 Dist. 4/31/27 Schmidt arrested - 5/2/27 held without bail by Allegretti. 6/22/27 - Schmidt acquitted - Gemmill. 4/6/28 Eugene McLaughlin brought back from Hayward, Wis. And turned over to the Sheriff. 5/15/25 - McLaughlin - Nolle Prossed - McGoorty.

On **December 16, 1926** Hillary Clements a member of the Ralph Sheldon gang was reportedly killed by Frankie McErlane and Joe Saltis. This fractured a short peace accord between the bootlegging gangs and the shooting commenced once more.

"Polack Joe" Saltis

On **December 19, 1926** John Wolwark 24 yrs. of 2732 N. Ridgeway was shot to death by unknown gangsters and found at 1548 Fulton St. in the rear. The investigation revealed that this victim ran a Beer flat at 1354 N. Lincoln St. It was also discovered that two off duty police officers were at the flat on the night of the slaying. The outcome of this murder is not known.

On **December 21, 1926** Samuel Cohen 32 yrs. of 6448 Eggleston Ave. was shot by unknown gangsters in front of 6412 Eggleston Ave. on his way home from work. He was a cobbler and was reducing prices in his shop which apparently angered Ike Sandler Sr. the President of the Cobblers Union. Thomas Burke, Irving Sandler Jr., Anna Sandler, William Lorimer, Clinton Thatcher, June Thatcher and Eileen Burke were all questioned in the killing, but it is unknown if anyone was charged.

By year's end there were 76 gangland killings reported in Chicago according to the CCC.

In **January 7, 1927** Santo Celebron was killed when it leaked out that he was a potential witness against Capone in an alcohol case.

On **January 7, 1927** John Costenaro 34 yrs. of 1346 51st Ct. in Cicero IL. was suffocated to death by unknown gangsters and found buried in a garage at 5435 W. 30th St. in Cicero, IL. He was a saloon-keeper and a potential witness in a government alcohol case against Capone et. al. and went missing. In May his body was excavated from the floor of the Cicero garage with a rope still around his neck and wrapped in a blanket.

On **February 6, 1927** John Petrack 22 yrs. was shot by Ralph Orlando and Ben Zion at 1341 S. Peoria St. The men were indicted in the killing, but the charges were later dropped **(Solved)**. *Police logs entered the case as follows:* February 6, 1927 Petrack, John - Age 22 - Fatally shot at 4:05 PM, 2/5/27, while sitting in a barber's chair at 1341 So. Peoria St. by a man who drove up and escaped in an auto. On 2/15/27 Ralph Orlando was turned over to the Sheriff on indictment. Ben Zion, still at large, was also indicted. Harry Wexler, Harry Tidler, Sam Schulman and Sam Kaplan were booked as accessories - released by Coroner and 2/21/27 discharged by Judge Eberhardt. 16 Dist. 3/8/27 Ben Zion surrendered at Sheriff's Office. 6/13/27 cases against Orlando and Zion stricken-off - Miller.

On **February 19, 1927** Vinerella Guadagni 31 yrs. of 2246 W. 24th St. was shot to death by unknown gangsters wielding a shotgun while seated in an auto in front of 2423 S. Oakley.

On **March 11, 1927** Frank "Lefty" Koncil 30 yrs. and Charles Hrubek 41 yrs. both gangsters for "Polack Joe" Saltis were gunned down by Capone gangsters in two cars at 1454 W. 39th St. No arrest was made in the killing. *Police logs entered the case as follows:* March 11, 1927 Hrubec, Charles, alias Hayes - Age 41 - Shot to death at 11:45 PM, together with Frank Koncil, well-known bootlegger, in front of 1454 W. 39th Sts., as they leaped from an automobile and attempted to escape on foot from several assassins in another machine. 15th Dist. March 11, 1927 Koncil, Frank - Age 30 - Shot to death at 11:45 PM, together with Charles Hrubec, alias Hayes, in front of 1454 W. 39th St., as they leaped out of an automobile and attempted to escape on foot from several assassins in another machine. 15th Dist.

Frank Koncil (left)

On **March 11, 1927** Tomaso Piazza 47 yrs. of 1041 W. Taylor St. was shot to death by unknown gangsters at 1307 Arthington St.

On **March 11, 1927** Benjamin Schneider 31 yrs. of 2839 Palmer St. was shot to death alongside his home by unknown gangsters. The murder supposedly involved a gambling feud.

On **March 14, 1927** Alphonse Fiori (ex-Genna operative) was found murdered and dumped in an alley off Taylor Street.

On **March 16, 1927** Frank Wright, Joseph Bloom and Rueben Cohen are machine gunned to death in Detroit. The men were Chicago gamblers and the suspected killer was Fred "Killer" Burke working on behalf of the Purple Gang. The Purples and Burke would carry out contract work for Capone on St. Valentine's Day in 1929.

On **March 23, 1927** Chin Poch 31 yrs. 202 W. 22nd St. was shot to death by an unknown Asian gang associate at 200 W. 22nd St.

On **March 24, 1927** Moy Sing 59 yrs. of 3208 W. Lake St. was shot to death by gang associates Lew Woo of 1360 E. 62nd St. and Mot Got of 3856 W. Madison Ave. in his laundry at 3208 W. Lake St. The victim was involved with the Hip Sing Tong of the On Leong Association that is heavily uninvolved in gambling operations. The outcome of this case is unknown.

On **March 24, 1927** Moy Yuk Hong 36 yrs. of 158 S. Ashland Ave. was reportedly shot to death by gang associates Gilbert Lee of 4728 Indiana Ave., Tommy Jue of 431 S. Clark St. and Lee Hung also of 431 S. Clark St. However the men were released when they were able to prove they were elsewhere by using a meter receipt from a yellow cab.

On **March 29, 1927** Frank Palumbo 44 yrs. of 1248 W. Grand Ave. was shot to death by unknown gangsters while seated in his auto in front of 529 Bickerdike Ave. The victim was the proprietor of a cigar shop and the police suspected Blackhand extortionist of the murder.

Officer Dan Healy (right)

On **April 4, 1927** Northside gang leader Vincent "Schemer" Drucci AKA: DiAmbrosio 33 yrs. was shot to death while in police custody at the intersection of Clark and Wacker. When asked to initiate an internal investigation, the Chief of Detectives stated the officer pulling the trigger (Det. Dan Healy) should get a medal. This killing came shortly after the March 14, 1927 failed attempt by Drucci to kill Capone in Hot Springs, Arkansas. The Northsiders were now under the sole leadership of Bugs Moran. After the killing of Drucci and in support of Moran, other racketeers allied themselves with the Northsiders to include: Gambling magnates Billy Skidmore and Barney Bertsche, Westside vice monger Jack Zuta and of course the Joe Aiello gang who would not let the leadership of the Unione Siciliana remain in the hands of Capone. *Police logs entered the case as follows:* April 4, 1927 Drucci, Vincent - Age 33 - Shot to death at 4:30 PM, at Clark St., and Wacker Drive in a police squad car while being driven to the station, by Patrolman Daniel F. Healy, whom he attempted to disarm. Jury composed of selected men from Evanston and Blue Island. 1st Dist.

On **April 8, 1927** Alexander "Alex" Burba 25 yrs. was killed at 2858 W. 39th St. He was the only witness in the murder of William Girard by Sam Giancana and after his death the case against Momo was dropped. *Police logs entered the case as follows:* April 8, 1927 Burba, Alex - Age 25 - Shot to death at 8:50 PM, after being called to the door of his grocery store at 2858 W. 39th St., by an unknown man who escaped. 15th Dist.

On **April 10, 1927** Anthony Sicoli 39 yrs. of 1459 W. Taylor St was shot to death in front of his home. The killing was suspected to involve Blackhand extortionist.

In May of 1927 St. Louis gangster Gus Winkler AKA: August "Big Mike" Winkeler, James Ray" arrived in Chicago soon to be joined by fellow St. Louis hoods Ray Nugent AKA: "Gander, Crane-Neck" and Robert Carey AKA: "Bob Conroy, Bob Newberry, Sanford". The men were associates of other hoods emanating from St. Louis namely Fred R. "Killer" Burke AKA: Thomas A. Camp and Byron "Monty" Bolton AKA: "O.B. Carter, Andy". The men were associates of the "Egan's Rats Gang" in St. Louis and developed the art of kidnapping. They also worked as guns for hire and carried out some contract work for the "Purple Gang" in Detroit. They came to the attention of Al Capone when they kidnapped one of his men. Instead of killing them Capone put them to work. The men would align themselves with Claude "Screwy" Maddox AKA: John E. Moore and his Circus Gang headquartered at Ashland and North Ave. very near the territory controlled by the O'Banion, Weis, Drucci, Moran-Northside Gang. This group would become known as the "American Boys" to the mostly Italian Torrio-Capone Mob. Capone could always put to work hoods unrecognizable to local authorities as demonstrated on St. Valentine's Day 1929 and in other killings.

Jones-Winkler-Burke

In **May of 1927** Carmen Ferraro was murdered and dumped in Bensenville, IL. Ferraro was a wealthy business owner and involved in bootlegging through a still he owned. The Feds arrested Ferraro and others on alcohol charges earlier in the month and it was speculated that he was killed for fear of him cooperating with the authorities or for running an independent operation outside of Capone's empire.

On **May 20, 1927** Frank Cremaldi 27 yrs. who lived in the Webster Hotel was shot to death by unknown gangsters on Grand Ave. two blocks west of Manheim Rd. in Leyden Township. He was a known bootlegger.

On **May 21, 1927** Paul Grandolfo 29 yrs. of 1108 N. Robey St. was shot by unknown gangsters and dumped in the DesPlaines River where he was found.

On **May 25, 1927** New York mobster Antonio "Tony" Torchie AKA: Tochio, Tocci, Tocco, A.M. Claugh 32 yrs. of Bellwood, New York was gunned down at Des Plaines and DeKoven Sts. when he appeared in Chicago to take advantage of a $50,000 reward to kill Capone that was offered by Joe Aiello. In all, four out of town assassins and four local assassins die for the same reason and "Machine Gun" Jack McGurn AKA: James or Vincenzo Gibaldi is suspected in all of the murders although he was never charged. *Police logs entered the case as follows:* May 25, 1927 Torchio, Tony, alias Antonio Tocci - Age 32 - Shot to death at 11:20 PM, 5/25/27 on sidewalk in front of 700 DeKoven St. by some unknown person or persons who escaped. 16th Dist.

On **May 31, 1927** Herman Carcelli 31 yrs. of 211 E. 24th St. Chicago Heights, IL. was shot to death by unknown gangsters using a shotgun from a speeding car at 22nd St. near State St. in Chicago Heights, IL.

On **June 1, 1927** Lawrence Lopresti 30 yrs. of 1019 Townsend St. was shot to death with a shotgun by unknown gangsters in front of 1011 Townsend St.

On **June 4, 1927** Jasper DiGiovanni 31 yrs. of 2449 W. Taylor St. was shot to death by unknown gangsters at 39th St. and Lombard Ave. in Stickney, IL.

On **June 6, 1927** Salvatore Vito Emma 27 yrs. of 210 Market St. in Waukegan, IL. was shot to death by unknown gangsters in front of 5730 W. 56th Pl. Waukegan, IL.

On **June 8, 1927** Joseph Agnello 35 yrs. of 1120 Townsend St. was shot to death by unknown gangsters in front of his home.

On **June 19, 1927** George Joseph Lauer 42 yrs. of 249 E. 17th St. Chicago Heights, IL. was shot to death by unknown gangsters in an auto on the side of his home.

On **June 26, 1927** Ignatius Guagliardo 46 yrs. of 1534 Kilpatrick Ave. was shot to death by unknown gangsters while on the corner of 72nd Ave. and Altgeld St.

On **June 29, 1927** Diego Altomonto AKA: Diero Attlomionte 32 yrs. was shot to death at 2002 Grand Ave. Lawrence Alagna AKA: Lorenzo Alagno 32 yrs. was shot to death at 1044 Taylor St. Garpare Alagna 35 yrs. was shot to death at 1025 W. Taylor St. on **July 11, 1927**. All were shot by unknown gangsters. Matt Lombardo and Peter Gardina were arrested as accessories, but later released. At this time Jack McGurn continued killing Genna Gang members at the behest of Capone and over control of the Unione Siciliana **(Solved)**. *Police logs entered the case as follows:* June 29, 1927 Alagna, Lorenzo - Age 32 - Shot to death at 11:40 P.M., 6/29/27, on sidewalk in front of 1044 W. Taylor St., by some unknown person or persons. On 6/30/27 Matt Lombardo and Peter Gardina were booked as accessories to murder and on 7/20/27 both were held by the Coroner on that charge. 16th Dist. Sept. 1927 No Bills on Gardina & Lombardo. June 29, 1927 Alttmonte, Diero - Age 32 - Shot to death at 12:26 A.M., 6/26/27, while seated in his automobile in front of 2002 Grand Ave., by a volley from shotguns fired by four men in a passing automobile. Otto Puppelo, a passenger, was wounded. Their unknown assailants escaped. 20 Dist July 11, 1927 Alagna, Gaspare - Age 35 - Shot in the back of the head and killed in alley rear of 1025 W. Taylor St., at 6:25 P.M., 7/11/27. His unknown assailants escaped. 16 Dist.

On **June 30, 1927** Numio Jamirriso AKA: Nunio Jamnerze 29 yrs. was killed at 614 Vedder St. during a time when McGurn continued killing remaining Genna Gang members, although no one was ever charged with this killing. ***Police logs entered the case as follows:*** June 30, 1927 Jamirriso, Nunio - Age 29 - Shot to death at 8:10 PM, 6/30/27, while entering his home on rear porch of 614 Vedder St., by some unknown person or persons who escaped. 29th Dist.

Jack McGurn

On **July 7, 1927** Peter Sansone 38 yrs. of 2631 Lowe Ave. was shot to death by Frank Talarico while on the corner of 26th St. and Union Ave. He was in the company of Charles Teravichia when the killing occurred. Talarico was acquitted and investigators suspected that Sansone was setting Teravichia up to be killed **(solved)**.

On **July 8, 1927** Sam Salerno 60 yrs. of 1400 North Park Ave. was shot to death by unknown gangsters in his grocery store at the same location. Joseph Galioto of 940 Milton St. was also wounded in the attack, but survived. Police suspected the killing was the result of the victim refusing to join the Italian Grocers Association.

On **July 9, 1927** Frank Albanise 34 yrs. of 1134 Townsend St. was shot to death by unknown gangsters in the rear of his store at that same location.

On **July 10, 1927** Joseph Montana was murdered. Jim Cervone was arrested, but the grand jury passed a no bill on a request to indict **(Solved)**.

On **July 12, 1927** Giovanni Blaucins AKA: Blaudins, Blandini 33 yrs. of 803 S. Morgan St. was shot to death and found in a prairie at 118th St. and Ashland Ave. It was suspected that he was a Genna Gang member and was killed by Jack McGurn who continued to kill Genna Gang members although no one was ever charged with the killing.

On **July 12, 1927** Simoni Galioto 31 yrs. of 940 Milton St. was shot by unknown gangsters on the corner of Townsend St. and Elm St.

On **July 13, 1927** Dominick Cinderello 35 yrs. of 5215 Augusta St. was found murdered with a rope around his neck in the Calumet Sag Canal at 86th Ave. and 111th St. in Palos Township. He was a Genna gang associate and Jack McGurn the prime suspect was arrested and again he was released and not charged **(Solved)**.

On **July 14, 1927** Adam Brzezinski 33 yrs. of 312 154th Pl., Calumet City, IL. was beaten to death by unknown gangsters and thrown into the Little Calumet River and found at 167th St. in Calumet City, IL.

On **July 20, 1927** Michael Stopec AKA: Stoper 22 yrs. of 148 W. Goethe St. was shot to death by unknown gangsters at 4047 Kenmore Ave. Robert Stanley was held by police, but was later released by a coroner's jury **(Solved)**.

On **July 25, 1927** Angelo Corona 55 yrs. of 1030 Newberry Ave. was shot to death by unknown gangsters and found at 826/830 W. Taylor St. in the gangway.

On **July 27, 1927** James DeAmato a hijacker working for Al Capone was killed and Frankie Yale AKA: Uale or Ioele was considered responsible for the slaying, although he was never charged.

On **July 27, 1927** Frank P. Hitchcock was found murdered. He was a saloonkeeper and distiller who apparently ran afoul of one of the bootlegging gangs and became a target of Capone lieutenant Johnny Patton.

On **August 3, 1927** Tony Cuiringlone was found dead in a cistern in Stickney, IL. He was a driver for Anthony Guisak a henchman for Al Capone. He was chased down with his wife by "Pollack Joe" Saltis and his men. His wife got away, but he was captured and severely tortured before he died. It is not known the outcome of this case.

On **August 6, 1927** Patrolman Thomas J. Healy succumbed to injuries he received on August 2nd. Healy was led to a gambling establishment at 71 E. 42nd

St. by Porter Simpson an informant. Once there the men exchanged gunfire when Simpson tried to rob the Officer. Both men died of their injuries **(solved)**.

On **August 9, 1927** Anthony Russo and Vincent Spicuzza were found shot to death and found in Melrose Park, IL. on August 11th. The two alky cookers who were from St. Louis and living in Little Sicily when they were allegedly offered $25,000 each for the murders of Capone and his associate Tony Lombardo by Joe Aiello. A St. Louis gangster by the name of Alex Blair was being sought for the crime, but it is unknown if he was ever questioned.

On **September 17, 1927** John Walsh 29 yrs. was murdered at 872 Cambridge Ave. Bert Hanson AKA: Bart Hart and Frank Seris AKA: Serio were wanted for the crime. It is unknown if they were ever apprehended **(Solved)**. *Police logs entered the case as follows:* September 17, 1927 Walsh, John - Age 29 - Found shot to death at 6:21 AM, 9/17/27 in alley rear of 872 Cambridge Ave., the actual time of occurrence being about 1:15 AM when in company of two men, Bert Hanson, alias Hart and Frank Seris, alias "Humpy". Seris had given him a dollar to get some cigarettes earlier in the day and he had not returned with either. On 9/24/27 arrest of the two men was recommended by the Coroner. On 10/3/27 Seris was arrested, he confessed to the murder and was turned over to the Sheriff on a Coroner's Mittimus. 28 Dist. 12/20/27 - to Joliet Pen. - Eller.

On **September 22, 1927** Salvatori Mozzapelle AKA: Mezzapelle, Sam Valenti 26 yrs. of 715 S. Morgan St. was shot in the head and struck with an axe by unknown gangsters and found on the Buecker Farm at State Rd. and 50th Ave. in Stickney, IL.

On **September 24, 1927** Sam Valenti was found dead with an axe in his head on a farm in Stickney, IL. By this point Aiello had upped the ante for the death of Capone. The victim came to Chicago from Cleveland to try and collect.

On **September 28, 1927** Samuel Guzzardo 39 yrs. of 355 W. Locust St. was shot to death by unknown gangsters using a shotgun near the corner of Locust and Milton Sts.

On **October 12, 1927** Frank C. Passani 28 yrs. of 31 E. 21st St., Chicago Heights, IL, was shot to death by unknown gangsters and dumped into a ditch at 167th St. and Cicero Ave.

On **October 12, 1927** Katherine Jones AKA: Kate S. Ware 38 yrs. of 13th and Berkley Ave. in east Chicago Heights, IL. was shot to death by unknown gangsters when she was summoned to the rear door of her home. She was suspected of providing information to authorities on local stills.

On **November 8, 1927** Frank Scallo 23 yrs. of 1440 N. Avers and Paul Scallo 32 yrs. of the same address were shot to death by gangster George Barratta of 823 Townsend Ave. while in the Scallo fish store at 608 N. Hamlin Ave. over a business deal. The Coroner's inquest directed police to apprehend Barratta and his wife Josephine. It is not know what the outcome of this case was **(solved).**

Green Mill Gardens

In November of 1927 nightclub entertainer Joe E. Lewis was attacked in his room at the Commonwealth Hotel on west Diversey Parkway. Lewis had allegedly broken a contract at the Green Mill night club at Lawrence and Broadway and was threatened by one of its owners, Capone killer "Machine Gun" Jack McGurn AKA: James or Vincenzo Gibaldi. Lewis did not heed the warning and took employment at another club and paid the price when his throat was slashed. He recovered and went on to have a stellar career in the movies. Reportedly in retaliation for the attack, Bugs Moran sent his men out to hunt down the attackers. They reportedly killed one of the attackers and fired shots at McGurn from their car. Other news reports state that Northside Gangster Schemer Drucci was said to have gunned down an Italian for the assault. Reports vary on this incident and the circumstances surrounding it. Some reports claim that all the attackers were killed within weeks, while others state that Sam Giancana AKA: Momo Salvatore, Mooney, or Gilormo Giangono was involved and possibly McGurn himself. Recent reports state that Sam Giancana admitted to his brother Chuck that he took part in this crime. Verified details have not been found.

On November 9, 1927 or March 7, 1928 "Machine Gun" Jack McGurn AKA: James or Vincenzo Gibaldi, chief killer for the Capone gang was in a phone booth at the Lenox Hotel on Rush Street and Chicago Ave. or the McCormack Hotel Smoke Shop at 616 N. Rush Street (both locations have been reported for the event) when Northside adversaries Peter and Frank Gusenberg and others opened fire at point blank range. Amazingly McGurn survived with only minor wounds and was able to enjoy revenge on St. Valentine's Day 1929. News reports at the time speculated that this attack was in retaliation for the knife attack on entertainer Joe E. Lewis.

Frank Gusenberg

On **November 10, 1927** Robert Aiello and Frank Aiello are murdered in Springfield, IL. The feud for control over the Unione Siciliana is thought to be the motive although no arrests were made.

On **November 14, 1927** Joe Vanela 32 yrs. of 569 W. Taylor St. was shot to death by unknown gangsters at 848 Taylor St.

On **November 17, 1927** Max Willner 34 yrs. of 1256 S. Springfield was shot to death by Steve Zaharchuck at 55 W. Washington while washing windows which was his trade. The killer prior to the shooting threatened the victim for not having a card from the Window Washers Union **(Solved).**

On **November 23, 1927** Sergeant Thomas Lynch of the Detective Bureau succumbed to wounds received accidentally from one of his own men. The men were on the lookout for gangsters involved in recent violence between the Capone and Aiello gangs. The officers became involved in a high speed chase at Western and Lake Sts. that ended at Lake and Hamilton when the Sergeant was shot. The Sergeant and several of his men were ordered to crack down on certain gangsters in order for Mayor Thompson to enhance his image in a potential run for the White House. The Police squad spotted a car containing suspected gangsters and pursued them while under gunfire from the suspects. No charges were ever placed in this incident.

On **November 24, 1927** Argyle G. Hartz 27 yrs. a government probation officer was murdered by John White Jr., John Nedles and Scotty McGowan, after the men forced him at gun point to leave the Alfalfa Gardens in Lansing IL. The body was found at the Calumet Sag Canal at Cicero Ave. in Worth Township. The men were wanted for the killing, it is not known if they were ever apprehended.

On **November 27, 1927** Roy A. Flynn 33 yrs. of 203 N. LaCrosse Ave. was shot to death in the rear of 1346 S. Ashland. In a dying declaration he accused gangster Mike Quirk of shooting him because Flynn knew where some beer was stored and would not tell Quirk and another so they could go steal it, the outcome of this case is unknown.

On **December 1, 1927** Fred A. Dullard 57 yrs. of 5741 Ridge Ave. was shot by unknown gangsters at 2235 S. Kenneth St.

On **December 6, 1927** George Clemens 45 yrs. of 1122 Cambridge Ave. was shot to death by an unknown gangster who was described as Italian while in front of 930 Milton St.

On **December 18, 1927** Peter Ruffalo 29 yrs. of 420 E. 22nd St., Chicago Heights, IL., was shot by unknown gangsters and found on Ridge Rd. just east of Halsted St., in Thorton Township, IL.

On **December 21, 1927** Michael James Loftus 27 yrs. was shot by unknown gangsters at 91st and California Aves. in Evergreen Park, IL.

On **December 28, 1927** Charles E. Miller was murdered by John Touhy AKA: Johnny Davis who was also killed during the assault. Touhy the brother of Mob leader Roger Touhy entered the Lone Tree Inn in Niles, IL. and while trying to negotiate with the bartender, was threatened by Charles Miller who was the brother of a rival Frank Miller. Apparently the conflict surrounded just who the bartender would by his beer from, Touhy or Miller. The Touhy gang beat Miller to the floor with a wrench and left. Upon their return sometime later, when Touhy saw that Miller was still there the shooting began. Miller was shot nine times and Touhy may have been accidently shot by one of his own men who was using a machine gun. Touhy was removed from the bar and dropped at the door of a hospital dead **(Solved)**.

On **December 31, 1927** Harry Portugias was murdered by unknown gangsters.

In **1928** Jimmy D'Amato was shot and killed on the street in Brooklyn, New York. He was a gangster working for Al Capone and was sent to New York to spy on Frankie Yale, a former protégé of Capone, who Capone suspected of betrayal. After the murder Capone reportedly learned that Yale ordered the killing and was stealing Capone booze and trying to take over some of the prostitution racket that Capone coveted.

On **January 1, 1928** Frank E. Carpenter 31 yrs. of 1434 Austin Blvd. was shot by unknown gangsters and found under the Chicago, Milwaukee and St. Paul Railroad viaduct between Kinzie and Carroll Aves.

On January 17, 1928 Members of the notorious 42 gang from Chicago threatened to raid the state reformatory for boys at St. Charles Illinois with machine guns unless they released associates of the gang from custody. The gang was a proving ground for criminals that wound up as leading members of the Chicago Mob. In response to the threat, the reformatory Superintendent requested the deployment of National Guard troops to the institution.

On **January 18, 1928** Joe Concialdi 18 yrs. of 1405 Emerald Ave. was shot by unknown gangsters and found at Western Ave. and Steger Rd. in Bloom Township. He was suspected of being a hijacker of Capone beer and booze.

On **January 18, 1928** Joseph Faso 24 yrs. of 269 E. 16th St. and Harry Fuller 34 yrs. of 7222 Cornell Ave. were shot by unknown gangsters and found in a prairie on Cottage Grove Ave. near Joe Orr Rd. They were suspected of being hijackers of Capone beer and booze.

On **January 30, 1928** Jack Mallardi 27 yrs. of 1126 Sinnott Pl. was shot by unknown gangsters at 1236 Sinnott Pl. The killers were suspected to be Blackhand extortionists.

On **February 1, 1928** Andrew DeLuca 32 yrs. of 1161 Townsend St. was shot by unknown gangsters using a shotgun in front of his residence. The killers were suspected to be Blackhand extortionists.

On **February 17, 1928** Isadore Goldberg 31 yrs. of 1439 S. Avers Ave. was shot by unknown gangsters in front of the garage at 1046 W. Harrison.

On **February 23, 1928** Phillip Leonetti 36 yrs. of 637 Miller St. was shot by unknown gangsters. He was killed in a candy store at 916 S. Loomis Street two doors from the restaurant he ran at 920 Loomis. He was the alleged leader of the 42 Gang and was known as an underling to Unione Siciliana President Tony Lombardo and his wife was a cousin to the wife of Diamond Joe Esposito. It was later reported that Leonetti was killed on the orders of Diamond Joe Esposito and that Leonetti was shaking people down for large amounts of cash using Esposito's name.

On **February 26, 1928** Robert J. Rutshaw 30 yrs. of 5245 S. Peoria St. was shot by unknown gangsters at 166 W. Washington St. in room #202 of the Cook County Federation Pleasure Club.

On **March 8, 1928** Joseph Cicala and Frank C. Siciliano 30 yrs. were murdered at 1727 Van Buren St. Joseph Terrvacchi was wanted in the killing and it is not known if he was ever caught **(Solved)**. *Police logs entered the case as follows:* March 8, 1928 Siciliano, Frank – Age 30 – Fatally shot and Joseph Sicola killed, at 4:40 AM 3/8/28, in The Dreamland Inn, 1727 Van Buren St., by the cook, Joseph Terravichio, part owner, because they interfered in a quarrel between him and his partner, Angelo Luci, whom he wanted to shoot. On 3/12/28 Bruno Anomanni was booked as an accessory. On 3/27/28 Angelo Luci and Richard Terravichio were also booked as accessories but on the same day all three were exonerated by the Coroner and their cases were nolle prossed 3/31/28 by Judge Schulman. The coroner recommended the arrest of Joseph Terravichio. 27 Dist.

On **March 21, 1928** Joseph "Diamond Joe" Esposito 55 yrs. was shot and killed near his home at 800 S. Oakley as he walked with two bodyguards Ralph and Joe Varchetti. He was a restaurateur, labor racketeer, political leader and the man who gave Paul "The Waiter" Ricca AKA: Felice DeLucia, his start in the United States with a job in his popular Taylor Street eatery the Bella Napoli Café at Halsted and Forquer streets. The victim was struck in the body and head with 58 pellets. Shortly before the killing "Dago Lawrence" Mangano approached "Diamond Joe" regarding his political support of a candidate running against Bill Thompson and his own candidacy for Committeeman. Apparently this was not acceptable to some gangsters. There were several different theories by police: first, he was killed by Joe Montana who was located nearby and who had previously killed two policemen before being acquitted, second he was killed by James Del Presco of 1033 S. Claremont who was previously shot and wounded and claimed Joe Esposito to be responsible, third, he was killed on the orders of Tony Lombardo in retaliation for having Phil Leonetti killed who worked for Lombardo, fourth, he was killed by the 42 gang who had previously killed a relative-Phil Leonetti and lastly he was killed by Paul Ricca who allegedly set up the murder using the up and coming Sam Giancana AKA: Momo Salvatore, Mooney, or Gilormo Giangono AKA: Momo Salvatore, Mooney, or Gilormo Giangono as one of the shooters, his body guards were held under suspicion, although no one was ever charged. ***Police logs entered the case as follows:*** March 21, 1928 Esposito, Joseph - Age 55 - Candidate for Ward Committeeman, 25th Ward, murdered in front of 810 So. Oakley Ave., at 4:50 PM, 3/21/28, by two unknown men who employed two double-barreled shotguns and a revolver which they discarded and escaped. 23rd Dist.

On **March 23, 1928** John Infantino 26 yrs. was murdered 1109 S. Peoria St. Sam Catandello was wanted in the killing and it is not known if he was ever caught. ***Police logs entered the case as follows:*** March 23, 1928 Infantino, John - Age 26 - Shot to death at 1 AM, 3/23/28, in a bedroom of his home, 1109 So. Peoria St., 2nd fl., for which his room-mate, Sam Catandello, alias Michael Armenci, is wanted. On 4/18/28 his arrest was recommended by the Coroner. 22 Dist. 6/14/28 Sam Catandello arrested and turned over to the Sheriff 6/18/28. July 1928 No Bill on Catandello.

On **March 27, 1928** John Zocoalo was murdered by unknown gangsters.

On **March 28, 1928** Jasper Montalbano 27 yrs. of 4250 N. Whipple St. was shot by unknown gangsters using a shotgun as he exited an auto in front of 870 Townsend St. The killers were suspected to be Blackhand extortionists.

On **March 29, 1928** Joseph Sakalanskas 40 yrs. of 4829 Nevada St. was shot by unknown gangsters in front of his home during an argument over alcohol. He was suspected of being a bootlegger at the time.

On **March 29, 1928** Charles Abragno 31 yrs. of 1424 W. Taylor St. was shot by unknown gangsters and found along Stony Island Ave. near Oak Glen, IL. He was a suspected bootlegger.

On **March 31, 1928** Thomas A. Johnson 35 yrs. of 5731 W. Addison was shot by unknown gangsters and dumped at Ogden Ave. near Kinzie St. He appeared to have been robbed and his auto was found at Polk and Kedzie Ave.

On **April 7, 1928** Charles Cook was murdered by Robert Nash. Nash was killed by the police 11 days later after killing a police officer **(solved)**.

On **April 10, 1928** Octavius Garady 43 yrs. was murdered at 13th St. and Hoyne Ave. He was a 20th ward committeeman candidate, a reformer and an attorney. This was another bloody primary election in what became known as the "Bloody 20th Ward". Earlier in the day carloads of gangsters terrorized voters shooting two other men and slugging scores of others. Granady a black candidate was running against a Thompson/Mob sponsored candidate, City Collector Morris Eller and the Mob delivered for Eller and Thompson. This case resulted in one of the largest election racketeering cases in Chicago history. As many as twelve men were arrested or indicted for the murder including two policemen, a judge, a State Senator, and a State's Attorneys Investigator, but all the charges were dropped. It was Special Prosecutor Frank Loesch that brought the charges, he would later be appointed as the executive Director of the Chicago Crime Commission. It was reported that a car load of gangsters chased Granady in his car until he crashed into a tree and was then shot to death. Sam Giancana AKA: Momo Salvatore, Mooney, or Gilormo Giangono was one of the mobsters suspected in the killing, years later Joe Annerino AKA: Genero claimed that James Belcastro admitted to him that he was one of the killers of Granady, but neither of the men were charged **(Solved)**. *Police logs entered the case as follows:* April 10, 1928 Granady, Octavius - Age 43 - Colored - Candidate for Ward Committeeman, 20th Ward, was shot to death at 13th St. and Hoyne Ave., while trying to escape in his auto from 6 or 7 assassins who pursued him in another machine. On 5/8/28 the Coroner recommended the arrest of his unknown assailants. 23 Dist. 6/18/28 John Armands arrested and indicted 7/2/28 Sam Kaplan arrested and turned over to Sheriff on indictment. 11/7/29 Kaplan - Armonds and Harry Hoelstein (also Ind. June 1928) cases N/P - David. The following arrests by State's Att. All indicted by Oct. 1929 G.J.: Louis Clementi, James Belcastro, John Armondo, Thos. Sammario, Lt. Phillip J. Carroll, and Patrolmen Michael B. Shannon, Walter F. Bailey, Geo. Tapling and Michael Loughney. 11/22/29 - Belcastro & Armondo N/P - David. 11/27/29 - all cases nolle prossed.

On **April 11, 1928** Thomas J. Johnson 42 yrs. of 1439 Jackson Blvd. was shot by unknown gangsters in a beer flat located at 1140 W. Adams. In a dying declaration to police the victim stated that he was shot by a man named "Nick". The outcome of the investigation is unknown.

On **April 13, 1928** an unknown white male approx. 45 yrs. was shot to death by unknown gangsters and found at 91st and Rockwell Sts. in Evergreen Park, IL.

On **April 15, 1928** Joseph Roberti was murdered by unknown gangsters.

On **April 18, 1928** Patrolman Emil Shogren was shot and killed while trying to interview two hoodlums at 39th and Michigan. The officer and his partner Sergeant John Shortwall approached the two men who opened fire killing Shogren immediately. The Sergeant pursued the assailants killing Robert Nash in the rear of 3958 S. Michigan in a shootout and capturing the second offender Joseph Copps who was wounded. Nash was wanted for a previous murder and Copps was charged as an accessory but never did any time for the crime **(solved)**.

On **April 23, 1928** Benjamin "Jew Ben" Newmark was killed when a shot was fired through his bedroom window at 7316 S. Merrill. Newmark was the former Chief Investigator for State's Attorney Robert Crowe who lost his re-election bid several days prior to the killing. Crowe referred to Newmark and his staff as Ali Baba and his forty thieves. It was reported that the victim was trying to form his own gang in opposition to Capone.

On **April 30, 1928** Pearl Eggleston 17 yrs. was machine gunned by a group of Westside hoodlums during the robbery of the Ritz Theater at 6337 W. Roosevelt Rd. The victim an usher in the show was killed during a $1,400 robbery by Sam Messeno, Jack "Puggy" White, Thomas McDonald, Madeline LaFleur, Yvonne LaFleur and two youths whose names were not released. The robber's vehicle was found at Archer and Long Aves. It led to gangster and labor racketeer Daniel Rooney who was not charged in the crime, he would be murdered in 1944. The remaining suspects plead guilty to the crime, but their sentences are not known **(solved)**.

On **May 8, 1928** William Jackson 28 yrs. of 5930 S. Park Ave. was shot by unknown gangsters and found in the rear of 6820 S. Chicago Ave. The deceased was a known gangster and was wanted for the Grand Trunk train mail robbery in Evergreen Park, IL.

On **May 14, 1928** Giuseppe Cavarretta was shot to death in an alley at 816 Milton Avenue. This was thought to be the aftermath of the mayhem of the recent election. However, the feud between Capone and Aiello continued with the shooting death of this alleged Aiello man.

On **May 26, 1928** William J. Watson 19 yrs. 311 S. Western Ave. was shot by Daniel R. Rooney and John J. Monahan AKA: Moynihan during a robbery of a soft drink parlor at the same address owned by the victim's father. The family of the victim, who identified Rooney from his hospital bed, complained of 55 continuances in the case and of the plea of guilty Rooney agreed to, allowing for a short prison sentence. In July of 1944 Rooney would be killed in front of a saloon **(solved)**.

On **June 12, 1928** James Lupino 29 yrs. of 2615 Rice St. was shot by unknown gangsters in the hallway of 814 N. Rockwell.

On **June 16, 1928** Frank Barnes 47 yrs. of 4743 Evans Ave. was beaten to death by unknown gangsters with a blunt object in the basement at 2701 South Park Ave. and then left in front of 2712 Cottage Grove Ave.

On **June 19, 1928** John Oliveri 45 yrs. of 1121 Cambridge Ave. and Joseph Salomone 30 yrs. of 1324 Wolfram St. were shotgunned to death by unknown gangsters in an auto in front of 503 W. Oak St. Both men were bootleggers.

On **June 19, 1928** Jimmie Raggio AKA: Raggie 40 yrs. of 5240 Calumet Ave. was shot by unknown gangsters while leaving his place of employment at 61 E. 51st St.

Big Tim Murphy home

On **June 26, 1928** Timothy D. "Big Tim" Murphy 45 yrs. was gunned down in front of his bungalow at 2525 W. Morse Ave. Murphy a feared labor racketeer was a tough thug from the back of the yards neighborhood and clawed his way to a leadership role by partnering with Mossie Enright a labor racketeer and killer along with TOC gambling impresario Mont Tennes before betraying both. He was suspected and arrested in several killings, but never convicted. In his final days he attempted a hostile takeover of a Capone fronted union that apparently cost him his life. John Hand, James Forsyth and Frank Noonan were sought in the killing, but later cleared. ***Police logs entered the case as follows:*** June 26, 1928 Murphy, Timothy, alias "Big Tim." - Age 45 - Shot to death at 11:00 PM,

6/26/28, in front of his home, 2525 Morse Ave., after he had answered a door bell summons, by three or four unknown men in an automobile, who, it appears, employed a machine gun. 41 Dist.

On **June 27, 1928** Willis Irving 36 yrs. of 2633 Federal St. was shot and beaten by unknown gangsters. He was found on 25th St. near Roosevelt Rd. in Broadview, IL.

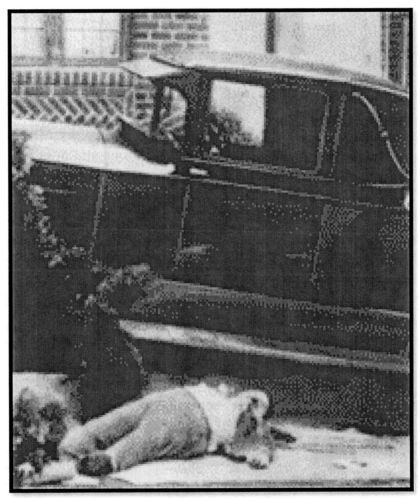

Frankie Yale dead

On **July 1, 1928** Frankie Yale was murdered. During the conflict between the north side gang and Capone, the Aiello's turned to Frankie Yale AKA: Uale or Ioele in New York for help after yet another failed assassination attempt on Capone and the installation of Capone's Unione Siciliana President, Tony Lombardo. Yale, National President of the Unione grew disenchanted with his former protégé and felt he was withholding dues and in turn he began hijacking Capone liquor shipments. He ordered Lombardo to step down and Joe Aiello to be placed as President of the Chicago Unione. In response Frankie Yale was murdered in a daylight pursuit on July 1, 1928 while driving down a Brooklyn

Street. Yale was called home from his saloon on a supposed emergency when the shooting occurred. "Machine Gun" Jack McGurn AKA: James or Vincenzo Gibaldi, Albert Anselmi, John Scalise, Tony Accardo, Paul Ricca and even Capone himself were some of the Chicago Mobsters suspected of the brazen crime. However, information reported at a later time indicated the killers in reality were Fred "Killer" Burke, Gus Winkler AKA: August "Big Mike" Winkeler, Frederick S. Goetz AKA: J. George "Shotgun" Zeigler and Louis "Little New York" Campagna. In this killing Chicago demonstrated to New York the utility of the machine gun in carrying out murders, it was reportedly New York's first by this method.

On **July 13, 1928** John Joseph Faul 31 yrs. of 1336 1/2 S. Austin Blvd. Cicero, IL. was shot by unknown gangsters while sitting in his auto at 5th Ave. and Troy St.

On **July 15, 1928** Danny Hartnett was shot by unknown gangsters in the Sterling Hotel. He was reportedly a notorious gunman.

On **July 19, 1928** Dominick Aiello 56 yrs. of 930 Milton St. was shot by unknown gangsters in front of his store at 928 Milton St. He is the uncle of gang leader Joe Aiello and the motive was suspected as the continual feud over control of the Unione Siciliana or Blackhand extortionists.

Dominick Aiello dead

On **July 24, 1928** Joseph Catironotta was murdered by unknown gangsters.

On **July 26, 1928** Sam Canalo AKA: Canale was shotgunned to death in his auto by unknown gangsters, he was an Aiello Lieutenant.

On **July 31, 1928** Benjamin Zion AKA: Benny Yanger 23 yrs. of 914 W. 14th St. was shot in the alley at 2418 W. Roosevelt Rd. by unknown gangsters. This murder was investigated by a grand jury looking into election racketeering in the 20th ward.

On **August 2, 1928** Lawrence Candan AKA: Canda 22 yrs. of 2509 W. 64th St. was reportedly shot by members of the Spike O'Donnell gang and found in the doorway of a saloon at 7434 S. Racine Ave. that was owned by Charles O'Donnell a brother of the notorious gangster. Police speculated a motive in that the victim posed as Ray O'Donnell in a shakedown of a motorist stemming from a traffic accident. The outcome of this case is unknown.

On **August 3, 1928** John Vella 29 yrs. of 448 W. Division St. was shot by unknown gangsters in front of his residence. Blackhand extortionists were suspected of the killing at the time.

On **August 5, 1928** Dominico Calandrino 34 yrs. of 1632 N. Girard St. was shot by unknown gangsters and thrown into a ditch at 175th and Central Park Ave.

On **August 7, 1928** Edward Divis 29 yrs. of 2636 W. 22nd St. was shot to death by three unknown gangsters in a soft drink parlor at 736 S. Paulina St.

On **August 8, 1928** Angelo Francisco was found shot to death in a cornfield near Mount Prospect, Illinois. The following day his wife Adeline Zaccard was found burned to death near Crown Point, Indiana. Angelo was part of a Bank robbery crew that robbed the West McHenry State Bank of $12,000 a few days earlier. The gang consisted of Carl Torraco AKA: Charlie Carr (a gunman for Torrio and Capone and the gangs' armorer), George Raymondi and David Taddio. One suspect matched the description of labor racketeer Mike Carrozzo, but he was never charged while the rest of the crew was convicted of the Robbery. The murder remains unsolved.

On **August 9, 1928** Virgillio Aleotto 51 yrs. of 1019 N. Larrabee was shot by unknown gangsters in front of his residence.

On **August 9, 1928** Tony Buttitta 40 yrs. of 920 Sedgwick St. was shot by unknown gangsters on Elm St. between Sedgwick and Townsend Aves.

On **August 13, 1928** a man known only as Michlevich 35 yrs. was shot by unknown gangsters and found in a ditch near Western Ave. and the Will County Line.

On **August 19, 1928** Frank Scarpinato 53 yrs. of 459 W. Division St. was shot by unknown gangsters in front of his residence.

On **August 19, 1928** Frank Alista AKA: Frank Barry, 30 yrs. of 446 Jackson St., Milwaukee, Wisconsin was shot at 24th and State Sts. by unknown gangsters in an auto.

On **August 22, 1928** Louis DiBirnardo 31 yrs. of 2827 S. Wells St. was shot by unknown gangsters at 28th and Stewart Sts.

On **August 29, 1928** Tony Soverino 22 yrs. of 2726 Flournoy St. was shot by unknown gangsters while seated in a Checker Taxi parked at 25ᵗʰ Ave. near Norwood Ave. in Melrose Park, IL.

On **September 3, 1928** Albert Pratt 32 yrs. of 12 W. Delaware St. was shot by Mike Riley, William Clifford and George "Red" Barker, all labor racketeers, in the Gould Garage at 868 N. Clark St. Another man and a police officer were also wounded during this incident. This was reportedly a labor dispute and the 3 men were arrested, tried and acquitted when the police officer changed his testimony and would not identify the accused in court **(solved)**.

George "Red" Barker

On **September 7, 1928** Antonio "Tony" Lombardo AKA: The Scourge, 36 yrs. of 2111 S. Austin, Cicero, IL. and one of his bodyguards Guiseppe Ferraro Morici 30 yrs. of 4825 W. 22ⁿᵈ, Cicero, IL., were murdered, Morici died on September 9, 1928, many thought this was a response to the Frankie Yale murder in New York. Two gunman killed Tony Lombardo and one of his two bodyguards as they left the offices of the newly named Italo-American Union (formerly the Unione Siciliana) in the Hartford Building at Dearborn and Madison in broad daylight. As the men walked through the busy downtown intersection of Madison and Dearborn Sts. 2 gunmen stepped from the doorway of the Raklios restaurant (now the site of the Chase Bank) and put two bullets in Lombardo's head at 61 W. Madison St. This opened the door for Patsy Lolordo another Capone man to assume the presidency and some historians suspected his brother Tony's (the uninjured Lombardo Bodyguard) involvement in the killing to make way for Patsy. It was also reported that Al Capone was angry over the victim having Joe Esposito killed and may have been involved in this murder, Historians later felt this killing was the motive for the spectacular St. Valentine's Day massacre several months later although it is doubted if any "one killing" was the true motive. Warrants were issued for north side gangsters Jack Zuta, Joe Aiello. Frank and Pete Gusenberg and Albert Kachellek AKA: "James Clark" were also suspected of the crime from descriptions of the killers. Frank Marco was identified but was killed before being brought to justice **(Solved)**. *Police logs entered the case as follows:* September 7, 1928 Lombardo, Anthony - Age 36 - Shot to death and one of his bodyguards, Anthony Ferrea, alias Ferraro, fatally wounded while walking west in front of #61 W. Madison St., at 4:30 PM. Murdered by some unknown person or persons who were lost in the crowds. Ferrea died on Sept. 9th. 1st Dist. 4/29/29 Warrant issued by Judge Lyle against Frank Marco after witnesses identified his picture at the B. of I. On 2/17/31 Marco, alias Marlo, was later murdered in New York City.

Tony Lombardo dead

On **September 22, 1928** Eugene G. Thivierge 35 yrs. was murdered at 68th St. and Cottage Grove Ave. He was a Checker Cab driver and embroiled in the "Cab Wars". Bernard M. Reister and Robert Moore AKA: Murphy, Mooney were charged with the crime and found not guilty **(Solved)**. *Police logs entered the case as follows:* September 22, 1928 Theviege, Eugene - Age 35 - Checker Cab - Fatally shot at 12:20 AM, 9/22/28, at the N.W. corner of 68th St. and Cottage Grove Ave., by two Yellow Cab chauffeurs when he parked near the Granada Café. One of the drivers, Bernard Reister, was captured while escaping from the scene. Arrest of the other, Robert Moore, alias Murphy, was recommended by the Coroner on 10/10/28. 7 Dist. Both men were indicted. 1/17/29 - Mooney and Reister both acquitted by Judge Miller. (Jury).

On **October 14, 1928** Eng Pake 40 yrs. of 508 S. Clark St. was shot by Leong Yuen and another Asian man as he entered a Yellow cab in front of 2113 Archer Ave. The murder was related to the Cab Wars of the day **(Solved)**. *Police logs entered the case as follows:* **October 14, 1928** Pak, Eng - Age 40 - Chinaman - Shot to death at 7:15 PM, 10/14/28, in front of 2113 Archer Ave., just as he boarded a taxicab, by another Chinaman, who escaped. On 10/17/28 Leong Yuen was booked for murder and on 11/1/28 held by the Coroner. 2 Dist. 6/12/29 - Acquitted - McGoorty.

On **October 15, 1928** Jung Bu Ging 60 yrs. was shot by unknown gangsters in his laundry at 1944 W. Madison.

On **October 17, 1928** Ralph J. Murphy 26 yrs. of 438 E. 62nd St. was shot by unknown gangsters with a machinegun while seated in an auto at 53rd St. and Union Ave.

On **October 19, 1928** Bazoo Sims 27 yrs. of 4637 Prairie Ave. was shot in front of his residence by unknown gangsters. He owned a grain store and sold alcohol and ran a gambling operation in the rear.

On **October 27, 1928** Peter Rizzito was killed by shotgun blasts in front of his Milton Street home. He was an associate of Joe Aiello and a candidate for the Unione Siciliana Presidency upon the death of Tony Lombardo.

On **October 28, 1928** a man known only as Darrow was killed. He was indicted for the August 6, 1926 murder of John "Mitters" Foley.

On **October 30, 1928** Vincent P. Signorelli 48 yrs. of 1025 N. Harding Ave. was shot by unknown gangsters while in his auto at 1434 Elgin Ave., Forest Park, IL.

On **November 5, 1928** Alfie Fricano 32 yrs. of 2455 N. Racine Ave. was shot by unknown gangsters while in front of his residence.

On **November 9, 1928** Charles R. Rice 44 Yrs. was shot by Michael McGovern in a soft drink parlor at 5213 S. Halsted. McGovern was arrested, but the grand jury passed a no bill when an indictment was sought **(Solved)**. *Police logs entered the case as follows:* November 9, 1928 Rice, Chas. - Age 44 - Fatally shot at 11:00 AM, 11/8/28, in a saloon at 5213 So. Halsted St., accusing one Michael McGovern as his assailant. On 11/5/28 McGovern's arrest was recommended by the Coroner. 18 Dist. 1/15/29 Michael McGovern arrested and held on Coroner's Mittimus. Jan. 1929 No Bill.

On **November 16, 1928** John G. Clay 59 yrs. of 2220 W. 113th St., a labor agent was shot by unknown gangsters while in his office of the Chicago Laundry and Dye House Drivers Union at 629 S. Ashland Ave. He was shot with revolvers and a shotgun through the front window.

On **November 30, 1928** Joseph Martino 40 yrs. of 161 E. 16th St. Chicago Heights, IL. was shot by unknown gangsters at 156 E. 16th St. Chicago Heights, IL.

On **December 6, 1928** Salvatore Lima 33 yrs. of 1432 Mohawk St. was shot by unknown gangsters at 1269 Clybourn Ave.

On **December 6, 1928** Leroy Gilbert the Police Chief of Chicago Heights IL. was shotgunned to death through a window in his own home. The "Heights" known by the tabloids as the "Center of Lawlessness" had been run for several years by Capone gangsters Jimmy Emery and Dominic Roberto. The Chief took action against them and paid with his life when he was killed.

On **December 8, 1928** John LaPrizza AKA: LaPuzza 23 yrs. of 139 25th Ave., Melrose Park, IL. was shot by unknown gangsters at 17th Ave. and 23rd St. in North Riverside, IL.

On **December 10, 1928** Dominick Sposato 45 yrs. of 17 Sheilds Ave., Chicago Heights, IL., was shot and beaten by unknown gangsters at 13th and Sheilds St., Chicago Heights, IL.

On **December 11, 1928** Frank Basile 28 yrs. of 722 S. Laflin was shot by unknown gangsters at 127th St. near Wallace St. in Chicago Heights, IL. Tony Felton was with the victim when he was killed and when he was arrested later he committed suicide. Frank Basile was a witness in the killing of Chief Gilbert on December 6th and was killed before he could provide any information in the case. These events led to a raid the following month by a collaboration of federal and local officials who took over the Heights in an effort to stabilize the area.

On **December 18, 1928** Ole Soully 47 yrs. of 7658 S. Laflin St. was shot by unknown gangsters while in the soft drink parlor at 1421 W. Taylor St. He was a witness in a kidnapping case and was killed by extortionist and kidnapping gangsters

On **December 18, 1928** Thomas Clyde Healy 34 yrs. of 755 E. 76th St. was shot by unknown gangsters and found in the parkway at 2510 S. California Ave.
On **December 20, 1928** Fillippo LaPaglia 39 yrs. of 643 S. LaSalle St. was shot by unknown gangsters while in his auto at 3205 S. Wells St.

On **December 27, 1928** Louis Nelson was murdered by unknown gangsters.

On **December 30, 1928** William J. Davern was murdered by unknown gangsters.

On **December 31, 1928** William McPadden 32 yrs. and Hugh "Stubby" McGovern 32 yrs. were murdered in the Granada Café at 6800 Cottage Grove Ave. by George Maloney. Some accounts state he was tried, convicted and sentenced to 14 years for the killings, while others state that the police mishandled the investigation and Maloney went free **(solved)**. *Police logs entered the case as follows:* December 31, 1928 McGovern, Hugh "Stubby" - Age 32 - Deceased and Wm. "Gunner" McPadden were shot to death at 2 AM, 12/31/28, in the Granada Café, 6800 Cottage Grove Ave., by George Maloney, who came in , spoke a few words to them, whipped out a gun and killed them both. Maloney was arrested immediately after the shooting, without resistance, and on 12/31/28 was held by the Coroner. 7 Dist. 1/22/30 - Nolle Prossed - McGoorty. December 31, 1928 McPadden, Wm. "Gunner" - Age 32 - Details in this case will be found in above murder of Hugh McGovern. 1/22/30 - Nolle Prossed- McGoorty.

Pasqualino Lolordo Dead

On **January 8, 1929** Pasqualino Lolordo 42 yrs. was shot dead in his home at 1921 W. North Ave. Following the Lombardo killing, Pasqualino Lolordo was installed as President of Unione Siciliana. Another Capone protégé, he struggled to keep the divided organization together when he received guests into his home. After some discussion he was shot dead by the men who were supposedly unknown to his wife. Lolordo's wife briefly identified Joe Aiello who may have just come out of hiding, as one of the killers before she assumed the customary code of silence "Omerta". After his death Joseph "Hop Toad" Guinta would assume the presidency while Joe Aiello felt he was in line for the position. ***Police logs entered the case as follows:*** January 8, 1929 Lolordo, Pasquale - Age 42 - Shot to death (13 times) at 5 PM, 1/8/29, in the parlor of his home, 1921 W. North Ave., by three unknown Italians with whom he had been drinking wine for a half hour. Arrest of the unknown men was recommended by the Coroner on 2/6/28. 29 Dist.

Joseph "Hop Toad" Guinta

On **January 31, 1929** Steve Kuczynski 23 yrs. of 5215 S. Paulina Ave. was shot to death in a flat at 4915 S. Ashland by gangsters Edward Maciejewski AKA: Eddie Mack and Joseph Bodner who were apprehended in the killing, while both were arrested the Bodner case was dropped and Maciejewski was killed by a police officer during a robbery before he could be tried **(solved)**. ***Police logs entered the case as follows:*** January 31, 1929 Kuczynski, Steve – Age 23 – Shot to death at about 4 AM, 1/31/29, in an alleged beer flat at 4915 So. Ashland Ave., by Edward Maciejewski, alias Mack, whose arrest was recommended by the Coroner, who held Joseph Bodnar, flat owner, as accessory. 17 Dist. 5/26/29 Edw. Maciejewski arrested and turned over to the Sheriff. 7/17/29 – Bodnar – Bond forf. & s/o – Kerner. 8/8/29 – Bodnar case reinstated – Sullivan. 1/27/30 – Maciejewski case s/o – Kerner. 1/27/30 Bodnar case s/o – Kerner. 3/30/30 – Maciejewski case s/o – Kerner. 6/29/33 – Maciejewski case reinstated and N/P – Prystalski. On 8/1/33 Maciejewski was killed by Police Officers during holdup.

On **February 4, 1929** William M. Cantwell 38 yrs. of 5239 Hirsch St. was shot by unknown gangsters in a saloon at 1842 W. Grand Ave. Police suspected labor racketeering as the motive behind this murder.

On **February 9, 1929** James A. Fee 43 yrs. of 3249 Walnut St. was shot by unknown gangsters while in front of 3221 Walnut St. Police suspected labor racketeering as the motive behind this murder.

On **February 14th 1929** Albert R. Weinshank, Peter Gusenberg, Frank Gusenberg, Albert Kachallek AKA: James Clark, Adam Heyer, John May a truck mechanic and Dr. Reinhardt Schwimmer an eye doctor who enjoyed hanging out with mobsters were executed in a garage at 2122 N. Clark St., at 10:40 AM. With Bugs Moran as their primary target, stemming from territorial, Unione Sicicliana and liquor disputes with Capone, seven members of the Northside gang were gunned down in the most infamous TOC murder in history, known as the St. Valentine's Day Massacre. Reportedly the killing plan was originally hatched at Cranberry Lake near Couderay Wisconsin in October or November of 1928. Those present at this planning session were reported to be: Al Capone, Gus Winkeler, George Zeigler, Louis Campagna, Fred Burke and politicos Bill Pacelli and Dan Seritella, although many other hoods were involved in the crime at different levels. After staking out the location for over two weeks by Capone operatives Byron Bolton, James "Jimmy the Swede" Morand and Jimmy McCrussen a signal was given and a killing team know to Capone hoods as the "American Boys" consisting of Gus Winkeler, Frederick S. Goetz AKA: J. George "Shotgun" Zeigler, Fred "Killer Burke", Ray Nugent and Bob Carey entered the Moran Gang office (two of which wore police uniforms) and slaughtered the seven men after lining them up against the wall.. While several local hoods that included Jack McGurn, Tony Accardo and Llewelyn Morris Humphreys AKA: "Murray the Camel", Curly were sought for questioning the names of the real perpetrators were confirmed several years later by one participant Byron Bolton. The case demonstrated to the public the worst case of investigative bungling by local and federal authorities in American history, while many legitimate investigators were stifled in the attempts to solve the crime. Several arrests were made along the way to no avail. The mass murder occurred in broad daylight in the S.M.C. Cartage Co. and even after the information came out authorities refused to pursue a real solution **(Solved)**.

Police logs entered the case as follows: February 14, 1929 Gusenberg, Frank - Age 36; Peter - Age 40 - Two of the seven Moran gangsters who were lined up facing a brick wall and mowed down with machine and shotguns in a garage at 2122 N. Clark St., at 10:40 AM, 2/14/29. When the killers left two had their hands in the air and two others, in police uniforms, followed pointing the machine guns at their backs. They all got into an auto disguised as a police squad car and escaped. 2/22/29 Sam Loverde and Michael Favia were booked. 2/27/29 John McGurn and Rocco Fanelli also booked and on 3/16/29 held without bail by Schwaba. 3/6/29 John Scalise was booked and indicted; he was found 5/7/29 murdered with Anselmi and Guinta in Hammond, Ind. 5/29/29 - Scalise cause abated - dead - Hopkins. 12/2/29 - McGurn case Nolle Prossed - Trude. Fred Burke captured 3/16/31 near Milan, Mo. 3/29/31 taken from St. Joseph, Mo. To St. Joseph, Mich. For the murder there of Officer Charles Skelly on 12/14/29. On 4/27/31 sentenced to Michigan State Pen. For life. Following Skelly's murder the massacre machine guns were found in Burke's St. Joseph, Mich. Home. Case number: 10002

<u>February 14, 1929</u> Heyer, Adam – Age 40 – One of the seven Moran gangsters who were lined up facing a brick wall and mowed down with machine and shotguns in a garage at 2122 N. Clark St., at 10:40 AM, 2/14/29. When the killers left two had their hands in the air and the other two, in police uniforms, followed pointing the machine guns at their backs. They all got into an auto disguised as a police squad car and escaped. 36 Dist. 2/22/29 Sam Loverde and Michael Favia booked on 7 charges each. 2/27/29 John McGurn and Racco Fanelli booked and on 3/16/29 held without bail by Judge Schwaba. On 3/6/29 John Scalise was booked and indicted; he was found murdered 5/7/29 with Anselmi and Guinta in Hammond, Indiana. 5/29/29 – Scalise cause abated – dead – Hopkins. 12/2/29 – McGurn case Nolle Prossed – Trude. Fred Burke captured 3/26/31 near Milan, Missouri. 3/29/31 taken from St. Joseph, Mo. to St. Joseph, Mich. for the murder there of Officer Charles Skelly on 12/14/29. On 4/27/31 sentenced to Michigan State Pen. for life. Following the murder of Skelly the massacre machine guns were found in Burke's St. Joseph, Mich. home. Case number: 10124

<u>February 14, 1929</u> Kachellek, Albert, alias Jas. Clarke – Age 40 – One of the seven Moran gangsters who were lined up facing a brick wall and mowed down with machine guns and shotguns, in a garage at 2122 N. Clark St. at 10:40 AM, 2/14/29. When the killers left two of them had their hands in the air and two others followed pointing the machine guns at their backs. They all got into an auto disguised as a police squad car and escaped. 36 Dist. 2/22/29 Sam Loverde and Michael Favia were booked on 7 charges. 2/27/29 John McGurn and Rocco Fanelli were booked and on 3/16/29 held without bail by Judge Schwaba. On 3/6/29 John Scalise was booked and indicted; he was found murdered 5/7/29 with Anselini and Guirta in Hammond, Indiana. 5/29/29 – Scalise cause abated – dead – Hopkins. 12/2/29 – McGurn case Nolle Prossed – Trude. Fred Burke captured 3/26/31 near Milan, Mo. 3/29/31 taken from St. Joseph, Mo. to St. Joseph, Mich. for the murder there of Officer Charles Skelly on 12/14/29. On 4/27/31 sentenced to Michigan State Pen. for life. Following Skelly's murder the massacre machine guns were found in Burke's St. Joseph, Mich. home. [THE MASSACRE] Case number: 10332

<u>February 14, 1929</u> May, John - Age 35 - One of the seven Moran gangsters who were lined up facing brick wall and mowed down with machine guns and shotguns, in a garage at 2122 N. Clark St., at 10:40 AM, 2/14/29. When the killers left two of them had their hands in the air and two others, in police uniforms, followed pointing the machine guns at their backs. They all got into an auto disguised as a police squad car and escaped. On 2/22/29 Sam Loverde and Michael Favia were booked on 7 charges each, 2/27/29 John McGurn and Rocco Fanelli were booked and on 3/16/29 held without bail by Judge Schwaba. 3/6/29 john Scalise was booked and indicted; he was found murdered 5/7/29 with Anselmi and Guinta in Hammond, Indiana. 5/29/29 Scalise cause abated - dead - Hopkins. 12/2/29 - McGurn case Nolle Prossed - Trude. Fred Burke captured

3/26/31 near Milan, Mo. 3/29/31 taken from St. Joseph, Mo. To St. Joseph, Mich. For the murder there of Officer Charles Skelly on 12/14/29. On 4/17/31 sentenced to Mich. State Pen. for life. Following Skelly's murder the massacre machine guns were found in Burke's St. Joseph, Mich. Home. Case number: 10541

February 14, 1929 Schwimmer, Reinhardt – Age 29 – One of the seven Moran gangsters who were lined up facing a brick wall and mowed down with machine guns and shotguns in a garage at 2122 No. Clark St., at 10:40 AM, 2/14/29. When the killers left two of them had their hands in the air and the other two followed pointing the machine guns at their backs. They all got into an auto disguised as a police squad car and escaped. 2/22/29 Sam Loverde and Michael Favia were booked. 2/27/29 John McGurn and Rocco Fanelli were booked and held without bail 3/16/29 by Judge Schwaba. On 3/6/29 John Scalise was booked and indicted; he was found murdered 5/7/29 with Anselmi and Guinta in Hammond, Ind. 5/29/29 – Scalise case abated – dead – Hopkins. 12/2/29 – McGurn case Nolle Prossed – Trude. Fred Burke captured near Milan, Mo. 3/29/31 brought to St. Joseph, Mich. from St. Joseph, Mo. for the murder there of Officer Charles Skelly on 12/14/29. On 4/27/31 he was sentenced to the Michigan State Pen. for life. Following Skelly's murder the massacre machine guns were found in Burke's St. Joseph, Mich. home. [THE MASSACRE] Case number: 11028

February 14, 1929 Weinshank, Albert - Age 26 - One of the seven Moran gangsters who were lined up facing a brick wall and mowed down with machine guns and shotguns, in a garage at 2122 N. Clark St., at 10:40 AM. When the killers left two had their hands in the air and two others, in police uniforms, followed pointing the shotguns at their backs. They all got into an auto disguised as a police squad car and escaped. On 2/22/29 Sam Loverde and Michael Favia were booked. On 2/27/29 John McGurn and Rocco Fanelli also were booked and held 3/16/29 without bail by Judge Schwaba. 3/6/29 John Scalise was booked and indicted; he was found murdered 5/7/29 with Anselmi and Guinta in Hammond, Ind. 5/29/29 Scalise cause abated - dead - Hopkins. 12/2/29 McGurn case nolle prossed - Trude. Fred Burke captured 3/26/31 near Milan, Mo. 3/29/31 taken from St. Joseph, Mo. To St. Joseph, Mich. For the murder of Officer Charles Skelly on 12/14/29. On 4/27/31 sentenced to Michigan State Pen. For life. Following Skelly's murder, the massacre machine guns were found in Burke's St. Joseph, Mich. Home.

St. Valentine's Day Massacre

On **February 22, 1929** Pete Locasto 36 yrs. of 1011 S. Oakley Blvd. was shot by unknown gangsters while on 22nd St. in North Riverside, IL.

On **March 19, 1929** William J. Vercoe 51 yrs. of 808 E. 49th St. was shot by gangsters in the Pony Inn at 5615 W. Roosevelt Rd. Cicero, IL. The victim was the President of Vercoe Fuel Oil Corp. The apprehension of George McNally of 5815 Roosevelt Rd. Cicero, IL., Michael Windle of 5615 Roosevelt Rd. Cicero, IL., and William Johnson of 223 N. Maplewood was ordered by the coroner's jury for their involvement in the killing. It is not known if they were brought to justice **(solved).**

On **March 22, 1929** Raymond Cassidy 30 yrs. of 5306 Emerald Ave. was shot by unknown gangsters while in front of 5213 S. Halsted St.

On **March 29, 1929** Settimio Conti 47 yrs. of 2330 74th Ave. Elmwood Park, IL. was shot by unknown gangsters in the basement of his home.

In April of 1929 the Cook County Coroner held additional Inquest hearings that brought Major Calvin Goddard to center stage to present scientific data regarding the ballistics of the St. Valentine Massacre firearms. This testimony led Coroner Bundesen to recommend the establishment of a modern crime detection laboratory in Chicago. The idea is furthered with the help of the Chicago Crime Commission (CCC). The lab was established at Northwestern University and provided training for officials from all over the country. Through this training the FBI stole the idea and established their own lab as they would do with the CCC Public Enemies List in years to come.

On **April 5, 1929** Frank Louis "Red" Krueger 40 yrs. of 4901 W. 14th St. was shot by two unknown gangsters while he sat in an auto at 736 W. 22nd St.

On **April 12, 1929** William F. Clifford 24 yrs. of Oak Park Arms Hotel, Oak Park, IL. and Michael F. Reilly Jr. 28 yrs. of 4315 Kedzie Ave. were murdered while in a LaSalle sedan in the rear of 4823 W. 22nd St. Cicero, IL. The men were involved in labor racketeering and the formation of the Midwest Garage Owner's Association. They were tried and acquitted of killing a garage attendant in September of 1928 along with Red Barker. This effort was headed by Capone gangsters George "Red" Barker and his brother-in-law "Big Tom" Sullivan and Dave Albin.

On **April 12, 1929** Michael McAndrews 39 yrs. of 7835 Langley Ave. was shot to death by Peter Peoria in the basement flat at 7639 Dobson St. where Peoria ran a speakeasy. It is not known if he was brought to justice for this killing **(solved).**

On **April 24, 1929** Frank Raday AKA: Frank Lee Brady 32 yrs. of 908 Grace St. was shot to death by unknown gangsters while in a dental office on the second floor of 2059 W. Madison St.

On **April 28, 1929** Enrico Arduini 43 yrs. of 714 W. Grand Ave. was shot by unknown gangsters in front of the 26th Street Grill at 237 W. 26th St.

On **May 3, 1929** Charles Folisi 46 yrs. of 801 S. Leavitt St. was beaten to death by unknown gangsters and dumped in a ditch at Hoxie Ave. near 135th St.

On **May 8, 1929** Joseph "Hop Toad" Guinta, John Scalise and Albert Anselmi were murdered in Hammond Indiana. Guinta was a flamboyant individual and he developed a close association with killers Anselmi and Scalise during his tenure as the leader of the Unione Siciliana. The three decided to rid the world of Al Capone. Capone set the men up with a staged falling out with his brother-in-law and bodyguard Frankie Rio AKA: Kline, Cline who was made privy to the plot. The three men were invited to a banquet in a near-by roadhouse in Hammond, Indiana where all three were beaten and shot to death. The media a step behind on this one, laid blame on the Northside gang of Bugs Moran.

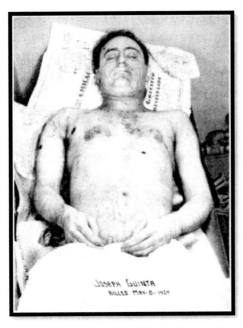

Joseph "Hop Toad" Guinta dead

On **May 15, 1929** Detective Raymond E. Martin 33 yrs. of 5058 N. Kedvale Ave., while acting as a decoy to capture a group of kidnappers, was shot and killed by the gang at Laramie Ave. near Van Buren St. The kidnapping victim was a former bootlegger named Philip Blumenthal who was released after the first payment of $15,000 was made by Henry Finkelstein a former Bugs Moran gang member. After the release he notified police who attempted to set up a sting to capture the gang with the murder victim posing as the victim's brother. The plan failed and the decoy was killed. The crew was later identified as Martin O'Leary, David Miller, Ernest Rossi AKA: Ross and Fred Fisher. However, justice was denied when Fisher and Miller were murdered in Kentucky and the other two were never captured although Rossi would be killed in 1934 **(solved)**.

On **May 21, 1929** John D. Hand 25 yrs. of 6706 Parnell Ave. was shot by unknown gangsters and found in his auto at 1415 S. 57th Ave. Cicero, IL.

On **May 22, 1929** Detective Joseph J. Sullivan 27 yrs. of 1037 S. Mayfield Ave. was shot in a speakeasy at 1610 W. Polk St. His body was then placed is his car and taken to 3131 W. Polk where it was discovered. The details of the killing were never verified, but the subsequent investigation and information presented by an informant verified the officer's death as a line of duty incident. One fact that was verified was that the speakeasy was owned by notorious gangster Joseph "Red" Bolton brother of State Rep. John Bolton and an associate of the Capone gang. Other individuals who were sought regarding the crime were the manager Elmo Clarke, bartender William "Dinky" Quan, gangster Willie Doody and a patron Bernard McComb. The different theories proposed were: that the victim was killed in revenge for his work under Lt. William Cusack, that he was following up on the beating of another officer at the establishment who was a friend of his, that he was investigating other individuals who were involved in the kidnapping of Philip Blumenthal and the murder of Detective Ray Martin or that he was searching for Willie Doody who was wanted for the shooting of a postal inspector. The aforementioned informant claimed that Clarke was the shooter, but enough evidence to charge him was never developed. A bit of justice came at a later date when Dinky Quan and two other hoodlums were killed by Sergeant P. B. O'Connell and his squad at 14 N. Sacramento in December of 1929.

On **May 26, 1929** Bruno Borrelli 31 yrs. of 215 W. 23rd St. was shot by unknown gangsters in a building at 265 Alexander St. where he followed a police officer into a the building to investigate a complaint about a moonshine still.

On **May 28, 1929** Charles Levy the Police Chief in west suburban Berwyn was murdered. Eddie Maciejewski was taken into custody for this and a previous killing and Willie Doody was wanted. Doody was also wanted for shooting a postal inspector and for questioning in the murder of Det. Joe Sullivan. The outcome of this case is unknown **(Solved)**.

On **May 30, 1929** Thomas McElligott 24 yrs. of 734 S. Kenneth was shot by unknown gangsters in the basement soft drink parlor at 361 W. Madison. The victim was involved in labor racketeering and the formation of the Midwest Garage Owner's Association. This effort was headed by Capone gangsters George "Red" Barker and his brother-in-law "Big Tom" Sullivan and Dave Albin.

On **May 31, 1929** Ettore Quaterri 54 yrs. of 1024 S. Racine Ave. was shot by unknown gangsters while seated on a bench in front of his home. Blackhand extortionists were suspected of the killing.

In **June of 1929** Joe Touhy was killed by a machinegun blast from one of his own men. He was one of the infamous Touhy brothers and was in the process of breaking up a Capone speakeasy in Schiller Park, a Chicago suburb, when one of his men, Paul Pagen attempted to shoot a bartender who reached for a weapon. Pagen claimed the shooting was an accident, but another brother named Johnny killed him a short time later. Johnny was charged in the killing and sent to Statesville prison. He was released after 4 years. A short time later Johnny was returned to prison where he died of consumption **(solved)**.

On **June 2, 1929** Herman Bloom was murdered by unknown gangsters.

On **June 5, 1929** Patrick Maloney 32 yrs. of 1213 Clarence Ave. in Berwyn, IL. was killed by James F. O'Connell AKA: Jim Dalton and other unknown gangsters in the office of the Kantainer Co. at 1722 Austin Ave. **(solved)**.

On **June 15, 1929** Louis Sevcik 22 yrs. of 2300 S. Cicero, Cicero, IL. was shot by unknown gangsters and found in a sewer at 27th St. and Blanchan St. in LaGrange Park, IL.

On **June 16, 1929** Ralph Cerra 35 yrs. of 1000 East Ave. in Kankakee, IL. was shot by unknown gangsters and found on Joe Orr Rd. near State St. in Bloom Township.

On **June 24, 1929** Frankie Marlow was murdered. It was discovered that he welched on a $250,000 debt to Capone.

On **June 26, 1929** Sam Muschia 37 yrs. of 2654 Thorndale Ave. was shot by unknown gangsters in front of 530 N. Morgan St.

On **July 3, 1929** Earnest Hoffman 57 yrs. of 3857 Cottage Grove Ave. was shot by unknown gangsters while driving his Checker Cab in front of 2501 Burling St.

On **July 10, 1929** Nathan Rossman AKA: Joseph Resnikoff 21 yrs. of 3024 Roosevelt Rd. was shot by unknown gangsters in front of 831 W. Maxwell St.

On **July 31, 1929** Thomas A. McNichols 37 yrs. of 4815 W. Adams St. a former court bailiff and James "Bozo" Shupe 34 yrs. of 1214 S. Ashland Ave. an ex-convict were shot to death as they assaulted each other at Madison and Aberdeen. Shupe was found to have purchased several machineguns including one used on St. Valentine's Day. However, he wound never testify at the Inquest hearings **(solved)**. *Police logs entered the case as follows:* July 31, 1929 McNichols, Thomas - Age 37 - Gangster. Fatally shot at 9:55 PM, 7/30/29, at Madison and Aberdeen Sts., in a duel with another gangster, James Shupe, whom he in turn also fatally wounded. The two had been gunning for each other as the result of alcohol hijacking. 26th Dist.

On **August 4, 1929** Yee Sun 60 yrs. of 2318 S. State St. was shot by opposing gangsters in front of 2223 Wentworth Ave. The victim a member of the On Leong had been in a protracted dispute with a rival Tong, Hip Sing since 1925. Ding Wing was suspected of the shooting, but Joe Tuck was arrested, tried and acquitted of the crime. The gangsters were probably disputing the gambling rackets or territorial concerns when the shooting occurred **(Solved)**.

On **August 9, 1929** Louis F. Heisler 25 yrs. of 5407 25th St. in Cicero, IL. was shot in the head, neck, chest and abdomen with a revolver and found in a prairie at 50th and Harlem Ave.

On **August 15, 1929** John Woytko 47 yrs. of 10316 S. Fairfield was shot by unknown gangsters as he parked his car in the garage at 2106 N. Mason Ave.

On **August 28, 1929** John F. Bowman 24 yrs. of 547 N. Pine Ave. was shot by unknown gangsters and brought to Henrotin Hospital by his business partner Frank Cudia who would provide no further information.

On **August 29, 1929** Tony Domingo 36 yrs. of 3021 Walnut St. was shot with a shotgun by unknown gangsters at 417 N. Ogden Ave.

On **September 2, 1929** Henry Connors 38 yrs. who lived in the Wacker Hotel was shot by unknown gangsters in the café at 509 N. Clark St.

On **September 5, 1929** Edward Wescott 26 yrs. and Frank Cawley 25 yrs. of 828 N. Harding Ave. were shot to death at Fullerton and Narragansett Aves. by unknown gangsters. The men were involved in labor racketeering and the formation of the Midwest Garage Owner's Association. This effort was headed by Capone gangsters George "Red" Barker and his brother-in-law "Big Tom" Sullivan and Dave Albin.

On **September 11, 1929** Charles Brown 30 yrs. of the Knickerbocker Hotel was shot by unknown gangsters and thrown from a vehicle at 54th and Lowe Ave. Brown was a known safe blower and a suspect in the 1923 murder of Lewis Hauschild.

On **September 16, 1929** Peter Pullizzi 26 yrs. of 1347 S. 59th Ct. in Cicero, IL. was shot by unknown gangsters while in his auto at 1247 W. Taylor St. Police claim he was a known bootlegger and ran roadhouses in Villa Park and Elmhurst IL.

On **October 13, 1929** Casmir Holzwork AKA: Riggins 29 yrs. of 1119 W. Madison St. was shot by unknown gangsters in his cigar store at the same address.

On **October 30, 1929** H. Myles Cannaven 46 yrs. of the Drexel Arms Hotel at Oakwood and Drexel Blvd. was shot by unknown gangsters while in his auto at the back of the hotel.

On **October 31, 1929** Rocco Maggio 33 yrs. of 1026 Newberry Ave. was shot by unknown gangsters while in his father in law's grocery store at 847 W. Taylor St.

On **November 10, 1929** Joseph Lopiccolo 30 yrs. of 4810 Northcott Ave. in East Chicago, Ind. was shot by unknown gangsters while in the rear of 212 Mason St. in Calumet City, IL. Police suspected the killing involved bootlegging disputes from northern Indiana.

On **November 24, 1929** Edward J. Tracey 28 yrs. was reportedly murdered by Melville Purves who was arrested and sentenced to 14 years in prison **(Solved)**. *Police logs entered the case as follows:* November 24, 1929 Tracey, Edward - Age 28 - Shot to death at 5:20 PM, while seated at a table in restaurant of the Club Arlington, 2418 W. North Ave., by his boyhood chum, Melville Purves, who, upon entering the place, deliberately walked up and shot him in the head. Purves was captured as he attempted to escape in a cab. He was booked for murder and his brother, William as accessory. On 11/25 Melville was held by the Coroner and William exonerated. The latter case was nolle prossed 12/11/29 by Judge Borelli. 30 Dist. 3/3/30 - John P. Sullivan booked - accy - 4/9/30 Nolle Prossed - Sbarboro. 5/1/30 - Melville - 14 yrs. Joliet Pen. - Trude.

On **December 1, 1929** Edward Baron 19 yrs. of 218 E. 26th Street in Chicago Heights was shot by unknown gangsters at 80 E. Main St. in Chicago Heights, IL. He was found with three bullet wounds to his head. He had recently been paroled and was wanted for local filling station robberies. Police at the time believed that he had a quarrel with his gang over the division of the proceeds and they killed him and dumped his body.

On **December 2, 1929** James Walsh 26 yrs. of 626 W. 18th St. was shot by gangsters at 87 W. Randolph St. Charles "Babe" Barron was held in the killing and police sought Joseph Coda AKA: Anderson and Robert Emmett Ryan for their involvement in the slaying, the outcome of this case is unknown **(solved).**

On **December 3, 1929** John Voegtle AKA: Paddy King 38 yrs. of 4321 N. Kilpatrick was shot by unknown gangsters on the 4th floor of 426 S. Wabash Ave., the victim was President of the Ushers Union.

On **December 11, 1929** Tomaso Tiritilli 50 yrs. of 3100 W. Polk St. was shot by unknown gangsters in front of 3109 W. Lexington St. The deceased was a plotter in the Ranierie kidnapping and was not identified at the time because of fear. Blackhand extortionists were suspected in this killing.

On **December 14, 1929** Police Officer Charles Skelly is shot and killed at the scene of a minor car accident in St. Joseph, Michigan. The killer escapes, but is identified as Fred "Killer" Burke a suspect in the St. Valentine's Day killings. Burke is eventually caught and imprisoned for killing the officer. Even after Major Calvin Goddard confirms that 2 machine guns recovered from the Burke farm were used in the Chicago Massacre and an indictment and murder warrant were issued, no attempt was made by federal authorities to bring him to justice in Chicago. Further testing later confirmed that one of the Burke guns was also used in the Frankie Yale murder in New York **(solved)**.

On **December 22, 1929** Roy F. Savery 42 yrs. of 25 N. Ogden Ave. was shot by unknown gangsters at 2824 W. Chicago Ave.

On December 31, 1929 Sam "Teetz" Battaglia shoots police Det. Sgt. Martin Joyce at the C & O Café at 509 N. Clark during a robbery. Joyce survived the attack and went on to a stellar career in law enforcement, however it is unknown if Battaglia was ever brought to justice for this crime. Teetz would go on to lead the OUTFIT in the 60s and died in prison in 1973.

The CCC recorded 261 TOC murders in Chicago between 1926 and 1929, 2 solved.

Approx. number of Chicago TOC related murders in the 1920s: 594
Approx. number of Chicago TOC related murders in the 1920s solved: 123
Approx. number of Chicago TOC related murders of Police Officers: 23

Chapter 3. The 1930s

By the beginning of the decade, TOC, like the rest of the country was suffering from the great depression. Many labor unions, a new source of revenue and power, came under the control of the mob, by using techniques such as: gunman, sluggers, hijackers, and extortionists. Truckloads of merchandise were destroyed, stores bombed, plants wrecked with axes and crowbars, acid poured into laundry vats/thrown on clothes, union officials kidnapped and people even killed when they resisted TOC demands. The Capone syndicate by this time was in clear control and became known as the OUTFIT. This OUTFIT was unique in its willingness to give considerable responsibility to non-Italians. Murray "The Camel" Humphreys of 7710 Bennett Ave. was a top gang leader for the old Capone Gang and was a genius when it came to developing new rackets. One of which was the formation of the Truck and Transportation Agency known as TNT. This organization through extortionate techniques would levy enormous fees on each driver and truck from different trucking enterprises and was said to make $1,000,000 a year from the coal business alone. A University of Chicago study estimated that racketeers cost the city $145,000,000 a year. By December of 1933 a Grand Jury investigation was initiated against TNT.

Murray Humphreys

By 1931 Chicago grew weary of Bill Thompson's big mouth, loose spending and close association with mobsters; they elected another pro-liquor Mayor by the name of Anton Cermak. Cermak was the head of a group that represented liquor interests and openly opposed Sunday closing laws, a bone of contention since the city formed. Cermak took the Democratic political machine to new heights and was said to have "systemized grand larceny".

Mayor Anton Cermak shot

Aldermen Kenna and Coughlin maintained control of the first ward political machine, but only with the approval of the Capone gang. Both faded from politics in the next several years only to be replaced by MOB sponsored politicians, something that would become endemic to the 1st ward for decades to come, until it succumbed to ethnic succession, indictments and redistricting.

In October of 1931 Al Capone was found guilty of failing to pay income tax on $1,038,654 between 1924 and 1929. He received a sentence of eleven years in prison. His reign over TOC in Chicago ended and he eventually died in Florida a sick and broken man in 1947. Other gangsters such as his brother Ralph "Bottles" Capone, Jake Guzik, Sam Guzik and Frank Nitti also were convicted of tax evasion, but survived prison terms and returned to their OUTFIT duties.

Upon Capone's incarceration Frank "the Enforcer" Nitti took his place. Nitti a trusted confidant', was supported by Paul "The Waiter" Ricca AKA: Felice DeLucia, an immigrant Italian who first came to the U.S. fleeing prosecution for a murder in Italy. He went to work for a major bootlegger and political power in Little Italy, "Diamond Joe" Esposito. He worked in Esposito's restaurant where he picked up his moniker and would later orchestrate Esposito's murder.

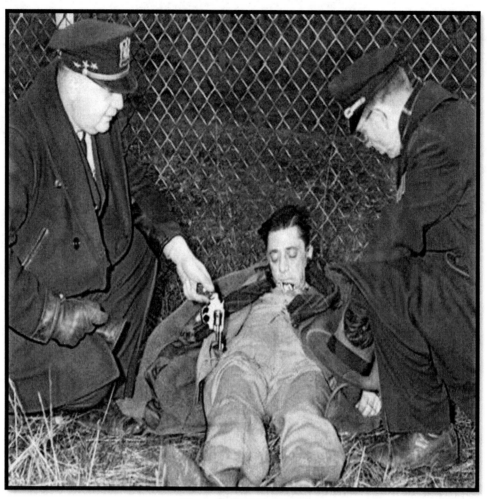

Frank Nitti dead

Of the new initiatives in the post-Capone OUTFIT, labor was pursued vigorously as indicated by the 1932 shooting of International Brotherhood of Teamsters Vice President Patrick Berrell. By 1934 the OUTFIT needed to diversify. The unions resisted as long as they could, but soon succumbed to OUTFIT muscle. During this decade Chicago TOC in trying to recover from the effects of the Volstead repeal, established an alliance with Frank Costello of New York and his Tammany Hall counterparts. In 1934 NY and Chicago TOC combined forces to move in on unions across the country i. e. Service employees, Theatrical-Stage & Motion Picture employees, Cleaning & Dying, Dairy-Milk Drivers, Retail Clerks and of course Labor. Torrio's national "Commission" held several meetings and plotted to expand throughout the country.

After the December 1933 repeal of the Volstead Act, the Chicago Mob knew this income had to be supplanted with other rackets and in due order diversified into related businesses that included: liquor, trucking and restaurants. In 1934 Nitti in cooperation with his east coast counterparts: Lucky Luciano, Lepke Buchalter, and Longie Zwillman, entered into a scheme to shake down the motion picture industry of millions of dollars. To accomplish this Nitti employed the services of George Browne a movie industry union official and Willie Bioff AKA: William Morris Bioff, William Nelson a local shakedown artist. This plan worked for several years and targeted some of the largest studios in Hollywood and threatened local theaters across the country. A friend recalled how his grandfather would take payments to a downtown hotel and hand them over to mobsters so he could continue to operate his movie theater.

Paul Ricca

During this era other crime figures emerged as leaders in the OUTFIT. The immediate successor to Nitti was Paul "The Waiter" Ricca. Ricca was a savvy leader, but encountered his own legal problems paving the way for Tony Accardo, who by the time of his death in 1992 established himself as the most successful OUTFIT leader of all time, only spending one night in jail for a minor gambling arrest.

While the "War on Crime" was actually something more of news reels than reality, local judges and prosecutors pursued gangsters now known as "Public Enemies" on minor charges of vagrancy, gun toting and labor racketeering. This was a minor inconvenience to the gang and they continued to flourish. At the federal level income tax charges had limited success and sent several of the more notable hoodlums to jail, usually returning to their gang positions after less than five years away.

Critical Events of the 1930s:

In 1930 Sergeant James McBride was shot by Capone gangster Claude Maddox. The Sergeant survived the shotgun assault and Maddox was arrested. The outcome of the case is unknown. What is known is that Sergeant McBride was the chief witness against another Capone gangster, Three Finger Jack White in the murder of a police officer. White was convicted, but only spent a couple of years in jail.

On **January 5, 1930** James Strangis 34 yrs. of 1535 Halsted St. was shot by unknown gangsters in the area about three miles east of Steger, IL. on 34th St. in Bloom Township. His body was then placed in his auto and it was set on fire.

On **January 7, 1930** Louis Antonucci 40 yrs. of 1020 Cypress St. was shot by unknown gangsters in a garage at 5532 Elston Ave.

On **January 8, 1930** James H. McManus 27 yrs. of 1139 N. Lawler Ave. was shot by unknown gangsters in the area of Diversey and Lincoln Aves.

On **January 11, 1930** Leo DeLorenzo 38 yrs. of 1911 Ogden Ave. was shot to death by unknown gangsters described as Italians during a dispute in a soft drink parlor at 3102 W. Harrison. He was found dead in an alley at 716 S. Kedzie.

On **January 30, 1930** Barney J. Mitchell 32 yrs. of 5040 Ridgeway Ave. and Glen Jackson 32 yrs. of 6417 St. Anthony's Ct. were shot in a cab by unknown gangsters at Ridge Ave. and Farwell St. Jackson drove the cab as Mitchell the treasurer of Checker Cab Co. was a passenger. The Cab Wars were a motivating factor in this killing which police felt was an inside job.

On **February 1, 1930** Julius Rosenheim 49 yrs. leaving his home at 3510 Dickens Ave. was gunned down by two men who exited a car at Ballou St. near McLean Ave. It seems that the government was seeking information in the tax case against Al Capone and Julius may have provided some. Months later it was revealed that the man known as a fixer and shake-down artist was also providing information to the gangs, police and press. This led to the assumption that this case was connected to the killing of newspaperman Jake Lingle some months later. Jack McGurn and Tony Accardo were questioned in the murder, but released without being charged.

On **February 2, 1930** Joseph Cada Jr. 29 yrs. of 2118 S. Scoville Ave. in Berwyn, IL. was shot by unknown gangsters while in his auto on Broadway near Leland Aves.

On **February 4, 1930** Phillip Marchese 39 yrs. of 2628 W. Monroe St. was shot by unknown gangsters in an alley near 2113 Lexington St. by unknown gangsters at about 2pm near a playground where children were playing. The victim beat murder charges against him in 1928 for killing Dominick Russo and Michael Pecore.

On **February 4, 1930** Guiseppe Bucheri 27 yrs. of 2709 W. 71st. St. was murdered by two gunshots to the head in his apartment. He was the proprietor of a grocery store on the west edge of the Loop. Neighbors said he had three men as guests in the flat at the time of the killing and Blackhand extortionists were suspected in this killing.

On **February 5, 1930** William Healy 36 yrs. of 7609 S. Normal was murdered by gun fire as he left a Beer flat at 3740 S. Lowe Ave. During a deathbed statement he named his assailants as: George "Monk" Campion of 3219 S. Union, Jerry Cotter of 523 W. 26th St. and Jack Neville address unknown. Campion and Cotter were arrested while Neville was being sought. Neville was murdered himself in 1939 and Danny Stanton was a suspect. It is not known if any of the men were ever prosecuted **(solved).**

On **February 14, 1930** Tony Lombardo 25 yrs. was shot by unknown gangsters in the alley behind 1413 Austin Ave. (Not to be confused with the Tony Lombardo who as a protégé of Al Capone and lead the Unione Siciliana until his murder in 1928).

On **February 23, 1930** Lorenzo Pizziferri 34 yrs. of 1129 S. Wood St. was shot by unknown gangsters in front of his residence. Blackhand extortionists were suspected in this killing.

On **March 4, 1930** Joe Cerrito 48 yrs. of 1217 W. Taylor St. was stabbed to death by unknown gangsters in the rear of 742 Sibley St. Blackhand extortionists were suspected of the killing.

On **March 5, 1930** Sam Maloga 27 yrs. of 4735 S. Hermitage Ave. was shot by unknown gangsters at 103rd St. and Roberts Rd.

John "Dingbat" O'Berta

On **March 5, 1930** John "Dingbat" O'Berta 29 yrs. of 1544 S. Richmond St. was found shot to death at 103rd and Roberts Road. O'Berta was a ward committeeman, bootlegger and associate of Frankie McErlane until a falling out which may have cost him his life.

On **March 16, 1930** John "The Billiken" Rito AKA: John Russo 27 yrs. was shot by unknown gangsters and dumped in the Chicago River and found near Irving Park Rd. His body had been tied up with wire when found. The victim was a collector for the northside liquor syndicate run by Ted Newberry who left the area for Toronto.

On **March 17, 1930** Peter Bica 42 yrs. of 118 W. Oak St. was shot by unknown gangsters in front of 2231 Lister Ave.

On **March 20, 1930** Cisaro Basile 54 yrs. of 632 S. Morgan St. was shot by unknown gangsters and thrown from an auto at 701 S. Miller St. Extortionists were suspected of this killing.

On **March 22, 1930** Andrew Racine 25 yrs. of 2136 W. 24th St. was shot by unknown gangsters at 93rd St. and Roberts Rd. where he was found in a ditch.

On **April 1, 1930** Martin "Babe" Mullaney 34 yrs. of 2847 W. Madison St. was shot by unknown gangsters while in his room (#238) at the Alto Hotel.

On **April 16, 1930** Joseph M. Cameron AKA: Blue 43 yrs. of 420 Surf St. was shot by unknown gangsters while riding in his auto at 1216 Blue Island Ave.

On **April 20, 1930** Frank Dire AKA: Delre, 33 yrs. Walter L. Wakefield 29 yrs. and Joseph Special 28 yrs. were all murdered at 2900 S. wells by Frank Delbano and it is unknown if he was ever convicted of the crime **(Solved)**. *Police logs entered the cases as follows:* April 20, 1930 Delre, Frank – Age 33 – Deceased, Walter Wakefield, his partner and Joseph Special, bartender, all alleged members of the Capone gang, were shot to death at 4 AM, 4/20/30, in their soft-drink parlor at 2900 So. Wells St., by a lone gunman who escaped. The next day a squad from the State's Attorney's Office lay in wait 8 hours in a flat at 3011 N. Halsted St. and captured one Frank Delbano, alias Dale, an ex-convict, whose gun was linked with these killings thru ballistics. On 4/24/30 Delbano was held by the Coroner. 3 Dist.

April 20, 1930 Special, Joseph - Age 28 - Deceased, Walter Wakefield and Frank Delre, partners in a soft-drink parlor at 2900 So. Wells St., all alleged members of the Capone gang were shot to death at 4 AM, 4/20/30, at that address by a lone gunman who escaped. The next day a squad from the State's Attorney's office lay 8 hours in wait for one Frank Delbano, alias Dale, whom they captured, in a flat at 3011 N. Halsted St. His gun was identified thru ballistics as the weapon used in these killings. On 4/24/30 he was held by the Coroner. 3 Dist. Case number: 11097

April 20, 1930 Wakefield, Walter - Age 29 - Deceased, Frank Debra, his partner in soft-drink parlor, and Joseph Special, the bartender, all alleged to the members of the Capone gang, were shot to death at 4AM, 4/20/30, in their place at 2900 So. Wells St. by a lone man who escaped. The next day a squad from the State's Attorney's Office lay in wait for eight hours in a flat at 3011 N. Halsted St. and captured one Frank Delbano, alias Dale, an ex-convict, whose gun was identified thru ballistics as the weapon used. On 4/24/30 Delbano was held by the Coroner on three charges. 3 Dist

On **May 7, 1930** Harry Anthony 28 yrs. of 615 Earl St., Toledo, Ohio was shot by unknown gangsters and found on Harlem Ave. near 92nd St.

On **May 8, 1930** Dominick Sciortino 55yrs. was shot to death in his home at 1233 Carmen Ave. The victim received a Blackhand letter and sent his family to stay with relatives. The case remains unsolved.

On **May 18, 1930** Police Officer George R. Neil 38 yrs. of 2936 Parnell Ave. was beaten and shot to death in a restaurant at 5435 S. Halsted St. by Daniel Lynch, John Kelly, William Connors and William O'Malley. He tried to stop the men from beating a black man and the men turned on him beat him and took his gun and shot him. While two of the assailants were arrested and the other two were sought, none were ever convicted in the slaying **(solved).**

On **May 25, 1930** Peter Plescia 42 yrs. of 4357 Palmer St. was gunned down by unknown gangsters in an alley at 1011 W. Grand Ave. He was thought to have been an organizer and collector for the reemerging Joe Aiello gang.

On **May 30, 1930** Dominick Costa was found beaten and shot to death. He was reported to be a thief and informant falling victim to Nitti's murder squad.

On **May 31, 1930** Peter Gnolfo AKA: Filippo Ignolfo, Abati 41 yrs. was trying to rebuild the Genna organization with support from the northside Aiellos. He was shotgunned for his efforts at Peoria and Eighteenth Streets by Terry Druggan and Frankie Lake on the orders of Al Capone. Within hours the revenge began and Michael Riley and William Clifford Valley gang members were found dead on the street. It was this killing that officially made Genna territory, Capone territory. ***Police logs entered the cases as follows:*** May 31, 1930 Gnolfo, Philip, alias Abatte - Age 41 - Shot to death at 9:45 AM, 5/31/30, while driving his auto south in Peoria St. between 18th and 19th Sts., by five unknown men in another machine who drove alongside and emptied shotguns into his car. Two other men with him, Carmi Guelvi of Toledo and Jos. Fiannaca of Rochester, NY, were wounded. 21st Dist.

Terry Druggan/Frankie Lake

On **June 1, 1930** Samuel Monestero 38 yrs. of 1365 Mohawk St. and his friend Joseph Ferrara AKA: Ferrari were shot by unknown gangsters at Locust and Clark Sts., both were reported to be Joe Aiello men.

On **June 1, 1930** Michael Quirk, Joseph Bertsche (brother of gambling magnate Barney) and Sam Pellar were gunned down and two others wounded in the Fox Lake resort known as Manning's Resort Hotel in the popular Chain of Lakes area, northwest of Chicago in McHenry County. The men and several others associated with Westside and northside bootlegging gangs were drinking in the wee hours when 5 gunmen entered the premise and opened fire. At first it seemed that the killings involved ongoing disputes between Capone and the Moran gang. Jack McGurn, Charles "Cherry Nose" Gioe, Frankie Diamond AKA: Frank Maritote and Frank Foster (a northside defector with Ted Newberry) were brought in for questioning, but later released. It was later attributed to gangster Verne Miller who was avenging a friends killing. Miller would go on to take part in the Kansas City Massacre in June of 1933. This case drew notoriety as the Fox Lake Massacre, but was never solved.

On **June 3, 1930** Thomas Sommerio 32 yrs. was found garroted in an alley at 833 W. Harrison. He was a ranking Aiello associate. ***Police logs entered the cases as follows:*** June 3, 1930 Somnerio, Thomas - Age 32- Found dead at 10:45 PM, 6/3/30, in the alley rear of 833 W. Harrison St., his wrists bound with wire and evidence that he had been garroted with a piece of wire or rope. Believed to have been tortured to reveal what he knew about the Fox Lake murders. The murder evidently was committed elsewhere and the body dumped in this alley. 22nd Dist.

On **June 3, 1930** Santo Mascellino 34 yrs. of 7515 W. 61st St., Summit, IL. was shot by unknown gangsters in his home.

On **June 7, 1930** Eugene "Red" McLaughlin 26 yrs. of 6315 N. Artesian Ave. was shot by unknown gangsters. He was a Valley gang protégé and brother of a large cab company operator and was pulled out of a drainage canal at Lawndale Ave. in suburban Summit, IL. He was shot in the head, his hands were bound and his body weighted down with iron.

On **June 7, 1930** Gasper Rokette 38 yrs. of 2153 Ridge Ave. Evanston, IL. was beaten to death by unknown gangsters and found at East Prairie Rd. and Main St. in Niles Center, IL.

On **June 9, 1930** Alfred "Jake" Lingle 38 yrs. of 125 N. Austin Blvd. the wealthy, tough talking gambler, OUTFIT associate and reporter for the Chicago Tribune was gunned down in the passage way to the Illinois Central Train Station at Randolph and Michigan Aves. in downtown Chicago. Lingle's murder was reported intensely by all the Chicago rags who raised questions of credibility about reporters who fraternized with gangsters as Lingle was known to do. While acting as a go between for corrupt police officials and gangsters, Lingle also maintained associations with Capone on the Southside and Jack Zuta on the northside. Suspects during the intense investigation included Frank Foster, Frank Nitti, James "Red" Forsythe and Leo Brothers, but in the end it was his double cross of Zuta, his talking to authorities (he was the liaison between Capone and Commissioner Russell) and his interest in a northside gambling operation that probably led to his demise. He grew up with Russell in the Valley neighborhood and when this came out after the murder Russell resigned. On April 2, 1931, Leo Vincent Brothers, (a hired gun from out of town who was wanted for murder in St. Louis) was sentenced to 14 years in prison for the murder, many speculate to this day that Brothers was just a fall guy in the whole episode, set up by Frank Nitti (**solved**).

Jake Lingle dead

On **June 9, 1930** Aloysius "Tough Guy" Kearney 36 yrs. was shot by unknown gangsters in front of 1115 S. Troy St. He was a collector for the National Garage Owners Association. Red Barker was sought for questioning in the killing, but never charged.

On **June 20, 1930** Lorenzo J. Juliano 48 yrs. of 12207 S. Wiley Ave. was beaten to death by unknown gangsters and found in an auto belonging to Daniel LaMorte at 123rd St. and California Ave. in a clay hole in Worth Township.

On **June 30, 1930** Frank Petito AKA: Mike Gallichia 16 yrs. of 1422 W. Polk St. was shot by Nicholas "The Little Man" Muscato and Peter "The Ape" Nicastro who then dumped him in a ditch on Joliet Rd. one mile southwest of Lawndale Ave. in Lyons Township. All members of the "42" gang, Petito was killed for violating gang rules by spending recklessly after the gang had hijacked alcohol from the Red Bolton gang. Nicastro was then taken for a ride himself, but survived long enough to name Muscato as the killer in both murders. The outcome of this case is unknown.

On **July 1, 1930** Anthony Amato 40 yrs. of 1339 S. 51st St. was strangled by unknown gangsters and found in a ditch at 30th St. and 1st Ave. in Riverside IL.

On **July 2, 1930** Elbert Lusader 43 yrs. of 7643 Berwyn Ave. was shot by unknown gangsters as he operated a northbound streetcar on State at Quincey Sts. The men were shooting at Police Lt. George Barker who was providing protection for gangster Jack Zuta through the downtown Loop district.

On **July 8, 1930** Vincenzo Phillipes 44 yrs. was shot by unknown gangsters at his newsstand at Throop and Madison Sts. Blackhand extortionists were suspected in this killing.

On **July 12, 1930** Leonard A. Perdenza 57 yrs. of 1019 Townsend St. was shot by unknown gangsters in front of his home.

On **July 15, 1930** Elsworth Moss 41 yrs. of 1829 Maypole Ave. was shot by unknown gangsters and found in the rear of 315 S. Lincoln St. He was a known bootlegger.

On **July 16, 1930** Barney "Murphy" McCone and Herman "The Kid" Diehn were shot by unknown gangsters in George Connor's Tavern at 7228 Circle Ave. in Forest Park, IL. The men were alleged to be union racketeers opposing James "Lefty" Lynch and his labor empire. Gunmen entered the saloon and acted as if they were sticking the place up when they killed the two men. Police quickly learned that three cars were found close by that were registered to Lynch's union office, however the outcome of the investigation is unknown.

On **July 21, 1930** Peter "Ash Can Pete" Inserra was killed by Frank Nitti's gang. He was an Aiello associate.

On **July 30, 1930** August Pusateri was shot by unknown gangsters in front of 2343 W. Ohio St.

On **August 1, 1930** Jack Zuta is killed. A Northside gang associate and Westside Vice monger, Zuta is tracked down to the Lake View Hotel near Delafield, Wisconsin by Capone gunman, Dan Stanton and other killers, possibly including Dago Lawrence Mangano. Zuta is found near the dance floor. Other patrons were directed out of the way before he is murdered by machine gun fire. In October, Danny Stanton is arrested on a Wisconsin warrant for Zuta's murder and extradited; the outcome of the case is unknown (**solved**).

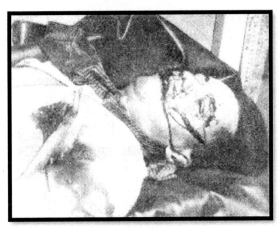

Jack Zuta dead

On **August 10, 1930** Samuel Siciliano 28 yrs. of 1006 Cambridge Ave. was shot by John Collura at Cambridge Ave. and Hobbie St. Collura was charged with the killing, but the outcome of that case is not known (**solved**).

On **August 14, 1930** Daniel Vallo 31 yrs. of 4853 West End Ave. was shotgunned by unknown gangsters in a vacant lot on Oakton St. in Niles Center, IL.

On **August 20, 1930** Charles Robert Mulcahy 52 yrs. of 7748 Constance Ave. and Bernard M. Ruberry 35 yrs. of 7737 Essex Ave. were reportedly shot by Charles Arthur Stein and Albert B. Courchene in a construction shack on the grounds of the new Lane Technical High School at Addison St. and Western Ave. Courchene was a plumbing inspector for the city and Mulcahy was a business agent for the Plumbers Union that was resisting a takeover by Red Barker on behalf of the Capone Mob. Mulcahy was a well-known labor racketeer and Ruberry was a former associate of the northside O'Banion gang. Capone's gang was suspected, the suspects surrendered themselves and were released on bond and Courchene was killed in 1931 while it is unknown if Mulcahy was prosecuted for the killing (**solved**).

On **August 24, 1930** Joseph Terravicchia 43 yrs. of 3405 S. 59th Ave. in Cicero, IL. was shot by unknown gangsters in the rear of his residence.

On **September 9, 1930** Peter Nicastro AKA: The Ape 22 yrs. of 1241 W. Taylor St. was shot by Nicholas "The Little Man" Muscato and thrown from an auto at 2346 S. Canal St. The victim and Muscato both participated in the earlier killing of Frank Petito. Nicastro made the mistake of bragging about the killing and was taken for a ride by Muscato and lived long enough to tell the police who shot him and killed Petito. Muscato was arrested and charged for the killings, the outcome of the case is unknown. The press touted the fact that these were the first Mob murders to be solved since 1924 **(solved).**

On **September 14, 1930** Angelo Spano AKA: Jack Costo 29 yrs. of 2053 N. Laramie Ave. was shot by unknown gangsters in the court way of a building at 4048 N. Sheridan Rd. He was accompanied by a Margaret Reardon and an unknown man. Reardon was held as an accessory and the unknown man was sought. It is not known what the outcome of this case was **(solved).**

On **September 18, 1930** John Roscoe 20 yrs. of 2719 Crystal St. was shot by unknown gangsters at Hoyne Ave. near Pierce St. Upon their arrival the police questioned the wounded hoodlum who refused to provide any information about his assailants.

On **September 19, 1930** George Peters AKA: Ollie Hassan 34 yrs. of 7603 W. 61st St. and Mike Lafakis 37 yrs. of 62nd Pl. in Argo, IL. were shot by unknown gangsters in a tavern at 6314 Archer Ave. in Argo, IL. Police suspected beer running as a motive in this crime.

On October 6, 1930 the wife of infamous Chicago Mayor William Hale "Big Bill" Thompson was robbed at gunpoint by future OUTFIT Boss Sam "Teetz" Battaglia. Teetz accompanied by William Carr took $17,000 in jewelry and the gun and star from Mrs. Thompson's police bodyguard. The men were tried and found not guilty by a jury of their peers.

On **October 12, 1930** Detective William P. Rumbler was shot to death in a soft drink parlor at 3174 N. Milwaukee Ave. The victim was visiting the owner who was an old friend when several armed gunmen enter and forced four people to the back of the store. Upon beginning to search them the Detective drew his revolver and exchanged gunfire with the men. The victim was shot eleven times and was able to fire four shots at the assailants. The investigation revealed that the officer and his partner Detective John Kratzmeyer had received death threats relating to their actions against beer runners. Three men were eventually identified: Walter Evenow, John Senow and Frank Mallen. Evenow and Senow were eventually sentenced to 60 years in prison and Evenow was paroled after serving 24 years while Mallen was never found **(solved).**

On **October 13, 1930** David W. Emmett 38 yrs. of 4728 Ingleside Ave. was shot by unknown gangsters while seated in his auto near his residence. Police suspected the killing had something to do with his partnership with Sam Hare in some gambling places.

On **October 23, 1930** Joe Aiello 39 yrs. of 2553 Lunt Ave. was ambushed by gunmen outside a Westside rooming house at 205 N. Kolmar. In 1929 Aiello, one of Capone's most tenacious enemies was installed as President of the Unione Siciliana after "Hop Toad" Guinta a Capone protégé was murdered by the big guy himself at an Indiana Roadhouse. Aiello was walking to a cab with a train ticket in his pocket for St. Louis. The heat was too much and he may have been headed to Mexico. He had left town before when things flared up leaving his minions to suffer the consequences. Aiello was machine gunned by assassins who set up sniper's nests in two apartments that trapped the man in a crossfire. A third apartment was rented by Jack McGurn and Tony Accardo, but apparently was not used in the assault. The men were questioned and released during the investigation. It was learned by police that as many as 5 individuals took part in this murder. The two men who rented the apartments used, went by the names of Morris Friend and Henry Jacobs. Police speculate that they may have been killers brought in from out of town. Soon after, the Northsiders broke up and the Capone gang took control of most of the remaining operations. Moran left Chicago to take up other criminal pursuits; he eventually died in federal prison while serving a term for Bank Robbery. After destroying the Northsiders, the Gennas and the Aiellos the only remaining resistance came from the Northwest side Touhy gang who fought Capone for control of certain alcohol operations and unions. The Skidmore and Johnson group who controlled much of the gambling on the Northside remained defiant also. Otherwise, this left the Capone syndicate in control of TOC in most of Chicago **(Solved)**. *Police logs entered the cases as follows:* October 23, 1930 Aiello, Joseph - Age 39 - Ital. - Married. Gang leader and partner of "Bugs Moran" was riddled with machine gun bullets in front of 205 N. Kolmar Ave., when he left the home of Pasquale Restegiocomo, alias Presto, to enter a cab. The fire was opened up on him from a "machine gun nest" in a flat across the street, 202 Kolmer Ave., and when he attempted to escape to the rear of the Presto home was felled from fire from a second nest from a window at 4518 West End Ave. Presto, who was his business partner and in whose home he had been rooming (it is believed in hiding) was booked 10-28-30 as accessory, but on 1/29/31 the case was nolle prossed by Padden before the inquest. Closed.

In 1930 following the murder of Joe Aiello, Capone was able to install his own president into the Unione Siciliana. Agostino Loverdo took the presidency and survived until he fell victim to a Cicero drive-by.

On **October 24, 1930** John Guida 24 yrs. of 1914 Potomac Ave. was killed by unknown gangsters in the soft drink parlor at 836 N. Racine Ave. Police suspect his membership in the "42" gang may have provided a motive in his killing.

On **November 1, 1930** Peter Zubulikis AKA: Jappas 42 yrs. of 5406 Jackson Blvd. was shot by two unknown gangsters in the driveway of his residence. Police revealed that he ran a "Book" downtown near the Board of Trade that may have provided a motive in the killing.

On **November 30, 1930** Leonard Sarno was killed during the robbery of a restaurant at 818 W. Randolph. Sarno had the misfortune of being a patron when Daniel Clementi, Joseph Catrino, Joseph Pupelli and Phillip Epstein committed the robbery while Chicago Police lay in wait. As the police moved in, shots were fired and patron Sarno was killed. Future OUTFIT Boss Sam Battaglia was wanted as the getaway driver in the crime, but the outcome of this case is not known **(Solved)**.

Teetz Battaglia

On **December 8, 1930** Tony May 54 yrs. of 2109 N. Lincoln Ave. was killed by unknown gangsters when a bomb exploded that was sent to his home in a package. The victim was a professional bondsman which may have contributed to his killing.

On **December 11, 1930** Marco Magnabosco 38 yrs. of 11354 Langley Ave. was shot by unknown gangsters in the hallway of his home.

On **December 12, 1930** Samuel Marino 26 yrs. of 1533 W. Ohio St. and his brother Rudolph Marino AKA: Tommasello 23 yrs. were shot by unknown gangsters and found at 91st and California Ave.

On January 1, 1931 Sam "Teetz" Battaglia along with John Wollek and George Bousk again robbed the C & O Café at 509 N. Clark. During the robbery the men shot 2 police officers in the restaurant one 3 times and one 2 times, but they survived. At trial the men were found not guilty by a jury and at a second trial the men plead guilty to assault with a deadly weapon. This was a good representation of justice in Chicago at the time.

On **January 4, 1931** August Battaglia 25 yrs. of 829 Gilpin Pl. was shot by unknown gangsters at the corner of Roosevelt Rd. and Halsted St.

August Battaglia

On **January 6, 1931** Pasquali Tardi 22 Yrs. of 905 Miller St. was shot by unknown gangsters at the corner of Polk and Miller Sts. He was a member of the infamous "42" gang.

On **January 6, 1931** Frank Candela 50 yrs. of 628 W. 25th Pl. was shot by unknown gangsters in front of 620 W. 25th Pl. Blackhand extortionists were suspected in this killing.

On **January 9, 1931** Petro Porto AKA: Pasquale Caruso 40 yrs. of 8312 S. Mat St. was shot by unknown gangsters while in an auto at 941 W. Taylor St.

On **January 10, 1931** Elmer Gasparino 33 yrs. of 10803 Ave. G was shot by unknown gangsters and found in an auto at 114th St. and Ave. F. He was reported to have been a member of the old Genna gang.

On **January 14, 1931** Enrico Bartocchi 28 yrs. of 2500 S. Avers Ave. was shot by unknown gangsters while riding in an auto with Dr. Wm. Henja in front of 2649 W. 25th St. He was suspected of being a member of the Capone gang.

On **January 28, 1931** Morris Berkowitz 29 yrs. of 3101 S. Turner Ave. was shot by unknown gangsters on the northeast corner of Roosevelt Rd. and Ashland Ave.

On **February 7, 1931** Joseph Tanzillo 34 yrs. of 627 S. Aberdeen St. was shot by unknown gangsters and found in the rear of 630 Miller St.

On **February 17, 1931** Frank Marlo AKA: Marco was shot by unknown gangsters on east 19th St. in New York City. It was reported that this victim was a journeyman killer and was suspected in the murders of Jake Lingle and Tony Lombardo although he was never charged in either. He also was the alleged killer of an Al Capone henchman which may have led to his death.

On **February 18, 1931** Albert B. Courchene 55 yrs. of 7701 Maryland Ave. was shot by unknown gangsters in front of 4222 Langley Ave. He was a Plumbing Inspector for the city and was awaiting trial for the murders of Charles Robert Mulcahy and Bernard M. Ruberry in 1930. The killing involved labor racketeering and may have been in retribution for the other killings. "Daper Dan" McCarthy a former official of the Plumbers Union and an associate of the northside O'Banion gang was being sought for questioning.

On **February 24, 1931** Francis J. Carr Jr. AKA: Junior 33 yrs. of 10627 S. Campbell was shot by unknown gangsters in the doorway at 12 W. Garfield Blvd. He was the Financial Secretary of the Painters, Decorators and Paper Hangers Union. The union was under the control of gangster Danny Stanton. This murder was just one incident of violence associated with the Mob takeover.

On **March 3, 1931** William J. Mayer 52 yrs. of 7322 Howard Ave. was shot by unknown gangsters as they attempted to place a bomb in the Blue Island Social Club at 11901 Vincennes Ave. Blue Island, IL.

In early 1931 during the Mob's takeover of numerous unions, Teamster Local 704 official James "Lefty" Lynch stood his ground and resisted MOB overtures. It nearly cost him his life when he was shot in both legs by Danny Stanton, Red Barker and Klondike O'Donnell while vacationing with his family at his summer home near Burlington Wis., though they were never charged with the assault and Barker assumed Lynch's post.

On **March 19, 1931** William J. "Wild Bill" Rooney the leader of the Sheet Metal Workers Union was gunned down in front of his home at 1517 N. Austin. Rooney was politically savvy and a union operative his whole live. He crossed swords with other union leaders over political opinions and TOC influence knowing the risks. He was tried for murder himself in 1916 after a killing related to a union election.

On **March 21, 1931** John Annerino AKA: Johnny Genero 37 yrs. of 515 W. 28th Pl. was murdered. Joe Annerino AKA: Peppy Genero reported that James "King of the Bombers" Belcastro killed his brother and also admitted to him that he killed Octavius Granady. Others implicated were Bruno Roti Sr. AKA: Rodi 51, Frank Tallarico, Louis DeLuca and Dominic "Potatoes" Valera, these men were charged in the killing based on information provided by the victim's younger brother August Annerino. Genero was driving with another man to his mother's home when his car became trapped at 29th St. and Normal Ave. where he was shot in the head. Several weeks later all the charges were dropped **(Solved)**.

On **March 30, 1931** Max Tender 42 yrs. of 719 Montrose Ave. was shot by unknown gangsters at Racine and Leland Aves. Police suspected the victim was involved in the dope business.

On **April 7, 1931** Anton Bagdon 28 yrs. of 2324 W. 22nd Pl. was shot by unknown gangsters and found dead in his auto at 1846 S. Spaulding Ave.

On **April 17, 1931** Walter Van DeWerken 30 yrs. of 1624 S. Newberry Ave. was shot by unknown gangsters and found in a ditch at Joe Orr Rd. near State St.

On **April 21, 1931** Edward Fitzgerald 33 yrs. of 7856 S. Union Ave. was shot by unknown gangsters in front of 7356 S. Peoria St. Four gangsters raided the tavern he was in and seized him. While trying to take him to a car he broke loose and was shot in the head. Police theorize the men were trying to have him lead them to Frank McErlane so they could kill him. It was later reported that Fitzgerald was a beer hustler and driver for the gang boss. It was also reported that the victim was killed by an opposing gangster named James L. Quigley who was released after being interrogated by police **(solved)**.

On **April 29, 1931** Mike "The Pike" Heitler, 54 yrs. of 2020 Humbolt Blvd., a pimp and suspected informant is shot to death and found burned in an icehouse in Barrington Township. "Dago" Lawrence Mangano and James "King of the Bombers" Belcastro were suspected, as he and others played cards with the victim before he went missing, but they were never charged. Mob Politician and future State Representative James Adducci was charged with the killing, but was not convicted or even held accountable by the voters of Chicago. It seems that Heitler was vying for a position as a gang leader and turned the suspects against him. In 1932 Adducci was a suspect in a kidnapping related to the pressure being applied by the police via Mayor Cermak. Another suspect in that case was Willie Bioff AKA: William Morris Bioff, William Nelson.

Mike "The Pike" Heitler

On **May 12, 1931** Harry Hyter 32 yrs. of 2019 N. Keystone Ave. was shot by unknown gangsters and found in the Jaranowski Woods near 157th St. and Torrence Ave. in Calumet City, IL. The victim was a minor gangster who once worked in the Wigwam Café for Bugs Moran and later was affiliated with the Capone gang. It was reported that he may have been a police informant that costs him his life.

On **May 24, 1931** Joseph Sobotka 43 yrs. of 1510 W. North Ave. was shot by unknown gangsters in his home. Police suspected this killing was the result of a quarrel between bootleggers.

On **May 28, 1931** Dan Agoa 36 yrs. of 1129 N. LeClaire St. was shot in front of 400 S. State St. He was secretary of the Chicago Window and Building Cleaner's Contractors Association. Benjamin J. Weber a business agent of the Window Washer's Union was suspected and later exonerated by a coroner's jury. This murder involved labor racketeering **(Solved).**

On **June 11, 1931** Dominick Latronica 21 yrs. of 6934 S. Wood St. was shot by unknown gangsters and found on 107th St. one mile east of Archer Ave.

On **June 13, 1931** Lorenzo Bua 45 yrs. of 1905 W. Taylor St. was shot by unknown gangsters in his grocery store at that location. He refused to name his assailants before he died.

On **June 19, 1931** James Janis 31 yrs. of 5514 Blackstone Ave. was shotgunned by unknown gangsters in front of 1139 W. 69th St.

On **June 20, 1931** Jacob D. "Jack" Kaufman 41 yrs. of 5024 Broadway Ave. was shot multiple times behind 305 E. 95th St. and died of his wounds. Jack was a rebel theater operator and fought the extortion attempts of Union Local 110 racketeer Tommy Maloy and his gangster friends. He was scheduled to testify the following day in front of a Grand Jury investigating the Union's affairs. Capone gunman Danny Stanton was sought for this slaying, but never charged.

On **June 23, 1931** Sam Pullano 29 yrs. of 2827 S. Wells St. was shot by unknown gangsters on 28th Pl. between Canal St. and Stewart Ave.

On **June 28, 1931** Frank Scavo 27 yrs. of 1321 W. Taylor Ave. was shot by unknown gangsters and found at 87th St. and 86th Ave. in Palos Township.

On **July 2, 1931** John P. Carr 31 yrs. of 1106 W. Huron St. was shotgunned by unknown gangsters from an auto at the northwest corner of Fry and May Sts.

On **July 10, 1931** Frank Caliendo 29 yrs. of 1428 W. Grand Ave. was shot by unknown gangsters at a beer flat he ran at 1438 Ferdinand St.

On **July 15, 1931** Edgar Smith AKA: New York Spike 35 yrs. of 1116 E. 67th St. was shot by unknown gangsters in the rear of 6230 Champlain Ave. and found in an auto in front of 5424 South Park Ave. He was a driver for gang boss Danny Stanton and was charged along with Stanton in the murder of Jack Zuta in Wisconsin.

On **July 16, 1931** Herman Diehm 52 yrs. of 1400 N. Lincoln Ave. and Bernard McCone 35 yrs. of 910 Lyman Ave., Oak Park, IL. were shot by unknown gangsters at 7228 Circle Ave. Forest Park, IL.

On **July 26, 1931** Elija H. Orr AKA: Ely of 2828 N. Kenneth Ave. was shot by unknown gangsters at 2405 Milwaukee Ave. He was the Secretary-Treasurer of the Newspaper Drivers Association and labor racketeering was suspected as a motive in this killing. In August it was reported that Jack Barry "Public Enemy" was suspected in the killing, but never charged.

On **August 11, 1931** Adolph J. Dumont 44 yrs. of 2008 Central Ave., Wilmette IL. was shot by unknown gangsters at Wilmette Ave. and Main St. in Evanston, IL. An investigation revealed that he had served time in Illinois and carried a $100.000 life insurance policy.

On **September 16, 1931** Carlo Piazza 22 yrs. of 5616 S. Kedzie Ave. was shot by unknown gangsters and found in his auto at 77th Pl. and Laramie Ave.

On **September 16, 1931** Joseph Pelligrino 33 yrs. of 1410 N. 15th Ave. Melrose Park, IL. was shot by unknown gangsters and found on the side of the road ½ mile north of Lake St. in Proviso, IL.

On **October 8, 1931** Elfrieda McErlane 29 yrs. of 7753 Bennett Ave. was shot by her husband, gangster Frank McErlane after a heated argument and found in a Packard Sedan at 8129 Phillips Ave. Police later suspected McErlane of the killing and that of James Quigley an enemy of his on the same day although he was never charged **(solved).**

On **October 8, 1931** James L. Quigley was shot and found floating in a drainage canal in Lockport, IL. He was a Southside gangster involved in the beer wars and it was reported that the McErlane gang, the Saltis gang or the O'Donnell gang killed him although no one was charged.

On **October 11, 1931** George Wilson 33 yrs. of 1511 W. 19th St. was shot in the head and body by unknown gangsters and found on Lincoln and 15th Sts. Police reported that the victim was a former police officer discharged in 1923 for extortion. He had recently been arrested for robbery and was said to be a member of the Westside Druggan/Lake Valley gang. George Druggan brother of gang boss Terry Druggan was being sought by police for questioning. It is not known if he was ever apprehended.

On **October 18, 1931** Mathias "Matt" Kolb 40 yrs. of 8819 Marmora Ave. in Morton Grove, IL. was killed in yet another handshake murder by two men in Kolb's "Club Morton Roadhouse" in suburban Morton Grove at Dempster and Ferris Aves. Kolb started his career in bootlegging at the beginning of prohibition. He was politically savvy and was an accomplished fixer for different gamblers, vice mongers and booze runners. He worked in the booze racket with associates of Capone and the Northsiders. He eventually left his associations with Capone because the violence scared him. He then restricted his activities to the northwest suburbs and became a fixer for and partner of the Touhy gang. Capone previously made overtures to Roger Touhy the head of the Touhy gang, about opening whorehouses and gambling establishments in what Capone considered as virgin territory. It was reported that Leo Shaffer a henchman of Kolb's was kidnapped by two Capone gunmen, Martin Accardo (brother of Tony) and John Matteis. They tried to force Shaffer to help them encroach on Touhy territory which led to a police sting and indictments. Touhy was not interested in any partnership with Capone and he was growing tired of the meddling by the Touhy gang in his affairs from bootlegging to labor racketeering. It was reported that Capone personally killed Kolb. However, this was at the time of Capone's tax trial and may be untrue as the case remains unsolved.

On **October 23, 1931** Michael J. Brannigan 42 yrs. was shot through the head by unknown gangsters at 75th and State Sts. in Stickney, IL.

On **November 5, 1931** Agostino Loverdo AKA: Salvatore Loverde 37 yrs. of 3649 Ferdinand St. who took the Unione Siciliana presidency and was shot in the head and body by unknown gangsters in the Italian American Republican Club at 1346 S. 51st Ct. in Cicero, IL. By this time Capone was removed via federal indictment, Moran left the area for other pursuits and the Unione lost its notoriety with the repeal of the Volstead Act. The organization went on for several more years with members of the new Chicago OUTFIT in its ranks. For the remainder of its existence Phil D'Andrea served as President from 1934 till 1941. From 1941 till 1943 Joseph Bulger a prominent Chicago attorney took the helm until the organization dissolved in 1943.

On **November 7, 1931** Richard Fishman 24 yrs. of 3861 Roosevelt Rd. was shot by unknown gangsters at 1319 Newberry Ave. Reportedly the victim had killed William Marzano in 1928 at the armory at 16th and Michigan Aves. It is not known if that contributed to his death.

On **November 9, 1931** Timothy Joseph Lynch 59 yrs. of 416 N. 4th Ave. in Maywood, IL. was shotgunned in the rear of his home. He was a business agent for the General Teamsters and Chauffeurs Union. He opposed Red Barker the mob emissary in union affairs.

In **November of 1931** Dan Tagnetti was murdered in Riverside, IL. He was a business agent for a Union local controlled by mobster Red Barker

On **November 30, 1931** John Alerri 33 yrs. was shot by unknown gangsters in front of 2000 Ogden Ave.

On **December 1, 1931** Vincent Petrikos 48 yrs. of 5800 S. McVickers Ave. was shot by unknown gangsters at 61st and Mead Ave. in Stickney, IL.

On **December 17, 1931** Joseph M. Barru 45 yrs. was shot by unknown gangsters six times in the chest and found at 116th St. and Kedzie Ave. by Willow Springs Highway Police.

On **December 21, 1931** Detective James J. Caplis was fatally shot in a restaurant at 804 W. Wilson Ave. The Detective was dining with his girlfriend when 5 bandits entered the restaurant and announced a robbery. The Detective drew his revolver and confronted the robbers and a gunfight ensued. A female diner was wounded and the officer killed during the melee. One of the robbers was identified as Herman Gleck AKA: Herman Cohen, Herman Glick. He was a Westside gangster associated with Mob Boss Lenny Patrick. He would be killed by Patrick in 1932 over a dispute. Other gang members Frank Freeman, Jack Burlison, Nicholas Bruno, Tony Pape, Rocco DeFillipis, Frank Piazza and Ralph DeFillipis who supplied the weapons were eventually arrested. Two young females were also arrested, but the charges dropped when they cooperated. Most of the men received lengthy prison sentences while Glick eventually received the ultimate sentence **(solved)**.

On **December 22, 1931** Daniel Fognotti 39 yrs. of 1446 S. Cuyler Ave., Berwyn, IL. was shot in the head by unknown gangsters and found at 23rd and Westover Sts. in North Riverside, IL.

On **December 22, 1931** Walter Schreffer 42 yrs. of 1641 Buena Vista Ave. was shot by unknown gangsters and found at Joe Orr Rd. and State St. in Chicago Heights, IL.

On **December 30, 1931** Abraham Schnieder 40 yrs. of 4131 Sheridan Rd. was shot by unknown gangsters and found on Wolf Rd. north of Grand Ave.

On **January 11, 1932** Benjamin Rosenberg 46 yrs. of 1100 S. 2nd St., in Maywood, IL. was shot by unknown gangsters at 3rd Ave. and Green St. in Maywood, IL. He was a member of the International Cleaners and Dyers Incorporated and ran his business at 2800 S. State St. with reasonable rates which took business away from competitors backed by Murray Humphreys and Jack McGurn. Before his death he was kidnapped by mobsters and ordered to get out of the business. He did not and paid with his life. Within days three suspects were taken into custody, one of which was a relative of an employee of the victim. The men were Patsy Clementi 19, Joseph Price 23, and Harry Robbins 26. The outcome of this investigation is unknown. The brother of a suspect Louis Clementi and Philip Mangano were known as Capone gangsters that were also arrested, but later released. Previously they were convicted of destroying trucks belonging to the victim's company **(Solved)**.

On **January 20, 1932** Morris Costabile of 431 S. Kedzie Ave. was found shot on Ogden Ave. near Downers Grove, IL. He was a former employee of the Abarbanell Bros. a chain of independent cleaners owned by Irving Abarbanell of La Grange whose life was threatened over the Cleaners and Dyers War. The victim reportedly opened a still for the Capone gang after leaving the Cleaning and Dying business. The conflict heated up when Ben Rosenberg was killed for undercutting prices of the union members controlled by Murray Humphreys and Jack McGurn. Bombings continued after the killings.

On **January 22, 1932** Michael J. Gallo 27 yrs. was shot by unknown gangsters in front of 1015 S. Parkway Ave.

On **January 22, 1932** Carmello Luchesi 50 yrs. of 2144 DeKalb St. was shot by unknown gangsters in front of 50 N. Hoyne Ave. The victim was a business agent in the Macaroni Union.

On **January 28, 1932** Philip Flavin 42 yrs. of 5055 Congress St. was shot by unknown gangsters and found in his car at 314 S. Hermitage Ave.

On **February 20, 1932** Joseph Morriss 44 yrs. of 644 Diversey was shot by unknown gangsters at Willow and Richard Sts. in Franklin Park, IL.

On **February 27, 1932** Joseph Dubet 49 yrs. of 3740 S. Austin Blvd. was shot by unknown gangsters at 56th and Ogden Ave. in Cicero, IL.

On **March 17, 1932** Joseph L. Lacheta 27 yrs. of 1510 Wentworth Ave. was shotgunned and found near Lincoln Highway and the Baltimore & Ohio tracks in Chicago Heights, IL.

On **March 20, 1932** Frank Battaglia 27 yrs. was murdered by unknown gangsters at 87th and Harlem Ave.

On **March 23, 1932** Otto Froneck 46 yrs. of 3053 Seminary Ave. was beaten and shot by unknown gangsters and found in a Buick sedan at Manheim Rd. and Buena St.

On **March 27, 1932** Carmino Spinelli 47 yrs. of 1750 W. Polk St. was shot by unknown gangsters on the northwest corner of Taylor and Hermitage Sts.

On **April 4, 1932** Charles O'Donnell 27 yrs. of 8255 Laflin St. was shot by unknown gangsters and found in the gangway of 1735 W. 91st St.

Lenny Patrick

On **April 5, 1932** Herman Gleck AKA: Herman Cohen, Herman Glick 21 yrs. of 1319 S. Sawyer St. was shot in the neck by prolific OUTFIT killer Lenny Patrick at Sawyer and 13th St. a week after Gleck knocked him down during a dice game on the Westside of Chicago. Sixty years later Patrick would admit to this and several other murders as he testified against his contemporaries in a federal courtroom. When questioned about this killing on the witness stand Patrick said "He hit me and I killed him a week later". This is one of the cases reviewed by Intelligence Detectives 1994, Patrick was arrested after the Cook County State's Attorney's Office had him indicted for three murders in 1995, however, this case was not charged as the file went missing. Patrick was later released by the State's Attorneys Office without explanation several months later **(Solved)**.

On **April 7, 1932** Benjamin Applequist 43 yrs. of 3402 Flournoy St. and Ernest Applequist 41 yrs. of 2848 S. Kostner were both shot by unknown gangsters in their business at 42 N. Paulina St. The victims were known associates of northside gangster Julian "Potato's" Kaufman.

On **April 9, 1932** Michael Carmen 47 yrs. of 11824 Wentworth Ave. was shot by unknown gangsters at Crawford and Vermont Sts. in Worth Township.

On **April 20, 1932** Sam Mule AKA: Morley 39 yrs. of 2046 Love Ct. was shot in the head and neck by unknown gangsters in the passageway at 327 Menominee St.

In **1932** American Boy and contract killer for Capone, Bob Carey was found dead in New York. The police investigated this as a suicide, but a short time later a former driver for Moran encountered Moran in a Waukegan, IL. tavern where Moran claimed he traveled to New York to take care of Bob Carey.

On **June 14, 1932** Dominick Scaturro 47 yrs. of 1522 N. Rockwell was found with his skull crushed in an alley at 648 N. Union. The victim was a labor racketeer and ran a beer flat at his home which police believe may have led to his death.

On **June 15, 1932** Fred DiGiovanni AKA: Cowboy Frank, Fred Pacelli, 35 yrs. was gunned down by Touhy killers. He was a Capone associate and bodyguard who was pictured by the press with Capone and Cubs great Gabby Hartnett at a Comiskey Park baseball game. He was gunned down at the Dells, an enormous speakeasy and casino operating in Morton Grove, IL. just inside Touhy's territory. The Touhy's had come to the Dells looking for the Pacelli, who was spotted by one of Touhy's people as he entered the club earlier in the evening. Pacelli was the younger brother of soon-to-be congressman Bill Pacelli. To kill him, Touhy sent his three best men, Willie Sharky, Leroy Marshalk AKA: Roy Marshank of Schiller Park and George Wilke who was also Touhy's business manager. The three hoods arrived at the Dells and knew exactly what to do. They quickly strolled into the bar where Marshalk shot Pacelli and Maryanne Bruce, Pacelli's girlfriend after she tried to wrestle the pistol out of Marshalk's hand. However, in the parking lot, unknown to them, the Cook County Sheriff's Police were waiting. Sgt. Joseph Cantello took the call about a robbery at the Dells and arrived to the casino's parking lot just as Touhy's men were leaving the building. At that point Cook County Highway Police Lt. James Meyering arrived with his brother Sheriff Wilbur Meyering and policeman Sam Lucas and a full-fledged gun battle was in place. While all three hoods were wounded, two of the hoods shot their way to safety. Wilke and Sharky were sent by Touhy to a Minneapolis Minnesota Hospital to recover and then recuperated at a Sheridan Ave. Hotel. Marschalk was arrested, but the outcome of the prosecution is unknown. The two year street war between Roger Touhy and the Chicago mob was on **(Solved)**.

On **June 17, 1932** George "Red" Barker 26 yrs. of 426 N. Austin Ave. was shot by unknown gangsters at 1500 N. Crawford Ave. He was a Capone gunman, labor racketeer and considered the most notorious racketeer of his time. He was allegedly killed by Touhy gunman. The Touhy gang while competing for control of several of the labor unions, provided protection from Capone gangsters for numerous labor leaders on the northwest side and Barker was their main threat. However, some mobsters blamed Paddy Berrell, a mobster who controlled an opposing Milk Wagon Drivers Organization, for the murder. Reportedly the shooter working for the Touhy gang was Willie Sharky firing a water-cooled machinegun in a tripod from a snipers nest across the street although he was never charged. Touhy gunman Willie Marks was also named as the shooter in later years although the case remains open.

On **June 29, 1932** George Brooks 39 yrs. of 162nd St. and Kenilworth Dr. Calumet City, IL. was shot by unknown gangsters in the yard of his home as they lay in wait for him.

On **July 21, 1932** Paddy Berrell was murdered by a group of men brandishing shotguns in his resort home in Shawano, Wisconsin. He was a union racketeer who was feuding with Chicago Mobsters and may have been responsible for the killing of Red Barker.

On **July 22, 1932** Jack A. Werner 36 yrs. of 7338 South Park Ave. was shot by unknown gangsters with a machinegun while in a Lincoln sedan at 354 E. 81st St.

On **August 10, 1932** Joseph F. Connell 33 yrs. of 1140 Hickory St. was shot by unknown gangsters in front of his residence.

On **August 16, 1932** Edward Hiller 46 yrs. of 123 W. 45th St. was shot in the doorway of 4431 S. Wells St. by Thomas Casey who was arrested and held for a grand jury, but the outcome is unknown **(Solved)**.

On **August 23, 1932** Herman Brin 28 yrs. of 1349 Newberry St. was shot by unknown gangsters in front of 1804 S. Michigan Ave.

On **August 24, 1932** Nello Pelligrini 24 yrs. of 2324 W. 24th St. was shot by unknown gangsters at 14th Pl. and Clinton St.

On **August 31, 1932** Charles Argento 37 yrs. of the Piccadilly Hotel was shot by unknown gangsters in Room 515 at the Blackstone Hotel.

On **September 2, 1932** Walter Zwolinski 28 yrs. of 2714 W. 56th St. was shot by unknown gangsters from a Chrysler auto with 1932 Illinois license plate 622-327 that was found in the rear of 5346 S. Artesian Ave. The outcome of this case is unknown.

On **September 25, 1932** Michael Tamburrino 27 yrs. of 1038 Massasoit Ave. was shot by unknown gangsters in the Palais Rue Café in Melrose Park, IL.

On **September 29, 1932** Iron Barger 37 yrs. was shot by unknown gangsters and found in an auto at 3100 W. 47th Pl.

On **October 11, 1932** Richard J. Roberts 35 yrs. of 5342 Fletcher St. was shot by unknown gangsters and found in the rear of 2737 Lexington St.

On **October 14, 1932** Thomas P. Kane 34 yrs. of 6837 Cornell Ave. was shot by unknown gangsters and found in an auto at 850 W. 54th St.

On **October 15, 1932** Sidney Masser of 5552 Warwick Ave. was shot in the office of the Ashland Lumber Company at 1800 N. Ashland where he was president.

Charles "Trigger Happy Charlie" Fischetti the first cousin of former Mob kingpin Al Capone was picked up for the murder although the charges were later dropped for unknown reasons **(Solved)**.

On **October 21, 1932** Tony Jerfita 31 yrs. of 7001 Altgeld St. was shot by unknown gangsters and found in an auto on the east side of a Schiller Park cemetery in Lyons Township.

On **October 26, 1932** Joseph Farinella AKA: Frank Amato 34 yrs. of 1117 S. Racine Ave. was shot on the street by unknown gangsters at 1007 S. Wood St.

On **October 29, 1932** Harry Lefkovitz 30 yrs. of 1219 S. Harding was shot by unknown gangsters and found in an auto at 5100 Lexington St.

On **November 5, 1932** Joseph Baron Sr. 48 yrs. of 1508 Mohawk St. was shot by unknown gangsters in the rear of his home.

On **December 1, 1932** Joseph Provengano 36 yrs. of 5236 Parker Ave. was shot by unknown gangsters while sitting in an auto at 73rd and Diversey Ave.

On **December 6, 1932** John Liberto 26 yrs. of 1956 W. Erie St. was shot by unknown gangsters at 73rd Ct. and Fullerton Ave. Elmwood Park, IL.

On **December 7, 1932** Anthony Persico 36 yrs. of 155 S. 23rd Ave. Melrose Park, IL. and Nicholas Maggio 35 yrs. of 1112 N. 23rd Ave. Melrose Park, IL. were shot by unknown gangsters and found at Irving Park and Cumberland Ave.

On **December 16, 1932** John Rinella 30 yrs. of the Club Road House was shot by unknown gangsters. He was the owner of a roadhouse at River Road near Higgins in Lyden Township; he was killed by John Ryan a member of the Touhy Gang and another gangster when he refused to buy beer from the gang. Ryan had an extensive record and was sentenced to 14 yrs. in 1919 for murder. He was paroled in 1927 and was shot on the Southside in 1940, but survived. The victim's girlfriend Marie Fleck identified Ryan as one of the killers. While Ryan was put on trial, he was found not guilty in front of Judge Fardy **(Solved)**.

On December 19, 1932 Frank "the Enforcer" Nitti AKA: Francesco Nitto, Ralph Nitto, Frank Raddo and Frank Sasso is shot by police Sgt. Harry Lang struggling during an arrest at his office at 221 N. LaSalle St. Rm. 554, Nitti survived and was cleared of all charges. Lang was indicted for assault on April 6, 1933. Northside gang boss Edward M. "Teddy" Newberry was suspected of arranging this event at the behest of Mayor Anton Cermak and both were possibly killed in retaliation. In February of 1933 Edward M. "Teddy" Newberry's body was found in a rural location and Cermak was killed at a political rally in Miami.

Sgt. Harry Lang

On **December 25, 1932** Ralph Pisano 16 yrs. of 2148 Flournoy St. was shot by unknown gangsters at 417 S. Western Ave. Two men only known as Ryan and Lamar were allegedly arrested for the killing and later both were acquitted **(Solved)**.

On **January 7, 1933** Edward M. "Teddy" Newberry is murdered and his body is dumped either in Ohio or near Chesterton, Indiana. He was the heir apparent to Northside Mob operations. Newberry was a rare individual who originally was a Lt. for the Moran gang but was able to switch sides after the St. Valentine's Day Massacre and work for Capone handling most of the newly acquired Northside operations. It turned out that Newberry was not happy with the split under Moran and thought with the connections of Cermak and his ability to switch to the Capone gang, would secure his future. After a period of time with Capone he allegedly retired only to reemerge in Gambling operations that the Capone-Nitti organization had no control over. Through his association with newly elected Mayor Cermak he provided intelligence to the Mayor's personal police squad. After members of the squad shot Frank Nitti, information surfaced that Newberry offered the officer responsible $15,000 for killing Nitti. Bert Delaney 54yrs., a Capone gangster was arrested during the investigation, several days after the killing, but was released by Municipal Judge Thomas M. Padden **(Solved)**.

On **January 19, 1933** Edward J. Fitzsimmons 32 yrs. of 4854 Blackstone Ave. was shot by unknown gangsters and found near 154th St. and Michigan City Rd. in Thorton Township. The victim was arrested for robbery in 1931 and carrying a concealed handgun in 1932.

On **February 7, 1933** Fred Petitti 32 yrs. of 4001 N. Menard Ave. was shot and killed. Frank Palome AKA: Chinchilla and another man were wanted for the killing. It is not known if they were ever caught.

On **February 8, 1933** William J. O'Brien 36 yrs. of 7332 Irving Park Blvd. was shot by unknown gangsters at 2042 N. Clark St.

On **February 15, 1933** Mayor Aton Cermak was assassinated. He was a powerful political force locally and nationally. His career was cut short by a bullet allegedly meant for Presidential Candidate Franklin D. Roosevelt in a Miami park by an immigrant Brick Layer by the name of Giuseppe Zangara who was immediately caught, tried and executed for the killing. Much like the Kennedy assassination 3 decades later, authorities ignored the possible Mob connections of Zangara and Mob implications to this killing and ruled that Zangara was simply insane and harbored socialist beliefs. Zangara is convicted by March 9th and executed by March 20th of 1933. Like they say Justice delayed is Justice denied. However, like the Kennedy assassination authorities in the federal government ignored intelligence that indicated that Cermak was the target and killed by the Chicago MOB after a failed assassination attempt on their Boss Frank "the Enforcer" Nitti AKA: Francesco Nitto, Ralph Nitto, Frank Raddo and Frank Sasso, that was reportedly orchestrated by Cermak and his close personal associate and Northside gang boss Edward M. "Teddy" Newberry. Reportedly, "Machinegun Jack" McGurn and "Three Finger Jack" White were in that Miami park the day of the shooting and both were armed and wearing Cook County Badges. Ted Newberry also paid for this indiscretion with his life **(Solved)**.

On **February 24, 1933** Dennis Bruce Ziegler 57 yrs. of 3716 N. Tripp Ave. was shot by unknown gangsters. He led the fight against the mob's takeover of Local 569 of the International Union of Operating Engineers. He was killed near his home for the trouble he caused.

On **March 1, 1933** Dan Lynch 33 yrs. was shot by unknown gangsters and found at Crawford and 40th Sts. Lynch a City Water Department employee reportedly killed Harold Cantrell in 1926 and was arrested for the crime, but it is unknown if he was ever convicted for that killing. He killed a police officer in 1930, but was not convicted in that killing either.

On **March 10, 1933** Samuel LaRocca 32 yrs. of 5137 Grand Ave. was shot by unknown gangsters in front of 1228 Larrabee St.

On **March 12, 1933** Fred Russo 25 Yrs. of 709 N. Cicero Ave. was strangled by unknown gangsters in an auto in the rear of 5910 N. Western Ave.

On **March 21, 1933** Joe Hanley 26 yrs. of 1223 Otto Blvd. Chicago Heights, IL. was shot by unknown gangsters near Sauk Trail on State St. in Bloom Township.

On **March 24, 1933** Fred F. Oser was shot and killed in the offices of the Motion Picture Operators Union by Ralph O'Hara. O'Hara was an associate of Tommy Maloy a union racketeer whom Oser opposed. O'Hara was tried and acquitted in the slaying claiming self-defense after Oser pulled a gun on him **(Solved)**.

On **April 5, 1933** Joseph Zurek 21 Yrs. of 613 N. Racine Ave. was shot by unknown gangsters and found on Harts Rd. between Touhy Ave. and Milwaukee Ave.

On **May 15, 1933** Rocco Belcastro 26 yrs. was shot and killed. Sam LaVerde, Dan Moretti, Louis Jacobs, Joseph Stopek and Charles Kumowski were all wanted for the crime, but it is unknown if any were ever brought to justice.

On **May 24, 1933** Edward Gambino 25 yrs. of 1134 S. Sacramento Ave. was shot in the head by unknown gangsters and found by tenants in the hallway at 2423 W. Grand Ave. The victim had previously been convicted of burglary and was arrested for a rape/robbery along with Mike Marino in 1932.

On **June 3, 1933** Carl Verdoni 35 yrs. of 1036 N. Hamlin Ave. was shot by unknown gangsters at 46th St. and Cicero Ave.

On **June 11, 1933** George Navigato 37 yrs. of 5301 Jackson Blvd. was shot by unknown gangsters on Lockwood Ave. just south of Jackson Blvd.

On **June 16, 1933** Joseph Petitte 44 yrs. of 800 S. Claremont Ave. was killed by unknown gangsters in front of 2334 W. Polk St.

On **June 18, 1933** Joseph Marzullo 22 yrs. of 2800 Wentworth Ave. was killed by unknown gangsters in front of 839 E. 47th St.

On June 26, 1933 Henry Berger 41 yrs. and his wife were forced to the curb in their automobile by two men at Central and Ohio Sts. and shot. The Bergers were on their way home to 5835 N. Kenton from a funeral parlor on the Westside. Berger was a general organizer for the International Brotherhood of Teamsters and was trying to force the Mob controlled Teamsters locals known as Outlaw locals into the International and thus into the Chicago Federation of Labor. Berger was struck in the head which resulted in paralysis and his wife was struck in both legs. Berger survived the attack and told responding police, Sgt. John Kratzmeyer that he would take care of the men that shot him, not cooperating any further.

Willie Marks

On **July 5, 1933** Willie Marks and Pat Burrell were killed while vacationing in Wisconsin. Marks was part of the Touhy gang that infuriated the Capone organization by protecting certain union leaders from the threats of takeover. He was also a suspect in the Red Barker murder and an attempt on Frank McErlane in the German Deaconess Hospital. He was with Burrell the Chicago's Teamster President at the time of the attack.

On **July 16, 1933** Tony Garrelli 12 yrs. was shot by Steve Aiello 17 yrs. AKA: Stovepipe, Joseph Spinnato AKA: Spin 18 yrs. and Mike Fellisho AKA: Jim 16 yrs. over a dispute between gang members in the Maxwell St. area. The boys were charged with the killing, but acquitted. Spinnato was killed later in the year and police speculated that he was killed by the victim's older brother Joseph in retaliation of this killing **(solved)**.

On **July 18, 1933** Emil Onesto 43 yrs. of 940 W. Polk St. was murdered. He was shot as he stood in his doorway at 1139 W. Taylor Street. Police learned that he was not the intended target. The killers were William "Irish" Madden 26 yrs. and Michael DeStefano both members of the notorious 42 gang. They were trying to raise defense funds for DeStefano's brother Sam who was serving a prison term in Wisconsin for bank robbery. The intended target was Frank Laino AKA: Mustari of 4649 Lexington St. a driver for "Dago" Lawrence Mangano who refused to contribute to the fund and was wounded in the attack. The two were arrested and DeStefano was released by police and disappeared becoming a fugitive while Madden was put on trial in front of Judge Benjamin P. Epstein. The outcome of the case is unknown **(Solved)**.

On **July 20, 1933** Aloysius Strook 35 yrs. of 7758 Jeffery Ave. was shot to death during an altercation at 8301 S. Chicago Ave. Charles Egan and John Curtin were arrested and indicted for the killing, but the outcome of the case is unknown **(Solved)**.

On **July 26, 1933** William E. Carr 24 yrs. of 2155 Cortez St. was shot by unknown gangsters in front of 1521 Elston Ave. In October of 1930 he along with future Mob Boss Teetz Battaglia robbed the wife of Chicago Mayor William Hale "Big Bill" Thompson.

On **July 28, 1933** Thomas Fredinordo AKA: Tony Rocco 28 yrs. of 1704 Sunnyside Ave. was shot by Pat Gordon and another man only known as Olson at

3946 Lincoln Ave. The victim was a beer peddler and apparently supplied beer to taverns under the control of Klondike O'Donnell, Westside gang boss. Four men attacked him, two of which had been partially identified as O'Donnell henchmen. It is not known if any of them were ever prosecuted for this crime.

On **August 1, 1933** Dominic Russo AKA: Tony Marino 42 yrs. of 1817 S. Home Ave. Berwyn, Il. was shot by unknown gangsters in front of 5337 W. 25th St. Cicero, IL. The victim was a Philadelphia gangster who became friends with Al Capone in jail there. He had been arrested by legendary lawman Eliot Ness several times in raids on Capone breweries in Cicero.

On **August 10, 1933** John Perillo 33 yrs. of 820 Miller St. was murdered at Polk and Miller Streets. Sam Battaglia and Ted Virgilio were wanted for the crime, in October of that same year a Cook County Grand Jury passed a No Bill on a requested indictment of the two men and they were never brought to justice **(Solved)**.

On **August 20, 1933** Sam Scrabino 29 yrs. of 4527 S. Laflin was shot by unknown gangsters in the rear of 4734 S. Bishop Ave.

On **August 21, 1933** Loreto Mule 48 yrs. of 1448 Cleveland Ave. was shot by unknown gangsters as he rode in a Lincoln sedan at Cambridge and Division Sts.

On **August 29, 1933** John Pippan 37 yrs. of 1319 S. 51st St. Cicero, IL. was shot to death on 51st St. between 12th and 13th Sts. in Cicero. Thomas Rosse and Gus Giovenco were wanted for the crime, but it is unknown if they were ever arrested for it.

In **August of 1933** Albert Bregar a former aide to Ted Newberry who landed on his feet and became a sidekick to Gus Winkler disappeared when he left the Lincoln Park Arms Hotel for a haircut and was never seen again. You would think events such as this may have enlightened Winkler and company, it did not.

On **September 8, 1933** James Tribble was shot and killed when he, along with a group of gangsters raided a union headquarters. He was an ex-convict and labor goon.

On **September 9, 1933** Nicholas Museato 32 yrs. of 1815 Garibaldi Pl. was shot by unknown gangsters in front of 908 S. Marshfield Ave.

On **September 16, 1933** Sam Incandella 22 yrs. of 621 Hobbie St. was shot by unknown gangsters at Bloomington Rd. and Ballou St.

On **September 22, 1933** Patrolman Miles Cunningham was shot and killed at Adams and Halsted Street in Chicago. The uniformed officer was approaching a vehicle that had been involved in an accident not knowing the suspected occupants were three of the most notorious gangsters in Chicago at the time and had just robbed a bank at Jackson and LaSalle. The first suspect was Gus Winkler AKA: August "Big Mike" Winkeler, who was a close associate of Al Capone and one of the masterminds of the St. Valentine Day Massacre. Winkler was killed on the street approximately two weeks later at 1414 W. Roscoe. The car used was registered to George R. "Machine Gun" Kelly a notorious bank robber. He was captured a couple days later in Tennessee and convicted of a kidnapping and sentenced to life in prison. The last suspect was Verne Miller, he was found dead near Detroit after the killing. While the last suspect who was driving a tail car was never identified three of them received justice in various ways **(Solved)**.

On **October 5, 1933** Joseph Pawlowski 36 yrs. of 5053 W. 32nd Pl. Cicero, IL. was shot by unknown gangsters at 5125 W. 29th St. Cicero, IL. William Evans a bank robber and gangster associated with labor racketeer and prolific gangster Red Barker was wanted for the crime, but it is unknown if he was ever apprehended. Evans would be murdered himself in 1934.

On **October 9, 1933** Gus Winkler AKA: August "Big Mike" Winkeler 33 yrs. of 3300 Sheridan Rd. was killed in front of the Charles H. Weber Beer Distributing Company 1414 W. Roscoe Avenue. Winkeler was a Capone gunman and favorite (American Boy) and a participant and one of the architects of the St. Valentine's Day Massacre, he was also under indictment for a mail robbery which aggravated new Mob Boss Frank Nitti to no end. He was also an associate of northside gangsters and worked both sides better than anyone. He was killed after Capone went to prison in front of the brewery he co-owned with County Commissioner Charles Weber. Like many of his contemporaries he reportedly was killed by two of his friends Frederick S. Goetz AKA: J. George "Shotgun" Zeigler and "Tough Tony" Capezio, on the orders of Nitti, although the men were never charged and the case was never solved. Other suspects were the Touhy gang, Martin Guilfoyle, Babe Baron and hood for hire Dominic Marzano.

On **October 10, 1933** Antonio Belmonte 44 yrs. of 2111 Kenilworth Ave. Berwyn, IL. was shot by unknown gangsters at his residence.

On **October 23, 1933** John Paplinski AKA: Flynn 37 yrs. of 904 S. Wentworth Ave. was shot by unknown gangsters in front of his residence.

On **October 27, 1933** Louis B. Cowan AKA: "Diamond Louis" 38 yrs. of 4819 W. 22nd St. was shotgunned to death in his car at 5935 W. Roosevelt in Cicero. He was there to pick up his bodyguard Joseph Corngold AKA: Fifke at a Cicero gambling joint, Corngold was also wounded in the attack from a passing car. Louis was a former bail bondsman, an investor in Sportsman's Racetrack and the owner of the Cicero Tribune since Capone days. He was a millionaire until the depression and a Capone favorite as his diamond belt buckle attested to. However, with Capone away he lost his luster to Nitti and had to go.

Joe Corngold

On **October 27, 1933** Patsy Damato 29 yrs. of 724 N. St. Louis Ave. was shot by unknown gangsters in a tavern at 4559 Diversey Ave.

On **November 4, 1933** Joseph Spinnato 19 yrs. of 807 S. Paulina St. was shot by unknown gangsters in the alley behind 1118 Blue Island Ave. Police suspected that he was killed by Joseph Garelli in retaliation for the murder of Garelli's younger brother Tony who was shot in July by Spinnato, Steve Aiello and Mike Fellisho who were arrested and acquitted of the charge. It is not known if this case was ever solved **(solved)**.

By the end of **1933** Verne Miller is killed in Detroit. Miller who gained notoriety for his part in the Fox Lake Massacre and the Kansas City Massacre drew the ire of Nitti and Ricca who did not have the same penchant for the American Boys and the subcontractors used by Capone. Many fell under the leadership of Nitti.

In **1934** Eli Daiches was killed by unknown gangsters. He was an advertising executive and police suspected Virgil Summers the leader of the "Summers Holdup and Murder Gang", but no charges were brought and the case remains unsolved.

On **January 1, 1934** Michael W. Reagan 29 yrs. of 9223 Houston St. was shot by Matthew Breen, Albert Zicha AKA: Ciha and a man only known as Pete and one other man at his residence. Eventually Breen and Zicha were arrested and tried for the crime. Breen was sentenced to 15 years and Zicha to 99 years **(solved)**.

On **January 13, 1934** Walter Stifaniak 23 yrs. of 2554 W. 45th St. was shot by unknown gangsters and found on State Rd. and 81st St. in Stickney, IL.

On **January 23, 1934** William "Three Finger Jack" White AKA: Henry J. Cerny was murdered. White was wanted by local authorities for an upcoming trial and while they could not find him, the FBI had been visiting the former gunman in his Oak Park apartment on Wesley Drive. He was laying low and suspected of being an informant, he had double-crossed "Fur Sammons" and was hated by the crippled Touhy gang. On the day he was killed he took two visitors into his suburban apartment, known as Joe and Bill to his wife, who was on her way out shopping at the time. The men drank for a while but drew guns and shot him before they left. Like many other victims he had lost his value to the Nitti/Capone gang and was more of a liability. The Oak Park police were able to gain a photo identification from residents of the building, who saw the assailants flee. They identified Murray Humphries and Klondike O'Donnell as the killers. While Murray Humphreys, Klondike O'Donnell, Claude Maddox and labor goon Marcus Looney were each suspected in the murder, none of the men were ever charged.

William "Three Finger Jack" White

On **January 31, 1934** William Evans 32 yrs. of 11546 S. Ave. L was shot by unknown gangsters in the rear of 1605 S. 51st Ave. Cicero, IL. The victim was a bank robber and associate of Red Barker. He was wanted in the 1933 murder of Joseph Pawlowski, but it is not known if he was ever apprehended.

On **February 4, 1934** Ernest Rossi AKA: Ross 37 yrs. of 5529 Flournoy St. was shot by unknown gangsters in the rear of his residence. He was suspected in the murder of Detective Raymond E. Martin in 1929, but was never captured for that crime.

On **February 19, 1934** Grover Cline 41 yrs. of 831 S. Laflin St. was shot by unknown gangsters in the passageway of his residence.

On **February 27, 1934** Joseph Smith 24 yrs. of 5016 S. Union Ave. was shot by unknown gangsters at 54th Pl. and Lowe Ave.

On **March 7, 1934** Daniel Losec 42 yrs. of 3853 Lake Park Ave. was shot by unknown gangsters in front of 2352 S. Ashland Ave.

On **March 7, 1934** Frank "Frankie" Pope 38 yrs. of 758 W. Jackson Blvd. Rm. 306 was shot to death in his hotel room at the Vernon Hotel. Pope an ex-millionaire newsman lost a management position in a Cicero gambling joint and dabbled in alcohol and drug dealing receiving prison sentences for both. Since his released from jail he resided in the hotel. On the day of the killing he received two men in his room while entertaining a lady friend. The men drew pistols and shot him dead. Both men and the women fled and were never found.

On **March 14, 1934** Charles Connors AKA: Ice Wagon, Marton 57 yrs. was shot by unknown gangsters and found on 107th St. near Archer Ave. in Palos Township. He was a member of the Northwest side Touhy gang and may have been killed for shorting other gang members. He was a prison escapee from Sandstone Federal Prison when he was killed.

On **March 17, 1934** Kay A. Jespersen 24 yrs. of 1730 W. Farragut Ave. was shot by unknown gangsters while riding in an auto with Fred Zehrol AKA: Enright, James when they were curbed by a car at 26th and Federal Sts. by two men who killed Jespersen.

On **March 21, 1934** Frederick S. Goetz AKA: Goitz, J. George "Shotgun" Zeigler 37 yrs. was killed on the Street outside the Minerva restaurant at 4813 W. Cermak (owned by "Dago" Lawrence Mangano) in Cicero, IL. He was a former Capone gunman (American Boy) and current Alvin "Creepy" Karpis-Red Barker kidnapping gang member at the time of the killing. In typical OUTFIT fashion shotgun blasts from a car passing by killed him on the spot. It has long been speculated that OUTFIT Boss Frank Nitti was cleaning up loose ends from the St. Valentine's Day Massacre some five years prior. Nitti never had the same penchant as Capone for contract employees especially those that were not Italian. Other speculation was that Goetz was killed by the Karpis-Barker gang for the mismanagement of ransom monies.

On **March 30, 1934** Joseph Garelli 18 yrs. of 923 Sholto St. was shot in a saloon at 914 Sholto St. Police suspected he was killed by gang members led by Steve Aiello. During recent gang disputes Garelli's younger brother Tony was killed earlier in the year by Joseph Spinnato, Steve Aiello and Mike Fellisho. Spinnato was then killed by Joseph Garelli in retaliation. And now Joseph has been killed possibly in retaliation for killing Spinnato. Ah yes, the circle of life!

On **April 26, 1934** Edward Dudeck was murdered by unknown gangsters.

On **April 26, 1934** Tony Canzoneri 42 yrs. of 1042 Orleans St. was shot by unknown gangsters in a tavern at 1142 Belmont Ave.

On **May 5, 1934** Chester Geisler 20 yrs. of 2009 W. 18th St. was shot by unknown gangsters in front of 2051 W. 18th St.

On **June 1, 1934** Clarence W. Haggerty 37 yrs. of 1512 W. Jackson Blvd. was shot by unknown gangsters on South Western Highway near Western Ave.

On **June 12, 1934** Peter Esser 37 yrs. of 503 Ingram St. was shot by unknown gangsters at a bar at 337 Plummer St.

On **June 21, 1934** Zigmund Masiong 20 yrs. of 3117 N. Drake Ave. was shot at Artesian and Diversey Aves., while dying in Cook County Hospital he named Charles Lewis AKA: Chuck, Miller as his assassin. Lewis was said to have killed the man on orders of a bootlegger. Lewis was killed several weeks later by Patrolman John Fogarty at 206 W. Randolph after a foot chase and after Lewis fatally shot another police officer **(solved)**.

On **June 28, 1934** Robert Millay 46 yrs. of 2428 W. 25th St. was shot by unknown gangsters while he talked to Nick Hodan on his front porch.

On **July 3, 1934** Fred Zehrol 26 yrs. of 2917 Logan Blvd. was shot by unknown gangsters in front of 1331 N. Clark St.

On **July 19, 1934** Michael H. Quinlan AKA: Bubs 37 yrs. of 6650 Stony Island Ave. was shot by unknown gangsters in a restaurant at 6325 Cottage Grove Ave. The union he was involved with was under the control of gangster Danny Stanton. This murder was just one incident of violence associated with the Mob takeover.

On **July 25, 1934** Sullivano Serpa 40 yrs. was shot by unknown gangsters and found on the sidewalk at 3330 Normal Ave.

On **July 30, 1934** Patrolman Anton Zapolsky died from a gunshot wound he received on July 27th in downtown Chicago while trying to capture a car thief. The offender Charles Lewis AKA: Miller of 2434 W. Moffet St. was killed a short distance away at 206 W. Randolph by Patrolman John Fogarty. Lewis was a killer employed by local bootleggers and killed Zigmund Masiong in June of this year **(solved)**.

On **August 12, 1934** John Imperato 26 yrs. of 717 N. Dearborn St. was shot by unknown gangsters and found at rear of 1221 W. Grand Ave.

On **August 13, 1934** Robert "Pudgie" Stamm 33 yrs. of 3304 Lexington St. was shot by unknown gangsters at 4950 Flournoy St. He was tried in 1926 for the murder of Howard Berkovitz at a poolroom at 1702 W. Roosevelt Rd. While the motive was reportedly involving the Yellow Cab Co., the outcome of the investigation is unknown.

On **August 19, 1934** Ray James Thompson AKA: Rob, Roy 42 yrs. of 8241 Dorchester Ave. was shot by unknown gangsters as he exited his car in front of his home. He was a union official for local 184 and the union he was involved with was under the control of gangster Danny Stanton. This murder was just one incident of violence associated with the Mob takeover.

On **September 10, 1934** Michael Lamperelli 24 yrs. of 13 E. 30th Pl. Chicago Heights, IL. was shot by unknown gangsters in an auto at 34th St. near State St. in Bloom Township.

On **September 10, 1934** John J. Sandrik 23 yrs. of 1018 Riese St., Whiting, In. was shot by unknown gangsters from an auto while he was waiting for a street car at 51st St. and Kedzie Ave.

On **September 15, 1934** Joseph Adduci 41 yrs. of 308 E. 117th St. was shot by unknown gangsters in a barber shop at 11857 S. Michigan Ave. Sam Mesi was questioned in the murder before the arrest of Sam Bruno who ultimately was convicted of the crime and sentenced to 14 years in prison **(solved)**.

On **September 29, 1934** Edward J. Meehan 31 yrs. of 6143 Whipple St. was shot by unknown gangsters in the alley at 5521 S. Carpenter St.

On **October 26, 1934** James Canzoneri 41 yrs. of 852 Fletcher St. was shot by unknown gangsters in the alley behind 3252 N. Clark St.

On **October 31, 1934** William Franceschi AKA: Francisco, Willie Francis 28 yrs. of 706 Buckingham Pl. was shot by unknown gangsters in front of his home. He was reportedly a bootlegger, extortionist and suspected jewel thief. He was also an associate of a hoodlum named Tommy Abbott. He was at the garage by his home inspecting some damage on a car when a car drove by and fired a shotgun and a revolver at him.

On **November 3, 1934** Joseph Carracio 28 yrs. of 325 S. Ashland Ave. was shot by unknown gangsters in a hallway at 1545 W. Van Buren St.

On **November 25, 1934** Anthony DiCaro 29 yrs. of 2956 Emerald Ave. was shot by unknown gangsters near the front of his residence.

On **November 25, 1934** John Wells 55 yrs. of 126 E. 31st St. was shot by unknown gangsters in front of 2252 Wentworth Ave.

On **November 27, 1934** Herman E. Hollis 31 yrs. of 4423 Sheridan Rd. and his partner Samuel Cowley both federal agents were shot by "Baby Face" Nelson and other unknown gangsters in Barrington IL., while the agents were trying to effect the arrest of the notorious gangsters and one woman. Agent Hollis died at the scene and Cowley died a couple of days later. After the gun battle the gangsters escaped to a home in Wilmette, IL, where Nelson died of nine bullet wounds. He was wrapped in a blanket and left at a cemetery on Niles Center Rd. north of Oakton St. near what is now downtown Skokie, Il.

On **December 16, 1934** Christ Peter Soupos 19 yrs. of 1941 Cleveland Ave. was shot by unknown gangsters in front of 2005 Lincoln Ave.

On **January 8, 1935** St. Valentine's Day participant and "American Boy" member Byron Bolton was captured by an army of FBI agents in a siege at 3920 N. Pine Grove. After Bolton's less than stellar performance as a lookout in the St. Valentine's Day massacre he changed employers joining the Barker-Karpis kidnapping gang. During the siege federal agents poured teargas into several apartments until they forced Bolton and his compatriot Russell Gibson along with two women out of the building. At this point Gibson while armed and wearing a bullet-proof vest was killed on a rear fire escape. Bolton surrendered peacefully. Eight days later agents carried out a second raid near Ocala, Florida where they poured gunfire into a home that killed Freddie and Kate "Ma" Barker, part of the same gang. He also spilled the beans and gave a full account of the St. Valentine's Day Massacre however authorities chose not to pursue it at this time.

On **January 13, 1935** Frank Panio 33 yrs. of 3033 S. Princeton Ave. was shot by unknown gangsters on the corner of 60th and Frontenac Sts.

On **January 14, 1935** Frank Abrignani 30 yrs. of 1022 S. Ashland Ave. was shot by unknown gangsters while he sat in his auto at 1512 Taylor St.

On **February 1, 1935** Joseph Catrino 27 yrs. of 914 S. Ashland Ave. was found shot by unknown gangsters.

On **February 2, 1935** Tommy Maloy 42 yrs. of 6806 Chappel Ave. was shot by unknown gangsters. Maloy was the czar of the Moving Picture Operators Union Local 110 and a member of the American Federation of Labor, he was killed while driving to work on Leif Erickson Drive (now Lake Shore Drive) at 25th St., and he was shot from another car. He was with his bodyguard Emmett C. Quinn as they left the apartment that Maloy kept for a Chorus Girl he was associated with. He had recently been indicted on tax charges. Maloy a tough and seasoned labor racketeer for years managed to keep TOC off his back. He placed gangsters on his payroll, assisted the Mob in taking over other locals and was quite heavy handed when he met resistance. However, like many who make deals with the devil he drew the wrath of someone or some group who eventually punched his ticket and probably feared his cooperation with authorities in light of his legal troubles.

On **April 16, 1935** John Donahue 35 yrs. of 815 Waveland Ave. was shotgunned by unknown gangsters in front of 809 Waveland Ave.

On **May 4, 1935** Frank A. Young AKA: Anthony Calatorius 40 yrs. of 4352 S. Mozart was shot by unknown gangsters. While driving his beer truck he was held up by three men and killed.

On **May 25, 1935** Clyde Osterberg 32 yrs. of 631 Oakdale Ave. was shot by unknown gangsters at 18th and Laflin Sts. He was a recalcitrant motion picture union operator who was an enemy of labor racketeer Tommy Maloy who was previously shot and killed. He attempted to start his own labor local and paid with his life.

On **June 3, 1935** Jack Magliola AKA: Magleo 38 yrs. of 2330 N. Meade Ave. was shot by unknown gangsters in a pool room at 5809 W. Grand Ave.

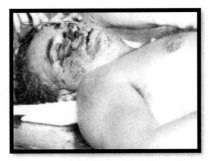

Louis Alterie dead

On **July 18, 1935** Louis "Two Gun" Alterie AKA: Leland Deveraigne, Leland Varain 49 yrs. of 922 Eastwood Ave. was ambushed from an adjacent apartment building as he left his swank abode. The killing was a classic setup by the Nitti gang. Alterie a Northside gangster and a labor racketeer who was President of the Janitors Union, was able to hang onto his Union interest after the fall of the Northside gang he was affiliated with, until Frank Nitti decided that he wanted that union to. He also gained some notoriety after the death of "Nails" Morton from a horse riding accident. He allegedly went to the stable where the horse that threw Morton was kept and shot it to death on the orders of Deon O'Banion. When O'Banion was killed Two Gun made an open challenge to the killers to meet him on State Street at high noon for a gunfight. Even his remaining northside colleagues thought that was over the top. When he was finally killed Labor discourse was proclaimed as the motive by investigating officials, although the case went unsolved.

On **September 24, 1935** Edward J. Arendt 32 yrs. of 5915 S. Fairfield Ave. was shot by unknown gangsters while on the front porch of 6444 S. Maplewood Ave.

On **November 14, 1935** Frank Stypulkowski AKA: Sloan 25 yrs. of 1612 Wabansia Ave. was shotgunned by three unknown gangsters while sitting in an auto at North Ave. and Paulina St. Reportedly the men were involved in the alcohol business.

On **November 15, 1935** Angelo Kleronomos 24 yrs. of 1313 S. 58th Ct. Cicero, IL. and Joseph Scaffidi 28 yrs. of 522 E. Resevoerie St. Milwaukee, WI. were shot by unknown gangsters while seated in an Auburn automobile at 2120 Custer St.

On **November 19, 1935** Sam Incandella 31 yrs. of 3825 W. Chicago Ave. was shot by unknown gangsters in front of his store at that location.

On **December 19, 1935** Joseph Annerino AKA: Pepi, Peppy Genero 47 yrs. of 310 W. 27th St. was shot to death as he sat in the window of a bar at 1543 E. 63rd St. from a car that pulled up in front. The former bootlegger, kidnapper and "Public Enemy" like so many others lost his status with the repeal of Prohibition. He was a former associate of James "King of the Bombers" Belcastro and it was speculated that he wanted to push his way into OUTFIT gambling operations. Belcastro was questioned in the slaying, but never charged.

Joe Genero

On **December 26, 1935** Sam Latella 38 yrs. was shot by unknown gangsters and found in front of 1450 W. Kinzie St.

On **December 29, 1935** Albert J. Prignano 43 yrs. of 722 Bunker St. (now Grenshaw) was shot by unknown gangsters in front of his home. He was a former alderman and state representative and was supported by Capone in his 1927 aldermanic race. He ran his own gambling interests under the protection of Capone. Prignano also had been a longtime associate of the Northside gang, but as their power waned he restricted his allegiance to the Capone/Nitti organization. Prior to his killing he was said to have argued with "Dago" Lawrence Mangano over protecting Westside gambling operations and was advised not to run for reelection. He survived two attacks on his life. Whatever the reason Nitti ordered his gunman into action and they killed him in a fake robbery. Anglo Lazzia was suspected of the killing, but it is not known if he was ever detained.

Alderman Albert Prignano and Al Capone

On **January 3, 1936** Elsie Henneman AKA: Kenneman 35 yrs. of 3116 Lowe Ave. was shot while sitting in an auto at 335 W. Root St. Her husband was George Henneman the Secretary-Treasurer of Painters Union Local 191. He was reportedly involved in the Mob takeover of the union that led to her death. William Schaaf was wanted for the killing, but it is unknown if he was ever arrested for it. Schaaf was killed in 1940 due to his union activities.

On **January 13, 1936** Eugenio Belmonte 32 yrs. 1330 Edgemont Ave. was shot by unknown gangsters who were riding in his auto with him in an alley at 3328 Flournoy St.

On January 23, 1936 the Chicago American reported that Byron Bolton an OUTFIT killer and former Navy machine gunner revealed from his prison cell after being arrested in a kidnapping case, his involvement in the St. Valentine's Day massacre. He named himself, Fred Goetz, Gus Winkler, Fred Burke, Ray Nugent and Bob Carey as the gunmen who executed 7 Northside gang members. The lookouts stationed to watch for Bugs Moran from a flat across the street were himself, Jimmy McCrussen and Jimmy "The Swede" Morand who both knew Moran on sight. He went on to say the crime was first planned at Cranberry Lake in Wisconsin around October or November of 1928. At this meeting were TOC luminaries that included Al Capone, Gus Winkeler, Fred Goetz, Louis "Little New York" Campagna, Fred Burke, and politicians Bill Pacelli and Dan Saritella. He went on to implicate Claude "Screwy" Maddox AKA: John E. Moore, and a man only known to him as "Shocker", both from St. Louis and affiliated with a gang known as "Egan's Rats" and "Tough Tony" Capezio from Chicago who burned one of the cars after the crime in a Wood St. Garage. Despite physical evidence that tied Fred Burke to the crime, FBI Director J. Edgar Hoover, who repeatedly denied the existence of TOC as a national issue, ignored the allegations and refused to investigate the report any further under the guise that murder was not a federal offense. This was during a time when the FBI did not investigate TOC, nor did they share intelligence with local police who were so corrupt that they had no interest in most TOC killings.

On **February 14, 1936** Vincenzo Gibaldi AKA: "Machine Gun" Jack McGurn, Gebardi, James was shot by unknown gangsters at the Avenue Recreation Parlor at 805 N. Milwaukee Ave. The infamous gangster did not hold his prior status with the old Capone-Nitti OUTFIT or any other gang for that matter. He had fallen on hard times, he spent most of his time on the golf course or involved in some minor gambling activities, but was trying to hold on to his gangster status. His last mistake may have been turning to politician Albert Prignano for help. Prignano who had fallen out of grace with the Capone-Nitti gang was murdered previously. A respite from his uncertain future may have been a couple hours of bowling, the establishment is said to have been owned by William "Smokes" Aloiso a Capone stalwart and suspected killer. During what was believed to be a staged robbery, turned into a hit on the feared killer. Near the body police found a Valentine Days card poking fun at his current status.

On **March 2, 1936** Anthony DeMory 22 yrs. of 622 S. Morgan St. was shot by unknown gangsters at Santa Cutia's poolroom at 1003 W. Polk Street in Little Italy. He was the half-brother of Jack McGurn and spoke of taking revenge for the death of his brother. Knowing the demeanor of the men ordering the killings, they took no chances, both cases went unsolved.

On **March 29, 1936** Claude Cooley 29 yrs. was shot by unknown gangsters on the second floor of 4907 S. Prairie Ave.

On **July 9, 1936** John M. Bolton 29 yrs. of 736 S. Ashland Ave. was shotgunned to death, while driving his auto, from a following car at Harrison and Washtenaw Aves. Bolton a State Representative and his brother "Red" were allies of the Capone gang in the twenties. However, in recent times he had operated gambling establishments, tried to take over others on the Westside not under the control of the Nitti gang. He also introduced legislation to legalize handbooks and established the Handbook Operators Association and the Handbook Employees Union without Nitti collaboration. The bill he and Mayor Kelly developed to legalize handbooks was killed by Governor Henry Horner. It was speculated that his death was caused by his new independence from the OUTFIT.

On **September 2, 1936** Joseph Campisciano 34 yrs. of 1041 Belden Ave. was shot by unknown gangsters just west of Willow Spring Rd. near Lemont, IL.

On **September 9, 1936** Paul Phemister 24 yrs. of 1047 Berwyn Ave. was shot by unknown gangsters in an alley at 1705 W. Madison St.

On **October 28, 1936** Adolph Anzona 30 yrs. of 3265 Warren Blvd. was shot by unknown gangsters in a tavern at 7225 Milwaukee Ave. in Niles, IL.

On **November 15, 1936** John Benedetto 33 yrs. of 1104 S. Main St. was shot by unknown gangsters and found in a car in front of 3450 N. Racine Ave. His death was the result of a dispute with his partner "Tough Tony" Capezio over the split of proceeds from the Robbery of John F. Cuneo and his wife at 3300 Lake Shore Drive. While the victims of the robbery were unable to identify Capezio, they did identify Benedetto's body as one of the stick-up men.

On **November 23, 1936** Michael Galvin 53 yrs. of 1222 Sherwin Ave. was shotgunned by unknown gangsters as he walked in front of 550 W. Madison St. He was a Teamster Union Secretary at the time of his death and four prior wives tried to claim his estate. It was reported that labor racketeer Marcus Looney was wanted for questioning in the killing.

On **December 17, 1936** Dominick Scaduto 25 yrs. of 457 Curtis St. was shot by unknown gangsters in the poolroom at 1032 W. Grand Ave.

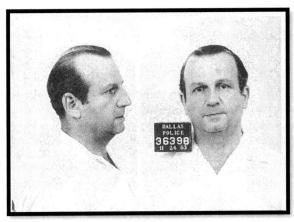

Jack Ruby

In 1937 former Westside gambling associate Leon Rubenstein AKA: Jack Ruby returns to Chicago from a respite in the western states and becomes involved with the Scrap Iron and Junk Handlers Union 20467 working as an organizer.

In **January of 1937** William Stanley was shot and killed by gangster Frank DeMere 26yrs. of 7118 S. Seeley after Stanley had shot and killed Frank Buglio the brother of gangster Ralph Buglio a partner of Pete Tremont.

On **January 8, 1937** Benjamin Greco 38 yrs. of 1062 W. Taylor St. was shot by unknown gangsters in a candy store at 1066 W. Taylor St.

On **June 14, 1937** Ambrosio Costello 55 yrs. of 731 W. Congress was shot by unknown gangsters in the doorway of his home. He was a bill peddler at the time of his death.

On **June 25, 1937** Robert A. Sheilds was shot and killed in front of his home at 3451 W. 61st St. He was the Financial Secretary of Local 184 of the Painters Union. He was the brother of labor racketeer Roy Shields and it was reported that this killing was an attempt by feuding gangsters to bring Roy out of hiding so they could kill him. The union the victim was involved with was under the control of gangster Danny Stanton. This murder was just one incident of violence associated with the Mob takeover.

On **October 3, 1937** Patsy Trotti 45 yrs. of 1543 Edgemont Ave. was murdered by unknown gangsters in an alley at 1011 Laflin St.

On **October 20, 1937** Joseph Locasio 27 yrs. of 3002 S. Wells St. was shot by unknown gangsters during a card game in a delicatessen at 3020 S. Wells St.

On **November 26, 1937** Fred Blacker AKA: "Bugs" was gunned down along with his wife outside the Argo Theater at 75th St. and 62nd Place in Summit, IL. by 3 masked gunmen. Blacker was the notorious Indiana Labor Racketeer, who under the employ of the OUTFIT controlled the MCA Company, who would terrorize nightclubs who did not hire MCA bands.

On **February 10, 1938** Lloyd B. Rourke 31 yrs. of 5533 Blackstone Ave. was murdered in an alley next to the Fairfax Hotel at 1639 Hyde Park Blvd early in the afternoon. He was an independent laundry driver and crossed a picket line to work. He was attacked with a baseball bat and struck in the head. He was killed by a hoodlum employed as a strike picket. This case is the result of gangsters and labor union racketeers struggling for power within newly organized laundry worker organizations.

On **May 16, 1938** Henry G. Schneider 42 yrs. of 4051 Southport Ave. was kidnapped and shot by unknown gangsters. His body was found at the west end of South Ave. in Glencoe, IL. He wanted a projectionist job held by a relative of gangster Nicky Dean. He was a member of the Projectionists Union and opposed Mob control and died for his efforts.

On **June 11, 1938** Eugene Dalassandro 41 yrs. of 1511 W. Adams St. was shot by unknown gangsters in front of 1301 W. Adams St.

On **June 29, 1938** Harry L. Minor 26 yrs. of 4708 W. Monroe St. was shot by unknown gangsters in front of 3110 N. Ashland Ave.

On **July 24, 1938** Nicholas Chiaramonte 58 yrs. of 336 W. 24th St. was shot by unknown gangsters in front of 316 W. 24th St.

On **August 6, 1938** Bruno Switaj 34 yrs. of 1369 Potomac Ave. an Alley Inspector and Leo Mosinski 27 yrs. of 1419 Noble St. an ex-policeman (both top precinct captains for Chicago Alderman Joe Rostenkowski) were shot multiple times as they slept in a car parked in front of the Rostenkowski home at 1349 Noble Street and next door to the alderman's insurance agency and the headquarters of the regular Democratic 32nd ward organization. Near dawn Joe heard shots and after the killings he took his family to the Rostenkowski summer home in Wisconsin. The killers were never caught.

On **August 8, 1938** James G. Dungan 35 yrs. was shot by unknown gangsters in front of his home at 3116 Lowe Ave. He was a business agent in the Painters Union Local 191 and was one of six members killed to this point during the Mob takeover. He survived a previous machinegun attack in 1934. He was suspected of involvement in union related bombings in the past. After this murder George Henneman took over his role and Roy Sheilds another union thug was reportedly a suspect in the killing. The union was under the control of gangster Danny Stanton.

On **August 9, 1938** Sam Picciotto 23 yrs. of 212 W. 24th St. was shot by unknown gangsters at 34th St. and Shields Ave.

On **August 12, 1938** Joseph LaPorte 25 yrs. of 1220 W. Polk St. was shot by unknown gangsters in an alley at 2539 W. Van Buren St.

On **August 24, 1938** Paul Battaglia 42 yrs. of 831 Cabrini St. is kidnapped off the street, shot in the head and tossed into an alley at 5115 Monroe St. from a speeding car. He was the older brother of future Mob Boss Sam Battaglia, but in these early years ran afoul with the Capone-Nitti gang by robbing horse betting rooms and handbooks. At the time he was a member of the 42 gang that spawned many top mobsters such as: Sam DeStefano, Felix "Milwaukee Phil" Alderisio, Leonard and Marshall Caifano, Chuck Nicoletti, Fifi Buccieri, Albert "Obie" Frabotta, William Aloisio, Frank Caruso, Willie Daddano, Joe DiVarco, Rocco Potenza, Leonard Gianola, Vince Inserro and of course Sam Battaglia.

On **September 22, 1938** John Bazula 33 yrs. of 1248 N. Campbell Ave. and Lucille Sommerfield Budasi 18 yrs. of 622 Patterson St. were shot in the rear of a handbook at 3633 N. Halsted by Charles Lane and William Wright who were held for the killing. It is not known what the outcome of the case was **(solved).**

On **October 21, 1938** Bert Delaney AKA: Barney Fresco 59 yrs. of 2300 S. Michigan Ave. was shot by unknown gangsters at 35th St. and Ellis Ave.

On **November 24, 1938** Joseph "Red" Bolton 40 yrs. of 30 N. Menard Ave. was shot by unknown gangsters at 35 N. Menard Ave., he was a brother of State Representative John Bolton (killed in 1936) and owned a speakeasy at 1610 W. Polk St. were police Det. Joe Sullivan was killed in 1929. For a time he was an associate of the Capone gang until he and his brother tried to move in on gambling operations which cost both men their lives.

On **December 23, 1938** or **April 12, 1939** John Minoque 32 yrs. of 7145 S. Claremont Ave. was shot by unknown gangsters in front of 7125 S. Claremont Ave.

In **1939** Jack Neville was murdered by unknown gangsters. Neville was named in 1930 as one of the killers of Michael Healy, but it is not known if he was ever apprehended for that crime. In October of 1939 gang boss Danny Stanton was arrested as a suspect in this murder, but it is not known if he was ever charged **(Solved).**

In **January of 1939** Walter Kelly is murdered. Kelly an operator of one of the lucrative Southside numbers wheels demonstrated to other wheel operators that the Chicago OUTFIT was dead serious in taking over their operations. The idea was first brought forth by Sam Giancana AKA: Momo Salvatore, Mooney, or Gilormo Giangono and it raised his stature in the OUTFIT.

On **April 5, 1939** George Sanders was shot to death and buried in quicklime. He was a business agent for the Chicago Waiters Alliance and bumped heads with OUTFIT labor racketeer and Capone gunman Danny Stanton.

On **April 12, 1939** James Lawrence 40 yrs. of 1124 Wilson Ave. was shot by unknown gangsters as he guarded a truck he was riding on at Walton St. between Paulina St. and Marschfield Ave.

On **May 1, 1939** Matthew R. Hyland 30 yrs. of 920 W. 35th Pl. was shot by Thomas "Toby" Rowan in an alley near 51st St. and Racine Ave. Rowan was arrested, charged and convicted of the killing. He was sentenced to Life in Prison **(solved)**.

On **July 5, 1939** Louis Schiavone 43 yrs. of 1045 N. Mason Ave. was shot by unknown gangsters as he drove his auto at 95th and 44th Sts. in Oak Lawn, IL.. He was a longtime associate of Frank Nitti in bootlegging and was designated as the OUTFIT's man to be placed in Local 66 of the Elevator Operators and Starters Union. At the time of his murder he was driving when a car pulled alongside his and an occupant shot him with a shotgun. He had Union ledgers in his car when he was found dead.

On **October 9, 1939** Amerigo Bertolini 42 yrs. of 260 N. Hamlin Ave. was shotgunned by unknown gangsters at 45 S. Albany Ave.

On **October 31, 1939** Paul Peters AKA: Paul King 50 yrs. of 3505 N. Oak Park Ave. was shot by unknown gangsters near his home. It was reported that the victim was a member of the International Printing Pressman and Assistant's Union, labor unrest is a motive in this killing.

On **November 8, 1939** Edward J. O'Hare 46 yrs. of 221 Franklin Rd. Glencoe, IL. was shotgunned in his car at 2613 Ogden Ave. O'Hare, a millionaire Dog Track operator became an unwilling partner with the Chicago OUTFIT in their track in Cicero and others across the country. He knew their secrets and helped run their business. He later became a very effective informant for the government in putting Al Capone away, allegedly with a deal to obtain an appointment to the Naval Academy for his son Eddie "Butch" O'Hare who went on to become a war hero in WWII and had the busiest airport in the country named after him, Chicago's O'Hare Airport.

Approx. number of Chicago TOC related murders in the 1930s: 325
Approx. number of Chicago TOC related murder cases in the 1930s solved: 44
Approx. number of Chicago TOC related murders in the 1930s of Police Officers: 7

Chapter 4. The 1940s

By 1940 it was clear that Chicago TOC known as the OUTFIT had finally consolidated into one syndicate, (the remnants of the Torrio/Capone gang). In 1940 the CCC publicly fought the OUTFIT over its control of local bookie establishments and for its efforts to seize control of the bartenders union. In fact, OUTFIT leaders Murray "The Camel" Humphreys, his new financial guru Frederick Evans, Paul "The Waiter" Ricca and Louis "Little New York" Campagna were indicted for attempting to embezzle $350,000 from the same union. However, after some skillful witness tampering the men were acquitted and a co-defendant who cooperated with federal authorities was **murdered**.

Louis Campagna

In May of 1941 the motion picture shakedown fell apart when a studio executive was indicted for income tax evasion and spilled the beans, implicating the OUTFIT's front men George Browne and Willie Bioff AKA: William Morris Bioff, William Nelson. The two men cooperated to save themselves and facilitated the indictment of Frank Nitti, Paul Ricca, Francesco Sacco AKA: Fillipo, Johnny Rosselli, Charles Gioe, Louis Campagna, Nick Circella, Phil D'Andrea, Ralph Pierce, Frankie Diamond along with NY TOC members Costello, and Genovese in 1944. The two men were eventually murdered for their cooperation.

George Brown

In 1944 Frank Loesch the highly respected and dedicated former Operating Director of the Chicago Crime Commission died at ninety two. In his published obituary it was detailed his feelings that the assassination of Mayor Cermak was certainly manipulated by the Mob.

Frank Loesch

Critical Events of the 1940s:

On **January 5, 1940** Leon Cooke died after being shot on December 8, 1939. Leon Cooke a union official with the Scrap Iron and Junk Handlers Union 20467 in Chicago became embroiled in a dispute over control of the union. Jack Ruby was suspected in the killing, but it was the Union's President John Martin who actually shot Cooke. Soon after Red Dorfman, who had never been a member of the union or a waste handler, showed up at a union meeting, paid his dues, and on the same night became the new secretary-treasurer. However, Ruby would also become involved with gambling on the Westside again, until a confrontation with Lenny Patrick, which motivated him to leave Chicago for Dallas, Texas where his sister owned a restaurant. Years later while a TOC operative, Ruby a night club owner would become involved in gun running with Cuban exiles, narcotics trafficking with French Connection associates, an informant for local police and the FBI and an operative with the CIA. Reportedly, Ruby became a participant in the assassination of President John F. Kennedy in 1963 reportedly on behalf of TOC leaders who arranged it. Two weeks earlier Ruby would talk to Lenny Patrick and Irwin Weiner, both well placed Chicago OUTFIT members, by phone before the assassination of President John F. Kennedy and Ruby's killing of Lee Harvey Oswald.

Red Dorfman

On **March 3, 1940** Peter Fricano 42 yrs. of 1510 N. Mohawk St. was shot by unknown gangsters while seated at the kitchen table in his home. He was charged in a double murder in 1922, but the outcome of the case is not known.

On **April 1, 1940** Joseph M. Carville 48 yrs. of 1623 E. 69th St. was shot by unknown gangsters and found in an auto at 64th St. and Harvard Ave.

On **June 14, 1940** Michael McGovern 34 yrs. of 8205 S. Laflin St. and James McGlade 29 yrs. of 1713 W. 83rd St. were shot by unknown gangsters as they sat in a Buick sedan at 70 E. 69th St. McGovern was the brother of Mobster and Labor Racketeer Hugh "Stubby" McGovern who was killed in 1928. He was the driver of a car involved in an accident in 1935 that left a passenger Cassa Jean Reeder dead and a second passenger John Timothy "Sandy" O'Brien a known labor racketeer injured while he escaped the scene. The men were known muscle for Danny Stanton and associates of OUTFIT boss Gus Alex.

On **June 23, 1940** Jerry Siegel 27 yrs. of 3215 Grenshaw St. was shot by unknown gangsters in front of 5523 N. Kenmore Ave.

On **July 26, 1940** John McLeod 37 yrs. of 5117 S. Wells St. was shot by unknown gangsters at 95th St. and Western Ave. An associate by the name of James Ryan was also shot, but survived his injuries. Ryan had an extensive record and was sentenced to 14 yrs. in 1919 for murder and paroled in 1927. He was charged with killing John Rinella in 1932, the victim's girlfriend identified Ryan as one of the killers. While Ryan was put on trial, he was found not guilty in front of Judge Fardy in 1933.

On **August 16, 1940** William D. Schaaf 36 yrs. of Highland, In. was shot by unknown gangsters at 78th and Ashland Ave. He was a former Business Agent for the Painters Union. He was wanted for the murder of Elsie Henneman in 1933, but it is unknown if he was ever apprehended. The union he was involved with was under the control of gangster Danny Stanton. This murder was just one incident of violence associated with the Mob takeover. James Dungan was questioned and released in this killing.

On **August 19, 1940** Carroll D. Corcoran 35 yrs. of 2455 E. 72nd St. was shot by unknown gangsters while backing his auto at 745 S. Exchange Ave.

On **March 31, 1941** Marvin Olson 42 yrs. of 8221 S. Laflin St. was shot by unknown gangsters using a shotgun and handgun and striking him in the face and head while seated in his car at 1219 Burling St.

On **April 15, 1941** John F. Arena 43 yrs. of 3124 Broadway was shot by unknown gangsters while entering his car at Irving Park Rd. and Kenmore Ave. The assassin fled in a vehicle with two other men.

On **April 20, 1941** Cyril V. Ryan 41 yrs. of 5252 S. Aberdeen St. was shot in the head and chest by unknown gangsters in the living room of his home. It was reported that his death was the result of a gang feud over control of Southside gambling. He was previously employed by a race news service and was wounded a year earlier in an attack that left his associate John McLeod dead.

On **April 23, 1941** Anthony "Anton" Gorczak 33 yrs. of 4938 S. Hermitage Ave. was beaten to death at a tailor and cleaning shop at 1745 W. 63rd St. Reportedly he was in conflict with mobsters involved in the cleaners and dryers industry. Murray Humphreys reportedly sent David Goldblatt to beat the victim to death with a baseball bat. He was arrested and convicted of the crime and implicated Humphreys, who was never charged **(solved).**

On **April 25, 1941** Joseph Todd 56 yrs. of 1822 Jackson Blvd. was shot in the head five times by unknown gangsters as he walked in front of 1658 W. Monroe.

On **May 23, 1941** Pete "Petey" Clifford was shot to death on Jefferson Ave. in Miami Beach, FL. Petey was an entertainer and owned a piece of the Paddock Club in Miami Beach. He received an urgent call from a woman before his death asking him to meet her. It was later suspected that he was having an affair with Frank Nitti's wife Anna.

On **September 24, 1941** Joseph LaSasso 27 yrs. of 3258 W. Congress St. was shot in the head by unknown gangsters in front of 743 S. Kedzie Ave.

On **November 20, 1941** Samuel Rothaiser AKA: Roth 53 yrs. of 3200 Arthington St. was shot in the head by unknown gangsters in front of 904 S. Kedzie Ave.

On **December 3, 1941** William E. Friesenhahn 31 yrs. of 2724 S. Wells St. was shot by unknown gangsters while in his auto at 26th and State Sts.

On **July 18, 1942** Loretta Youngblood of 2227 Monroe St. and Arthur W. Wallace were both shot during a shootout between Wallace and Charles Youngblood the husband of victim Loretta Youngblood in their home. Both men were associated with the Painter's Union. The union the men were involved with was under the control of gangster Danny Stanton. These murders were just one incident of violence associated with the Mob takeover. It is unknown if Charles Youngblood was ever charged in this incident.

On **September 27, 1942** Salvatore Coriglione AKA: Solly 32 yrs. of 641 N. Damen Ave. was shot by unknown gangsters in a tavern at 2000 Erie St. He was reportedly a handbook employee who was shot down by two gunmen in front of 40 witnesses although no one was identified or charged.

On **October 22, 1942** Mrs. Paul V. Galvin and Edna Sibilski were shot to death in the Galvin home at 3038 Normandy Pl., Evanston, IL. The victims were employer and maid and were killed during a robbery of the home. In 1946 police recovered two guns used in this murder from a Bookie Bandit gang responsible for the death of two police officers and one of their associates, however the outcome is unknown.

On **October 20, 1942** John Ragucci 39 yrs. of 1649 Warren Blvd. was shot in the neck and body by unknown gangsters who fled in an auto from the rear of 907 S. California Ave.

On **November 16, 1942** Carlos M. Boscarino AKA: Cullybugs 18 yrs. of 248 W. Alexander St. was shot in the chest by unknown gangsters and found in the vacant lot at 320 W. Alexander St. Carmen DiGiacomo AKA: DiGiaco and Frank Piegari AKA: Biegari were questioned by the police, but not charged with the killing.

On **December 3, 1942** Charles Vinci of the "Violent Vinci's" 33 yrs. of 718 W. 25th Pl. was found shot to death in the Point Inn tavern at 2501 S. Halsted. Joe and Sam DiCaro were held in the killing and Mike Rancatore was wanted, but it is not known if the case was ever adjudicated. The Vinci brothers Charley (a deputy sheriff), Joe, Jim and Mike were minor political players which put them in close proximity to TOC. In 1925 brother Jimmy Vinci (killer of Union racketeer Mossie Enright) died in a Bridgeport duel with Joe Granata, brother of 1st ward political powerhouse Bill Granata, who would himself be murdered in 1948. Mike Vinci was killed in 1925 in a dispute over money at a gambling house **(solved)**.

On **December 25, 1942** Robert E. McLaughlin 42 yrs. of 704 S. Wesley Ave. was shot in the face by unknown gangsters and found at 731 N. Albany Ave. McLaughlin was the owner of a large cab company and resisted the OUTFIT's takeover of the business. Guiseppe Glielmi AKA: Joey Glimco was suspected in the killing, but never charged.

On **February 2, 1943** Estelle Carey 34 yrs. of 512 Addison St. was beaten and tortured before being set on fire by unknown gangsters. The victim was a vivacious gangster "moll" and girlfriend of OUTFIT member Nicolas Circelli aka: Nicky Dean, she was murdered in her apartment. Carey was a successful 26 girl in Circella's Rush Street club. Reportedly she was holding extortion money for Circella since his 1941 arrest. When Circella started to cooperate with authorities in New York, Carey was briefed by OUTFIT bosses and traveled to New York to urge him to say no more. This had little effect and put her in harm's way. During the investigation police learned that while her boyfriend was in jail for the Hollywood extortion case she continued to see several other men. On the day of her death she allowed her attackers entre' and she suffered a terrible beating, with most of it directed at her face, but it was the fire that killed her. After word of her death reached Circella his cooperation ceased and gangsters Dominic Nuccio, Ralph Pierce, Les "Killer" Kruse and Marshall Caifano were all questioned as suspects before being released **(Solved)**.

On **May 6, 1943** Daniel "Danny" Stanton 46 yrs. of 7558 Kingston Ave. and Louis Dorman 41 yrs. of 6103 Evans Ave. were shot as they sat in Harry's 6500 Club at 65th and May in Chicago. Stanton a Capone gunman, knew people were looking for him two weeks earlier in one of his haunts at 6100 S. Halsted when he was able to give them the slip. It was speculated that Nitti was keeping the killer alive. The men were killed by shotgun blasts coming through a back door of the tavern administered by unknown assailants. Police quickly focused on Martin "Sonny Boy" Quirk who Stanton tried to kill once, before he went to work with the renowned gunman. The next suspect was James J. "Red" Fawcett who at one time worked as a Stanton bodyguard and Samuel McPherson Hunt AKA: Golf Bag Hunt a friend of Fawcett's. In 1947 William Block a mob assassin was suspected in the killing after a shotgun he used in the shooting of James Ragen matched the one used in this case. The last on the list of suspects was labor racketeer Edward Piech, gambling may have provided a motive.

On **May 15, 1943** Walter J. Smith 28 yrs. of 343 Center St. Aurora, IL. was shot four times in the body by unknown gangsters while he changed a car tire in front of 3856 W. Chicago Ave. He was part of a robbery crew in 1940 that robbed the Chicago Tribune and wounded security officer Harry Walsh. He was arrested and cooperated in the investigation leading to the arrest and imprisonment of 3 of his conspirators all of whom went to jail while he received probation. Shortly after the murder the Chicago Crime Commission received a tip that named Gus Zapantis, Peanuts Panczko, Johnny Sorenson and Michael Wilkes as suspects in this case. The police held for questioning: Frank Spiteri, Harry Regner, Frank Fata and Vito Borselino who was held by military authorizes. Kenneth May AKA: Joseph Masters was later questioned in the case as was Emil and Edwin Grudecki. While a great deal of effort was put forth by the police it is unknown what the outcome of this case was.

On **June 7, 1943** Aldo Razzins 30 yrs. of 2253 W. 24th St. was shot twice in the head and found in his car at 545 N. Wabash Ave.

On **September 8, 1943** Martin J. Quirk AKA: Sonny Boy 39 yrs. of 6646 Stony Island Ave. was shot in the abdomen by unknown gangsters near 6618 Stony Island Ave. Quirk an outsider to OUTFIT gambling operations and a former employee of Danny Stanton, was desperate to be part of the action, wanting a take of Stanton's action and tried to force his way in. James Egan, Anthony DeLardo, John J. Williams, John Enright, James Forsythe, Ray Deskovich, J. DeJonckheere, Mike Doe and Robert Block were all indicted and tried in the killing, yet none were convicted. Bail bondsman Charley Cohen in 1948 informed the CCC that James "Red" Fawcett was the man who killed Quirk, but by that time Fawcett was also dead **(Solved)**.

On **October 27, 1943** John Pisano AKA: Giovani Ippolito 47 yrs. of 3000 Washington Blvd. was shot three times in the head by two different guns and found in front of 2515 W. Congress St. in his car. The Chicago Crime Commission received a tip regarding the murder allegedly from a woman who lived in the Ambassador Hotel. From this tip it was surmised that the killing may have involved illicit gambling operations as Pisano was in the mobbed up Juke Box business. This led police to interview the son-in-law of politician Botchy Connors, but the man was cleared. Police then arrested Frank Padula who stated he had entered into a business deal with the deceased and the victim reneged, however Padula was released **(Solved)**.

On **December 1, 1943** William Wytrykus 42 yrs. of 2050 Berwyn Ave. was shot by unknown gangsters in his radio store at 1180 Milwaukee Ave. Police speculated that the intended victim was Ralph Czernik an employee of Wytrykus who was a key witness in a $30,000 liquor highjacking. The police revealed a long term affair the married victim was having and eventually questioned the highjackers Czernik testified against, but released them without charging.

On **December 6, 1943** Thomas Oneglia AKA: Neglia 47 yrs. of 6118 N. Campbell Ave. was shot to death while sitting in a barber chair in the shop at 1608 N. Sedgwick. Two gunmen entered the shop while the victim was being shaved, fired several shots into him, threw their weapons at him before fleeing to a waiting auto. Throwing the weapons was a gesture of " Black Hand" extortionist although it was unlikely a Black Hand killing. It was speculated that several men were murdered who had ties to the Grande Cheese Company in Wisconsin, this victim was one of them. The others were Vincent Benvenento, Sam Gervase, James V. DeAngelo, Onofrio Vitale, Frank Diamond (Maritote), Marcus Lipsky, Nick DeJohn and Leroy Sommers. This Company was suspected of OUTFIT connections for years and dealt in some kind of black market, possibly narcotics. His exact position in this organization is unknown. Other victims mentioned were also part of the 42nd wards "little syndicate".   This victim was also a business partner of future northside Mob Boss Ross Priolo AKA: Prio. It was possible that he was informing on the OUTFIT to authorities. The Chicago Police Intelligence Unit reviewed this Cold Case from 1994 through 1997 to no avail.

In **December of 1943** Julius "Loving Putty" Annixter was killed. He was the gambling boss in the 24th ward.

DiVarco-Cerone-Prio at McClellan

On **December 17, 1943** Sidney Rossman AKA: Edward Ross, Eddie English 38 yrs. of 444 St. James Pl. was shot in the head by unknown gangsters in his room. Gangsters Paul Labriola and Maurice Barad were both questioned by police in the killing, but neither were charged. Both men would die by gangster bullets.

On **January 14, 1944** Ben Zuckerman AKA: Zookie the Bookie, Little Zookie 49 yrs. of 4046 Wilcox St. was gunned down outside his residence. Zookie was a long time killer, bootlegger, and gangster who took control of gambling in the 24th ward after the previous gambling overseer Julius "Loving Putty" Annixter was killed. However, Zookie rubbed the local political leader Arthur Elrod and gangster "Dago" Lawrence Mangano the wrong way when he began to sell watered down spirits out of a string of liquor stores he bought along Roosevelt Road. Renowned killer Lenny Patrick and his crew were suspected of the killings on orders of Jake Guzik, but were never charged. Patrick would emerge as the OUTFIT Boss in the Jewish quarter and followed their migration to the northside Rogers Park neighborhood.

On **March 2, 1944** Sam Gervase AKA: Geruase 38 yrs. of 3339 N. Pierce Ave. was found shot to death in his Refrigerator repair shop at 609 w. Division. He was an ex-convict and an OUTFIT associate. He was shot several times and 38 & 45 cal. handguns were found at his side. This too was an indication of "Black Hand" extortionist activities, but doubted. It was speculated that several men were murdered who had ties to the Grande Cheese Company in Wisconsin, this victim was one of them. This Company was suspected of OUTFIT connections for years and dealt in some kind of black market, possibly narcotics. His exact position in this organization is unknown. Other victims were also part of the 42nd wards "little syndicate".

On **March 11, 1944** James V. D'Angelo 42 yrs. of 2413 N. Spaulding Ave. was found after he was beaten to death and left in the trunk of his car at 1526 N. LaSalle. He too was an associate of OUTFIT figures and the Grande Cheese Company. It was speculated that several men were murdered who had ties to the Grande Cheese Company in Wisconsin, this victim was one of them.

In **April of 1944** J. Livert "St. Louis" Kelly was killed in a gun battle allegedly over policies. Kelly was a friend of Nitti and a partner of Danny Stanton in gambling and labor racketeering.

Joe Aiuppa

On **April 18, 1944** James D. Larkin AKA: Jens Larrisen was shot and found at 1337 S. Kildare Ave. He ran an OUTFIT hangout called "The Dome" at 7466 W. Irving Park Rd. Matt Capone Brother of Al was suspected of the killing in his Cicero bar "The Hall of Fame" at 4839 Ogden Ave. Matt fled for 11 months and returned when the case went cold. However, he was eventually indicted by a Coroner's Jury for the killing, but was not convicted. He lived until January of 1967 when he died of natural causes under an assumed name. Joey Aiuppa was also arrested in connection with this murder **(Solved)**.

On **April 22, 1944** Frankie Abatte AKA: Abate was killed by unknown gangsters stemming from suburban discourse. He was the Calumet City OUTFIT Boss and was found shot in the face and naked in a ditch near Hot Springs Arkansas. He was an associate of James V. D'Angelo who was an associate of the Little Syndicate on the near north side and was killed himself in March of 1944. It was speculated that due to tax problems he may have been talking to government agents. The victim was a race horse owner and took some of his horses to the mob getaway, but never returned.

On **July 4, 1944** Daniel Rooney 37 yrs. of 4856 Washington Blvd. was shot by unknown gangsters in front of a saloon at 3117 Fifth Ave. He was a labor racketeer and the younger brother of Bill Rooney. Bill was a labor boss who was killed in 1931 when Red Barker was a suspect, but never charged. Bill was also arrested for a murder in 1928 during the robbery of a soft drink parlor; the outcome of that case is unknown.

On **August 3, 1944** "Dago" Lawrence Mangano and his bodyguard Michael Pontillo were killed in an ambushed on their way home from the Paddock Club in Cicero, Illinois. Mangano was the Westside OUTFIT overseer and was driving with Pontillo and a woman in the car and was being followed by what he thought were the police that curbed his vehicle at Blue Island and Taylor streets. As he exited his car he was shot by a shotgun and 45 automatic. The car left and when Pontillo went to his aid the car returned and shot Pontillo. The 3 DOMS (Dominic "Bells" DiBella, Dominic "Nags" Brancato, and Dominic "Libby" Nuccio) were suspected of these murders at the time, but never charged.

Lenny Patrick at 95 arrest

On **December 11, 1944** Harry Krotish tried to take over the gambling and loan shark operations of Lenny Patrick and was shot to death by Patrick. At the time no one was charged with the killing, but Patrick would admit to this crime in his federal court testimony in 1992. The Chicago Police Intelligence Unit reviewed this case and others in 1994 and arrested Patrick for this killing and 2 others in 1995 after the Cook County States Attorney indicted him. He was released several months later and the charges dropped without explanation by the Cook County State's Attorneys Office **(Solved)**.

Lenny Patrick Arrest Report

On **December 28, 1944** Joseph J. Mundo 33 yrs. of 3245 Lexington St. was shot by unknown gangsters and found in his auto at 14th and Wolcott Sts. It appeared he was shot at close range by a passenger in his car who escaped the scene in a trailing car according to witnesses. He was the nephew of notorious State Rep. James Adduci and an associate of Dago Lawrence Mangano. He reportedly was a partner in a gas coupon scam that took a Detroit gang for over $30,000. His partner was Mike Dooman who was killed a couple of days later.

On **January 1, 1945** McKinley "Mike" Dooman 37 yrs. a northside racketeer was shot in a coffee shop at 938 W. Belmont. He was reportedly a partner in a gas coupon scam that took a Detroit gang for over $30,000. His partner was Joseph J. Mundo who was killed a couple of days before him. Peter Boulahanis was indicted and convicted in this killing, but the case was reversed on appeal and the State chose to drop the charges and not retry the case **(solved)**.

On **March 15, 1945** Wencel Urban was found murdered in a ditch in Kankakee County. Urban was a gangster from St. Louis and considered by some as the best safe cracker in the country. He was a member of a Robbery gang along with Willie Niemoth, Patrick Flaherty, Llewellyn Morgan, John "Jiggs" Sullivan, Michael Kosar (killed in 1947) and Thomas Leahy. In 1944 the gang pulled off a $2,000,000 safe deposit robbery from the E. H. Rumbold Real Estate Company at 624 W. 119th St. After his arrest Kosar and Leahy cooperated and testified against Niemoth and Flaherty resulting in life terms for both men. Reportedly the robbery funded the defense for gangster Danny McGeoghegan who had robbed a bank in 1930 and was acquitted around the time of this killing. Reportedly Urban was the brains of the crew and was taken for a ride because he demanded a larger portion of the proceeds than the others.

On **March 27, 1945** Andrew DiFiore 56 yrs. of 1125 Webster Ave. was shot in the head in the kitchen of his home by unknown gangsters. He was a successful building owner and businessman. His nephew and two in-laws were questioned in the slaying, but neither was charged.

On **March 29, 1945** Maurice Barad 39 yrs. was shot by unknown gangsters and dumped from a vehicle into a ditch near Irving Park Rd. and the Mohawk Country Club in Bensenville, IL. He was an associate of Dago Lawrence Mangano, was an ex-con and involved in cigarette highjackings and gas coupon scams. Federal investigators suspected he was killed for cooperating with authorities. In 1948 it was reported that the victim's wife named Paul Labriola and Martin Ochs as the killers. It is not known if they were ever questioned in the killing **(solved)**.

On **April 6, 1945** Onofrio Vitale AKA: Ono Fris 51 yrs. of 7 E. 157th St. Calumet, City was found after he was beaten to death and dumped into a sewer at Ohio and Union Aves. in Chicago. He was reported missing from Calumet City where he lived with his family. He was bound in a similar fashion as was murder victim James V. DeAngelo. They were last seen together and were both associates of the Grand Cheese Company. It was speculated that several men were murdered who had ties to the Grande Cheese Company in Wisconsin, this victim was one of them.

On **April 6, 1945** William Tarsch AKA: Galatz, Kalach 45 yrs. of 1855 S. Komensky Ave. was shot gunned in the passageway of 3710 W. Roosevelt Rd. after running afoul with the local gambling operation. He was an associate of Benny "Zookie the Bookie" Zuckerman and fired Lenny Patrick and his brother Meyer. In retaliation Patrick killed him. No one was charged with this killing at the time, but Lenny Patrick would admit to this crime in federal court during his 1992 testimony. The Chicago Police Intelligence Unit reviewed this case in 1994 and arrested Patrick for three other killings in 1995 after the Cook County States Attorney indicted him. However, after being unable to find the file he was not charged on this case. Patrick was released several months later and the charges dropped without explanation by the Cook County State's Attorneys Office **(Solved)**.

On **May 25, 1945** James J. "Red" Fawcett 45 yrs. of 8041 South Shore Dr. was shot in the head by unknown gangsters in a tavern at 2468 E. 75th St. Red was a suspect in the Danny Stanton killing and a close friend of Samuel McPherson Hunt AKA: Golf Bag Hunt who was also suspected in the Stanton killing. However, in 1948 bail bondsman Charley Cohen informed the Chicago Crime Commission that Frank Quattrochi killed Fawcett, but by this time Quattrochi was dead.

On **July 13, 1945** Morris H. Margolis 30 yrs. of 4300 Marine Dr. was shot in the head by unknown gangsters and found in his auto in front of 1622 W. Ontario St. He was a longtime associate of Chicago mobsters and worked for the Snow Ice Company and Gold Seal Liquors. He was also involved in the black market. He was indicted with several Mob associates in 1941 for labor racketeering in the misappropriation of union funds belonging to the Retail Clerks International Protective Association.

On **July 21, 1945** Carl Carramusa 37 yrs. of 837 N. Lawndale Ave. was shot by unknown gangsters while in an auto in front of his home. His cousin Phillip Morreale an associate of the Chicago OUTFIT was a suspect, but never charged. It was later reported that he was a front man for a Kansas City Narcotics Syndicate and in 1942 he cooperated and testified before a federal grand jury leading to indictments of several Kansas City mobsters.

On **August 2, 1945** Mike Favia AKA: Little Mike was found dead in a field near Crystal Lake IL. The victim had been dead approximately two weeks and was clad only in shorts and socks. He was identified through dental work. His vehicle was found and contained 10,000 gasoline ration coupons, a black market business of organized crime during the war. He was arrested and booked on 7 charges 2/27/29 during the investigation of the St. Valentine's Day Massacre. He was never charged with the killings.

On **August 28, 1945** Joseph F. Randazzo 27 yrs. of 2826 S. Emerald Ave. was shot by unknown gangsters and found in an auto at Lexington and Loomis Sts. The Mercury auto belonged to June E. Giacolo of 3841 W. Division St., but the case went unsolved. The victim was a known Thief, highjacker and black marketer. In 1943 he was indicted with several other hoodlums for highjacking a truck carrying alcohol. He eventually cooperated and testified against his co-defendants for a light sentence. Police theorize that as a motive in his death.

On **September 2, 1945** Detective George H. Helstern 50 yrs. of 2312 Devon Ave. and his partner Detective Charles A. Brady 34 yrs. were shot and killed on the south east corner of Clark St. and Lunt Ave. by a gangster named Cecil "Red" Smith, 45 yrs. of 105 Eugene St. The detectives attempted to question Smith, Tiny Mazzanars and a third man named Frank Nitti (unrelated to the gang chief) as they appeared to be casing a drug store when Smith opened fire on the detectives. An investigation led police to identify the killers. Smith was killed by Mazzanars and Renoto Lolli, both members of the "Summers Holdup and Murder Gang", before he could be captured **(solved)**.

On **September 28, 1945** Alex Chase was killed. The OUTFIT attempted to take over his local gambling operations in Hammond, Indiana. When he resisted he was murdered, Teetz Battaglia was questioned, but never charged for lack of evidence.

On **November 30, 1945** Cecil "Red" Smith 45 yrs. of 105 Eugene St. was shot in the head by Renoto J. Lolli while riding in a car driven by Laurence Mazzanar and accompanied by Christ Perres on Rose St. near Irving Park Rd. The men were all associated gangsters and planned the killing after Smith murdered two Police Detectives months earlier. They then buried Smith's body near Kinsington and Eastwood Sts. in Schiller Park IL. Mazzanar and Lolli were arrested and held to a grand jury while Perres was killed by Sgt. Frank Pape while the officer arrested Mazzanar, both Lolli and Mazzanar pled guilty and received long prison sentences for this murder **(solved)**.

On **December 8, 1945** John Kowalski AKA: Polack John, Little Johnny Polish, John Gerven 31 yrs. of 2326 W. Grand Ave. was shotgunned by two unknown gangsters in a tavern at 1801 W. Huron St. The victim was working on a Juke Box when he was killed. Reportedly he was a central figure in the Juke Box racket. He was also said to be an associate of gangster "Baby Face" Nelson. At the time the industry was quit mobbed up through the Coin Machine Acceptance Corporation, the Associated Phonograph Owners Inc. and the Illinois Phonograph Owners Inc. Labor racketeers also had a hand in the corruption through the electrical workers union. Two of the main competitors were the Wurlitzer Company and the Seeburg Company. Other distributors vied for territories around the city, often encroaching on each other and leading to violence as in this case.

On **January 5, 1946** Frank Quatrocchi AKA: Torpedo, Quirk, Marshall 41 yrs. of 1249 W. Ohio St. was shot in the head by unknown gangsters in front of a restaurant at 34 S. Clark St. The victim was a known mob torpedo for the Moran gang and associated with Nick DeJohn, Potato's Kaufman and Smokes Aloisio. At the time of his death he was sought for the shooting of Vincent Benevento. Prolific gangster Marshall Caifano, gambler Izzy Lazarus, John Cairfello and Frank Yario (the secret owner of the restaurant were the murder occurred) were all questioned in the killing, but none charged. At the time police sought Paul Labriola, Martin "The Ox" Ochs and Frank Santore for questioning. In 1948 bail bondsman Charley Cohen confirmed to the Chicago Crime Commission that Caifano was in fact the killer, but he was not charged.

On **January 10, 1946** Sam W. LaMargo 35 yrs. of 1206 W. Taylor St. was shot in the head six times by Victor Sufaro who sat in an auto with the victim in front of 853 Wolfram St. Police speculated that this killing involved gambling activities and the outcome of the investigation is unknown.

On **January 21, 1946** Frank Covelli 39 yrs. of 1310 Jackson Blvd. was shot by unknown gangsters who sat with him in an auto in front of 4120 W. Van Buren St. Reportedly the victim was a handbook and was killed in the midst of a police crackdown on gambling.

On **April 10, 1946** Louis J. Laino AKA: Tiny 33 yrs. of 4649 W. Lexington St. was shot by unknown gangsters and found in his auto at 4701 W. 5th Ave. Subsequent to the police investigation Sam Battaglia, Marshall Caifano, Patsy Clementi, Dominic and Michael Messina and Joseph DeStefano were all wanted for questioning in the killing. It is not known if they were ever detained in this case.

Marshall Caifano

On **April 18, 1946** Harry Richmond AKA: Red 38 yrs. of 511 Independence Blvd. was shotgunned by unknown gangsters in front of 509 Independence Blvd. The victim was reportedly a restaurant owner, member of the so called "Summers Holdup and Murder Gang" and the operator of several handbooks in the Madison and Paulina Sts. area with gangster Walter McComb. He was also a former member of the infamous "42" gang. It was speculated at the time that he may have provided police with information as to the location of another gang member Renoto Lolli or that he changed his wire service away from the service controlled by the Capone gang which could provide motive for the killing.

On **July 17, 1946** William Quinn 40 yrs. of 3315 W. Madison St. was killed in front of his home. He was involved in the Juke Box Racket and replaced John Kowalski when he was killed in December of 1945, working for Capone gangster Tough Tony Capezio. Albert Spagnola was arrested for the killing, but said it was an accident that occurred when he tried to rob the victim and was eventually acquitted **(solved)**.

Tony Capezio

On **August 14, 1946** James M. Ragen Sr. 66 yrs. of 107 S. Seeley Ave. succumbed to mercury poisoning after being shot by gangsters. He was the General Manager and part owner of Continental Press at 431 S. Dearborn, part of the General News empire. They produced a Racing Form known as the Midwest News Service and the Continental Wire Service. Reportedly before his death, he was informed by OUTFIT emissary Congressman Daniel Serritella that members of the Chicago OUTFIT again wanted this enterprise and wanted him out of the business. The Chicago OUTFIT had established its own wire service known as Trans-American Publishing & News Service Inc. that was in direct competition with Continental. Many customers were threatened and forced to pay for both services during this feud. Ragen received numerous Death threats from Tony Accardo, Murray Humphreys and Jack Guzik and had been followed. This caused Ragen to hire retired police officers Walter Pelletier and Martin Walsh to provide bodyguard services for him. Attempting to protect himself, seven weeks before he was shot he gave a detailed statement to the Cook County State's Attorney regarding OUTFIT activity, mainly about political corruption. Murray Humphreys met with Regan afterword and informed him that his affidavit was about Nitti and he was dead, but Regan would not budge. On June 2, 1946 with his bodyguards tailing him James Regan was shot while in his car at the corner of 39th and State St. by men in a pickup truck. He survived the shooting but died of mercury poisoning while recuperating in Michael Reese Hospital under heavy police guard. In 1947 William Block a mob assassin was suspected in the killing after a shotgun he used in the shooting was recovered and matched the gun used in several mob killings including this one. A least one witness was located (George Buckley) and eventually Lenny Patrick, Davie Yaras and William Block were identified and indicted in the case in March of 1947. They were later released and the arresting officers were suspended for allegedly accepting reward money. This lead to investigating officer Lieutenant Bill Drury to be fired and he too was killed the day before he was to testify in front of the Kefauver Commission about OUTFIT activities in Chicago. The Chicago Police Intelligence Unit reviewed this case in 1995 after arresting Lenny Patrick on three other murders, but prosecutors and federal authorities were unwilling to pursue it **(Solved)**.

On **September 21, 1946** Vincent Benvenento AKA: The Don 45 yrs. of 1057 Grand Ave was shotgunned near Lake Zurich, IL. by two unknown gangsters. He was asleep in a cabin when the gunman broke through the door. He was a former bookmaker in Chicago with his nephew Nick DeJohn (killed in 1947) and Dominick Nuccio. He was a leader of the Unione Siciliana a position coveted by Tony Accardo. He was the leader of the 42nd ward's (Little Sicily) Little Syndicate. It was speculated that several men were murdered who had ties to the Grande Cheese Company in Wisconsin, this victim was one of them. Prior to his death he was involved with the near northside lush racket district that was taken over by the 3 Doms after this killing. The Chicago Police Intelligence Unit reviewed this case in 1994 through 1997 to no avail.

In **October of 1946** Leahm Kelly was shot to death as he exited his car at his home in Joliet, IL. He was deeply involved in the Juke Box racket and was known as the Will County Juke Box King and owned Kelly's Juke Box Co. in Cicero, IL. It was speculated by police at the time that Kelly was expanding his business into territory coveted by the OUTFIT's slot machine boss Eddie Vogel and paid with his life.

In **1947** John Dolf was killed by unknown gangsters. Jack Cerone was arrested for the killing, but later released for a lack of evidence.

On **February 14, 1947** John E. Golding 47 yrs. of 619 S. Lombard Ave. was shot by unknown gangsters as he sat in his auto in front of 31 S. Halsted. The victim was a slot machine owner and hijacker. Police speculate that he was stealing slot machines from Chicago under the control of Dutch Vogel slot king of the OUTFIT and would place them in LaSalle and Peru counties. William Block a prolific mob assassin was suspected in the killing after a gun he used in the shooting of James Ragen matched the one used in this case. The outcome of the investigation is unknown.

On **March 17, 1947** James Crowley and his wife Elizabeth L. "Betty" Crowley were returning home from a St. Patrick's Day party downtown when their car was hit with a hail of shotgun pellets. James was not hit, but when he looked, his wife who was driving was slumped over the wheel dead. Crowley was the boss of the Bartenders Union and fought hard to try and keep the OUTFIT out of his union. It cost him his wife.

On **May 9, 1947** Nicolas "Mike" DeJohn AKA: Vincent Rossi 37 yrs. of Santa Rosa, CA. was strangled by unknown gangsters and found in the trunk of his expensive convertible in San Francisco, CA. He was a former bar owner and bookmaker with his uncle Vincent "The Don" Benevento and Dominick Nuccio. The Chicago Crime Commission also considered him as the gambling boss and political fixer in the 42nd ward (Little Sicily). Additional information from the Commission considered him as a representative of political powerhouse Senator William "Botchie" Connors and an associate of former City Sealer and political figure Daniel A. Serritella. He left Chicago after a dispute with other gangsters over gambling or narcotics according to narcotics investigators. It appeared he intended on staying in California as he purchased a night club there. It was speculated that several men were murdered who had ties to the Grande Cheese Company in Wisconsin, this victim was one of them. His exact position in this organization is unknown. Lenny Patrick was suspected in this murder, but local police never shared this with California authorities. Leonard Calamia and the 3 Doms (Dominic "Bells" DiBella, Dominic "Nags" Brancato, Dominic "Libby" Nuccio) were also suspected in this killing. The Chicago Police Intelligence Unit reviewed this case in 1994 through 1997 to no avail.

In **1947** James Barcella was murdered by unknown gangsters. He was an underling to the 3 Doms (Dominic "Bells" DiBella, Dominic "Nags" Brancato, Dominic "Libby" Nuccio) in running the near northside lush racket district.

On **June 20, 1947** Ben "Bugsy" Siegel of New York City was shot by unknown gangsters as he sat in the living room of his girlfriend Virginia Hill's Hollywood home. It was always speculated that he was killed for mishandling Mob money in the construction of the Flamingo Casino is Las Vegas, Nevada. He was also found to be the local representative of the Trans-American Wire Service run by the Chicago OUTFIT. What was later reported was that he was stealing money from the Mob and the contract was issued to the Chicago OUTFIT at the Commission meeting of National Mob leaders at the Havana Mafia Conference on December 25, 1946. This murder contract was specifically issued to Charles and Rocco Fischetti first cousins of Al Capone and ranking members of the Chicago OUTFIT who attended the conference with Tony Accardo and Frank Sinatra. The Fischetti's also provided a $300,000 loan for the construction of the Flamingo.

Reportedly the Chicago bosses recruited the Los Angeles Mob run by Jack Dragna who provided the shooter who used a carbine rifle in the attack. Other reports indicated that Lenny Patrick, Dave Yaras and William Block were sent to California by Murray Humphreys to kill Seigel although the case remains unsolved.

On **August 2, 1947** Vince Bozic was shot and killed by Gus Alex. He lived long enough to provide the police with his killer's name, but the case remains unsolved.

On **September 18, 1947** Catherine "Tina" Jacobs was found murdered in a ditch in Southwest Michigan. The victim worked as a dice girl in a night club which exposed her to many gangsters. Dominic Nuccio was one of the gangsters who was questioned in the slaying, but not charged.

On **November 12, 1947** Michael Kosar 43 yrs. of 1007 N. Central Park Ave. was shotgunned in the kitchen of his home by unknown gangsters and his wife was wounded in the attack. He was a member of a robbery gang along with Willie Niemoth (a former Capone gangster), Patrick Flaherty, Llewellyn Morgan, John "Jiggs" Sullivan, Wencel Urban and Thomas Leahy. In 1944 the gang pulled off a $2,000,000 safe deposit robbery from the E. H. Rumbold Real Estate Company at 624 W. 119th St. After his arrest the victim and Leahy cooperated and testified against Niemoth and Flaherty resulting in life terms for both men. There was an attempt on his life in September of 1947, but he escaped injury. Police seemed secure in the fact that this killing was in retaliation for his testimony and were seeking the other members of the gang for questioning. It was reported that Urban had been killed in 1945 and Sullivan had never been apprehended. Reportedly the robbery funded the defense for gangster Danny McGeoghegan who had robbed a bank in 1930 and was acquitted in March of 1945.

On **May 13, 1948** Joseph Washulski 38 yrs. of 2225 W. Cortez St. was shot in the head by unknown gangsters in the alley at 2239 W. Cortez St.

On **May 22, 1948** George Statkatos AKA: Bulldog, Barboot King 27 yrs. of 623 S. Halsted St. was shot in the head by unknown gangsters and found in his auto at Troy and Ohio Sts. He was known to run a dice game known as barbudi. He probably died for not cutting the OUTFIT in on his action.

On **May 24, 1948** Leo "Little Sneeze" Friedman 34 yrs. of 2958 W. Jackson Blvd. was shot by unknown gangsters on the northeast corner of Sacramento Ave. and Jackson Blvd. He was an associate of Statkatos and was suspected of being part of a crew that had robbed OUTFIT gambling joints in Elmwood Park, IL. He also worked as an enforcer for Lenny Patrick.

On **June 9, 1948** Norton Polsky 27 yrs. of 1865 S. Springfield Ave. was shot in the head by unknown gangsters in the vicinity of 3849 W. 19th St. He was an associate of Statkatos and Friedman and was suspected of being part of a crew that had robbed OUTFIT gambling joints in Elmwood Park, IL. In the 1940s Westside gambling impresario Lenny Patrick tried to expand his operations to the northside area of Broadway Ave. between Belmont and Diversey Sts. The problem was this area was already controlled by Capone cousin Rocco Fischetti who probably had Patrick enforcers Friedman and Polsky killed during the dispute. It was reported that the dispute was arbitrated by the OUTFIT Boss Tony Accardo without any further bloodshed.

On **July 10, 1948** Doward Falcoln was gunned down by two gunmen in the doorway of his apartment at 1837 N. Lincoln Ave. Falcoln was the head busboy at the Pump Room of the Ambassador East Hotel near Rush Street and a rapist. His biggest mistake was attempting to rape the 35 year old wife of mobster Dominic Nuccio in Lincoln Park while walking her dog near the Nuccio home. The 3 Doms (Dominic "Bells" DiBella, Dominic "Nags" Brancato, Dominic "Libby" Nuccio) were questioned in the slaying, but never charged.

On **July 28, 1948** Nathan Gumbin 55 yrs. of 1356 Madison was shotgunned in the head by unknown gangsters while in his auto at 39th and Wallace Sts. At the time mobster Ben "Foggy" Fillichio was questioned by police regarding this killing, but never charged. In May of 1954 intelligence was developed that indicated that Sam Battaglia and Marshall Caifano were responsible for this murder. It is not known if police ever acted on the information.

On **August 31, 1948** Phillip Spagnola of 1405 S. 51st Ave. Cicero, IL. was strangled by unknown gangsters and found in an alley in the rear of 1533 Flournoy St. His brother Albert was arrested in 1946 for the murder of William Quinn over the Juke Box racket and apparently the victim was killed in a case of mistaken identity. Gang killer James Barsella was a suspect in the killing and was killed himself the next day.

On **September 1, 1948** James Barsella AKA: Jungle Bells 33 yrs. of 849 N. Avers St. was shot in the head by unknown gangsters and found in his new auto in front of 5701 S. Kilbourn Ave. In 1946 the victim was arrested with mobster Paul Labriola and two others for attacking two Army veterans in a Wabash Ave. nightclub. After a court hearing they were questioned by narcotics officers regarding the 1946 murder of Carl Carramusa, then released. Over the years he had been questioned in several murders. Barsella and his compatriots Martin "The Ox" Ochs and Paul Labriola were in conflict with the old Capone Mob over the Southside numbers racket being run by Pete Tremont for Jake Guzik. Reportedly the victim was also involved in hijacking OUTFIT slot machines in McHenry County.

On **October 8, 1948** William Granata was hacked to death in the lobby of his apartment building at 188 W. Randolph. Granata an attorney, state legislator and candidate for circuit court clerk was a powerful figure in Westside politics. His family had long ties to the Chicago Mob. While dealing with representatives of the west bloc and their hoodlum sponsors it became dangerous when Granata took a stance toward reform.

On **October 28, 1948** Jack Veronsky 50 yrs. of 6 N. Hamlin Ave. was shot in the head by unknown gangsters and found in front of 4428 Wilcox St.

On **December 20, 1948** Anthony Pellegrino 33 yrs. of 3103 W. Lexington was shot in the head by unknown gangsters and found in the rear of 2416 W. Lexington St. He recently sold the Re-Fined Oil Products Company he owned at 1315 S. Oakley Blvd. The victim was the head of a narcotics gang that was convicted in 1943 of shipping heroin and cocaine from New York to Chicago. He was sentenced to 3 years for the crime and may have been killed because of his continued involvement in the drug business. He was involved in Democratic politics and worked for the city upon his release from prison in 1946.

On **January 7, 1949** Frank Hyman AKA: Al Thomas 50 yrs. of 177 N. Leamington Ave. was machine-gunned by unknown gangsters in front of his home.

On **October 10, 1949** Elmer Madsen AKA: Whitey was killed by unknown gangsters. He was an associate of Arthur "Fish" Johnson who was known to deal in stolen property. Charles Szelog was questioned in the killing and released only to be killed himself several weeks later.

On **November 6, 1949** Charles Szelog 29 yrs. of 3146 Monroe St. was shot by unknown gangsters and found in a garage at 4646 W. Polk St. He was identified after his death as a participant in a jewelry theft from a car at Monticello and Fullerton Aves. Police speculated at the time that he may have been killed over a dispute with gang members over proceeds or for talking too much. He was an associate of Peanuts Panczko, Martin Ochs, Bruno Tassione, John Andrews, Carl Fiorito and Walter Jedynak. He reportedly left his post as a lookout for the gang during a burglary which led to some of the men being arrested. Police were looking to question his associates regarding the killing.

On **December 9, 1949** Frank J. Christianson 44 yrs. of 1637 51st Ave., Cicero, IL. was murdered by unknown gangsters in front of his home. In 1948 an honest candidate was elected president of Cicero by the name of John Stoffel. He selected a police officer named Joe Horejs to close the gambling dens. For this the village board took away Stoffel's authority over the police and Horejs was fired, leading to Stoffel's resignation. He continued to fight corruption in the town and was assisted by former Cicero Township Assessor and Assistant State's Attorney Frank Christianson who was murdered for his efforts. No charges were ever placed in the killing.

On **December 22, 1949** Frank Orofino 23 yrs. of 5150 S. Kedzie Ave. was shot in the head by unknown gangsters at 92nd and Cork Ave. Palos, IL. The victim had worked for Aaron Goodman AKA: Gino Martin as a bartender in his tavern and the men partnered in a handbook. The gun used in the killing was found by children playing in Stickney, IL. Goodman and several people listed in the victims address book were questioned by the police, but no one was charged.

Approx. number of Chicago TOC related murders in the 1940s: 98

Approx. number of Chicago TOC related murder cases in the 1940s solved: 13

Approx. number of Chicago TOC related murders in the 1940s of Police Officers: 2

Chapter 5. The 1950s

In 1950 the Kefauver Commission held its first session in Miami, Florida and several weeks later they came to Chicago where they were assisted greatly by the Chicago Crime Commission whose investigators worked to locate hoodlums and serve subpoenas. On the day of the first session, the Attorney General of the United States declared that the Kefauver Commission had no reason to exist. Maybe that attitude was why the FBI had no interest in TOC enforcement up to this time. During the Commission's time in Chicago many hoods went into hiding. The committee disclosed political activity related to gambling. During their weeks here, the murder of two prospective witnesses, Lt. Bill Drury and OUTFIT Attorney Martin Bas put the city in turmoil. These hearings were credited with the democrats taking a beating in the November election. This lead to the firings of Capt. Dan "Tubbo" Gilbert and a second firing of Capt. Tom Harrison of the Chicago Ave. station, both were known by the press as "Millionaire Cops" for their wealth and tolerance to gambling operations. In July of 1950 Chicago Crime Commission, Operating Director Virgil Peterson spent two days in front of the Commission explaining Traditional Organized Crime in the United States and in Chicago specifically. At this session in the Nation's Capital he represented the American Municipal Association and provided a great deal of information to the Commission members. Mr. Peterson also explained the close association between Chicago and New York hoodlums in rackets such as Unions, Juke Boxes, Gambling and the National Horse Racing Wire Service just to name a few. Race Tracks in the Chicago area and Florida were depicted as bastions for Chicago hoodlums and OUTFIT investments in Hotels was also brought to the fore.

Mayor Kennelly & Sen. Estes Kefauver

While these commission hearings captured the headlines of the day, behind the scenes and far from Chicago, TOC entities from Chicago and across America were expanding their interests and power throughout the Caribbean. Places such as Havana, Cuba, Guatemala and the Dominican Republic became strongholds for American TOC through their gambling operations and narcotics trafficking. What this decade would bring about would be an unholy alliance between gangsters and American Intelligence Agencies. Before it was over, American TOC would be an important component in the Cold War and would use this status to help eliminate foreign leaders, an American President and plot against others in the name of Democracy. What we have learned from these practices is to never underestimate the cunning of TOC and their ability to manipulate federal agents, intelligence operatives and American Politicians at the highest levels.

Reportedly in the 1950's the Chicago OUTFIT controlled beef processing plants in Lake Zurich and elsewhere, in order to increase profits they introduced horsemeat to the public. While horsemeat was about a quarter of the cost of beef, these plants would blend it with the beef at 40 percent horse, 60 percent cow mixture until authorities caught onto it and stopped the practice in 1952. The ensuing investigation found that state inspectors were paid off by the OUTFIT to look the other way. The investigation resulted in several indictments and some convictions. While the news reports of the day put the blame on Sam Giancana AKA: Momo Salvatore, Mooney, or Gilormo Giangono only low level mobsters were held accountable.

Critical Events of the 1950's

On **January 18, 1950** Rosario Davi 52 yrs. of 14448 S. Marshfield Ave. Dixmoor, IL. was shot by unknown gangsters and found in a prairie at 167th St. near Halsted St. in Hazelcrest, IL. He operated a tavern where he lived in the rear. After his body was found his tavern was found abandon, no money or belongings were missing.

On **March 21, 1950** Edward Murphy was killed by unknown gangsters in Indiana. It was revealed that rival Lenny Patrick ordered the killing. Years later Lenny Patrick would admit to this in Federal testimony. The Chicago Police Intelligence Unit reviewed this case in 1994 through 1997 **(Solved)**.

On **April 5, 1950** Ernest D. Potts 64 yrs. of 3217 Washington St. was shot by unknown gangsters in front of his residence. He was a local precinct Captain, but was involved in gambling his whole life.

On **September 25, 1950** William Drury was shot to death as he backed into his garage at 1843 W. Addison. The victim was a former Police Lieutenant in Chicago and at one time ran the Anti-Organized Crime Unit. He arrested three suspects in the infamous James Ragen murder case (June, 1946) that apparently cost him his career when it was alleged that he beat OUTFIT suspects during the investigation and accepted a reward for his work. He was scheduled to appear (at the time of his murder) in front of the Kefauver Commission, a Congressional Commission looking into Organized Crime's infiltration into legitimate business. Some background on Drury questioned his integrity while others described him as a hard charger against the OUTFIT. Marshall Caifano was a suspect in this murder. Lenny Patrick emerged as the prime suspect in this killing, but was never tried. The Chicago Police Intelligence Unit reviewed this case in 1994 through 1997 and learned that suspect Patrick had admitted to this crime during his federal prison stay, but authorities chose not to pursue the case **(Solved)**.

Lt. William Drury

On **September 25, 1950** Marvin J. Bas 45 yrs. was killed near his home by unknown gangsters at 1540 Orchard St. He had been a Republican candidate for Circuit Court Clerk, an attorney for independent taxi companies and had just met with a jitney cab insurance czar about a proposed city ordinance on taxi fares before he was killed. Like Drury, he was scheduled to testify at the Kefauver Commission the next day to provide information about a corrupt police official running for Cook County Sheriff by the name of Dan "Tubbo" Gilbert when he was murdered. His talking apparently made someone mad. His killing was never solved.

In November of 1950 "Big Jim" Martin an operator of a black policy wheel in Chicago resisted the Mob takeover and was shot. He survived the shooting and fled Chicago. Jackie "The Lackey" Cerone was suspected in the shooting and later bragged about it on a federal wiretap blaming the victim's survival on bad ammunition.

On **April 19, 1951** Albert Isaacs 36 yrs. of 3838 West End Ave. was shot in the head by unknown gangsters and found in his auto at 2145 W. DeKalb St. Reportedly the victim owned the Parkway-Ritz Grill at 2740 N. Clark St. Police learned he was a heavy gambler and found a large amount of clothing in his car as if he was leaving town. He recently borrowed a large amount of money from a relative. His former wife, a stripper and a suitor of hers were questioned by police then released.

On **June 12, 1951** John Jankovsky 36 yrs. of 2219 N. Monitor St. was found shot and beaten to death along a road near Hinsdale, IL. He was slated to become a business agent for Local 705 of the Teamsters Union and was considered a victim of Labor violence with the OUTFIT.

On **June 18, 1951** Lenny "Fat Lenny" Caifano was killed during an attempt to kidnap Teddy Roe, the head of the black policy wheel on the south side. Roe was eventually killed by the Outfit in 1952. Lenny was the brother of Marshall Caifano an OUTFIT enforcer and future Las Vegas overseer.

Brancato-Trombino dead

On **August 6, 1951** Anthony Brancato and Anthony Trombino both in their 30s were found in their 1951 Oldsmobile at Ogden near Hollywood Blvd. in Los Angeles, CA. shot to death from behind. The victims started their criminal careers in Kansas City and came to LA in the 1940s where they were known associates of LA Mob Boss Mickey Cohen. Brancato was related to Cleveland crime syndicate underboss Frank Brancato and was the younger brother of LA mobster Norfia Brancato. The men proceeded to carry out their own crime wave amassing over 40 arrests some of which were unsanctioned by their Mob Bosses. The men stepped over the line when they robbed the sports book at the OUTFIT controlled Flamingo Casino in Las Vegas where manager Hy Goldbaum recognized Brancato who wore no mask. That was the last draw and Mob Boss Jack Dragna ordered Jimmy "The Weasel" Fratianno to set the men up and kill them. Fratianno was placed in the LA Mob through Chicago overseer Johnny Rosselli. Fratianno set up a meeting about a score and along with Charley "Bats" Battaglia shot the men from the rear seat. They shooters were questioned and released and the case went unsolved until 1978 when Fratianno became a government witness **(solved).**

On **December 1, 1951** Samuel J. Rinella 49 yrs. of 7755 Chappell Ave. was shot by 2 unknown gangsters in front of his home as he was entering his Cadillac. The victim a well-known police character dating back to the Capone era had interests in the Palace Gardens on N. Clark St., the Paddock Club 2847 Broadway Ave., Curley's Tavern at 2147 S. Canal St., the Brown Derby Nightclub at 104 S. Wabash St., the Copacabana Nightclub 201 N. State St. and several handbooks over the years. At the time of his death questions arose regarding his associations with police officials and their regular presence at the Brown Derby. It was also revealed that retired Police Capt. Thomas J. Duffy had invested some $205,000 in the Copacabana. Rinella was described as a former beer and alcohol peddler for the Capone Mob. The victim's attorney revealed a pending 3 month tax investigation against the mobster and suggested that he was silenced to keep him from spilling Mob secrets. Reportedly Charles and Rocco Fischetti (Capone cousins) had given the hood financial backing at various times over the years. Several persons of interest were being sought for questioning to include: Joe Fusco, the Fischetti brothers, Dan Barone, George Cherones, Duffy and other misc. investors.

In **1952** Jems Larrisen was shot and killed. He was a racehorse trainer and reportedly Robert "Bobby" Ansoni appeared before a Grand Jury regarding the murder and was never charged. Ansoni was a Capone era gangster that ran the Town hotel in Cicero for Mob Boss Joey Aiuppa.

On **February 6, 1952** Charles Gross was gunned down at 1546 N. Kedzie. Three men armed with two shotguns fired seven rounds from a vehicle striking him in the right side of his body. Gross was a business man and owner of Gross Beverage Company. He was very active politically and was slated to run for Republican Committeeman in the 31st ward. His opponent was James Mesi an OUTFIT connected candidate from the Westside. Mesi's brother Sam was a suspect in the murder and the 1934 murder of Joseph Adduci. Threats against Gross to back out of the political race were recorded and came from the lips of Lenny Patrick himself. Eco James Coli a Mob labor racketeer and reportedly a member of an OUTFIT hit squad was a suspect in a previous robbery connected to Gross and the murder itself. Prolific OUTFIT killer Chuckie Nicoletti was questioned when the car he used fit a description provided to police of the vehicle the shooters escaped in. At one time Smokes Aloiso was questioned in the killing. Tough Tony Capezio was also considered a suspect in the case. A Minor hoodlum by the name of Michael Joyce was arrested during the investigation, but not charged with the killing. Joyce would be found in a burning car at 819 N. Harding after being shot in the head nine years later. At a later time Lenny Patrick became a suspect, but was never charged. The Chicago Police Intelligence Unit reviewed this in 1994 through 1997 to no avail.

Nicoletti and Alderisio

On **May 5, 1952** David Zatz 39 yrs. of 5060 Sheridan Rd. was shot and found in the trunk of his Oldsmobile parked at 2743 Orchard St. The victim was a bookmaker in a cigar store at 160 N. LaSalle St. He was a rival bookmaker to Lenny Patrick and met with Patrick at the Park Row Restaurant at Roosevelt and Keeler Aves. He was then shot by Patrick's associate Davie Yaras on Patrick's orders and put in the car. Patrick would admit to this crime in federal court in 1992. The Chicago Police Intelligence Unit reviewed this case in 1994. Patrick was arrested for this killing after he was indicted by the Cook County State's Attorney Office along with 2 other murders in 1995. He was released several months later and the charges dropped without explanation by the Cook County State's Attorneys Office **(Solved)**.

On **July 2, 1952** Robert Paglia AKA: Robert Page 26 yrs. of 1738 N. Natoma Ave. was murdered by unknown gangsters and found along Bateman Rd. near Route 62, in Algonquin, IL. He was under indictment for hijacking telephone company trucks. The victim was reportedly with three of his co-defendants when he was taken for a ride and killed. One of the men Ernest Rocco Infelise was arrested for lying during the inquest and James "Turk" Turello was picked up by police in Morton Grove for questioning as was Joseph Rossi and William Case all members of the gang. All the men were then released.

On **August 4, 1952** Teddy Roe, the Black Policy King was ambushed and killed while walking on south Michigan Ave. This was in retaliation for the "Fat" Lenny Caifano killing during an attempted kidnapping of Roe in 1951. At this point the OUTFIT secured a total takeover of the black policy operation on the Southside. Sam Battaglia was later identified as a possible suspect in the killing, but it is not known if he was ever detained.

In **1953** Bobby Greenlease was kidnapped and murdered; he was the son of a prominent Kansas City auto dealer. Carl Austin and Bonnie Brown were arrested and police recovered about half of the $600,000 ransom. The results of the prosecution are unknown. Several Chicago area hoodlums were murdered and were suspected by police of involvement with the crime. Other ransom funds were recovered all over the United States, mostly at race tracks.

On **January 4, 1953** Milton Glickman a rival bookmaker to Lenny Patrick was killed on orders of the Westside gambling Boss and prolific hitman. Patrick would admit to this crime in federal court in 1992. The Chicago Police Intelligence Unit reviewed this case in 1994. Patrick was arrested after his indictment for this killing and he was also charged with 2 others in 1995. He was released several months later and the charges dropped without explanation by the Cook County State's Attorneys Office **(Solved)**.

On **June 11, 1953** Clem Graver of 976 W. 18th St. was a State Representative and 21st Ward Committeeman. He was also a candidate for U.S. Representative of the 5th District although he was ordered to get out of the race by Sam Giancana AKA: Momo Salvatore, Mooney, or Gilormo Giangono who wanted someone else in that seat, to which Graver refused. Giancana had also given Graver money to get someone out of prison which he could not do. Finally, Momo had him kidnapped from his garage. He was never seen again and rumor has it, his body was deposited under the new underground garage being built at Grant Park. Intelligence at the time indicates that Sam Battaglia, Gus Alex and Frank Sortino were assigned to carry out this crime. On November 24, 1953 members of the Chicago Police Intelligence unit known then as Scotland Yard raided Celano's Tailor shop at 53 W. Jackson and took Jake Guzik and Gus Alex into custody interrogating the men in the Graver disappearance. They were released when their attorneys intervened. It is not known if the other suspects were ever questioned in the case. Graver's brother-in-law Harry Hochstein AKA: Weisman was also suspected of complicity in the murder of Mayor Anton Cermak. In 1955 after the election of Richard J. Daley as Mayor of Chicago, the Scotland Yard unit was disbanded.

In **April of 1953** Louis Strauss AKA: Russian Louie was strangled to death in California. He attempted to blackmail Las Vegas developer Benny Binion. Binion turned to a local Mob Boss Jack Dragna who employed several mobsters to do the job including OUTFIT members Marshall Caifano, Albert "Obie" Frabotta and

Felix "Milwaukee Phil" Alderisio although none of the men were ever charged **(Solved)**.

On **June 15, 1953** Patrolman Anthony Cannata was fatally injured in a tragic vehicle accident at Chicago Ave. and Noble St. while pursuing a vehicle that matched the description of the car used in the kidnapping of State Rep. Clem Graver. Graver was presumed dead on the orders of Sam Giancana AKA: Momo Salvatore, Mooney, or Gilormo Giangono and both cases remain unsolved.

On **October 4, 1953** OUTFIT Underboss Anthony Ragucci was shot and dumped into a sewer on 35th Street. He had begun his career under Capone, but recently developed tax problems and was suspected of talking to federal authorities. His brother was only able to identify him by his ring that bore the initials AR.

In **1954** John D. Trepani was murdered in Milwaukee, Wisconsin. Like many other Mob killings the services of OUTFIT killer Felix "Milwaukee Phil" Alderisio were employed. As his moniker indicates, he was originally from the dairy state.

On **March 15, 1954** Angelo Paul "Needle Nose" Labriola 37 yrs. of 1226 S. Austin, Cicero, IL. and James Weinberg 53 yrs. of 4434 N. Dover St. were doped, strangled and found in the truck of a car parked in a vacant lot at 2013 Lawler Ave. The men formed the Cook County Licensed Beverage Association with offices at 2452 Harlem Ave. Elmwood Park, IL. Reportedly the organization enlisted 3,500 saloons and was viewed by police as a shakedown operation. The men's activities allegedly angered OUTFIT leadership and police sought the men who met with the victims in their offices just before their disappearance and others associated with the organization. They were: Gerald Covelli, Stanley Boryca, Sam Mesi, Walter Kawalski, William Pisano, Frank Laino, Joseph Nicoletti, Johnny DiBiase, Tony Capezio, Cowboy Mirro, Hot Dog Lisciandrello and Joseph Sorences (victims found in his car). It was also speculated the men were killed for possibly being informants against the OUTFIT, threatening to kill restaurant association lawyer Abraham Teitelbaum, robberies of handbooks, involvement in the horse meat scandal and being part of a drug ring. Sam Mesi was questioned in the murders as he was seen speaking with the men just hours before they were killed. In 1970 gangster Chuckie Cremaldi admitted involvement in the killings. It is not known if any of these men were ever brought to justice for this murder **(Solved)**.

On **April 10, 1954** James Pape 37 yrs. of 1612 W. Roosevelt Rd. and Anthony Pape 40 yrs. of 1277 W. Cabrini Pl. were both shot in the head by unknown gangsters while in an auto at the corner of Flournoy and Lawndale Ave. The brothers were gunned down over OUTFIT violence in labor unions or their involvement in narcotics trafficking that brought heat on Tony Accardo. However, it was reported that James was not involved in the narcotics racket like his brother. It was also reported that mobster Albert "Obbie" Frabotta and 3 black narcotics dealers were questioned in this killing and then released. This was one of several killings related to the indictment of a drug gang that was precipitated by a federal agent infiltrating the gang and other agents buying drugs from the members.

On **May 14, 1954** Frank "Shorty" Caduto 46 yrs. of 3056 W. Jackson Blvd. was shot in the head by unknown gangsters in front of 1919 W. Cullerton St. He was a Mob drug dealer and caught in the middle of Labor violence. This killing and that of the Pape brothers along with Labriola and Weinberg were reportedly stemming from the release of Paul "The Waiter" Ricca and his displeasure of Accardo's leadership while he was incarcerated. Five of the remaining members of this drug gang feared for their lives and two eventually disappeared, they were Joe Iucullo and Tony Sperna.

On **August 18, 1954** Charles "Cherry Nose" Gioe was shot to death after entering his car. Cherry Nose was former OUTFIT powerhouse and one of several mobsters imprisoned in the Hollywood extortion case and one of the last to be paroled. He anticipated being rewarded for his service when he was released and apparently he was wrong. Gioe had been trying to work his way back into the unions and was the subject of an immigration investigation which made him susceptible to informing on the OUTFIT. Guiseppe Glielmi AKA: Joey Glimco and Claude Maddox and were both suspected in the killing, but never charged.

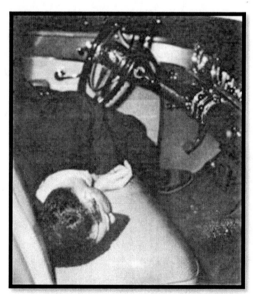

"Cherry Nose" Gioe dead

On **August 21, 1954** Frank Maritote AKA: Frankie Diamond was killed by machine gun and pistol fire while opening his garage to park his car at his home at 710 S. Keeler in Chicago. He was one of the Chicago OUTFIT members indicted in the Hollywood Extortion case in March of 1943. He was one of the last to be paroled. Maritote anticipated being rewarded for his service when he was released and apparently he was wrong. Diamond like other old timers were attempting to get back in the game after prison time. He began bullying people and had become the subject of an Immigration investigation which made him a threat to the new OUTFIT of Tony Accardo. Labor racketeer Joey Glimco, Milwaukee Phil Alderisio, Marshall Caifano, Albert Frabotta and Claude Maddox were all suspected in the killing, but never charged.

On **September 22, 1954** Arthur Ebenroth 35, was stabbed to death on the street at 3510 S. Central Ave. in Cicero. He was killed by Vincent J. Inserro AKA: "The Saint", Frank Relli. The men became involved is a dispute after Inserro falsely accused Ebenroth of whistling at his wife Mary 27 yrs. The victim was one of several men building a new home on that block when Inserro approached the victim and stabbed him after a brief argument. Inserro immediately left the area and was captured in 1956 by federal agents in Maywood, IL. Reportedly he was acquitted after the trial **(Solved).**

On **March 6, 1955** Emil R. Grudecki AKA: Grumpy 37 yrs. of 821 N. Ashland Ave. was shot by unknown gangsters while standing in front of a tavern at 2000 W. Erie St. He was a known burglar and a member of the notorious Panczko burglary gang. He was known to short his compatriots when he could get away with it. Several people were questioned by police and they included: Rocco Cassella (bar owner/witness), Mike Lucurcia (witness), Michael Joyce, Anthony Girignoni, and Nick Digoria, all of them were eventually released.

On **September 17, 1955** Michael DeStefano was killed by his brothers Sam and Mario and found in a car in Cicero, IL. This was due to a litany of drug problems and came under the orders of Sam Giancana AKA: Momo Salvatore, Mooney, or Gilormo Giangono after being alerted to problems by associates in a Cicero gambling joint.

Mario DeStefano

On **September 18, 1955** Dominick F. Christiano 37 yrs. of 8034 42ⁿᵈ St., Lyons, IL. was found shot and dumped from an auto at Route 66 and Willow Springs Rd. The victim's car was located in McCook, IL. and blood stains indicated the victim was shot in his car. He owned a restaurant at 3941 Roosevelt Rd. with George Wilson. The victim was under indictment for shooting Wilson in a dispute regarding the victim's wife.

On **November 4, 1955** Willie Bioff AKA: William Morris Bioff, William Nelson was murdered in front of his Phoenix home years after cooperating with federal authorities in the Hollywood Extortion Scandal that sent several top mobsters to prison in the early 1940s. Bioff changed his identity, but that did not work as he was known to local law enforcement and he was spotted in Las Vegas by OUTFIT overseer Marshall Ciafano who reported the sighting to Accardo back in Chicago. He was working at the Riviera for Gus Greenbaum. Accardo then ordered the killing and a dynamite bomb was placed under Bioff's car and he was blown to bits. The investigation led authorities to Clarence Michael Campbell a suspected bomber with connections to Chicago and St. Louis. He was suspected of renting a car at a nearby location two days before the killing. However, before authorities could locate him he was blown to bits while planting a bomb in Chicago on **May 25, 1956** and the investigation ended **(Solved)**.

Willie Bioff explosion

On **December 10, 1955** John Coletta was shot in the head by unknown gangsters and found in a blazing auto near Elgin, IL. Police speculated the victim was involved with the 1953 kidnapping/murder of Bobby Greenlease, the son of a prominent Kansas City auto dealer.

On **December 18, 1955** Alex Louis Greenberg was murdered as he and wife Pearl were leaving the Glass Dome Hickory Pit Restaurant on south Union Ave. and Twenty Eighth St., Greenberg for years had handled the personal finances and savings for Frank Nitti and his family. He was also the man that allegedly introduced Nitti to the Chicago Mob in the twenties. After Nitti committed suicide, Greenberg was slow in providing their fortune to the family of his former confidante, even after receiving direct orders from OUTFIT leadership. Greenberg was flush with cash owning or having an interest in the following: Manhattan Brewery, Prima-Bismarck Brewing Company, Hawthorne Hotel, Town Hotel, Seneca Hotel, Ace Distributing, Lawndale Enterprises and City Management Realty. He also could link Chicago OUTFIT monies to prominent people outside of Chicago, especially in California and Las Vegas. In the end it was revealed that Tony Accardo and Jackie Cerone were associated with the Foxhead Brewery of Wisconsin which may have developed into a competition with Greenberg's breweries in Chicago. Either way Tony Accardo, Jake Guzik, Joe Fusco, Ralph Pierce, Sam Giancana AKA: Momo Salvatore, Mooney, or Gilormo Giangono, Marshall Caifano, Gus Alex, Sam Battaglia, Albert "Obie" Frabotta and Felix "Milwaukee Phil" Alderisio were questioned or identified as suspects in the killing, but no one was ever charged with the killing.

Lou Greenburg murder scene

In **1956** Ralph Rizza 40 yrs. was found shot by unknown gangsters in his car on the Calumet expressway. Reportedly the killing was associated with the murder of John Coletta in 1955 and Police speculated the victim was involved with the 1953 kidnapping/murder of Bobby Greenlease, the son of a prominent Kansas City auto dealer.

On **March 27, 1956** Gustave Johnson AKA: August, Gus, Fred Jensen 69 yrs. of 7534 N. Octavia Ave. was shot in the head by unknown gangsters at Birchwood and Oconto Ave. He was a retired carpenter and an excessive gambler. In the 1940s he began to shake down book makers by letter and threatening to inform authorizes if they did not pay. The investigation revealed that the victim was a former associate of Al Capone during prohibition and provided gambling tips to the Chicago Police, the Chicago Crime Commission and the State's Attorneys Office. Police attribute his death to these activities. Mob luminary Sam Giancana ran two gambling joints (the Forest and the Retreat) near the victim's home in the 6500 block of Milwaukee Ave.

On **June 8, 1956** Max Epstein 54, Lois Gates 28 and John Keller 49 were shotgunned to death in Mickey's Miracle Bar at 1114 W. Argyle St. in the Uptown neighborhood of Chicago. The killer was Lawrence "Crazy Larry" Neumann 28 yrs. the son of a wealthy family who wound gain notoriety in the 1970s as a member of Tony Spilotro's Hole in the Wall Gang in Las Vegas. Neumann came into the bar brandishing a shotgun a month after a dispute with the bar owner Mickey Epstein and his brother Max claiming he was short changed less than two dollars. As he entered the bar screaming he would kill everyone there he cornered Max behind the bar and shot him as he begged for his life. He then turned the gun on a Dice Girl named Lois Gates and killed a newspaper vendor named John Keller as he came through the front door. The police hunted him for 8 weeks and finally caught him in a neighborhood just west of Cook County Hospital where the police fittingly fired a shotgun at him as he fled. After Nuemann was convicted of the three murders he was sentenced to 125 years for each death and would not be eligible for parole for 40 years. However, his well-paid lawyers filed many appeals and in the end Nuemann was paroled after only 12 years and would go on to kill again **(solved).**

Larry Neumann center

On **July 13, 1956** Joseph John Restagno 38 yrs. of 3358 W. Jackson Blvd. was found murdered by drowning at the hands of unknown gangsters who weighed the victim down with 65 lbs. of metal and dumped him in the Calumet Sag Canal at 104th Ave. and Route 83 in Palos Township. He was identified by authorities as part of a stick up gang that robbed an OUTFIT Handbook in Cicero before the murder. He formerly resided at 2158 Harrison St. and was under indictment for a $300,000 hijacking. He may have been part of the kidnapping gang that snagged Tough Tony Capezio. The men were reportedly fingered by Chuckie Nicoletti before the killings. Police also speculated the victim was involved with the 1953 kidnapping/murder of Bobby Greenlease, the son of a prominent Kansas City auto dealer. The case remains unsolved.

On **July 15, 1956** Peter Salanardi AKA: William Payone 44 yrs. of 126 S. Central Ave. was found murdered in a car at 5212 Adams St. The car belonged to murder victim Joe Restagno killed July 13th. He was identified by authorities as part of a stick up gang that robbed an OUTFIT Handbook in Cicero before the murder. Police learned that he was a hood from New York and his bullet riddled body had over $3,000 hidden in his socks. He was found in an auto northeast of Carpentersville, IL. He may have been part of the kidnapping gang that snagged Tough Tony Capezio. The men were reportedly fingered by Chuckie Nicoletti before the killings. Police also speculated the victim was involved with the 1953 kidnapping/murder of Bobby Greenlease, the son of a prominent Kansas City auto dealer. The case remains unsolved.

On **July 22, 1956** Thomas Kaskas 36 yrs. of 3836 W. Adams St. was shot in the head by unknown gangsters behind 1514 S. Keeler Ave. He was beaten, stabbed and shot behind his right ear. He was part of a robbery crew that had members killed in two different shootouts with the men assigned to robbery details led by Lt. Frank Pape. He may have been part of the kidnapping gang that snagged Tough Tony Capezio. The men were reportedly fingered by Chuckie Nicoletti before the killings. The case remains unsolved.

On **July 25, 1956** Carmen Gallo Jr. 26 yrs. of 3230 Lexington St. was found murdered on Naperville Road just west of Route 66. The victim had been bound with tape and he was shot in the head 3 times. He was last seen by his brother after the men spent the evening with their parents. However, it was the brother John Gallo who was implicated as part of a stick up gang that robbed an OUTFIT handbook in Cicero. It appeared that Carmine was mistaken for John and killed. Police speculated that the brother John was involved with the 1953 kidnapping/murder of Bobby Greenlease, the son of a prominent Kansas City auto dealer. The case remains unsolved.

On **September 26, 1956** Dallas Lamar Carroll 42 yrs. of 2735 Austin Blvd. was shot by unknown gangsters as he sat in an auto at Harlem Ave. and Riverside Dr. in Berwyn, IL. He was a former police officer from Miami. At one time he was married to the ex-wife of Martin Accardo brother of Outfit Boss Tony Accardo. The victim managed the Wishingwell restaurant at 5838 W. 26th St., Cicero, IL. a restaurant his wife obtained during a previous divorce. Reportedly two mobsters were overheard threatening his life. Police worked to identify those men, but the case remains unsolved.

Martin Accardo

On **November 29, 1956** Alan "Duke" Holt 28 yrs. of 2757 Pine Grove Ave. was shotgunned by unknown gangsters in front of 4330 S. Clinton, Stickney, IL. The victim was the head of a gang of slot machine thieves. They would use special tools to break into the machines and remove their contents. Many of the machines were placed and controlled by OUTFIT hoodlums. Police considered this a mob killing from the victim's activities.

On **March 31, 1957** Banker Leon Marcus who handled many of Sam Giancana's investments was indicted for embezzling. He pressed Giancana for help with his legal problems and apparently this made Giancana nervous and he had Willie Daddano take care of the problem. He used an ex-police officer by the name of Salvatore Moretti dispatched to make sure Marcus told the FBI nothing. When Marcus's body was found at 2136 W. 51st St. the police recovered a bill of sale for a River Road Motel. This oversight cost Moretti his life **(Solved)**.

On **April 17, 1957** Salvatore Moretti was tortured and murdered then found in the trunk of his own car on Canton Farm Rd. southwest of Chicago. It was later reported that Willie Daddano was responsible for this killing although he was never charged. The ex-police officer was reportedly employed by OUTFIT Boss Sam Giancana to kill Banker Leon Markus and recover incriminating documents from his person. However, police recovered the documents on the banker after the murder that put the Boss in a bad situation and Moretti paid for this mistake with his life. Moretti's twin brother Vincent would later be killed for his part in burglarizing Tony Accardo's home. A third brother Michael was convicted in 1951 of killing two youths. All three Moretti brothers were police officers at one time.

On **June 29, 1957** Frank Mustari AKA: Frank Laino was murdered. He was an OUTFIT hitman, former driver and bodyguard for "Dago" Lawrence Mangano and was killed by the man he was stalking, William O. Bates AKA: Willard who was identified as the killer, however Bates was murdered on **November 1, 1957** apparently before he could be held accountable for the crime or claim self - defense. Reportedly Frank Fratto was a suspect in the Bates killing.

On **August 6, 1957** Donald Kramer 26 yrs. of 9446 Lotus Ave. Skokie, IL. was shot by unknown gangsters and found in the trunk of a rented Oldsmobile parked in front of 4810 N. Harlem Ave. The victim was a glazier by trade, but police learned he was a heavy gambler and owed $14,000 to a bookmaker. He was also embroiled in union conflicts within his trade. It was reported that a Melrose Park Glass Co. the victim worked for was owned by Capone gangster Tough Tony Capezio.

On **December 17, 1957** Alex "Sonny" Michas was murdered by unknown gangsters.

In **February of 1958** Santiago Rosa Gonzalez was murdered. Gonzalez was involved in Bolita wheel operations and resisted the mob takeover. He was lured to a meeting at 1813 W. Washburn and reportedly stabbed to death by Angelo and James LaPietra. This information was provided by OUTFIT associate Ken Eto after a failed attempt on his life in 1983, but for some reason the pair were never charged **(Solved)**.

Gus Alex

On **May 10, 1958** Lacey L. Rankins 50 yrs. of 8230 S. Michigan Ave. was shot in the head by unknown gangsters at 743 E. 61st St.

On **May 28, 1958** Frank J. "Starchy" Pullano Jr. 41 yrs. of 7800 Yates Ave. was stabbed and his throat slit by unknown gangsters when he was found at 121st and Page Sts. in Calumet Park, IL. Reportedly he was involved in hijacking and gambling although never convicted. Police speculated that he was killed elsewhere and dumped at this location.

On **May 29, 1958** Dominick "Little D" Albano AKA: Michael Sipari, Vincent Costa, Danate 38 yrs. of 318 S. Kostner St. was shot in the head by unknown gangsters in front of 346 S. Kostner Ave. He was identified by authorities as part of a stick up gang that robbed an OUTFIT Handbook in Cicero before the murder. The case remains unsolved.

On **December 3, 1958** Gus Greenbaum was murdered in his Las Vegas home at 115 N. Monte Vista Rd. along with his wife. Greenbaum considered the Mayor of Las Vegas was a masterful gambling impresario who made millions for the OUTFIT running Las Vegas Casinos and was encouraged to take over the troubled Riviera in 1955. Gus resisted the offer and because of that his sister-in-law was found murdered. Gus then complied with his overseers in Chicago and during the next couple of years picked up the struggling business, but along the way he picked up a bad drug habit. Much to his detriment he became sloppy in his work while running the casino and was also suspected of stealing from the OUTFIT. He also made the mistake of hiring noted snitch Willie Bioff who was spotted by Marshall Ciafano. Apparently that was not acceptable and he and his wife were found brutally killed and Gus was decapitated as a message to others.

In **1959** Harry Figel 38yrs. of 2448 47th St. was shot to death in downtown Chicago by Police Officer and Mob operative Richard Cain. Cain claimed that Figel resisted arrest and Cain was forced to shoot him. Reportedly Figel was part of a ring of Homosexual hustlers who worked out of the downtown Greyhound Bus Station and would shake down victims during sexual encounters. When Cain found out he tried to take part of the action and Figel was killed when he resisted. Cain was cleared of the charges, but was arrested a short time later for extorting $30,000 from a local hooker **(solved)**.

On **March 10, 1959** Hyman "Heinie" Wainer 54 yrs. of 3622 McLean Ave. was shot by unknown gangsters in the rear of 3270 N. Lake Shore Drive where his wife lived. He had been secretly married for two years. The victim was a former Capone bootlegger and had interests in liquor stores and was a known fence. Reportedly he was involved in Liquor Racketeering in which the racketeers falsely label liquor or sell stolen liquor. Police were looking for a known whiskey hijacker and ex-convict by the name of Daniel Bakovich for questioning and it is not known what the outcome of this case was.

On **June 20, 1959** Leo "Lippy" Goldsand 48 yrs. of 240 E. Delaware was shot in the back of the head by unknown gangsters and found behind the front seat of his car at 4515 N. Wolcott Ave. The victim was a World War II black marketer and currently a fence. He was a partner with Heinie Wainer who was killed in March of this year. Reportedly he was a heavy gambler and deeply in debt when he was killed.

On **July 8, 1959** Mario Melchiore 35 yrs. of 2104 S. Euclid Ave. Berwyn, IL. was shotgunned by unknown gangsters at 4000 W. Gladys St. The victim was an attorney and real estate speculator with a family office at 347 1/2 S. Pulaski Rd. He was subjected to the ire of Westside residents for buying homes from white families and selling them to black families. While driving he was curbed by a yellow convertible and taken from his car at gunpoint by two men. As he broke away from the men he pleaded for his life before being shot in the back. The men fled and police speculated that his death resulted from his business practices as other realtors received threatening letters warning the same results if they sold to blacks.

On **July 18, 1959** Nicholas "Nick" Versetto 30 yrs. of 248 W. 26th St. was found strangled and shot by unknown gangsters in a vacant lot at 26th and Federal Sts. Reportedly he was tortured before being shot. He had recently been implicated with Gene Tanuta and Frank Bradlo in a $30,000 burglary in the building he lived in. The burglary victim was Joseph Frisco the building owner who informed Nick of a party he would attend in the suburbs. Apparently he then recruited the two accomplices to carry out the crime and then provided their names to the police trying to illicit a reward. The outcome of the burglary case and the murder are unknown.

On **August 14, 1959** John Miraglia 42 yrs. was shot in the head and back by unknown gangsters while seated at the bar of the Orange Latern Inn at 1904 W. Division Ave. He was an ex-convict, burglar, black marketer and passed bad checks during his criminal career. He was one of the few remaining members of a gang headed by the late Paul "Needlenose" Labriola.

On **August 14, 1959** Edward Kochanski AKA: Kane 41 yrs. of 4638 Cermak Rd., Cicero, IL. was shot in the head by unknown gangsters and found behind 1505 S. Kolin. The victim had been clubbed in the head and his pockets turned inside out and his shoes were missing. He had recently worked in Cicero gambling joints specifically the Barton Hotel at 2324 S. Cicero Ave. He was also a bartender who shot his girlfriend in 1957 and tried to commit suicide himself only to survive and be murdered. A black 1956 Ford sedan was seen leaving the alley.

On **August 22, 1959** Fred Evans 57 yrs. of 5000 Marine Dr. was killed. During his career he operated a chop shop with his partner Murray Humphreys. During the World's Fair he partnered with Capone and Humphreys in running the Popcorn Concessions. He then worked to take over the laundry business starting with Ruby Cleaners at 2801 W. Montrose. As a confidant of Humphreys and financial genius, he was gunned down in front of the Lake Street laundry that he owned with Humphreys and Guiseppe Glielmi AKA: Joey Glimco reportedly because they suspected him of stealing. As he entered his car at 5409 W. Lake St. two men pulled alongside and shot him. At the time of his death he was under federal subpoena involving his partner Joey Glimco. He was the second of 3 witnesses to die. No one was ever charged in the killing.

On **November 2, 1959** Sam A. Gironda AKA: Grecco, Grinda 40 yrs. was shotgunned by unknown gangsters in the driveway of his home at 6455 W. 89th Street in Worth Township. He was an employee of the Chicago Water and Sewer Department and was from a large family in the 26th and Wentworth area who were politically active. His criminal record indicated he was arrested for purse snatching, assault, extortion, robbery and counterfeiting. The killing was in the midst of a payroll scandal that Sam was part of. He owned a used car lot (Forest Motor Sales, Robbins, IL.) with a partner Gus Rubino and also ran a mob sanctioned handbook out of the business. Reportedly he had a violent quarrel with Rubino three weeks before the murder and shut down the business. Police speculated the men may have dealt in stolen cars. The outcome of the investigation is unknown.

On **November 6, 1959** Joe Bronge died after being shot by unknown gangsters on July 19, 1959. He was a local beer distributor and resisted the OUTFIT's overtures to muscle into his business. He died of his injuries and prolific killer Felix "Milwaukee Phil" Alderisio and Albert "Obbie" Frabotta were reportedly suspected of the killing, but never charged. Bronge was the President of Tri Bee Supply Company which was run by Tom Eboli. Eboli's father for a time ran the Genovese crime family in New York. It was also learned that Bronge was feuding with Steve Anselmo another beer distributor and close friend of Sam Giancana. The reason for the feud was over who would provide beer for the Our Lady of Mount Carmel Italian Fest in Melrose Park, IL. He was also under federal subpoena regarding syndicate activities and was the first of 3 witnesses to die.

On **December 16, 1959** Roger Touhy was murdered. Like Bugs Moran, Roger "The Terrible" Touhy fought the Capone syndicate for control of liquor distribution in Chicago and the suburbs and went as far as protecting labor leaders from Capone overtures. With the help of TOC emissary Jake "The Barber" Factor AKA: Iakow Factrowitz, Touhy was incarcerated for the bogus kidnapping of Factor in 1935. Upon his release from prison he was gunned down on the steps of his sister's home in the Austin neighborhood of Chicago at 125 N. Lotus. His killers were reportedly Marshall Caifano, Teetz Battaglia and Sam Giancana who was wounded during the assault. None were ever charged.

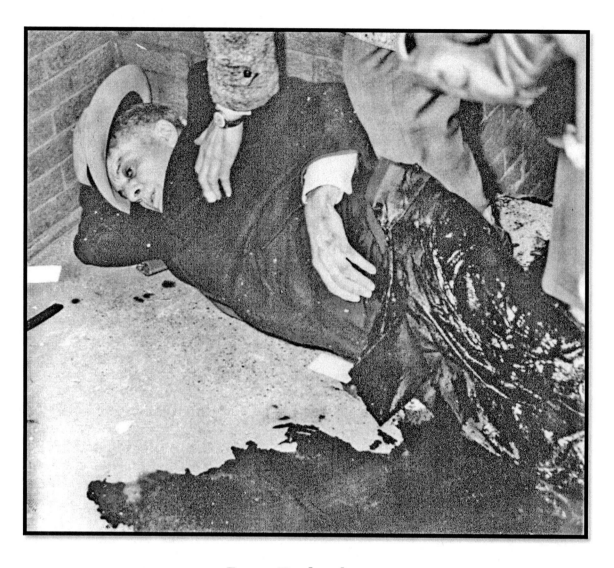

Roger Touhy shot

Approximate number of Chicago TOC related murders in the 1950s: 70

Approx. number of Chicago TOC related murder cases in the 1950s solved: 13

Approx. number of Chicago TOC related murders in the 1950s of Police Officers: 1

Chapter 6. The 1960s

As we enter a decade best remembered for social revolution, modernism and activism, locally the Chicago OUTFIT appears to be the same beast it has been since the end of World War II. Locally, that may have been the case, but internationally TOC in America and the OUTFIT through a small group of its members and associates had become major players in the drug trafficking trade most notably, in a case that would receive a great deal of attention in coming years and be portrayed on the big screen in a movie titled: The French Connection. These same operatives by this time had also ingratiated themselves as informants for the FBI and as operatives for covert CIA operations in an attempt to topple Fidel Castro in Cuba through gun running activities and complex coup plots. The OUTFIT had proven its value in other South American coup plots and assassinations in the 1950s. But, now TOC in America found itself in a unique role to stop the onslaught of investigations and prosecutions brought about by the administration of President John F. Kennedy and his brother Attorney General Robert Kennedy. What the 1960s presents are some of the greatest mistakes ever committed by the federal government that ultimately cost this country the life of the first and maybe only President to seriously pursue TOC in America.

Critical events of the 1960s

In **1960** Joseph Albanese was murdered. He was an associate of mobster Willie "Potato's" Daddano and at one time was a cellmate of Daddanos' in prison. Reportedly he was killed for money he owed Potato's and did not pay back. Daddano was the number one suspect in the killing, but never charged.

On **January 6, 1960** William "The Saint" Skally was found murdered in River Forest, IL. He was a Chicago Burglar and Bureau of Narcotics informant, but after his cooperation with law enforcement was reportedly discovered and reported to Sam Giancana by an OUTFIT attorney he died.

On **February 9, 1960** Herman Posner 72 yrs. of 125 N. Pine Ave. was stabbed, slashed and found behind his residence. He was a projectionist and a rebel against Union Local 110 Motion Picture Operators officials associated with the OUTFIT. He had reports detailing embezzlement, kickbacks and shakedowns which he provided to federal authorities that he was working with when he was killed. He had planned to travel to Washington and provide testimony to the Senate Rackets Committee. The victim's 3 sons all members of the union received threatening letters after their father's death warning them not to pursue his union work. Intense investigations after the murder led to indictments of labor racketeers. Blood relatives of several OUTFIT leaders were members of the union since the Mob's complete takeover in 1935 and after the murder of union racketeer Tommy Maloy. Vice President of the Local Frank Galluzo was questioned in the murder, but no charges were ever filed.

On **March 22, 1960** Michael Saporito disappeared. Reportedly, he was a Chicago Police Officer who assisted the OUTFIT by committing jury tampering in a high jacking case. He passed money onto his brother who sat on the jury that was trying several OUTFIT members and he was promised a promotion. The case backfired and he was indicted. The OUTFIT reportedly knew he was the only one who could link the bribe to Joe DiVarco. The Mob bonded him out of jail, planted his car at Midway Airport and he was never seen again. It was clear to his family what had transpired.

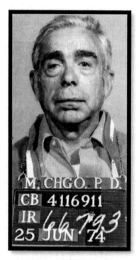

Joe DiVarco

On **March 28, 1960** Arthur Adler 43 yrs. of 7601 S. Chappel St. was found murdered in a sewer at 1625 N. Neva St. by city workers. The victim's nude body was found 3 weeks after being disposed of and lead to a controversy at the coroner's office when an exact cause of death was not determined 2 months later. Coroner's personnel would only state that the victim could have died from fear. Adler was a prominent figure on Rush St. and was the former owner of the Trade Winds restaurant at 857 N. Rush and the Black Onyx at 104 E. Walton St. His wife openly complained about gangsters that hung around there to include: Milwaukee Phil Alderisio, Joe "Cesar" DiVarco, Marshall Caifano and Obbie Frabotta. Even without the cause of death the police conducted a homicide investigation that revealed the victim's latex distributing company at 749 W. Roosevelt Rd. was hurting financially and the victim's wife claimed to be penniless. Adler openly complained about being pushed out of his restaurant and supposedly borrowed $100,000 from the OUTFIT which he could not repay. Adler was also under federal subpoena regarding crime syndicate activities in the nightclub business, but claimed he was not a front for Marshall Caifano in the Trade Winds as suspected. He was the third federal witness to be killed. Obbie and Joe Frabotta were among many gangsters quizzed in the killing which remains unsolved.

On **March 31, 1960** Charles B. Vaughn 29 yrs. of 1705 Diversey Ave. was shot by unknown gangsters at 2741 N. Paulina St. He was shot by two assailants who drove up in a car. He was a member of a stick-up gang that while associated with the OUTFIT, made a fatal mistake of robbing a card game held by several mobsters' wives. One of the wives was pistol whipped during the robbery. Other members of the gang were kidnapped and shot, but Vaughn was the only one to die. Years later it was revealed that Chuckie Cremaldi a federal informant and collector for Sam DeStefano participated in this killing; however I do not know if that information was ever shared with Chicago Police or if the case was ever solved.

On **October 13, 1960** Michael J. Urgo 31 yrs. of 7800 Cortland Dr. Elmwood Park, IL. was shot by unknown gangsters in front of 1911 North 78th Ave. Elmwood Park, IL. The victim was an Attorney and the son-in-law of Guido DeChiaro described as a distant relative of Paul Ricca and a juke box distributor and associate of mobsters: Jackie Cerone, Chuckie English, Joe Gagliano and other Accardo hoodlums. At the time of the shooting Urgo was coming to the aid of DeChairo who was being accosted and possibly kidnapped. As he approached gun in hand he was shot to death. This crime was an affront to the Outfit and was part of a crime spree carried out in which 10 Outfit associate's homes were reportedly burglarized by a crew consisting of Joachim Silva, Dominick Motto, Frank DelGuidice, Lester Belgrad and Richard Fanning. Most of the men went missing or were killed by the end of the year.

Tony Accardo & Jackie Cerone

On **November 15, 1960** Michael DeMarte 50 yrs. of 1533 W. Congress Parkway was shot by unknown gangsters in front of 1523 W. Congress Parkway. He was known by police as a "Walking Bookmaker" meaning he would take bets at various locations. He was on unemployment and was working as a waiter and had no police record to speak of. The intent of his assailants was quite unusual as their car slowed by its target as he walked along and shots were fired from a black sedan. When the victim collapsed the men approached on foot and fired more shots into him. The police investigation revealed that he received a threatening call 3 weeks prior. They also learned that the victim was the brother of Edward D'Aquila the owner of the Trade Winds restaurant that received a great deal of attention recently because of the murder of its former owner Arthur Adler along with the fact that it was a hangout for notable hoodlums.

On **December 6, 1960** Lester Bugrad AKA: Belgrad 43 yrs. of 2626 N. Richmond St. was shot in the head and found in an auto at 1649 W. 13th St. His wife told police that he was a salesman for a company at 5 S. Wabash, but the owner of the company denied that Belgrad worked for him. She went on to say the victim left the house abruptly after a phone call and was dead 4 hours later. He had a minor police background for impersonating a policeman, carrying a gun, selling phony police badges and running a confidence game. He was a member of a crew that carried out a crime spree in which 10 Outfit associate's homes were burglarized by a crew consisting of Joachim Silva, Dominick Motto, Frank DelGuidice, and Richard Fanning. Most of the men went missing or were killed by the end of the year.

On **December 10, 1960** Richard Fanning 29 yrs. of 6714 Clyde Ave. was found tortured to death in the rear seat of his car parked at 3565 S. Wells St. He was a known safe cracker and was part of a crew consisting of Joachim Silva, Dominick Motto, Frank DelGuidice and Lester Belgrad. The men were involved in a crime spree carried out in which 10 Outfit associate's homes were burglarized. Most of the men went missing or were killed by the end of the year.

On **December 12, 1960** Frank DelGuidice 51 yrs. of 466 N. Ashland Ave. was shot in the head by unknown gangsters and found at 1705 W. Ohio St. The victim was an unemployed sheet metal worker and sign hanger. He was a member of a crew that carried out a crime spree in which 10 Outfit associate's homes were burglarized by a crew consisting of Joachim Silva, Dominick Motto, Lester Belgrad and Richard Fanning. Most of the men went missing or were killed by the end of the year.

On **February 2, 1961** Theororos Sampaniotis age 33, was murdered. He was found in an abandon garage at 642 Blue Island Ave. He had been shot 3 times in the head and twice in the chest at close range. Police theorize that the killers had a personal grudge against him because of marks indicating he was kicked after being shot. He was known to be a gambler and it was believed gambling activities may have led to his death.

On **March 31, 1961** John Arthur Powers age 38, was murdered. He was ambushed by gunman who shot him 5 times as he was entering his apartment. He was a bartender at the Velvet Lounge, 3551 W. North Ave. He stopped for something to eat at Crawford and North Ave. and took a taxi to his residence. He was a known patron of Cicero gambling joints and was heavily in debt. He was an ex-convict who was sentenced to the IDOC for Robbery in 1941. Following his parole in 1946 he was violated 3 times before being discharged in 1956. While in prison he became friends with Morris Litberg a principle figure in a vending company. Several months before the slaying, Felix "Milwaukee Phil" Alderisio and other OUTFIT representatives became connected to the vending company. Litberg complained he was being muscled out of his business and sought aid. The victim brought Edward J. McNally into the picture to help.

On **May 15, 1961** Edward J. McNally 33yrs., was murdered. He was ambushed a short time after leaving the Velvet Lounge, 3551 W. North Ave. He was shot 3 times in an alley behind 3441 W. Fulton. McNally frequented Cicero gambling joints and was in debt to loan sharks. McNally once participated in holding up a Cicero bookie. Before the murders he and John Powers were offered $15,000 to kill 3 OUTFIT members who had muscled their way into Morris Litberg's vending company. Instead, the two men reported the offer to the mobsters who gave Litberg a beating causing him to flee Chicago.

On **June 13, 1961** L. C. Smith 39 yrs., was murdered. His body was found in his parked car in downtown Chicago's loop area. He had been shot in the head 5 times with a 45 cal. Automatic, after being abducted while driving his car around Pulaski and 16th St. His car was forced to the curb at 4006 W. 16th st. Two of the men got into his car and forced him to drive away while the other 2 men followed. Smith was known to be a customer of juice racketeers and a Cicero gambler. On July 21, 1961 a Cicero gambler was identified by a witness as one of the four men who abducted the victim, a Cook County Grand Jury failed to indict the man and the case remains unsolved.

On **June 14, 1961** Shelby Faulk 36 yrs. of 7120 S. Emerald Ave. was found murdered next to his 1961 white Cadillac, in the alley at 7304 S. Union Ave. Police found bullet holes over his left ear, in his left chest and in his chin. Two bullets had been fired through the right front and right rear doors. Investigators felt that robbery may have been the motive since the victim's pockets were empty and his wallet and an expensive ring were missing. Previously Faulk had been convicted of selling narcotics and was sentenced from two to three years in prison in 1955. He had also served a prison term for manslaughter in his native state of Tennessee. Police intelligence revealed that Faulk was last seen with $7,000 to purchase narcotics.

On **June 20, 1961** Ralph DelGenio 57 yrs. from Cicero, IL, was found murdered in his car at 626 S. Wells St. The car, a battered 1954 model was ticketed by police at 11:55 am and the officers remembered seeing the car there the previous day, they ordered the car towed to the auto pond. A pond employee appeared and after driving the car found the body under a blanket in the back seat. The victim had been beaten to death with a blunt object. The body was disfigured and had additional cuts and bruises and appeared to have been there for two days. DelGenio was due in U.S. Bankruptcy Court the day before his body was found and failed to appear. Police at the time theorized that he was killed because of his debt and probably owed money to Juice operators most of which were associated with the OUTFIT.

On **July 29, 1961** Michael Joyce 30 yrs. of 2329 N. 76th Ct. Elmwood Park, IL. was found shot in the head by unknown gangsters in a burning car at 819 N. Harding St. When firefighters put out the fire the body was found slumped over on the floor next to the drivers' seat. He had been shot twice in the head, his penis cut off and shoved in his mouth and the car doused in gasoline and burned. Joyce was an associate of Frank Cullotta and had a habit of starting trouble in OUTFIT sponsored bars. He had been arrested numerous times for burglary, traffic violations and narcotics violations; he gained some notoriety in 1952 as a suspect in the Charles Gross murder, although he was never charged. Police speculated that he talked too much and may have died at the hands of other thieves, while Cullotta claimed he was killed by the OUTFIT for annoying them.

On **August 1, 1961** Carl Wiltse 27 yrs. was shot to death by multiple shotgun blasts into his apartment. The victim was watching television and his assailant(s) removed a screen and fan from a kitchen window to get access to the victim. He was struck in the neck and chest. Police described him as a small-time burglar and hoodlum. His wife reported, 2 months before the murder assailant(s) fired six shots into the apartment and six shots into the victims' 1953 vehicle. It was also revealed that he was an informant.

On **August 11, 1961** William "Action" Jackson AKA: William Kearney, 30 yrs. of Cicero, IL. was found murdered in the truck of his car, a green, two door 1957 Cadillac, on lower Wacker Drive between Wells and Franklin Sts. in the evening hours. It was later learned that Jackson an OUTFIT juice collector, was kidnapped off the street by the very mobsters he worked with. He was then taken to a meat rendering plant on the Southside where he was hung on a meat hook, tortured and beaten for three days before he died. Police speculated that he was killed for several reasons that included hijacking trucks he did not have permission to do, shorting his bosses on collections he made, cheating burglars he would fence property for, ignoring warnings to stop stealing from other thieves and cooperating with federal authorities regarding a pending federal theft case he was fighting. He had a scheduled court date in front of Federal Judge William J. Campbell on September 21st regarding the theft of $70,000 worth of electrical appliances from a railroad yard. Whatever the reason, fabled FBI Agent Bill Roemer later wrote that Jackson was not a snitch and an FBI microphone picked up conversations of several high ranking OUTFIT members laughing and joking about the torture and murder. This group included: Fioravante "Fifi" "The Nose" Buccieri, Jackie "The Lackey" Cerone, James "Turk" Turello, Dave Yaras, Frank "Cowboy" Mirro and Felix "Milwaukee Phil" Alderisio. Roemer also speculated that OUTFIT members may have seen him talking to Jackson on the street shortly before the murder. Years later Frank Cullotta would report that Jackson was killed by Tony Spilotro and Chuckie Crimaldi among others, for skimming money from his Boss Mad Sam DeStefano. Apparently this information was never passed on to local authorities who were responsible for homicide investigations and the case was never solved. Jackie Cerone was questioned regarding this murder by federal authorities. In 1972 Federal Investigators developed information on this case from Charles Crimaldi a juice collector for Sam DeStefano who claimed he was at the murder scene. This led to an indictment in the case that was suppressed. This case reflected the pure disregard the OUTFIT had for the lives of their own people **(Solved)**.

Wm. Action Jackson

On **October 20, 1961** John A. Kilpatrick 54 yrs. of 5231 S. Lawndale was found murdered in his car at the rear of 3312 W. 61st St. by 3 city forestry workers two blocks from his office. Kilpatrick was the President of the United Industrial Workers of America and was President of Local 300 of the UIWA in Chicago. He had been shot once under the left ear. Two sticks of dynamite were found wired to the ignition of his car apparently from a previous assassination attempt. Apparently he provided information to authorities on the theft of funds ($420,667) by Angelo Inciso who ran local 286 of the UIWA. Inciso blamed Kilpatrick for his 10 year prison term and probably arranged the killing. Dana Nash and William Triplett were convicted of the crime and Nash was sentenced to 99-150 years and Triplett to 14 years in prison **(solved)**.

On **November 4, 1961** Albert Brown 39yrs. of 604 S. May was shot to death. He was shot four times outside the plant of the Lonergan Dye Company at 4651 Arthington St. in Chicago. He was discovered by a plant foreman who found him face down next to a car he borrowed from his brother. He was shot in the chest and the back of the head. A 7.65 mm Italian Beretta automatic pistol was found in the weeds about 100 feet from the victim. On October 31st he was convicted and sentenced to 5 to 10 years for burglary and remained free on an appeal bond and police speculate he was killed by juice operators.

On **November 8, 1961** Joseph Gentile 51 yrs. of 1631 W. 19th St. was shot to death while seated in his car with two companions in front of his home. Six shots were fired from another vehicle and one struck Gentile in the temple. Reportedly police knew him as a stick up man and theorized that he was killed by juice operators.

On **November 9, 1961** Albert "Transom" Testa 48 yrs. of 700 N. Monticello Ave. was found in a coma in an alley at the rear of 1031 N. Francisco Ave. He had been shot twice in the head and died that day at Cook County Hospital. Testa was a burglar of small stature (less than 100 lbs.) and gained his nickname from his ability to use transoms to make entry to his targeted scores. Police advanced multiple theories: an 18 yr. old stripper whom Testa had introduced to high ranking OUTFIT members had turned informant, Testa was a longtime friend of Action Jackson who was suspected of informing and was killed 3 months earlier, Testa was a bookmaker associated with mobster Chuckie English which may have led to his death. He was in prison for counterfeiting in 1948 and was sentenced to prison in 1934 for Rape.

On **November 14, 1961** Louis DiMeo 24 yrs. was found beaten to death in the closet of his apartment at 1910 Lake St. in Melrose Park, IL. Firemen responding to a fire in the flat discovered a couch and bed on fire, gas jets on a stove open and the victim in a closet. Although a weapon was never found, police speculate that he was beaten with a 5 lb. caulking hammer purchased at a local hardware store on the morning of the murder by a man described as swarthy, 30 years old and 5'6 in height.

On **November 16, 1961** John "Red" Hennigan 43 yrs. of 2638 W. 25th St. was shot to death in the early morning hours across the street from his home. He was seated in his car and was struck by a shotgun blast in the groin; a second blast missed its mark and hit the window of the car. An empty shell casing was found nearby. He was an unemployed truck driver and his body was found by his wife when she returned from her job. At the time of the slaying Hennigan was on bail for an Armed Robbery indictment returned on March 23rd of that year. In his pocket police found a receipt from a Melrose Park gambling den and other addresses of Cicero gambling locations. Multiple theories were advanced by police: he was an informer, he was involved with extorting from other burglars and stick-up men such as himself, he ran up gambling debts and was involved in gambling house robberies. An FBI report later listed Fiore "Fifi" "The Nose" Buccieri as a suspect in the killing. However it remains an open case.

In **1962** John W. McCarthy was found dead in the trunk of a car on the southwest side of Chicago. He was the cousin of Thomas McCarthy who would be killed in 1977 and left in the trunk of his car.

Fifi Buccieri

In **1962** a man only known as Padone was murdered. At first it was surmised that he had interfered with the OUTFIT takeover of Bolita operations, but it was later revealed he was attempting to seduce the wife of a mobster involved in Bolito. After being provided with the information, Northside gambling Boss Ross Priola AKA: Prio arranged the killing and Padone was shot to death on north LaSalle St. This information was provided by OUTFIT associate Ken Eto after a failed attempt on his life in 1983 **(Solved)**.

In **1962** Elmer "Dutch" Dowling and Mel Beckman were murdered on the eastside of St. Louis, Mo. Starting around 1940 Frank "Buster" Wortman operated an organized crime gang in St. Louis that for all intents and purposes was a franchise of the Chicago OUTFIT. Wortman was recorded by FBI agents meeting with Sam Giancana at the Armory Lounge talking about illicit businesses in St. Louis. Dutch Dowling was a top lieutenant for Wortman in the vending machine rackets and Bechman was his bodyguard. The Wortman gang was at odds with other mobsters namely John Vitale and Tony Giordano. Wortman became friends with OUTFIT luminary Murray Humphreys during a prison term. It is not know if the case was ever solved.

On **January 20, 1962** August "Gus" Vivirito 35 yrs. was murdered. Gus was shot 6 times on January 6, and was allegedly a police informant. A Cicero gambler was identified as the perpetrator, but a grand jury failed to indict him.

On **February 4, 1962** Henry Volanti 24 yrs. of 218 W. 24th St., was found strangled to death with his hands tied behind his back in the trunk of a car parked for two weeks in the parking lot of 2328 S. Dearborn.

In February of 1962 the Chicago OUTFIT reportedly sent a team of assassins to Florida to kill yet another one of their own, Frankie "The X" Esposito a labor racketeer. This crew was made up of Jackie Cerone, Fifi Buccieri, David Yaras, Turk Torello, Frank Cerone, Lou Rosanova and possibly Vincent Inserro. However, the FBI was made aware of the contract and was able to monitor the crews' activities and avert the crime according to FBI Agent Wm. Roemer.

On **April 24, 1962** Gerald J. Valente 58 yrs. of 3450 W. Ohio St. was shot and killed in front of Bea's lounge at 4634 Cermak Road in Cicero, IL. He was known as a gambler.

On **April 26, 1962** Phillip Scalvo 38 yrs. of 2554 Rose St. in Franklin Park, Ronald J. Scalvo 28 yrs. of 1444 W. Ohio St. and Lydia Abshire 28 yrs. of 2817 N. Newland were all shot and killed as they sat in an auto in Elmwood Park, IL. The two men managed a saloon called the Black Door in Rosemont, IL. and their father was a personal friend of OUTFIT Boss Tony Accardo. The owner Frank Pondeleo was an associate of OUTFIT Boss Paul Ricca. Another hood by the name of Billy McCarthy got into an altercation at the Black Door and the Scalvo brothers beat him up. Frank Cullotta an associate of McCarthy reported that Billy told him he wanted revenge and a couple of days later he and Jimmy Miraglia reportedly followed the men from the bar and killed them along with a woman they were with. Police reported someone approached the car and fired into it leaving local police to claim it was one of the best planned executions they have ever seen. John Lardino a prominent mobster was questioned in the killing, but never charged. A short time later the two assassins were found murdered, but the case went unsolved.

On **May 8, 1962** Michael Ragenese 25 yrs. was found shot twice in the head in a car parked in the garage of a building under construction in Stickney Township. The victim was being sought by the FBI for questioning in a $1,750,000 Florida jewelry robbery. He was a former bartender and tavern manager.

On **May 14, 1962** James "Rocco" Roscoe Miraglia 25 yrs. of 1845 N. Mulligan Ave. and William J. McCarthy 25 yrs. of 4336 W. Gladys Ave. were found murdered and in the trunk of Miraglia's car parked at 3855 W. 55th Place. The case became known by authorities as the M & M murders. They had been beaten and strangled and police speculated that they were killed for cooperating with police after receiving a light prison sentence for a recent conviction that they were scheduled to surrender for on May 15th. It was learned years later that the men had committed the killing of the Scalvo brothers in Elmwood Park against the edict of the Chicago OUTFIT. McCarthy was reportedly captured first by mobsters and tortured before revealing the location of his associate Miraglia. His head had been put in a vise and closed causing one of his eyes to pop out of its socket before he was killed. Tony "The Ant" Spilotro was indicted for the killings, but was not convicted **(Solved)**.

Tony Spilotro

On **May 20, 1962** Peter J. Bludeau 50 yrs. of 5115 W. 32nd St. in Cicero, IL. was found murdered in the trunk of his car in front of 2658 S. Christiana. He had been arrested on March 21st of that year in a gambling raid in Chicago. One of the Cicero gambling bosses by the name of Joe Corngold AKA: Fifke was questioned regarding this murder, but no charges were placed and the case remained unsolved.

On **May 22, 1962** Leroy Sommers is murdered in Wisconsin. It was speculated that several men were murdered who had ties to the Grande Cheese Company in Wisconsin, this victim was one of them. The others were Vincent Benvenento, Sam Gervase, James V. DeAngelo, Onofrio Vitale, Thomas Oneglia, Frank Diamond (Maritote), Marcus Lipsky and Nick DeJohn. This Company was suspected of OUTFIT connections for years and dealt in some kind of black market, possibly narcotics. His exact position in this organization is unknown. The Chicago Police Intelligence Unit reviewed this case in 1994 through 1997 to no avail.

On **May 31, 1962** Leo Johnson 22 yrs. was found dead from a bullet wound to the head in an alley at 1521 W. Harrison St. He was employed as a car hiker for a beauty shop. He had been arrested for larceny and spent some time in prison. Reportedly Police believed he was connected with the Guido-Yonder stick-up gang.

On **June 18, 1962** Herbert Kwate 23 yrs. was found shot to death in a ravine north of Carpentersville, IL. Police believe he was killed by members of a bandit gang he belonged to. They blamed him for helping police set up a trap for the gang in which two of his fellow bandits were slain while invading the home of Herbert Freed at 5505 N. Francisco. Members of the gang were Nick Guido 41, a former bank robber, Gary Dellasandro 25, a known burglar-forger and Frank Yonder 22, a former friend of the victim. It is not known if the case was ever cleared by police.

On **June 18, 1962** Sidney Frazin AKA: Sidney Craigin 52yrs. of 4422 W. Monroe was shot to death by two men who chased him into the Community Friends Social Club at 765 W. Taylor St. He was a gambling collector for the OUTFIT in the Loop and had been arrested for gambling on this date at 845 S. Wabash and charged with being a keeper of a handbook. Police believed he was killed for double crossing the OUTFIT he worked for. For years police reported that the victim was a gambling collector in the Loop area for OUTFIT luminaries Gus "Slim" Alex, Frank "Strongy" Ferrarro and Louie Briatta. Briatta reportedly a brother-in-law to corrupt first ward alderman John D'Arco held a city job until an expose' led to his dismissal. The case remains unsolved.

On **August 7, 1962** Eddie Robinson was murdered. Robinson ran a Bolita wheel on the Westside and resisted the OUTFIT takeover. He was shot to death at Independence Blvd. and the Eisenhower expressway by Joseph "Joe Shine" Amabile and Vincent "The Saint" Inserro although his body was never found. This information was provided by OUTFIT associate Ken Eto after a failed attempt on his life in 1983 **(Solved)**.

On **August 24, 1962** Alex Sorrentino 54 yrs. was found shot to death in a field at 501 Parnell Ave. in Chicago Heights, IL.

In **February of 1963** the body of Eugenia "Becca" Pappas was found in the Chicago River, she had been murdered. In December of 1962 OUTFIT enforcer and bodyguard for Felix "Milwaukee Phil" Alderisio, Frank "The German" Schweihs was dating the beautiful girl named Becca. Naturally her parents became upset with this unholy union, to the point they moved the family out of Chicago. However, Eugenia came back to Chicago and became deeply involved with "The German". After a few months the relationship soured and when Becca tried to break it off she vanished. The young beauty was last seen alive driving the German's car which he disposed of shortly after the murder. And lastly it was learned that the case was investigated by corrupt lawman Riccardo Scalzetti AKA: Richard Cain who himself was killed gangland style with Schweihs as a suspect. When found she had been in the water a couple of weeks after being shot in the head.

Frank Schweihs

On **February 28, 1963** Benjamin F. Lewis 53 yrs. of 3949 W. Fillmore was found shot to death in his ward office at 3604 W. Roosevelt. He was the democratic alderman of the 24th ward and one of the first powerful black leaders on the west side of Chicago. Police speculated he was demanding more money from the OUTFIT for the gambling spots in his ward than they were willing to pay. Allegedly he was also a bookmaker and was running book out of his ward office. Chicago Police learned that he was warned by Westside gambling Boss Lenny Patrick to stop making book or pay a portion of his proceeds to the OUTFIT. He failed to take heed and was killed. It was reported that during the initial investigation Frank "One Ear Frankie" Fratto was a suspect in the killing. Ultimately Patrick, Angelo "The Hook" LaPietra, David Yaras and an active police officer were suspects from information provided by a federal informant when the Chicago Police Intelligence Unit reviewed this and several other OUTFIT killings in 1994; However, federal authorities chose not to pursue the case at that time **(solved).**

On **May 6, 1963** Irving Vine 58 yrs. was found bound gagged and beaten to death in his swank Hyde Park apartment at 5307 Hyde Park Boulevard by a maid who noticed his legs were tapped together, his hands tied behind his back and a sheet was over his head. He was said to be a salesman but, Vine was a small time gambler and ran handbooks for OUTFIT slot machine boss Eddie Vogel. The only thing that could have caused his murder was his failure to back up OUTFIT Boss Murray Humphreys' claim that unreported income being investigated by the IRS came from Vine's wife before they were married. By the way, Humphrey's wife was married to Vine before she left him for Humphreys, so much for the code and honor in the OUTFIT.

On **June 7, 1963** Kenneth C. Gordon 41 yrs. of 418 Webster Ave. was found shot to death in a car at 3006 Waterloo Court. He was said to be a salesman of jewelry.

On **August 24, 1963** Mario Liberatore 34 yrs. was found stabbed to death in a car at 2209 S. Ridgeway Ave.

On **October 18, 1963** Robert Carpenter 31 yrs. of 6541 S. Peoria Ave. was killed by shotgun blasts fired from a passing car. The car was found parked at 7410 S. Peoria; he was the manager of the Jazz Lounge at 3221 Fifth Ave.

On **November 18, 1963** Leo S. Foreman AKA: Leo Wilson, 42yrs. of 4817 Neva Ave. was found shot and stabbed to death in the trunk of a car parked at 5204 W. Gladys. He was president of LeFore Insurance Company 7050 W. Belmont and was said to be an acquaintance of Sam DeStefano. In reality he was a collector for Mad Sam. It was learned years later by the testimony of Chuckie Crimaldi, another DeStefano crew member, that he had become involved in a disagreement with DeStefano at his insurance company office and had the nerve to throw Sam out. DeStefano became infuriated and decided to kill his underling. He lured Foreman to the basement of his Brother Mario's Cicero home and Mad Sam, Crimaldi, Mario DeStefano and Tony Spilotro beat and tortured him until he begged Mad Sam to kill him. In 1972 the three participants were charged based on the testimony of Crimaldi who was cooperating with federal authorities by this time. Tony was found not guilty at trial. Sam was killed in 1973 while awaiting trial. He was reportedly killed by his brother Mario and Spilotro. Mario was the only one to be convicted of Foreman's murder, but the case was reversed on appeal and he died of natural causes before he could be retried **(solved)**.

"Mad Sam" DeStefano

On **November 22, 1963** President John F. Kennedy was shot to death in a motorcade in Dallas, Texas. Over the years the true details were obscured in one of the most complex investigations in American history in the name of national security. However, by the 1970s Congressional Committees starting with the

Church Committee and later the House Select Committee on Assassinations began to develop a real sense of just what happen on that infamous day in Dallas. By the writing of this book it has become clear that TOC in America and the Chicago OUTFIT very likely played a key role and may have been responsible for the President's murder according to authors Waldron and Hartmann. This became apparent to Chicago Police Intelligence Unit Detectives in 1994, while investigating several unsolved OUTFIT murders they were made aware that a prolific killer they arrested in 1995 by the name of Lenny Patrick would often brag about how the OUTFIT wacked the President of our country. What is most troubling is the fact that the mistakes this country made that allowed this to happen are still happening today. The Chicago OUTFIT members that were reportedly involved in this killing were: Sam Giancana, Murray Humphreys, Francesco Sacco AKA: Fillipo, Johnny Rosselli, Sam DeStefano, Riccardo Scalzetti AKA: Richard Cain, Chuckie Nicoletti, Lenny Patrick, Irwin Weiner and Jack Ruby. Most of these men died or were murdered before committee investigators could debrief them or bring them before it. It has long been asserted that the Chicago OUTFIT supported presidential candidate John F. Kennedy, however this has been disputed through the research of Professor John Binder of the University of Illinois at Chicago and appears to be of urban legend. Giancana was reportedly incensed when the White House turned its back on the OUTFIT despite overtures from Frank Sinatra et. al. and allowed Attorney General Robert Kennedy and federal law enforcement to initiate the greatest attack by law enforcement the Chicago OUTFIT had ever faced. While the debate rages on, it would be a disservice to exclude this case.

Richard Cain

On **January 21, 1964** Anthony Moschiano 26 yrs. of 914 Oakley was stabbed to death in a garage at 10656 W. 28th St. in Westchester, Illinois. The home was that of Chicago Police Officer Thomas N. Durso. The victim's body was not found until April 13, 1964 in the DesPlaines River near River Grove. He was an ex-convict and a narcotics informant. Thomas Durso and Michael Gargano were convicted of the killing and both were sentenced to 100 to 150 years in prison **(solved)**.

On **March 6, 1964** Albert Louis Romano 41 yrs. of 209 N. Pulaski was found face down shot to death from close range in an alley behind 4137 Grenshaw St. He was an ex-convict who had been found guilty of armed robbery, assault to murder, and extortion. He was a suspected narcotics dealer and the son of Louis Romano, a onetime labor slugger and Capone Mob associate. Reportedly he was killed over a labor dispute. Harold Johnson was convicted of the killing and sentenced to 40-60 years in prison **(solved)**.

On **March 30, 1964** Duane Seavey AKA: David Smiley left his home, never to return. He is assumed dead for his cooperation with authorities that led to the arrest of Joey Aiuppa and several associates in a raid on the Towne Hotel in Cicero on November 1, 1962. Seavey a steel salesman was known to frequent the gambling establishment at the hotel and provided information to the staff of State's Attorney Daniel Ward. In preparation of an affidavit, a mistake was made and Seavey's real name was divulged. For over a year after the arrest he was afforded police protection that was finally ended. It was reported that Aiuppa had lured Seavey to a meeting the day he disappeared although no one was ever charged in the case. State's Attorney Ward gained a reputation for trying to build cases against the OUTFIT and was known for characterizing Cicero as "The Walled City of the Mob".

On **August 31, 1964** Guy Mendola Jr. 39 yrs. of 1554 N. 43rd Ave., Stone Park, Illinois was shotgunned to death by his associates as he parked in the garage of his home at 1554 N. 43rd Ave. in Stone Park, IL. Mendola was a member of the Paul Panczko burglary crew and was also part of a crew under Willie Daddano who were arrested for a Franklin Park bank robbery. He was free on bond regarding federal charges of unlawful flight to avoid burglary prosecution at the time of his killing. After the bank robbery arrest, suspecting one of the crew talked to the police, Daddano through corrupt police official Richard Cain had all the crew members take a polygraph tests in which Mendola failed and was killed. Cain was eventually jailed for his part in the bank robbery. In 1970 Chuckie Cremaldi admitted involvement in this murder, he was never charged **(Solved)**.

On **September 7, 1964** Charles W. White 33 yrs. of 4710 N. Kenmore Ave. was found murdered in a ditch along Naperville Road. He was shot twice in the head three miles southeast of Elgin, IL. He was a convicted killer with a lengthy arrest record. Frank O'Connell was convicted of the crime and sentenced to 40-60 years in prison **(solved)**.

On **March 21, 1965** Bertha Mae Bullock 27 yrs. was found shot to death while sitting in her sports car at 47ᵗʰ St. and the Lake. She was shot three times and was known to be a narcotics informant.

On **April 24, 1965** Willie Horn 39 yrs. was shot and killed at 72ⁿᵈ and Wabash Ave. while sitting in a car with a woman who was also wounded. At the time he was a co-defendant in Federal Court with OUTFIT member Americo T. DePietto.

On **September 9, 1965** Joan Williams 18 yrs. and Eddie Mae Harrison 19 yrs. were found shot in the head alongside the Westlawn Cemetery at 4300 N. Thatcher Road south of Norridge, IL. Both victims had their eyes and mouths taped and both had lengthy police records as prostitutes.

On **May 29, 1965** Leslie R. Vanna AKA: Vana 25 yrs. of 1949 W. 21ˢᵗ St. was murdered. Vanna a uniformed security guard was found bound at his hands, feet, and mouth. While the Tribune reported that Tom Sprovieri was suspected, Mario Sprovieri was charged with the killing and after several continuances the case was stricken by Judge Power with a leave to reinstate, which it never was. Mario was later shot to death in 1970 in a social club at 2620 W. Huron **(Solved)**.

In 1965 Chicago OUTFIT hit men Charles "Chuckie" Nicoletti and Felix "Milwaukee Phil" Alderisio were caught by Chicago Police slumped down in the front seat of their work car apparently preparing to carry out a contract killing. The customized "Hit Car" boasted compartments to hide weapons, was extremely fast, and had switches to turn off the tail lights if police were following. The men and the vehicle gained such notoriety in this arrest they became a topic discussed during congressional hearings in Washington D. C. regarding organized crime. These men were reportedly part of a Mob inspired conspiracy to kill President John F. Kennedy.

On **September 11, 1965** OUTFIT entrepreneur Manny Skar 41 yrs. was gunned down in the entrance of the parking lot of his high rise apartment building at 3800 north Lake Shore Drive. Skar came from the Jewish near west side of Chicago to open two Chicago area hotels with nightclubs using $5.8 Million dollars in loans that were underwritten by the OUTFIT. In less than a year he defaulted on the loans and it was learned that some of the cash was diverted to his personal use. Reportedly Tony Spilotro bragged about the murder and was credited with it, but never charged and Chuckie Cremaldi later admitted involvement. Family Secrets testimony revealed that Tony Spilotro and Joey Lombardo were involved in the killing **(Solved)**.

On **November 24, 1965** Angelo J. Boscarino 33 yrs. was found murdered, he was beaten, stabbed and his throat cut at 4214 W. 24ᵗʰ Place. Boscarino was part of a crew run by Willie "Potatoes" Daddano that high jacked a $380,000 shipment of silver bullion in LaGrange, IL. After someone provided information to authorities the crew was arrested and charged. He was purportedly killed for being an informant, which was denied by authorities. In 1970 Chuckie Cremaldi admitted involvement in this killing. It is not known if he was ever charged **(solved).**

On **December 15, 1965** Anthony P. Ponzio was murdered, he was found in the trunk of a stolen car in the parking lot of O'Hare Airport on January 10, 1966. He had been strangled. He was the nephew of Dominic Galiano who would later succumb to Mob violence himself.

On **February 5, 1966** Mitsuri Wakita 43 yrs. died from gunshot wounds to his chest after replacing a flat tire on his car in front of 243 W. 28th Street. He was the brother-in-law of Daniel Escobedo who gained notoriety for suing the State of Illinois for a violation of his sixth amendment right to counsel.

On **February 28, 1966** Leonard Centrone 29 yrs. was found dead behind a building at 2074 George Street in Melrose Park, IL. He was shot eleven times in the head, heart and groin probably while in his car. He had been implicated in a high jacking in which several men went to prison.

On **February 28, 1966** Clarence A. Forest 26 yrs. of Worth, IL. was found in the trunk of his car in St. John, IN. He had been shot twice in the chest and right thigh. He had been a part-time bouncer in three joints operated by mobster Frank LaPorte. He was believed to be associated with Louis Practico who was killed at a later time. Found on the victim was a diary outlining activities at the Eagles Club where he was a bartender and information about other notorious vice dens in Willow Springs, IL.

Frank LaPorte & Al Capone

March 10, 1966 Dominick "Hunk" Galiano an OUTFIT vice purveyor and manager of the OUTFIT controlled Talk of the Town Club, was murdered while playing cards by Jasper Campise an OUTFIT loan shark operator who was arrested for the murder, although the outcome of that case is unknown. Campise would gain Mob notoriety for his botched assassination attempt on Ken Eto in 1983 that cost him his life.

On **July 20, 1966** Sam Panveno AKA: Van Corbin was shot and killed by two unknown men using handguns equipped with silencers outside the Country Club Motel 8303 North Ave. Melrose Park, IL. He was staying there temporarily with his wife and family. He was an associate of mobsters and had been the contractor in the 1963 construction of Tony Accardo's new home at 1407 Ashland in River Forest, IL.

On **August 30, 1966** Louis "Gigi" Pratico 42 yrs. of 42 West 14th Street, Chicago Heights was found in a ditch at Joe Orr Road and West End Avenue on the outskirts of Chicago Heights. He had been beaten and shot twice in the head. He was alleged to be a front man for Frank LaPorte and had been a Chicago Heights police officer until he was dismissed from the department. It was believed that he was trying to maintain some of LaPorte's rackets after the gang boss retired to CA. Fifi Buccieri, the future OUTFIT Boss, was suspected as he moved in on LaPorte's operations.

On **September 17, 1966** Lawrence "Larry" Stubitsch AKA: Stubich was shot to death during an alleged Robbery at the Bistro Room, a Go-Go on Higgins Road. Four armed men entered the establishment at 4:15 am and a struggle ensued in which Stubich and the manager Richard DeAngelo were both shot, but DeAngelo survived. Family Secrets testimony revealed that the victim was a business partner with Frank Calabrese in the 1960s putting juice loans on the street and DeAngelo was the killer. However, Frank Calabrese was denied permission to avenge the killing by Angelo LaPietra at the time **(solved)**.

On **November 22, 1966** Charles C. Crispino 51 yrs. of 1738 N. Natoma was killed. He was shot five times while exiting his car near his home. He had worked at the office of the Illinois Secretary of State.

On **February 22, 1967** Robert T. Hannah 31 yrs. of 1058 N. Marshfield was found dead and frozen in a snow bank on 31st Street near the Tri State Tollway in Lyons Township outside of Chicago. He had been shot 8 times. He was to testify in court regarding a narcotics case.

On **February 27, 1967** Wesley Funicella 39 yrs. of South Holland, IL. was found dead in the trunk of his car parked in Blue Island, IL. He left his home the previous day at 5:30 pm to "see a man". Police believe he was a victim of juice operators whom he had borrowed $17,000 from in January of 1964, repaying only $4,600. He was beaten and strangled.

On **March 7, 1967** Joseph F. Polito 33 yrs. was shot-gunned to death near his home at 4121 N. Spaulding. He was an admitted swindler and game fixer. He was heavily in debt to mob juice operators and had testified in 1965 as a sports fixer.

On **March 16, 1967** Alan R. Rosenberg 36 yrs. of Skokie, IL. was murdered. He was found in the back seat of a rented Cadillac with his hands cuffed in front of him, he was shot seven times. Police believed he was slain between 9:00 am and 3:00 pm the previous day. Rosenberg was an ex-convict and an associate of Felix "Milwaukee Phil" Alderisio. It was later learned that Rosenberg and Alderisio were involved in a major scam of a travel agency that may have contributed to his death. He was also believed to be a juice collector for the OUTFIT. Frank Schweihs was questioned in the killing, but never charged.

On **May 3, 1967** Louise Covelli was murdered at her Encino CA. home. The 31 year old was the wife of Chicago mobster turned informant Gerry Covelli. While she was found bruised and beaten, the official coroner's report stated that she had overdosed.

On **June 18, 1967** Gerry Covelli was killed in Encino, CA. He was a career mobster in Chicago and associated with the Rush street crew of James Policheri AKA: "Monk" Allegretti. He became involved in a Mob hijacking case and ultimately turned informant moving to California after testifying against his associates. However, the long arm of the OUTFIT located him and placed a bomb in his car that literally blew him to pieces.

Monk Allegretti

On **July 12, 1967** Arthur "Boodie" Cowan 46 yrs. of 7307 Crawford, Lincolnwood, IL. was found dead in the trunk of his car parked at 418 S. Kilpatrick. He was shot once behind his left ear with a .32 cal. weapon. Cowan was last seen alive as he left his home on July 5th for a three hour meeting on the Southside. The car had been parked at that location since July 7th. He was a juice collector for the OUTFIT.

In **November of 1967** Eugenio Lopez AKA: James Crizell was murdered. Lopez had interfered with OUTFIT Bolita operations and Ken Eto lured him to a meeting at 642 N. Clark where OUTFIT killers Anthony DelMonte, Frank Orlando and Vincent Inserro strangled the victim with a wire. Northside gambling Boss Ross Priola AKA: Prio ordered the killing. This information was provided by OUTFIT associate Ken Eto after a failed attempt on his life in 1983 **(Solved)**.

On **August 6, 1969** Harry D. Carlson was murdered. He was a business partner to murder victims Steve Ostrowsky (killed 76) and Harry Holzer (killed 75) and the first of 30 to 40 killed allegedly during an OUTFIT struggle to control the Chop Shop Racket between 1969 and 1983 known as "Car Wars" by the press.

On **December 5, 1969** Earl Omer Addlesman 47 yrs. of Zion, IL. just north of Chicago, was found on the floor of a 1967 Chevrolet station wagon parked at 14th and Peoria. He was bound gagged and shot in the head with a .22 cal. weapon. The victim was heavily in debt to juice operators.

Between 1969 and 1983 close to 40 murders occurred in what Law Enforcement felt was the attempted OUTFIT takeover of the Auto Theft Rackets and subsequent Chop Shop operations in the Chicago area. Jimmy "The Bomber" Catuara was replaced by Albert "Cesar" Tocco in running the operations after a bloody takeover. Local media appropriately referred to the killings as the "Car Wars" in Chicago.

Approx. number of Chicago TOC related murders in the 1960s: 88
Approx. number of Chicago TOC related murder cases in the 1960s solved: 2
Approx. number of Chicago TOC related murders in the 1960s of Police Officers: 0

Chapter 7. The 1970s

The Chicago Crime Commission in 1970 voiced a concern over the OUTFIT's infiltration into local movie theaters; this was followed by a 1971 CCC report in conjunction with the Illinois Institute of Technology titled "A Study of Organized Crime in Illinois". The report contained a strategic plan for Illinois Law Enforcement in the battle against TOC. Several well-known OUTFIT members have placed their relatives in the local projectionist union.

In the 1970s federal legislators were finally dedicated to attacking TOC and started to focus on the hierarchy with the introduction of the "Racketeering Influenced and Corrupt Organizations Statute"(RICO). This allowed local and federal prosecutors to work together in their efforts using local and federal statutes, targeting leaders and seizing their assets.

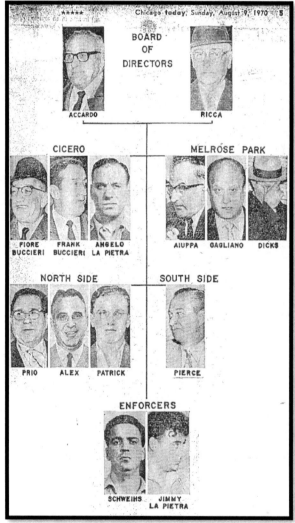

OUTFIT Leadership 1970

Critical events of the 1970s

On **March 21, 1970** Carmen Trotta 28 yrs. of Crestwood, IL. a southwestern suburb of Chicago was shot twice in the side and pursued through a parking lot in Lyons, IL. near Chicago. He had been convicted of high jacking $138,000 worth of cigars. A female motorist saw the pursuit and saw one of the assailants with a gun. When the victim fell a passing motorist stopped causing the assailants to flee in a car driven by a third man that almost hit a truck as it left.

In **August/September of 1970** Michael "Hambone" Albergo, an OUTFIT loan shark and enforcer who was assigned to muscle those late on their payments, disappeared before standing trial in a criminal case where he was arrested for making loans to undercover police officers. It was always thought he died at the hands of his OUTFIT associates for making such detrimental mistakes. Nick Calabrese in his cooperation with the FBI led them to the Bridgeport construction site where Hambone was supposedly buried. The site on the edge of the new Chicago White Sox stadium known as Cellular Field or "The Cell" by the media yielded only a tooth and some bone fragments that did match Albergo after DNA analysis. Nick Calabrese provided details on how he, Frank his brother and Ronnie Jarrett picked the victim up in a stolen car, where they strangled him to death before disposing of his body. (Case cleared through Operation Family Secrets in 2005, Frank Calabrese Sr. was held responsible at trial) **(solved)**.

On **September 28, 1970** Mario Sprovieri was shot to death in a storefront social club at 2620 W. Huron St. five bullets entered his face and head. The case remains unsolved. He was previously charged with the murder of Leslie R. Vanna in 1965. After numerous delays that case was stricken on leave by Judge Power and never reinstated.

On **January 7, 1971** Rosario "Ross" Corriero 41 yrs. of 19211 S. Emerald in Crete, IL. was found dead, shot twice, once in the head and once in the chest. His body was found in the rear of his station wagon by the Crete Police Department. Police reported that hundreds of football parlay cards printed by OUTFIT gamblers were found in the car and they surmised that he was an OUTFIT gambling associate.

On **October 19, 1971** Sam "Sambo" Cesario 53 yrs. of 917 S. Bishop was clubbed and shot to death while seated on a lawn chair in front of a building he owned at 1071 W. Polk Street. The assault was carried out by two masked men who kept Sam's wife and a friend at gun point during the attack. Sambo was an OUTFIT gambling boss who oversaw gambling and juice activity in the Maxwell Street area. It was learned at a later time that Sam had taken up with the girlfriend of imprisoned OUTFIT Boss Felix "Milwaukee Phil" Alderisio. Harry Aleman, Tony Spilotro, Butch Petrocelli and Joey Lombardo were suspected of this murder, but never charged.

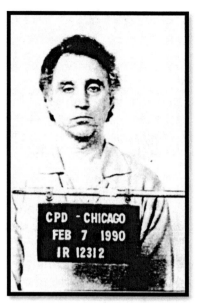

Harry Aleman

On **December 1, 1972** Charles Krulik was found murdered in a shallow grave in Maine Township along Algonquin Road near the TriState Tollway. A telephone tip to police led to the discovery. The victim testified regarding OUTFIT jargon in the trial of Sam DeStefano who himself would be murdered several months later. The case remains unsolved.

On **March 10, 1972** Charles W. Carroll 39 yrs. of Hickory Hills, IL. was found dead in the trunk of a parked car at 8119 S. Ada. The victim was bound, gagged, blindfolded and shot once in the back of the head. He was a long time bookmaking lieutenant for OUTFIT gambling boss Ralph Pierce.

Ralph Pierce

On **August 8, 1972** Guido Fidanzi 45 yrs. of Chicago Heights, IL. was shot to death in the office of a gas station in Chicago Heights. Two killers fired 10 shots from two handguns into the victim. He was known as a Mob member and ex-convict.

On **September 27, 1972** William Logan 35 yrs. of 5916 W. Walton was murdered on the street in front of his home. He was on his way to work when a car pulled up with two men in it and shotgunned him. Harry Aleman was charged with the killing when his driver Louie Almeida informed police of what happened. Logan was married to Aleman's cousin and she turned to Aleman for help during their divorce. During the first trial Aleman was acquitted by a corrupt Judge. Years later, after a corruption scandal known as Operation Greylord, the truth came out, the corrupt Judge committed suicide and Aleman was retried and convicted and ended up dying in prison **(Solved)**.

On **October 1, 1972** Patrolman Anthony Raymond 25, of the Hillside P.D. was murdered after being abducted during a traffic stop on the westbound entrance ramp to the Eisenhower Expressway at Mannheim Road. Patrolman Raymond was unaware the three occupants in the suspicious vehicle he stopped had just committed an armed robbery. The suspects abducted him, taking him to one of the suspect's homes where he was strangled with a guitar string. He was then stabbed four times in the back which proved to be fatal. The suspects placed his body in a 55-gallon drum which was transported to a farm owned by the sister of one suspect near Rhinelander, WI. His body was then buried in a shallow grave and not found until nearly 11 months later. Two suspects were convicted of conspiracy, aggravated kidnapping and murder. The offender who committed the strangling and stabbing was sentenced to three concurrent terms of 100 to 200 years and died in prison in 2009. The other offender was sentenced to four concurrent terms of 75 to 150 years in prison. The third suspect was killed during an attempted robbery in Indiana in 1973. Robert Harder a partner in a burglary and jewel theft ring provided information in this killing and was killed himself in 1974. Louis Almeida a partner of hit man Harry Aleman claimed that Aleman informed him that the killers in this case were associates of Aleman and called him to tell him of this incident after it occurred **(solved)**.

On **April 14, 1973** "Mad Sam" DeStefano 64 yrs. of 1656 N. Sayre was shotgunned to death in his garage. On March 6, 1972 DeStefano and Edward Speice were arrested for threatening a government witness with death. At the trial DeStefano represented himself making a total mockery of the trial process and angering his OUTFIT superiors and sealing his fate as a loose cannon. Speice was an associate of DeStefano and a career criminal. DeStefano was known as an OUTFIT juice collector, killer and Mob terrorist. He had become a liability to the OUTFIT by his public challenge to law enforcement and his psychotic behavior. Sam Giancana did not like Mad Sam and requested several times to take him out, but was always thwarted by Paul Ricca who protected Mad Sam. Maybe with Ricca's recent death Mad Sam lost his protection. At the time of his death he was awaiting trial for the 1963 murder of Leo S. Foreman. Two of his soldiers Tony

Spilotro and his own brother Mario were suspected of killing Mad Sam, but never charged. They used the ruse of having information on the whereabouts of turncoat Chuckie Cremaldi to set up the slaying. As they approached the garage Mario provided a cover for Tony who was carrying a shotgun, when Mario stepped aside Tony's first shot took Mad Sam's arm off. He never knew what hit him.

Mad Sam DeStefano dead

On **June 23, 1973** William "Red" Klim was shot to death in the parking lot of Churchill Down Race Book in Las Vegas, Nevada. The victim was an employee of Ceasar's Palace Casino and may have been murdered for several reasons to include: he was cooperating with authorities in an investigation of illegal bookmaking that targeted Chicago OUTFIT operative Lefty Rosenthal, he had information regarding Tony Spilotro's involvement in the Teamster Pension Fund investigation or that he was a loanshark that refused to pay street tax to Spilotro. Spilotro was ultimately charged but the case fell apart when witnesses were unable or unwilling to identify the killer **(solved)**.

On **June 30, 1973** Frank Gallo died from gunshot wounds he received on June 28, 1973. Gallo was an OUTFIT associate who was shot while allegedly breaking into the home of mobster Nicholas Sarillo Sr. AKA: Ricardello at 6021 Emerson in Rosemont, IL. Apparently police ruled the shooting justifiable and Sarillo was not charged. Several years later Sarillo was arrested with a number of men in a high stakes poker game at the Happy Days Tavern in Island Lake, IL. Among the men arrested were notable OUTFIT figures Joe Amato and Michael Posner. In 1982 Sarillo survived a car bomb in Wauconda, IL. Police investigating the explosion suspected that Sarillo may have been transporting the car bomb when it went off.

Joe Amato

On **June 30, 1973** Frank Giammarese and his wife Marlene of 2035 W. Belle Plain were gunned down in a hail of gunfire from an automobile in front of 3442 N. Lincoln Ave. They had just left the Cordon Blue Lounge a couple of doors south in the early morning hours. Reportedly Frank was involved in the Bolita racket indicated by a 1968 arrest. Little information was available on this case and it occurred approximately 2 blocks from the scene of the murder of former police Captain William Drury in September of 1950.

On **December 20, 1973**, Riccardo Scalzetti AKA: Richard Cain 49 yrs. was murdered at Rose's Snack shop at 1117 w. Grand Avenue. Cain was lured to his death under the guise of accepting an OUTFIT contract to kill Las Vegas oilman Ray Ryan. Ryan had pressed charges against Las Vegas overseer Marshal Ciafano for extortion in 1963. Ryan was eventually killed in an explosion in October of 1977, while leaving his tennis club. Cain a former law enforcement operative with the Chicago Police Department and later a Chief Investigator for the Cook County Sheriff, worked as an informant for the FBI and was an operative for the CIA all while maintaining his loyalty to Sam Giancana. These connections emerged in 1964 and he was fired from the Sheriff's Office. He was later convicted in his role in a 1963 Franklin Park bank robbery and sentenced to a 3 year prison term. When he was paroled in 1971 he traveled to Mexico and the Middle East with Sam Giancana, he resided in Mexico with Giancana helping him to build his Caribbean gambling empire and acted as a courier for other business interests as far away as Europe. On this cold December day, he had been back from Mexico for only about 3 weeks, when two men wearing ski masks and carrying a shotgun and a pistol staged a hold up, Cain was conferring with four other men when the robbers stood all 7 patrons against a wall when the killers took his face off with a shot gun. Harry Aleman, Marshall Caifano, Tony Spilotro, Joey Lombardo and Frank Schweihs were all suspects in this murder, but never charged. Cain probably obtained more access to law enforcement than any other hood in history. In 2005 it was reported that Cain along with Chuckie Nicoletti, Francesco Sacco AKA: Fillipo-Johnny Rosselli, Jack Ruby, Murray Humphreys, Sam DeStefano, Lenny Patrick, Irwin Weiner and Sam Giancana played key roles in the assassination of President John F. Kennedy. Cain was actually on a list of people congressional investigators sought to interview in the 1970s, although most were killed before testifying before the House Select Committee on Assassinations. It was rumored that possible motives for this slaying were that Cain was trying to establish his own crew while another theory states that Marshall Caifano learned of his informant status and obtained permission to have him killed. Reportedly John Monteleone, Angelo and James LaPietra, John Fecarotta, Turk Torello and Joey Aiuppa were responsible for this killing **(Solved)**.

Angelo LaPietra

On **January 6, 1974** David Yaras was murdered. Reportedly before congressional investigators could question him about the assassination of President John F. Kennedy. While details of the Yaras murder are unknown, at this time much is known about the background of Davie Yaras. He was born in Chicago and became friendly with Jack Ruby and Lenny Patrick at a young age and he worked as a hit man for the Chicago Mob. Yaras was also a close associate of Jimmy Hoffa and helped establish Teamster Local 320 in Miami. After WWII, Yaras worked for the OUTFIT in Cuba. According to a federal narcotics officer, Yaras "ran a number of gambling operations on the island". After the fall of Fulgencio Batista, Yaras was the "Chicago OUTFIT's liaison to the Cuban exile community". Yaras, considered to be the prime suspect in several gangland killings, was arrested 14 times by the police. In 1947 he was arrested for the murder of James M. Ragen, the national manager of the Continental Press

Service, an organization that was in conflict with the OUTFIT. Four witnesses identified Lenny Patrick, Dave Yaras, and William Block as the gunmen, but after one witness was murdered, two recanted, and another fled, the indictment was dropped. The night before the assassination of President John F. Kennedy, federal investigators eventually learned that Yaras telephoned another hit man, Robert Barney Baker. A few days earlier, Jack Ruby also received a 17 minute telephone-call from Baker. Yaras was interviewed by the FBI and admitted that he had known Ruby for about 15 years in Chicago. However, as Bernard Fensterwald has pointed out: "The FBI never asked Yaras about his own Mafia connections, but did ask him whether he thought Ruby was connected with the syndicate". Yaras, as one might guess, stated that he doubted that Ruby had such connections."

On **January 27, 1974** Wayne Cascone 27 yrs. of 3412 S. Bell was found shot to death in a parked car at 3335 S. Western. An informant claimed two men had lured the victim to a car in an alley near his home before he was killed. Cascone boasted to a girlfriend that he had information on the death of Sam Rantis who was missing since December and later found in February. Cascone was involved in Bolita operations and linked to a scandal involving counterfeit money being passed through the operation. An ex-con friend of Rantis said 5 deaths were linked to in-fighting over the counterfeit money. James Irwin was suspected of the killing, but never charged, he was killed in May of 1976.

On **February 24, 1974** Socrates "Sam" Rantis 43 yrs. of 7912 W. North Ave. in Elmwood Park, IL. was found murdered. His frozen body was found in the trunk of his wife's Buick parked at O'Hare airport. He was last seen on December 7, 1973. He had puncture wounds to his chest and his throat was slashed. He owned Albano's restaurant formerly the Korner Sandwich Shop at 1015 S. Western where the bodies of 2 of his contemporaries Joe Grisafe and Sam Marcello would be found stuffed into 55gal. drums on July 6, 1974. Sam had owned the Motor World West Hotel at 5255 W. 47th St. in Forest View where federal agents confiscated counterfeit bills and equipment in June of 1970. Rantis served 11 months in prison for those charges. He was involved in Bolita operations. Police eventually learned that James Irwin and Wayne Cascone were two of the killers in this and other related murders. However, Irwin was killed on May 1, 1976 and Cascone was found dead on January 27, 1974 before either was brought to justice for these crimes. The cases were exceptionally cleared and closed by the Chicago Police Department. It was later reported that Harry Aleman was also involved in this murder **(solved)**.

On **April 21, 1974** William Simone 29 yrs. of 2415 N. Laramie was found by a passerby shot in the head in the back of his parked car at 2446 S. Kedvale Avenue. His hands and feet were bound and his mouth was gagged. He was an associate of Sam Marcello and was tied to the Cicero faction of the OUTFIT and Fifi Buccieri. His death was linked to the killing of 4 others and related to a Bolito and counterfeiting operation. It was later reported that Harry Aleman was involved in this killing but never charged.

On **June 14, 1974** Anthony J. Dichiarinte AKA: Tony D. 56 yrs. of 6336 N. Kolmar was found badly decomposed in the trunk of a rented car parked in the parking lot of a Holiday Inn in Willowbrook, Illinois. He was last seen in April and was reported missing on May 10th by his wife. He had been dead for approx. four weeks. He had an arrest record ranging from hijacking to armed robbery and reportedly was known to be in the narcotics trade. He had identification in his clothing and the case remains unsolved.

On **July 6, 1974** Samuel J. Marcello Sr. 57 yrs. of 6017 N. Emerson in Rosemont IL. and Joseph "Big Joe" Grisafe 34 yrs. of 742 W. Dempster, Mount Prospect, Illinois were found murdered. Marcello disappeared in November of 1973 after collecting a juice loan from a Chicago restaurant owner. Both men were found stuffed into 55 gal. drums behind the Korner Sandwich Shop at 1015 S. Western Ave. Information provided to the police revealed that these were just 2 of 5 murders related to the same dispute. The former owner of the restaurant Sam Rantis was also slain over this feud. All the men were involved in Bolita operations and linked to a scandal involving counterfeit money being passed through the operation. Police eventually learned that James Irwin and Wayne Cascone were the killers in this and other related murders, however Irwin was killed on May 1, 1976 and Cascone on January 27, 1974 before they were brought to justice for these crimes. These murder cases were exceptionally cleared and closed by the Chicago Police Department **(solved)**.

On **July 13, 1974** Orion Williams 38 yrs. was found shotgunned to death in the trunk of his girlfriend's 1972 Chevrolet at 70 E. 33rd Street. He was believed to be involved in highjackings and may have withheld information from the OUTFIT. He was also set for trial on July 9th for a federal indictment and may have been cooperating with authorities. Several years later information was presented that linked long time Cicero, OUTFIT member James Inendino to the murder during a sentencing hearing in Federal court. However, the case remains unsolved. Harry Aleman was also named as a suspect, but never charged **(Solved)**.

On **September 27, 1974** Daniel Seifert 29 yrs. of Bensenville, IL. was shotgunned to death in front of his wife and 4 year old son at his Bensenville business. Four masked gunman in two vehicles appeared at 8 am. The victim tried to flee to a neighboring plant where he was hit by a shotgun blast. He was again shot with a 38 cal. pistol and shotgun. When he went to the ground a shotgun was placed to his head. Seifert was involved with Irv Weiner and Felix "Milwaukee Phil" Alderisio in the International Fiber Glass Co. in Elk Grove. The OUTFIT fabricated the company to bilk money in the form of loans from the Teamsters Central States Pension Fund. In February Seifert, Joey Lombardo, Felix Alderisio, Irv Weiner, Ron DeAngeles, Tony Spilotro and Allen Dorfman were indicted for the fraudulent loans coming out of the pension fund for years. The OUTFIT at this point could not afford for Seifert to testify the following January against Lombardo in the Teamster Pension Fund case. Lombardo et. al. was accused of defrauding the Teamsters of 1.4 million in loans to American Pail

Company in Deming New Mexico. Joey Lombardo, Frank Schweihs, Joey Hanson, Jimmy LaPietra and Tony Spilotro reportedly caught up with Seifert and killed him. (Case cleared through Operation Family Secrets in 2005, Joey Lombardo was held responsible at trial) **(solved)**.

On **September 28, 1974** Robert W. Harder 39 yrs. of Hoffman Estates, IL. was found near Dwight, IL. He was shot in the face in a bean field and a pistol was found under is body. His wife's car was nearby. Harder was an informant in the killing of Hillside Police Officer Anthony Raymond in 1972. Reportedly he was also part of a burglary/jewel theft ring and had flipped on one of his partners Silas C. Fletcher and was due to testify against Fletcher in an upcoming trial. In 1974 Joey Lombardo was suspected in the murder of Harder, but not charged. In 1978 federal authorities had claimed that James Inendino and Harry Aleman had previously tried to kill Harder. His murder remains unsolved.

On **December 27, 1974** Richard J. Mazzone 40 yrs. of Melrose Park was shotgunned to death in the driveway of his home. He was struck in the abdomen and back after parking his car. He claimed to be a self-employed plumber and owner of Mazzone Plumbing, Sewer and Rodding Service.

On **January 16, 1975** Carlo DeVivo 46 yrs. was shot and killed as he walked to his car from his apartment at 3631 N. Nora Street. Two masked gunman shot him with a shotgun and pistol 3 times in the head and 3 times in the body. The men fled in a waiting van with a car following them to obstruct any pursuit. The van was abandon behind 7062 W. Belmont Avenue. The victim was a bookmaker and an associate of the Chicago OUTFIT under Turk Torello as far back as 1951 and worked as muscle in the juice business. His murder was reportedly planned and executed by Harry Aleman although he was never charged.

The Last Supper: Accardo, Amato, DiVarco, Torello, Aiuppa, DiBella, Solano, Pilotto, Cerone, Lombardo

On **April 29, 1975** Anthony P. Battaglia 61 yrs. of LaGrange Park, IL. was shot once under the chin with a 38. cal. handgun in the driveway of his home. He was a member of the OUTFIT and the brother of the late boss Sam "Teetz" Battaglia. He owned Cicero Amusement Devices, a pinball machine distributor. At the time there was friction between Cicero mobsters and a group known as the Hillbilly Mafia which resulted in 4 deaths in 1975. The victim operated out of the Annetta Hotel in the 2400 block of Laramie and the Silver Spur Lounge in the 2100 block of Cicero Avenue.

In **April of 1975** Joseph Lipuma 33, was reported murdered in the basement of Chalmers Elementary school on the Westside of Chicago where he was a janitor. At first police ruled the death natural, probably a heart attack until a mortician found a small bullet hole behind the man's ear. The victim was an associate of Ronald Magliano and Sam Annerino who were both killed later in OUTFIT fashion. Police suspected his killing was related to the others, but no charges were ever placed.

On **May 12, 1975** Ronald T. Magliano 43 yrs. of 6232 S. Kilpatrick Avenue was found shot to death, gagged and blindfolded. He was shot with a 25. cal. handgun behind his left ear. His home was set on fire using gasoline at three separate locations, which blew the windows out, presumably to conceal the murder. The victim was an underworld fence and was scheduled to be sentenced on May 20th for a recent conviction. Harry Aleman was later reported to be involved with the killing, but never charged.

On **May 12, 1975** Edward "Marty" Buccieri was shot to death while sitting in his car in the parking lot of Ceasar's Palace Casino in Las Vegas, Nevada where he was a pit boss. Marty was a cousin of Chicago Mob Boss Fiore Buccieri. Law Enforcement learned that Buccieri had approached Allen Glick the head of Argent Corporation and the Mob's man running casinos in Vegas namely the Stardust, Hacienda, Fremont and Marina casinos. Marty demanded a finder's fee for his help in introducing Glick to Mob connected financial backers in obtaining loans. He went as far as physically threatening Glick. Glick informed Lefty Rosenthal of the incident. Rosenthal allegedly reported this problem back to Bosses in Chicago and Tony Spilotro was given the contract to take out Marty. Police arrested a low level hood by the name of Horton for the crime although he stated that he was trying to rob Marty when he shot and killed him **(solved)**.

On **June 6, 1975** Harry Holzer and his girlfriend were found murdered in a summer home in Fennville, MI. near the vacation mecca of South Haven. Holzer was a business partner to murder victims Steve Ostrowsky (killed 76) and Harry D. Carlson (killed 69) and one of 30 to 40 reportedly killed during an OUTFIT struggle to control the Chop Shop Racket between 1969 and 1983 known as "Car Wars".

On **June 19, 1975** Sam Giancana AKA: Momo Salvatore, Mooney, or Gilormo Giangono 67 yrs. was murdered in his home at 1147 S. Wenonah in Oak Park, Illinois. Momo recently returned to Chicago, from his exile in Mexico (from 1966 to 1974), after being expelled by Mexican authorities. Momo was shot 7 times with a .22 cal. handgun in the head, mouth and chin at approximately 10:30 pm in the basement kitchen of his home. He had returned recently from a Houston Hospital regarding health issues. His body was discovered around midnight by caretaker Joe DiPersio. At the time it was speculated that he was killed for several possible reasons that included: he withheld profits from Chicago Bosses for his lucrative gambling empire in the Caribbean, he was hoping to resume his leadership role in the Chicago OUTFIT, or a fear of Momo talking to federal authorities regarding the OUTFITs' involvement in numerous TOC/CIA coup and assassinations plots against Fidel Castro, when in reality they were allegedly an important cog in the assassination of President John F. Kennedy through Chicago operatives such as Riccardo Scalzetti AKA: Richard Cain, Francesco Sacco AKA: Fillipo- Johnny Rosselli, Charles Nicoletti, Murray Humphreys, Sam DeStefano, Lenny Patrick, Irwin Weiner and Jack Ruby. Chicago Police at the time were conducting surveillance on the home which led to Dominic "Butch" Blasi and Chuckie English, both close to Giancana, subpoenaed to appear before a Grand Jury regarding the murder that appeared to be sanctioned by OUTFIT leadership. Giancana was the first of several witnesses to be murdered before they could be interviewed by Congressional Investigators as to their involvement in the JFK assassination. Reportedly Angelo LaPietra disposed of the gun.

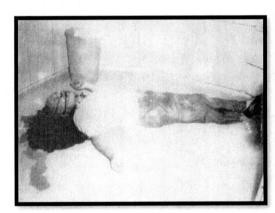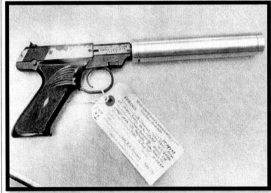

Giancana dead and Gun used

On **July 14, 1975** Christopher Joseph Cardi AKA: Chris, Richard 43 yrs. of Elmwood Park, IL. was approached by two masked gunmen inside Jim's Beef Stand at 1620 N. River Road in Melrose Park, IL. and shot to death. The assailants used .45 cal. handguns shooting the victim 8 times in the back and once in the face. An employee was wounded during the assault. This occurred at 12:11 pm as the victim's wife and 3 of his children looked on. Cardi was the nephew of mobster William "The Beast-Wee Willie" Messino who was a juice operator for Joseph "Joe Gags" Gagliano. He was a police officer from 1957 to 1962. He ran afoul of the OUTFIT when he was sentenced to 10 years in prison for selling heroin in 1971. The OUTFIT did nothing to assist him and he was paroled on June 18th. Harry Aleman and Butch Petrocelli were reported to be the killers, but never charged.

Willie Messino

On **July 30, 1975** Chicago OUTFIT confidant and Teamster Union Leader Jimmy Hoffa disappears on his way to a planned meeting outside of Detroit. An FBI wire years earlier recorded Murray Humphries and Guiseppe Glielmi AKA: Joey Glimco a union powerhouse, describe Hoffa as "the best man they ever knew". Hoffa's willingness to make available Teamster Pension Funds to TOC across the country was no doubt the reason behind such praise. It was reported in 2005 that Hoffa also played a part in the assassination of President John F. Kennedy. Hoffa was never seen again and assumed dead. The strongest suspect in the murder was Russell Bufalino an east coast gangster and labor racketeer, but he was never charged.

Joey Glimco

On **August 28, 1975** Frank Goulakos 47 yrs. of 601 Charing Cross Road in Elk Grove Village, Illinois was approaching his vehicle parked at Seminole and Parkside when a masked gunman jumped out of a car and shot him 6 times striking him in the head and chest. The attacker jumped back in the car and fled the scene. The victim was a cook at DiLeo's Restaurant 5700 N. Central, about 2 blocks from the murder scene. His front tire had been flattened apparently in an effort to detain him during the attack. Harry Aleman was reported to be a suspect in this murder, but never charged.

On **August 30, 1975** Nick Galanos AKA: Keggie or Kegee, 48 yrs. of 6801 W. Wabansia was found shot to death in the basement recreation room of his home. He was shot seven times in the head, back and chest with a .45 cal. handgun. Police estimate the shooting to occur after 10pm the previous evening. The victim was a city-dump foreman who had an interest in a Broadview discount store. He had been subpoenaed by the Illinois Crime Investigating Commission in 1969 and was a bookmaker who was warned by the OUTFIT not to move his operations into Forest Park. He apparently ignored the warnings and seemed to have known his killers. Harry Aleman was reported to be a suspect in this murder, but never charged.

On **September 11, 1975** August Maniaci a member of the Milwaukee crime family and gambling purveyor under the control of the Chicago OUTFIT was murdered by several gun shots outside his Milwaukee home. He was a suspected informer and it was reported that Chuckie Nicoletti a prolific killer was seen in the area around the time of the shooting. It was also reported that Chicago Mobster Albert Tocco was involved in the killing but never charged.

On **October 6, 1975** Louis Bombacino was killed in Tempe, Arizona when his car blew up. He was a known OUTFIT member turned FBI informant who had testified against OUTFIT Underboss Jackie Cerone and others in 1970.

On **October 8, 1975** Frank Plum 43yrs., of 2117 N. Western Ave. was shot in the head four times and killed in the alley behind 939 N. California. Harry Aleman was a suspect in this crime, but never charged.

On **October 31, 1975** Anthony J. Reitinger 34 yrs. of 5302 N. Magnolia was murdered. Reitinger was an independent bookmaker who made an estimated $30,000 a day out of his home. He resisted OUTFIT threats from prolific killer Harry Aleman demanding street tax on his operation. He was in Mama Luna's Pizzeria at 4846 W. Fullerton to meet someone when two masked men entered carrying a sawed off shotgun and carbine. Both men fired striking him six times and killing him immediately. Harry Aleman and Joe Lombardo were suspected of the crime, but never charged.

On **November 9, 1975** Tamara Rand was killed in her home in San Diego, California. She was a friend and business partner of the Mob's Las Vegas front man Allen Glick. She invested in his Casinos and was hired as a consultant at the Hacianda for $100,000 dollars a year. She was led to believe that she had purchased a percentage of the casinos that Glick ran for the Mob, when Glick denied this she sued him. A trial could have revealed the Mob's hidden interests in the casinos. The murder occurred just days after an argument with Glick. The weapon used was a 22cal. handgun the weapon of choice of Tony Spilotro who was a suspect, but never charged.

On **December 3, 1975** Ned C. Bakes AKA: Ignatius Spacchesi 70 yrs. of Addison, IL. was found by his daughter dead in the trunk of his 1975 Chevrolet Caprice one half mile from his home in the parking lot of the Torch-Lite restaurant. He was shot twice in the top of the head with a large caliber handgun and he was strangled. He was reported missing by his wife who last saw him at 8:30 am on Saturday November 29th. The victim was a Capone era gangster who served as a county bailiff in the 30's and a Deputy Sheriff in the 40's. He acted as a courier for Paul Ricca in the 40's and 50's when Ricca was in prison. He served time for tax evasion and stolen securities convictions and was paroled in 1973.

On **January 20, 1976** Frank DeLegge Jr. 38 yrs. of Melrose Park, IL. was found frozen with his throat slashed in a ditch at Roman Road and the Tri-State Tollway in Elmhurst, IL. He was reported missing that night. He was released from prison in 1974 for a 1963 bank robbery that also saw Frank DeLegge Sr., Riccardo Scalzetti AKA: Richard Cain, Willie Daddano and Rocco Montagna convicted. He was also convicted of robbing a Crystal Lake jewelry salesman twice. The victim was the son-in-law of Nick Palermo and worked at Palermo's Mayo Plumbing Company.

On **January 31, 1976** Louis DeBartolo 29 yrs. of 1514 N. 35th Ave. in Melrose Park, IL. was found murdered in the rear of International Discount Sales at 5945 W. North Avenue where he worked. He was on a prison release program for a robbery conviction of the Columbia National Bank of Chicago. His wife reported him missing on January 29th. His body displayed marks on his arms indicating someone stood on his arms while he was tortured with a mop handle that was found jammed down his throat. He had puncture wounds in his neck and was shot in the right ear with a small caliber handgun. Police learned he was deeply in debt and may have been a juice customer. Harry Aleman was reported to be a suspect in this murder, but never charged.

On **May 1, 1976** James Erwin 28 yrs. of 1937 W. 33rd Street was murdered as he exited his car at 1873 N. Halsted. He was shot 13 times with a shotgun and .45 cal. handgun and hit in the abdomen, back and shoulder. Erwin was identified by police as a killer in 4 of 5 murders related to the Bolita racket in 1974. All the victims were involved in Bolita operations and linked to a scandal involving counterfeit money being passed through the racket. Irwin was killed before he was brought to justice for these crimes. Harry Aleman was reported to be a suspect in this murder, but never charged.

On **June 30, 1976** Paul Haggerty 27 yrs. was found bound, gagged, blindfolded and strangled in the trunk of his car at police auto pond #7 at 3200 S. Western Avenue after he was reported missing June 24th when he was last seen alive. At the time he was residing in a halfway house at 15th and Indiana after his release from prison. The car had been towed from a parking lot at 902 W. 19th Street. Haggerty was a convicted thief and burglar and had just finished a prison stretch for burglary and grand theft. Frank Schweihs and Frank Calabrese Sr. were suspected after the murder. However, the Family Secrets case revealed that Nick Calabrese, his brother Frank, Frank Saladino and Ronnie Jarrett were all part of the crew that surveiled and then hunted down the victim (Case cleared through Operation Family Secrets in 2005) **(Solved).**

Frank Calabrese Sr.

On **July 22, 1976** David Bonadonna 61 yrs. was shot and killer and found in the truck of his car. He was a Kansas City, Missouri business man who was trying to infiltrate nightclubs that featured go-go dancers. Harry Aleman was reported to be a suspect in this murder, but never charged.

On **August 9, 1976** Francesco Sacco AKA: Fillipo, Johnny Rosselli born in Italy in 1905, disappeared after leaving his sister's home in Florida. After the death of Sam Giancana it was reported that Rosselli, one of Giancana's top lieutenants and his overseer in Las Vegas and California was in fact working with the CIA and Cuban dissidents since 1959 in a plot to assassinate Fidel Castro. Information reported in 2005 confirms that this unholy alliance with the CIA provided Roselli and his Chicago counterparts, Teamster officials Jimmy Hoffa and Tony Provenzano, New Orleans Mob Boss Carlos Marcello and Florida Mob Boss Santo Trafficante with the means to orchestrate the assassination of President John F. Kennedy in 1963. The Cuban plot caused one of the most extensive cover- ups in United States history under the guise of National Security. Rosselli who claimed to be an American was not. Roselli's body was found in Biscayne Bay, near Ft. Lauderdale Fl. in August of 1976 in an oil drum. This was near Frank Nitti's former winter home. He had been shot and cut into pieces. Congressional investigators were looking to interview him at the time of his death.

On **September 21, 1976** Paul Gonsky a purveyor of Porn was gunned down in a parking lot at 1317 North Wells Avenue. This occurred during a time when the OUTFIT was squeezing porn dealers out of business or into partnerships. Gonsky shunned these advances and continued to expand in Chicago. He made the mistake of opening an X-rated theater near one owned by Felix "Milwaukee Phil" Alderisio. The parking lot he was killed in was owned by Frank Schweihs who lived in an apartment nearby. Of course Schweihs was a suspect in the killing, but never charged.

On **October 5, 1976** Steven H. Ostrowsky 34 yrs. of Flossmoor, IL. was murdered as he exited his Cadillac across the street from his auto parts store at 7370 South Chicago Ave. He was struck by 5 .30 cal. rifle rounds fired from a van that pulled alongside his car. Ostrowsky was convicted in 1973 with Billy Dauber for interstate auto theft charges and served one year in prison. Dauber who also served one year in prison for this conviction was an OUTFIT killer and a subordinate to Jimmy "The Bomber" Catura an OUTFIT Lieutenant. Dauber was also involved in an interstate auto theft business that the OUTFIT was trying to take over. Labeled as "Car Wars" by the media in Chicago the struggle for control of the auto theft racket left 30-40 individuals dead including two former partners Harry Holzer and Harry Carlson along with Mob Bosses Catura and Dauber, between 1969 and 1983.

On **December 15, 1976** Frederick "Rick" Manzie was found murdered in his Las Vegas home. He was an associate of Chicago mobsters and the husband of entertainer Barbara McNair. McNair was friends with Tony Spilotro who invested in her career. Manzie was a heroin addict and had run up gambling debts in Vegas that he could not pay back. The case remains unsolved.

In mid-**December of 1976** Joseph LoPiccolo 59 yrs. of 3170 N. Sheridan Road vanished under the watchful eye of Bureau of Narcotics investigators. He was considered at the time the top OUTFIT narcotics figure in Chicago. He was an ex-convict and thought to be dead at the time. On May 21, 1978 his body was found in a cemetery on Staten Island. He had over 50 stab wounds and investigators suspected that he was killed by New York Mob Boss Carmine Galante over a feud, although no one was charged.

In 1977, prolific OUTFIT assassin Harry Aleman was acquitted in the murder of a union employee. This case later became part of the "Operation Greylord" investigation when it was learned that this judge in fact had taken a bribe to throw this case. The judge committed suicide before he could be tried. Aleman was re-tried and convicted in 1998.

On **February 12, 1977** James Villerreal 24 yrs. of 1364 W. Ohio Street was stabbed to death in an alley behind 1439 W. Augusta Blvd. He recently went into a tavern in the area with a sawed-off shotgun and forced five people against a wall demanding to know the whereabouts of Henry J. Cosentino a minor hood who disappeared January 24th and was found dead later in a car trunk on March 15,

1977. On this same night a friend of his, Sam Rivera was shot and killed in a tavern at 1326 W. Grand Avenue.

On **February 12, 1977** Sam Rivera 27 yrs. of 1649 W. Ohio Street was fatally shot and his wife wounded in a tavern at 1326 W. Grand Avenue. Earlier in the day his friend James Villerreal was stabbed to death while looking for Henry J. Cosentino who was also found dead. Police charged Robert Bonamici 32yrs. of 2435 W. Huron St. with the Rivera murder and the wounding of his wife. He was released on a $35,000 bond and the outcome of that case is not known **(Solved)**.

On **February 25, 1977** Mickey Cogwell was shot and killed. He was a prominent street gang leader in Chicago. He led a gang the bore his named called the "Mickey Cobras", this gang was once part of the Black P-Stone Nation. Cogwell was also President of Local 304 of the Hotel and Restaurant Employees Union. Chicago Police in 1970 considered him a link between the gang and the Chicago OUTFIT. He angered OUTFIT leadership and it was reported that OUTFIT Boss Joey Aiuppa had him killed.

On **March 4, 1977** Patrick J. Marusarz 21 yrs. of west Huron Street was shot 5 times in the knee, face and chest with an automatic pistol while he played cards at Flash Messenger Service, 543 N. Ogden Avenue with OUTFIT associates Phillip Cozzo, Arthur Bravieri and a fourth man at about 4:00 am. The killer apparently having a key to the location of the killing entered wearing a gorilla mask. Police speculate the killing was linked to the mob takeover of gambling or juice activities.

On **March 15, 1977** Henry J. Cosentino 52 yrs. of 5726 N. St. Louis Avenue was found decomposed and murdered in the trunk of his car at Chicago Police auto pond #5 at about 7:20 am. The car had been tagged abandon on February 7th and was towed on February 18th from 2963 N. Wisner Ave. His wife reported him missing January 24th. The body was found bound, gagged and the death was caused by a blunt instrument forced through his neck. Cosentino was a convict (served 1 year for interstate theft) and small time hood with a record that dated back to 1942 for Burglary, cartage theft and bad checks. He may have been into loan sharks and was a part owner of Flash Messenger Service at 543 N. Ogden. He was the brother-in-law of Grand Ave. Underboss Jimmy Cozzo, whose family (Father Sam) owned Rose's snack shop on Grand Avenue where Riccardo Scalzetti AKA: Richard Cain was gunned down in 1973. At the time Police thought the murder involved a war over the messenger service or the juice business. Family Secrets testimony revealed that the victim had a dispute with Frank Saladino who he shot in the leg. Soon after he was targeted, when permission was granted by OUTFIT Boss Angelo LaPietra to kill him. The Calabrese brothers along with Ronnie Jarret searched for him and Frank Calabrese Sr. found him and was responsible for this killing. (Case cleared through Operation Family Secrets in 2005) **(solved)**.

Ronnie Jarret

On **March 29, 1977** Charles "Chuckie" Nicoletti 60 yrs. of 1638 N. 19th Ave. in Melrose Park, IL. is found shot in the head in his Oldsmobile parked at the Golden Horns Restaurant at 409 E. North Avenue in Northlake, IL. He took three .38 cal. bullets to the back of the head and died about six hours later at Northlake Community Hospital. The engine of the car caught on fire after the shooting. During his career he was a suspect in over 20 killings. He also made the mistake of voicing his opposition to the murder of Sam Giancana AKA: Momo Salvatore, Mooney, or Gilormo Giangono to OUTFIT Bosses at the time. At the time of this murder there appeared to be a power struggle inside the OUTFIT. It was also speculated that the murder occurred over internal disputes and problems related to off-track betting parlors the mob was involved in. In 2005 it was also reported that he was one of a handful of Chicago mobsters involved in the assassination of President John F. Kennedy in 1963. At the time of his death Congressional investigators sought to interview him about the assassination and his presence in Dallas on that fateful day. Harry Aleman was reported to be a suspect in this murder, but never charged.

On **April 4, 1977** John D. Lourgos 53 yrs. of 8501 S. Springfield Avenue was shot to death in front of his home. He was followed from his business, Lorenzo's Pizza and Gyros at 315 S. Halsted Street. The two assailants wearing ski masks were driving a silver Camaro and were armed with a twelve gauge shotgun. One of the men fired 4 shots, 2 of which hit the victim.

On **June 13, 1977** Richard Ferraro 36 yrs. of Oak Lawn, IL. was found dead. He was last seen on this date at 13th and Condesa Del Mar in Alsip, IL. His wife reported him missing and his 1977 Lincoln was found at his place of business, Statewide Auto Wrecking Company Inc., at 630 State Street in Calumet City, IL. He was an associate of Joseph F. Theo a robber who was killed a couple of days later and Joseph Scalise, Theo's partner who had worked at Statewide.

On **June 14, 1977** Thomas McCarthy 37 yrs. of 10217 W. Belden Avenue in Leyden Township was found decomposed in the trunk of his 1974 Cadillac parked at O'Hare International Airport. His wife reported him missing on June 6th and he had been shot in the base of the skull with a .38 cal. handgun. The body was discovered after a Sheriff's Investigator called the airport to see if the car was there. It was first recorded at the airport garage on June 7th. The victim was last seen leaving his home on June 4th at 10:30 am. He was under investigation by the FBI for cartage theft and his arrest record dated back to 1969 for burglary. His cousin John W. McCarthy was found dead in the trunk of a car on the southwest side in 1962. Reportedly Butch Petrocelli was responsible for this killing, but never charged.

On **June 15, 1977** Joseph Frank Theo 33 yrs. of 665 W. Diversey Parkway was found on Wednesday morning shot to death in the back seat of a car parked at 1701 N. Cleveland Ave. across the street from the shuttered Pegasus Company off-track betting office at 1720 N. Cleveland Avenue. He was shot twice in the head with a shotgun. The victims arrest record dated back to 1961 when he was a member of a burglary ring that was known for wearing disguises and were arrested in 1971 for burglaries at the Carriage House Apartment Hotel at 215 E. Chicago Ave. He was a friend of Richie Ferraro a car parts dealer who was killed a couple of days before and employed Theo's burglary partner Joe Scalise. Police believed this death may have been the result of a dispute over burglary proceeds or the OUTFIT warfare over the stolen auto parts business. Harry Aleman was reported to be a suspect in this murder, but never charged.

On **July 3, 1977** John R. Schneider 27 yrs. of 1030 N. State was found decomposed in the trunk of a rented Chevrolet Caprice in the parking lot of O'Hare Airport on Sunday when a police officer noticed a foul odor. He had been shot once in the head with a .25 cal. handgun and wrapped in plastic. The car was rented by his roommate John Sochacz and he was last seen by him on June 29th. He was a friend of Sam Annerino who was himself killed three weeks later. He had credit problems at the time of his death.

On **July 12, 1977** Earl S. Abercrombie Jr. 34 yrs. of Chicago Ridge, IL. was found dead in the trunk of a car at O'Hare Airport by police after parking lot attendants detected a foul odor. His body was naked and he was shot twice in the head and the car was parked there for a week before it was found. His mother stated that he was last seen on July 7th when he left for his job as a baker. He was from Mississippi and was known to sell stolen cars there. His arrest record dated back to 1967 and he was believed to be involved in auto theft and narcotics dealing.

Police believed the motive to involve drugs, burglary proceeds or the stolen car parts war that was raging in Chicago.

On **July 13, 1977** Morris Saletko AKA: Maurice or Maishe Baer 63 yrs. of 4255 W. Chase in Lincolnwood, IL. was found murdered in the trunk of his 1977 Oldsmobile in the parking lot of the Brickyard Shopping Center at Narragansett and Diversey. He was shot in the left side of the face and head. A previous attempt to kill him and a friend George Weinberg occurred in May of 1975, after he was paroled for his involvement in a silver high jacking. He was part of a crew run by Willie "Potatoes" Daddano, that high jacked a $380,000 shipment of silver bullion in Lagrange, IL. After someone provided information to authorities the crew was arrested and charged. He may have been killed for being an informant or for shorting OUTFIT bosses.

On **July 22, 1977** Joseph LaRose, John Vische, Donald Marchbanks and Malcolm Russell were found shot to death at U.S.Universal 216 West Higgins, Park Ridge, IL. The four men reportedly sold home fire and burglary alarms. Three of the victims LaRose, Marchbanks and Russell had their pockets ripped out. But they still had some cash and their jewelry. The men were found in an elevator that led to the underground parking garage. At the time Park Ridge police theorized the men were victims of a robbery. Earlier in the evening the victims had shown a large amount of cash to people who attended a meeting with them. This money wasn't recovered. The date of this multiple homicide coincides with the OUTFIT purge of burglars in the wake of the Tony Accardo home break in. Reportedly Paul Schiro was a suspect. Insurance Company Executive and Teamster Official Allen Dorfman maintained an office in this building. One or more of the victims was associated with murder victim Steven Garcia. Garcia was one of a group of burglars who allegedly burglarized Levinson's Jewelers' on the near northside. Harry Levinson an associate of Tony Accardo turned to the Boss for help and the proceeds were quickly recovered. But, during an Accardo vacation the burglars hit the boss's suburban home to retrieve the loot they thought was kept in the home at 1407 Ashland in River Forest, IL. The burglars all paid with their lives. In Park Ridge the dead men's business practices were also in question and two of the men were under federal investigation. The fact that valuable property was left behind and the scene was cleared of casings convinced Investigators that the crime was related to TOC, but were never able to solve it. Years later authorities named OUTFIT member Paul Schiro as a suspect, but the case remains unsolved.

Park Ridges Murders

On **July 22, 1977** Mark C. Thanasouras 49 yrs. of 9601 S. Southwest Highway in Oak Lawn, IL. was shotgunned to death at 5:15 am at 5507 N. Campbell. He was struck in the head and abdomen as he was walking a lady friend to her residence. He was a disgraced Chicago Police Department Commander assigned to the Austin District from 1966 to 1970 and who was sent to prison for 18 months for shaking down taverns. He received an early release after testifying against four Police Captains who were later acquitted. Chicago Police Detectives learned a suspect who was a Police officer with OUTFIT ties was seen acting suspiciously in the area before the killing, but the case remains unsolved. The same officer was also a suspect in the killing of a Westside politician. The victim was working as a bartender at the L & L Club at #2 Buckley Road in Lake Bluff, IL. The owner of the club where Thanasouras worked, George Nicholas Christofalos AKA: George N. Lardas was killed there in March of 1979. Police speculate he was killed by OUTFIT loansharks, due to unrest in the Greek community or because of being a government witness.

On **July 25, 1977** Sam Annerino 34 yrs. of 9520 S. Mayfield in Oak Lawn, IL. was murdered at 4:20 pm on Monday as he left the Mirabelli Furniture and Appliance store at 10550 S. Cicero in Oak Lawn, IL. He was shot by a masked gunman who fired 5 shotgun blasts into him. The killer then fled in a red vehicle driven by a second man. Annerino was a Lt. for Jimmy "The Bomber" Catuara and may have been killed in the OUTFIT's struggle between Jimmy Catuara and Albert Tocco to take over the Auto theft rackets between 1969 and 1983 in which some 30 to 40 individuals were murdered. Joey Lombardo and Frank Schweihs were suspected in the killing of Annerino, but never charged. Family Secrets testimony revealed that Angelo LaPietra sanctioned this murder suspecting Annerino was an informant. He assigned the Calabrese brothers, Gumba Saladino and Ronnie Jarrett to the case but those plans fell through and it is not clear who actually carried out the hit.

On **August 25, 1977** James A. Palaggi 46yrs. of 4700 S. Harlem Ave., Lyons, IL. was found shot to death and wrapped in moving blankets in the rear of his van parked at 3221 N. Keating Ave. He was last seen on August 19th and was reported missing by his wife. He was an associate of Richie Ferraro and Sam Annerino and probably died during the "Car Wars" dispute of this era.

On **October 18, 1977** Ray Ryan was killed in an explosion as he left his tennis club. Ryan a wealthy oilman had pressed charges against Las Vegas overseer Marshal Ciafano for extortion in 1963. Caifano was sent to prison, but never forgot. Tony Spilotro, Joey Lombardo and Frank Schweihs were suspected, but never charged.

On **December 13, 1977** Leo Frank Filippi 43 yrs. of Cicero, IL. was found shot to death on the back seat floor of a car parked at 4730 W. 46th St. He worked at a Cicero disco and was last seen leaving work on December 7th. He previously served time for Income Tax Evasion.

On **January 16, 1978** John Mendell 31 yrs. of Lincolnwood, IL. was killed. He was found in the trunk of his 1971 Oldsmobile parked at 6304 S. Campbell on February 20, 1978. The car had been there since the day after he was last seen alive. The body had signs of torture and his throat was cut. The victim was an electronics expert and was part of the Accardo residence burglary crew. Mendell was suspected of disabling the burglar alarms at Levinsons Jewelry Store and the Accardo residence. At first the police suspected this crew of failing to cut the OUTFIT in on a score, but later learned of the Levinson and Accardo scores. Family Secrets testimony revealed that Ronnie Jarrett who was an associate of Mendell set up a meeting with the unsuspecting victim and drove with him to the garage of his mother-in-law in Bridgeport where Frank and Nick Calabrese along with Frank Saladino waited. Once there the men beat, strangled and cut his throat, stripping him naked before putting him in the trunk of his own car for disposal. (Case cleared through Operation Family Secrets in 2005) **(Solved).**

Frank Saladino

On **January 20, 1978** Bernard F. Ryan 34 yrs. of 2727 W. 111th Street was found behind the wheel of a 1976 Lincoln Continental that was registered to his brother John. He had been shot 3 to 4 times in the head. The car was covered with snow and was not found for several days after the killing, it was parked at 1657 S. 44th Court in Stone Park, IL. The victim had a police scanner in his hand when he was found. He was the second of the suspected Accardo residence burglars found murdered. He was a known burglar to the police and served time for numerous burglary and federal securities forgery convictions. Also during this month and the next the bodies of burglars Steven Robert Garcia, Vincent Morretti a former police officer and leader of the ring (brother of former police officer Sal Moretti the killer of Banker Leon Markus) were found dead with Donald Renno AKA: Donald Swanson, John Mendell (electronics expert who disabled the Accardo alarm), Robert A. "Bobby" Hertogs and John Charles McDonald all found beaten and murdered throughout the Chicagoland area. The last to go was the Accardo house keeper Michael Volpe after his Grand Jury testimony who simply vanished off the face of the earth, he was suspected of setting up the job. They were all part of the Accardo break in. Family Secrets testimony revealed that Tony Spilotro, Frank Schweihs, John Anthony Borsellino and his understudy Ronnie Jarrett were suspected in the killings. (Case cleared through Operation Family Secrets in 2005) **(Solved)**.

On **January 31, 1978** Vincent Moretti 51 yrs. of Elmwood Park, IL. and Donald R. Renno AKA: Donald Swanson 31 yrs. of 2554 N. Neva were found murdered in the rear seat of Renno's Grandfather's Cadillac parked in the parking lot of Esther's Place at 5009 S. Central in Stickney, IL. Both men were badly beaten and both men had their throats cut and were stabbed. Moretti was believed to be the leader of the Accardo residence burglary ring and was suspected of fencing loot in Las Vegas against the wishes of OUTFIT leadership. Renno may not have been part of the burglary, but only died for being with Moretti (Moretti's twin brother Salvatore was murdered in 1957 for the botched killing of Banker Leon Markus). A third brother Michael was convicted in 1951 of killing two youths. All three brothers had been police officers at one time. Family Secrets testimony revealed that Moretti and Renno were driven to a closed restaurant in Cicero at 22nd and Laramie by John Fecarotta. Waiting at the restaurant were OUTFIT bosses John Monteleone, Jimmy LaPietra and Joe Ferriola. Other crew members who were there were Frank and Nick Calabrese, Butch Petrocelli, Tony Borsellino, Frank Saladino and Ronnie Jarrett. Once in the restaurant the men were ceased and while the Calabrese brothers strangled Moretti, Saladino jumped up and down on his chest soon causing his death. While this was going on other members of the group where strangling Renno until he met the same fate. (Case cleared through Operation Family Secrets in 2005) **(Solved)**.

John Monteleone

On **February 2, 1978** Steven Robert Garcia 29 yrs. of 5615 N. Cumberland was found murdered in the trunk of a rented 1977 Ford Granada parked at the Sheraton Motor Hotel at 6810 N. Manheim Rd. in Rosemont, IL. The victim had multiple stab wounds and his throat was cut. He had been missing over two weeks and was thought to be a member of the Accardo residence burglary crew. Police knew him to be a jewel thief. **(Solved).**

On **March 17, 1978** Dino J. Valente 41 yrs. of 954 E. 171st Place in South Holland, IL. died from 4 shotgun wounds delivered from a 12 ga. shotgun the day before in front of his 1977 Continental. He was parked next to Rukavina's Restaurant at 645 Torrence Avenue in Calumet City, IL. He died at St. Margaret Hospital in Hammond, IN. He was a long time associate of Mobster Frank LaPorte in a music company in Chicago Heights, IL. The victim also ran a juke box and billiard business out of his home which police theorize lead to his death.

On **April 3, 1978** Frank J. Smith Jr. 63 yrs. of 1247 Ashland Avenue in River Forest, IL. was shot to death in a residential alley behind 4149 N. St. Louis Ave. The victim ran F & M Vending Company at 1112 W. Westgate in Oak Park, IL. He was making business collections when he was killed and police speculate that he and Dino Valente who was killed on March 17th were both victims of an OUTFIT takeover of vending rackets in Chicago. The victim's car was missing and probably contained important records related to the business.

On **April 6, 1978** Robert A. Hertogs 22 yrs. of 2119 W. Iowa Street was found shot to death in the trunk of a 1972 Oldsmobile parked in the Jewel grocery store parking lot at 3552 W. Grand Avenue. The victim was clad only in shorts and the car had been reported stolen on March 30th, the same day the victim was last seen alive. He was a professional burglar and two of his associates, Patrick Marusarz and Henry Cosentino were both murdered in 1977. The reality was he was part of the burglary crew that hit Levinson's Jewelry Store and the Accardo residence. **(Solved).**

On **April 14, 1978** John Charles McDonald 42 yrs. of 5001 Carriageway in Rolling Meadows, IL. was found shot in the head and neck in the alley behind 446 N. Racine. He was a co-defendant in a 1972 burglary case with Bernard Ryan who was killed in January and had been questioned by police after Ryan's murder. He had a prior conviction for attempted burglary in 1966 with George Fedoruk. Police originally felt that these murders were carried out by the OUTFIT in an attempt to exert control over the burglary rackets that was lost in 1969 when OUTFIT Lieutenant Willie "Potatoes" Daddano was imprisoned. However, it was learned that all the associated burglars were killed for their involvement with the Accardo residence burglary. (Case cleared through Operation Family Secrets in 2005) **(Solved).**

In **January of 1978** Michael Volpe 75 yrs. the housekeeper for Tony Accardo when his house was burglarized vanished off the face of the earth after testifying in front of a grand jury. Police speculate that he helped set up the burglary.

On **June 30, 1978** August Palmisano was slain by a car bomb in the Milwaukee area. He was associated with the Milwaukee Mob that was under the control of the Chicago OUTFIT. The victim was a suspected informant and probably killed at the hands of the Chicago OUTFIT similar to the killing of August Maniaci in 1975.

On **July 28, 1978** James "Jimmy the Bomber" Catuara 72 yrs. of 9600 S. Kilbourn in Oak Lawn IL. was shot to death on the street at Hubbard and Ogden Sts. in Chicago. The victim was shot twice in the head, once in the neck and back and was face down in the street near his red Cadillac. It was reported that several hitmen were waiting near-by in a blue van in a remote industrial area before the killing. The Bomber was in a struggle to control the auto theft rackets against Southside OUTFIT Boss Albert Tocco and William Dauber after several of his underlings were killed including Lt. Sam Annerino, Richie Ferraro and Steve Ostrowsky. This conflict lasted from 1969 to 1983 and resulted in 30 to 40 murders and became known in the media as "Car Wars".

On **September 8, 1978** Melvin Young 42 yrs. of Elk Grove Village, IL. was found shot to death in the trunk of his 1978 Lincoln Continental Mark V in the parking lot at O'Hare Airport. He was shot in the chest and it was estimated the car was parked there several days before it was discovered. He was recently employed as a salesman at Custom Metal Polishing and Plating Company at 1750 N. Campbell. He specialized in custom motorcycles and had a couple of arrests for possession of stolen vehicles.

On **September 27, 1978** Robert Martinez Vaca 46 yrs. was found shot to death seated in a stolen vehicle parked in a parking lot next to the Village Pub at 8839 22nd Place in North Riverside, IL. He was found by a co-owner of the pub, and was shot several times with a .38 cal. handgun in the back and neck and it was discovered that the car was parked there between 3 and 6 am. He was known to police as a professional burglar and robber. The victim, a juice client himself was once a driver for OUTFIT Lieutenant Marshall Ciafano as reported in the mid-1960s by the Illinois Legislative Investigating Commission (ILIC) and was associated with other mobsters such as OUTFIT cartage thief Anthony Legato. Federal tapes revealed that mobster James Inendino had Vaca collecting juice for him and speculated that he may have been silenced to keep him from talking to the government as he did in the 1960s before the ILIC.

James Inendino

On **March 11, 1979** George Nicholas Christofalos AKA: George N. Lardas 41 yrs. of Lake Bluff, IL. was killed in the parking lot of the L & L Club at #2 Buckly Road in Lake Bluff, IL. while warming up his 1976 Cadillac Eldorado at 4:00 am. Two masked gunman approached and one held an employee at bay in the doorway of the establishment while the other pumped three 12 gauge shotgun blasts through the car window striking the victim in the left upper part of his body. The victim had a long record for vice and immigration violations. He was born in Greece, was a naturalized Canadian and married an American woman. He was a former business partner of John Lourgos who was killed in April of 1977 and befriended former Police Commander Mark Thanasouras after he was released from prison and employed him before he was gunned down in July of 1977. It was reported that Joey Borsellino, Gerry Scarpelli and Jerry Scalise were responsible for this killing, but never charged.

On **May 22, 1979** John Anthony "Tony Bors" Borsellino 48 yrs. of 744 Magnolia Circle in Lombard, IL. was found dead alongside a road or in a farmer's field near Frankfort, IL. He was shot five times in the back of the head with a small caliber handgun. He was fully clothed including a tee shirt that bore the name of Brown's Bingo Hall, 6060 W. Belmont a location frequented by mobsters. He was suspected of being one of the assassins assigned to track down and kill the burglars that hit Tony Accardo's house in 1978. He was also part of a crew run by Willie "Potatoes" Daddano, that highjacked a $380,000 shipment of silver bullion in LaGrange, IL., known by law enforcement as the Spector Freight silver robbery. He had done time for his part in the crime. After someone provided information to authorities the entire crew was arrested and charged. The Family Secrets trial later revealed that this killing was the idea of Butch Petrocelli and a crew he was associated with known as the Wild Bunch, yet remains open **(Solved)**.

On **June 1, 1979** Timothy W. "Timmy" O'Brien 39 yrs. of 8750 S. Merton in Oak Lawn, IL. was found shot to death in the trunk of his car on Old Western Avenue in Blue Island, IL. He was dressed in black slacks and a black sport shirt pulled up over his head and was shot in the head with a shotgun. The victim owned Irish Keystone Auto Parts in Robbins, IL. and was under indictment for receiving stolen property as part of his chop shop operation. His arrest record for auto theft dated back to 1957. It was speculated that he too, was another victim of "Car Wars".

On **September 25, 1979** Robert Brown was strangled, beaten and hacked to death in his store at 3120 N. Nordica St. in Chicago, IL. He sold clothing and Jewelry from the store and was an associate of mobster Frank Cullotta, Wayne Matecki and Allen Dorfman. He would sell jewelry in a nightclub that Cullotta owned and the killing appeared to be a result of a robbery as the safe was found open. Police had no suspects in the case until 1982 when Frank Cullotta became a government informant. Cullotta targeted the victim for a robbery and Lawrence "Crazy Larry" Nuemann and Wayne Matecki (all members of the Spilotro crew in

Las Vegas) traveled to Chicago from Las Vegas to carry out the crime and returned with the proceeds. During the robbery the men decided to kill the victim fearing arrest as the victim knew Matecki. The men were charged in Cook County Criminal Court where Matecki was acquitted and Nuemann was found guilty receiving a life sentence **(solved)**.

On **September 28, 1979** Gerald V. "Ding Dong" Caruseillo 47 yrs. of Melrose Park, IL. was found dead at a condo development at 951 N. Highway 53 in Addison, IL. The victim was wearing jeans, a dark sweatshirt, a scarf and gloves. He was carrying a screwdriver and $1,750 in cash, but no identification. He was shot seven times in the back. He was known to police as an armed robber and burglar and was once a driver for Joseph Aiuppa a high ranking OUTFIT member. He had an arrest record that dated back 26 years. Two men were seen leaving the scene in a late model green Dodge.

On **October 11, 1979** Sherwin "Jerry" Lisner 46 yrs. was found at home by his wife Jeannie (a cocktail waitress at the Aladdin Casino in Las Vegas) dead in the swimming pool at 2303 Rawhide Ave. in Las Vegas, NV. Lisner was an associate of Chicago OUTFIT Boss Tony Spilotro and was facing federal charges for transporting stolen merchandise and was suspected by Spilotro of being a police informant. Spilotro dispatched his top Lieutenant Frank Cullotta to take care of the problem. Cullotta and a partner Wayne Matecki went to Lisner's home and after entering the house Cullotta started shooting and pursued the victim through it. Lisner was found in the pool shot 10 to 12 times in the head **(solved)**.

Approx. number of Chicago TOC related murders in the 1970s: 105
Approx. number of Chicago TOC related murder cases in the 1970s solved: 22
Approx. number of Chicago TOC related murders in the 1970s of Police Officers: 1

Chapter 8. The 1980s

In 1980 the Chicago Crime Commission called for a Grand Jury investigation into allegations of OUTFIT influence in the ranks of the Chicago Police Department. In 1998 an OUTFIT sponsored thief named Bobby Siegel turned state's evidence against a group of co-conspirators that included a former Chief of Detectives (1980) known for his associations with TOC types.

In 1980 the CCC developed evidence of abuse in Bingo licensing and regulation in Illinois, including TOC involvement in the game as warned against by the CCC back in 1969.

In 1980 the CCC urged Senator Charles Percy of the U. S. Permanent Subcommittee on Investigations to appoint a special federal prosecutor to investigate the Teamster Union's Central States Pension Fund that was later discovered to be a piggy bank for the OUTFIT during a federal probe known as "Pendorf".

Critical events of the 1980s

In **1980** Tommy McCarthy a juice loan agent for Frank Calabrese Sr. is found murdered in a car at O'Hare Airport. Butch Petrocelli was suspected in the crime but never charged. This hit was not sanctioned and was believed to be one of the reasons that Petrocelli was killed. Family Secrets testimony revealed this information **(solved).**

In March of 1980 "Big" Joe Arnold the OUTFIT overseer of operations in the Rush Street area for Joe "Cesar" DiVarco was shot by a disgruntled loanshark victim in the basement of the Candy Store an infamous Rush Street Strip Club. He survived the shooting and refused to cooperate with Police and no one was charged.

On **July 2, 1980** William Earl "Billy" Dauber 45 yrs. and his wife Charlotte 37 yrs. of Monee Road in Crete, IL. were shot to death by rifle and shotguns while driving to their home in Crete from a court appearance in Joliet. The gunman rode in a stolen 1978 Blue Ford van and assaulted them at Monee and Manhattan Roads in rural Will County, IL. Billy was facing federal gun and cocaine charges. He was an OUTFIT associate who worked as a killer for Albert Tocco in southern Cook County. Dauber was killed during a struggle between Tocco and Jimmy Catura who were fighting for control of chop-shop and auto-salvage businesses for street taxes. This situation started in 1969 described as "Car Wars" by the media. 30 to 40 murders were associated with that feud and Dauber was suspected as the hit man of choice. When Dauber was arrested on cocaine and weapons charges by the federal government he began to talk. His OUTFIT bosses may have feared the damage he could do to the organization and Frank Calabrese, Jerry Scalise, Butch Petrocelli, Gerry Scarpelli, and Ronnie Jarrett reportedly went hunting for him and bagged his wife too. (Case cleared through Operation Family Secrets in 2005, Frank Calabrese Sr. was held responsible at trial) **(solved)**.

Billy Dauber

On **November 28, 1980** Eleftherios "Nick" Valentzas 34 yrs. of 546 East Park in Villa Park, IL. was shot to death while entering his car in a parking lot at 2222 N. Harlem in Elmwood Park, IL. He was struck in the head and chest by multiple pistol and shotgun rounds by two men wearing dark clothes. One of the men seen leaving the scene with a shotgun walked with a noticeable limp. The victim ran a Greek coffee house at 6000 W. Belmont Avenue and was paying $300 a month in street tax for a gambling operation he maintained. He made the payments to Donald Scalise, Nick Boulahanis and Frank Rinella. From there the money went to Bobby Salerno and Phillip "Philly the Fruit" Latorre and then on to Butch Petrocelli. The victim was to have testified in a federal extortion case against three of the hoods.

In **1981** Tommy Mock a west suburban bar owner and mortal enemy of corrupt suburban police officers was shot to death in the driveway of his home. In secretly recorded conversations two of the officers were heard talking about the killing and admitting involvement. The officers involved were also involved in protecting OUTFIT sponsored video poker operations in several west suburban municipalities. However the case remains unsolved.

On **March 14, 1981** William Joe "Butch" Petrocelli 43 yrs. of 342 Forest Avenue in Hillside, IL. was found tortured and murdered in the back seat of his car parked at 4307 W. 25th Place. His hands were bound with tape, his mouth and nose were covered with surgical tape, his face was burned with lighter fluid and his throat was cut. The cause of death was asphyxiation. He had been reported missing to the FBI by his girlfriend. Butch was a reputed hit man for the OUTFIT and rose under Joe Ferriola to oversee bookies at race tracks. He was suspected of enacting a street tax on burglars who were already paying Jerry Scarpelli, an equally sinister hood. It got worse when it was revealed that Butch used the Boss's name in this scam and he was thought to be withholding money from his superiors. He was also accused of withholding $100,000 collected for the family of his former partner, Harry Aleman who was Ferriola's nephew. He defied orders to turn the money over and was accused of carrying out unsanctioned hits. An Underboss at the time, Joe Ferriola ordered the murder with Angelo LaPietra's approval. It was reported by a government informant that Angelo LaPietra, James LaPietra, Gerald Scarpelli, Frank and Nick Calabrese, Frank Santucci, John Monteleone and Frank Furio carried out the murder. Other reports claimed Ernest Infelise was also involved in the murder. (Case cleared through Operation Family Secrets in 2005) **(Solved)**.

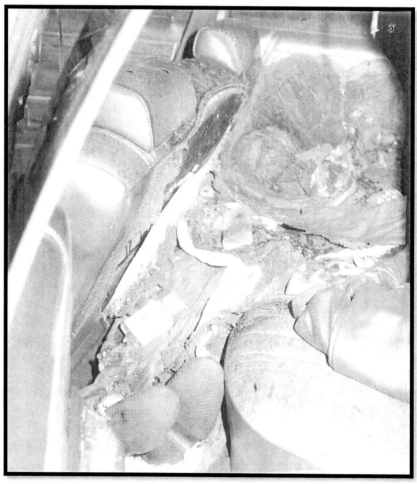

Butch Petrocelli dead

On **May 6, 1981** Fiore Forestiere 58 yrs. of Glen Ellyn, IL. was found shot to death in a van near 8140 O'Connor Drive in River Grove, IL. He was shot five times, once in the head and four times in the chest. He was an ex-convict with a record.

On **May 18, 1981** Sam Faruggia 60 yrs. of 906 Franklin St. in River Forest, IL. was found wrapped in a rug in the rear of a station wagon at 758 N. LaClaire, he was stabbed at least five times and his throat was cut. His daughter reported him missing to the River Forest Police Department three days earlier after he failed to appear at work on a Monday morning. He operated Melody Music, a Juke Box Firm and Leyden Acceptance at 3809 W. Grand Avenue. Both firms were formerly run by Chuckie English (murdered in 1985) an OUTFIT Lieutenant close to Sam Giancana AKA: Momo Salvatore, Mooney, or Gilormo Giangono.

On **June 2, 1981** Ronald Scharff 37 yrs. and Patricia Freeman were found shot to death in an apartment in the rear of the P.M. Pub at 238 West Rand Road in Lakemoor, IL. a small town northwest of Chicago. Ron was the owner of the Pub and Patricia was a barmaid. A short time before the killings, Scharff had an altercation with the former wife of hoodlum Larry Nuemann. Nuemann was working for the Tony Spilotro crew in Vegas and admitted the killing to Frank Cullotta a Spilotro Lieutenant. The police were provided with Neumann's name at the time, but never pursued the lead. Nuemann died in jail in January of 2007 and was never charged **(solved)**.

On **June 24, 1981** Michael Cagnoni a successful trucking company executive was blown up in his car in Hinsdale, IL. Cagnoni made the mistake of entering into a partnership with the OUTFIT in order to expand his business. When the partnership soured Cagnoni knew he was dead. On that fatal day Frank Calabrese Sr. reportedly waited for him in a stolen car and when Cagnoni pulled onto the nearby tollway Calabrese used a remote control to detonate a bomb attached to the bottom of the car killing the executive immediately. Family Secrets testimony revealed that Frank Calabrese, John Fecarotta, Jimmy DiForti and John Monteleone were all involved in the planning of this murder that was sanctioned by Angelo LaPietra (Case cleared through Operation Family Secrets in 2005, Frank Calabrese Sr. was held responsible at trial) **(solved)**.

Michael Cagnoni's car

On **June 27, 1981** Joseph D. Testa Jr. was blown up as he started his car after a round of golf in Oakland Park, FL., he died 2 days later. Testa a millionaire builder and bank owner lived in an elegant home in LaSalle County, IL. Reportedly he was a long time associate involved in OUTFIT building projects and laundering money. Reportedly, he was sent by the OUTFIT to secure gambling interests in Australia in the early 1970s. While there he posed as a high ranking police official from Illinois and this cost him the Cook County Sheriffs badge he carried upon his return. He had a dispute with mobster Marshall Caifano over money Caifano claimed he was owed. Reportedly Caifano was given permission by Joe Lombardo to kill Testa and Frank Schweihs and Anthony Panzica were identified as suspects in the case, but never charged. After his death his estate valued at over 2 million dollars and the subject of a will, gained much attention when 2 police officials were left sizable amounts of cash.

On **August 5, 1981** Charles F. Monday AKA: Charles Mondzyk 44 yrs. was found dead in the trunk of a car parked in the 6200 block of west Schubert. He had been beaten to death and was missing for 13 days. Neighbors finally called the police about the suspicious auto and they made the discovery. He allegedly worked with Anthony Legato an OUTFIT associated drug dealer.

On **August 7, 1981** Anthony Legato 50 yrs. of Berwyn, IL. was found murdered in the trunk of a 1975 Ford parked at 4759 West George. The body was wrapped in a blanket and this victim was reported missing the same day as murder victim Charles Monday as the two were allegedly associates in the drug business.

On **September 13, 1981** Nicholas D'Andrea 49 yrs. of Chicago Heights, IL. was murdered and found in the trunk of a burning car near Crete, IL. He left his home at 2:00 pm and was found in the car at 9:30 pm the same day. The victim in this case showed signs of torture. He worked for the Southside crew of Al Tocco who may have ordered the murder. It is believed this killing was connected to the attempted murder of Southside Boss Alfred Pilotto earlier in the month on a golf course. According to the testimony of Nick Calabrese who was present, James Marcello, Sam Carlisi, Anthony Chiaramonte and Angelo LaPietra took part in this killing before placing the victim in a car. (Case cleared through Operation Family Secrets in 2005, James Marcello while not convicted by the jury was held responsible by the judge at trial) **(solved)**.

Albert Tocco

On **October 3, 1981** Samuel Guzzino 51 yrs. of Chicago Heights, IL. was found murdered in a ditch in Beecher, IL. He had been shot in the head and his throat cut. He also worked for Albert Tocco and had worked as a bodyguard for Al Pilotto as he was golfing with the Southside Boss when he was shot. It is suspected that he had something to do with the shooting that costs Nick D'Andrea his life too and the torture of D'Andrea may have revealed Guzzino's involvement in the shooting of Pilotto. The case however, remains unsolved.

Al Piloto

On April 24, 1982 Nicholas Sarillo Sr. is blown up in his van as he was driving in Wauconda, IL. He survives the explosion and according to Family Secrets testimony, it was revealed that Frank and Nick Calabrese, Joe Amato, Angelo and Jimmy LaPietra, Sam Carlisi, John Fecarotta, and James Marcello were involved in the planning and execution of this crime. Apparently this victim would not pay street tax for the gambling operations that he ran. In 1973 the victim killed Frank Gallo while Gallo was trying to forcefully enter Sarillo's house in Rosemont, IL. He was reportedly an associate of many mobsters and was arrested with several in a gambling raid years earlier.

On **October 8, 1981** John Klimes was blown to bits when a bomb was detonated in his pick-up truck as he drove in McCook, IL. The victim was a leader in the Outlaws Motorcycle Gang and had been running his mouth about taking out OUTFIT Boss Joey "Doves" Aiuppa. The motorcycle gang was allied with the OUTFIT in matters of drugs, prostitution and weapons and apparently the victim thought he could take over the OUTFIT and do a better job than Doves. As you can imagine Aiuppa was not too pleased when this got back to him and he assigned Jimmy DiForti to take care of it. Family Secrets testimony revealed that DiForti obtained a detonator from Nick Calabrese and the task was completed by DiForti, Jimmy Marcello and others. The media at the time credited this killing to a protracted war between motorcycle gangs. However this case was not cleared at the Family Secrets trial and remains unsolved **(Solved)**.

On **March 28, 1982** Richard L. Campbell was found shot to death behind the wheel of a truck at Molick's Standard Station 1596 Miner Street in DesPlaines, IL. The victim worked at various gas stations that reportedly were involved in OUTFIT gambling. Chicago Police Intelligence Detectives became involved in this murder as a cold case and worked with numerous other agencies connecting this case with two other murders. The case remains unsolved.

On **June 3, 1982** Robert Hayden Plummer 51 yrs. of Lake Forest, IL. was found murdered in the trunk of his car in a Motel parking lot at US 45 and Route 83 in Mundelein, IL. The victim was reported missing on May 23rd by his wife. The body indicated he was struck 3 times on the back of his head and 1 time on the left side of his head above his ear. He was part of a multi-million dollar interstate gambling ring that was indicted in 1971. He may have resisted paying his OUTFIT associates street tax. In 1990 Rocco Infelise was convicted of this killing **(solved).**

On **October 8, 1982** Leo "John" Manfredi AKA: Leonard Corfini, John DuBois 67 yrs. of Cicero, IL. was found shot four times in the head in the basement of a shuttered Pizza Parlor at 6233 W. Roosevelt Road in Berwyn, IL. Police suspected he was using juice proceeds to finance drug deals that fell through and he could not repay the funding.

On **December 30, 1982** Mark Tortoriello the 29 year old son of James Tortoriello (who was found murdered in an abandon Ft. Lauderdale, Florida warehouse in 1984) was shot and killed in front of a house in the 8200 block of Southwest Fifth Court, North Lauderdale FL. a block from his home. The shooting was apparently the result of minor drug dispute according to police. In January 1983, North Lauderdale police issued a warrant for Nick D`Ambrosio in the slaying. New York State Police arrested Nicholas J. D`Ambrosio, 24, of Brooklyn, (the son of a New York Mobster) about 60 miles north of New York City. The outcome of the case is unknown. The victim and his brother James Jr. were scheduled to go on trial in January of 1983 for attempting to sell stolen paintings valued at 1.4 million dollars **(Solved).**

On **January 11, 1983** Robert P. Subatich 44 yrs. of Michigan City Road in Calumet City, IL. was found shot once in the head in the trunk of his 1981 Lincoln Mark IV parked at O'Hare Airport. The victim was reported missing since January 4th and was parked in the garage since December 27th. Police suspected him of being involved in dealing cocaine and being involved in Chop Shop operations.

On **January 20, 1983** Allan Dorfman 60 yrs. of Deerfield, IL. was shot to death in the parking lot of a Lincolnwood, IL. hotel at Touhy and Lincoln Avenues. He was hit 8 times in the head with a .22 cal. automatic handgun. Dorfman was an OUTFIT associate, former consultant to the Teamster's Central States Pension Fund and owner of Amalgamated Insurance Agency Inc. The company handled premiums/claims on millions of dollars of Teamster business. Dorfman was killed by 2 gunman while his protégé who walked through the parking lot with him, a long time OUTFIT operative and former bail bondsman by the name of Irwin Weiner, went unscathed. Previously, Weiner had negotiated a 1.4 million dollar loan from the Pension Fund with the help of his friend Dorfman. Dorfman entered the insurance business with his father Red who was a close associate of Teamster Boss Jimmy Hoffa and OUTFIT Boss Tony Accardo. Allen Dorfman eventually became a trustee of the teamster pension fund and turned the fund into a piggy bank for TOC across the country. In 1967 two masked gunman shot up Dorfman's car as a warning to him from out of town gangsters about his greed in their dealings. Shortly before the killing Allan along with Teamster Boss Roy Williams, Thomas O'Mally, Amos Massa and Chicago hood Joey "The Clown" Lombardo were convicted for attempting to bribe a Nevada Senator. The OUTFIT became concerned that Dorfman may begin cooperating with authorities while he was awaiting sentencing and killed him. Investigators concurred with the possibility of him cooperating. Shortly after the crime, investigators tentatively identified the shooting suspects as Frank Schweihs and Ray Spencer. In 1986 authorities named Paul Schiro as a suspect in the case and later John Fecarotta was suspected.

On February 10, 1983 OUTFIT gambling overseer Ken Eto was taken for a ride but survived 3 GSWs to the back of his head at 7129 W. Grand. The bungled hit caused the OUTFIT great consternation when ETO turned into a cooperating informant from witness protection (WITSEC). The assigned assassins Jasper Campise and Cook County Sheriff's Police Deputy John Gatusso were reprimanded for the sloppy work and killed a short time later. The killing was ordered by Northside Boss Vince Solano. Eto provided the most detailed look at the inner workings of the Chicago OUTFIT to date. At a sentencing hearing for Southside OUTFIT Boss John "Johnny Apes" Monteleone in Milwaukee, Eto described setting up 4 individuals for murder as they interfered with gambling operations.

Ken Eto testifies

273

On **March 2, 1983** Michael G. Chorak of 17205 S. Burnham in Lansing, IL. was found shot to death in his car at his place of business M & J Auto Wreckers at 1463 E. 130th St. The victim was shot in the back of the head with a .38 cal. handgun. He was in the auto salvage business and was a victim of the OUTFIT's struggle to control the auto theft and chop shop rackets that resulted in 30 to 40 killings between 1969 and 1983. Joe Radisch an escapee, convict and former employee of Chorak was arrested and convicted in the slaying **(solved)**.

On **July 14, 1983** John Gattuso 47 yrs. of 2324 W. Taylor Street and 1721 Sunset Ridge in Glenview, IL. and Jasper Campise 68 yrs. of 1535 Forest in River Forest, IL. were both found murdered in the trunk of Campise's 1981 Volvo parked in the parking lot of the Pebblewood Condominiums at 55070 Pebblewood Lane in Naperville, IL. Gattuso was stabbed once in the neck and four times in the abdomen with a rope around his neck indicating he may have been tortured. Campise was stabbed 5 times in the left side of his body. Gattuso while a Cook County Deputy Sheriff ran OUTFIT sponsored gay bars, taverns and restaurants in the past. Campise was an OUTFIT loan shark operator who was arrested for the murder of Dominick "Hunk" Galiano, an OUTFIT vice purveyor in 1966, the outcome of that case is unknown. The two men had been identified as the hitmen in the attempted murder of Ken Eto in February of 1983, Gattuso being the actual triggerman. Their failure was a devastating blow to the OUTFIT as Eto became a valuable source of information about OUTFIT operations, but overtures by federal authorities to join Eto in witness protection were rejected by the two men. Ernest "Rocco" Infelise a top enforcer and hitman was suspected in the killings, but never charged. Family Secrets Testimony identified Jimmy DiForti and Sam Carlisi as operatives in this killing **(Solved)**.

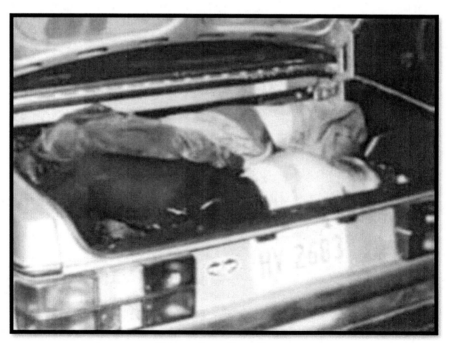

Campise death car

On **July 23, 1983** Richard Ortiz and Arthur Morawski were shotgunned to death while sitting in a car in front of a Cicero tavern. Morawski was not the target of this hit that was planned and was reportedly carried out by Nick Calabrese, Frank Calabrese Sr. and James DiForti. Police believed Morawski was not a target, but the man was in the wrong place at the wrong time. It is believed though, that Ortiz was the true target and it involved a drug deal and an unsanctioned killing. Frank Calabrese Jr. later revealed the details of the killing that his father provided to him. In that scenario Frank Sr. drove and Frank's brother Nick and James DiForti exited the car and opened fire on the men. Family Secrets testimony revealed that the Calabrese brothers, John Fecarotta, Jimmy DiForti and John Monteleone helped plan this killing after Angelo LaPietra sanctioned it. (Case cleared through Operation Family Secrets in 2005, Frank Calabrese Sr. was held responsible at trial) **(solved)**.

On **November 24, 1984** James "Mugsy" Tortoriello 73, was found in an abandon Ft. Lauderdale, FL. warehouse. He had been shot in the head several times with a small caliber handgun. He was muscle for the Chicago OUTFIT running gambling and prostitution in the suburbs until 1971 when he had a falling out with his superiors. He then moved to Deerfield Beach, FL. where he allegedly was involved in dealing guns and drugs. On September 14, 1982 there was an attempt on his life and he disappeared. Several months later his 29 year old son was killed after a failed drug deal. This case demonstrates the long arm of the Chicago OUTFIT. His arrest record dated back to 1930 and included the theft of a truck carrying shoes and stockings during World War II.

On **December 16, 1984** Anthony V. Crissie 49 yrs. of 337 N. East River Road in Des Plaines, IL. was found dead in Countryside, IL. He was shot once in the chest and three times in the head. Police surmise he was shot with a .22 cal. handgun with a silencer. He was deeply involved with OUTFIT business dealings for more than a decade. He was the former director and a stock holder in the River Grove Bank & Trust. He also ran the Mutual Development Corporation at 10330 Roberts Road in Palos Heights, IL. which was known to finance OUTFIT business deals. In the late 1970's he was a partner with OUTFIT gambling boss Ken Eto and Sam Sarcinelli in Taco-Si a Skokie, IL. based food business. Shortly before his death he had been questioned by federal agents regarding OUTFIT money matters which could have led to his death.

On **January 10, 1985** Leonard "Lenny" Yaras 44 yrs. of 4001 W. Chase in Lincolnwood, IL. was shot to death sitting in his car in front of All American Laundry and cleaners, A-1 Industrial Uniforms both located at 4224 W. Division Street. Yaras had an interest in both businesses and was president of A-1. He was shot 11 times, 4 times in the head and neck by two gunmen in a four man hit squad. Yaras a long time OUTFIT associate, and Lenny Patrick confidant was in a struggle to maintain his interest in Northside Rogers Park gambling operations that were being taken over by operatives of Joey Lombardo. His father was David Yaras a long time member of Patrick's assassination crew and a renowned killer. Apparently his resistance to the takeover led to his death.

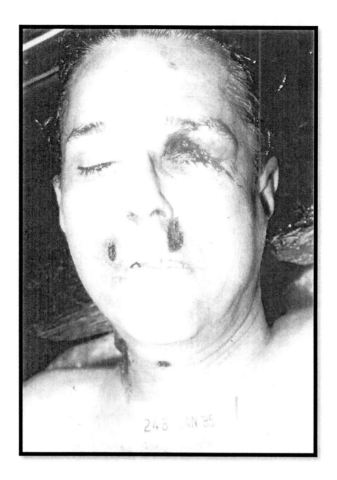

Lenny Yaras dead

On **February 9, 1985** Charles "Chuckie" English 70 yrs. of 1131 N. Lathrop in River Forest, IL. was shot to death as he walked to his Cadillac in the parking lot of Horvath's restaurant at 1850 N. Harlem Avenue in Elmwood Park, IL. Horvath's restaurant was a popular nightspot frequented by many Chicago OUTFIT figures. Allegedly the victim had just left a meeting with mobster John Lardino AKA: John Nardico, two circuit court judges and two local politicians. It was reported that Lardino made a phone call just before English left for his car. Chuckie, at one time the number one Lieutenant for Sam Giancana AKA: Momo Salvatore, Mooney, or Gilormo Giangono, had also worked as his bodyguard, confidante and was designated as the OUTFIT's Jukebox Boss. Police believe that English refused to set up Giancana for his murder and was stripped of his ownership in a record company known as Lormar Distributing at 2311 N. Western. After Giancana's death English was a lieutenant for Tony Accardo, but was vocal about the way Giancana was terminated. In 1976 he was put out to pasture by the OUTFIT and stripped of his position as head of gambling in the 29th ward, the head of bookmaking, vending machines and loanshark operations in Cicero. He had changed his allegiance from the imprisoned Joe Lombardo to the future Boss Joe Ferriola just before his murder. No solid motive was ever established and the case went unsolved.

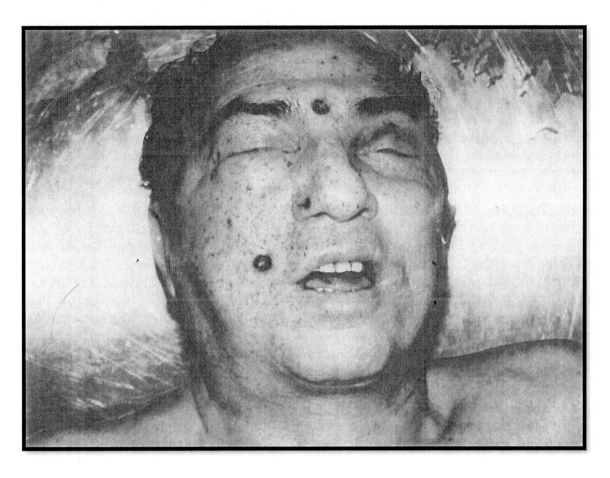

Chuckie English dead

On **February 12, 1985** Hal Smith 48 yrs. of 315 Kenilworth Drive in Prospect Heights, IL. was found murdered in the trunk of his Cadillac Seville in the parking lot of the Arlington Park Hilton Hotel in Arlington Heights, IL. He had been badly beaten, his neck slashed during torture and his throat was cut and he died of strangulation with a belt or rope. Smith was a sports betting kingpin and was considered by Justice Department Officials as the largest independent bookmaker in the area. A Crime Commission Investigator had an opportunity to discuss this murder with Smith's friend, federal informant and WITSEC participant William B.J. Jahoda after BJ appeared at a sports gambling conference at Northern Illinois University in January of 1999. In this discussion it was revealed just how close BJ and the victim were and how BJ was being pressured by OUTFIT gambling Boss Rocco Infelise to reign in (make them pay street tax) all the independent bookmakers including his friend Smith. BJ talked to Smith several times warning him of the impending violence, but Smith dismissed his warnings. Then in February of 1985 Rocco Infelise and several of his minions appeared at BJ's Long Grove, IL. home and ordered him to go get Smith and bring him back. BJ felt that his friend was now out of time and was probably going to get a beating. He knew that if he did not follow orders, he too would get a beating or worse. BJ then called his friend under the guise of going to

277

have drinks and after they met he said he forgot something and had to stop by his Long Grove home. He said as they entered the home through the kitchen, Smith froze when he saw Infelise and the others. BJ was then ordered to leave and as he walked to the car, he could hear Smith screaming in pain. BJ knew after his friend was found tortured and dead that he would accept the proposal of IRS investigators and help them bring down the Infelise crew, 20 in all, which he did, sending all of them to prison for racketeering. Of the men, Rocco Infelise, Louis Marino, Robert Bellavia and Carmen "Bobby" Salerno were convicted of Smith's murder with the help of BJ who passed away in 2004 of natural causes while living in an undisclosed location **(solved)**.

On **July 26, 1985** Patrick A. "Patsy" Ricciardi 59 yrs. of 5348 N. Virginia was found murdered in the trunk of a stolen car after it had been towed to a police station parking lot. He was shot once in the head. Patsy operated the Admiral Theater for the OUTFIT in the 3900 block of west Lawrence Ave. He was able to turn a good profit for the OUTFIT and was suspected of laundering money through it by inflating attendance records. He was also a cousin of Felix "Milwaukee Phil" Alderisio and allegedly held some $5 million dollars for Phil when he died. In the end he was reportedly the OUTFIT's porno-movie Boss, but was suspected of being a federal informant. He simply knew too much about the porno business and the secret of the $5 million.

On **January 13, 1986** Michael S. Lentini 44 yrs. of 9110 Grant, Brookfield, IL. was shot three times as he started his car while leaving for work. Assailants fired multiple shots through the car windows as the victim headed for work as a pressman at Regensteiner Publishing Enterprises Inc. at 1224 W. Van Buren.

On **January 27, 1986** Richard N. DePrizio 36 yrs. was shot twice in the head and was left in a parking lot at 2520 S. Wolf Road in Westchester, IL. He owned V. N. DePrizio Construction which held city contracts before going into bankruptcy in 1983. He was about to be indicted by the federal government regarding those contracts and he owed everybody and just maybe juice operators to.

On **March 15, 1986** Giuseppe "Joe" Coccoza 54 yrs. of 708 W. Bittersweet was found shot to death in a parked car at Keeney and Forest in Evanston, IL. Chicago Police Intelligence Unit Detectives reviewed this murder as a cold case in 1994. At the time they learned that Joe was employed in Chicago at a gas station. Joe was a degenerate gambler who owed money to at least two different OUTFIT juice loan operators. He was having work done on his car at a northside gas station that was frequented by Outfit juice collectors. He was intending to flee Chicago and his debt. Joe would regularly make payments at his place of employment to collectors from the street crew of Lenny Patrick. The case was eventually linked to other murders in 1982 and 1987. All three cases were tied together by local gas stations. The FBI initially cooperated with the investigation by Chicago Police, Evanston Police and the Cook County State's Attorney. A federal proffer described the murder and identified the killers as 2 juice collectors. However, for unknown reasons the FBI and the Cook County State's Attorney terminated their support. Federal authorities would not provide access to the 2 witnesses that they controlled and the case was never solved.

On **June 6, 1986** Jeff Vandermark was beaten to death with a hammer in his Las Vegas apartment, he was the son of Jay Vandermark. Franks Schweihs a brutal OUTFIT assassin was suspected in this killing. Family Secrets testimony revealed that the father Jay was being sought for stealing from the OUTFIT and was being protected by Emile Vaci who was also murdered. Jay Vandermark was last seen at the Arizona Manor, a hotel and nightclub in Phoenix. Reportedly he was given an all expenses trip to Mazatlan, Mexico. He disappeared and was never seen again and is assumed dead.

On **June 7, 1986** Emil "Mal" Vaci 73 yrs. was found murdered in Phoenix, AZ. where he worked in a restaurant. He had appeared before a federal grand jury regarding the skimming of Las Vegas casinos. He was a trusted associate of the Chicago OUTFIT and was really in charge of the skim and simply knew too much. When appearing in front of a federal grand jury he was offered immunity which made his Chicago superiors very nervous. It was also learned that he had helped a second man, Jay Vandermark who was stealing from the OUTFIT and a suspected slot skimmer years before. He actually hid the man in his home which was unforgivable. These were irrefutable circumstances to the OUTFIT and his death warrant was signed. Vandermark's son Jeff paid for his father's indiscretions when he was beaten to death in his Las Vegas apartment the day before. Early on, Frank Schweihs and Paul Shiro were accused of this killing, but Family Secrets testimony revealed Joey Hanson was also involved and Nick Calabrese was the one to pull the trigger and later dumped the victim into a nearly dry drainage ditch wrapped in a tarpaulin while Paul Shiro and Jimmy DiForti watched from a look out car (Case cleared through Operation Family Secrets in 2005) **(solved).**

On **June 22, 1986** Anthony J. "Tony the Ant" Spilotro 48 yrs. and his brother Michael P. Spilotro 42 yrs. were found buried in a 5 foot deep grave in Northwest Indiana. The men were reported missing on June 14th and the Lincoln they drove was found in the Howard Johnson Motel parking lot at Mannheim and Irving Park Road. Joe Ferriola upon his appointment as OUTFIT Boss in 1986 held Tony "The Ant" Spilotro responsible for the OUTFIT's problems in Las Vegas. While the Vegas position gave Tony great notoriety he seemed out of control and was suspected in as many as 25 murders in Vegas, most not sanctioned by his bosses in Chicago. His burglary ring and the wealth he amassed from it were not approved either. Tony and his brother Michael were ordered back to Chicago under a guise of promotions for both and they were killed in Bensenville, IL. Family Secrets testimony revealed that James Marcello had picked the brothers up and drove them to a home in Bensenville where they were beaten to death by a dozen OUTFIT associates including Nick Calabrese, Louis Marino, Louie Eboli, John Fecarotta, Jimmy LaPietra, John DiFronzo, Sam Carlisi and Joe Ferriola. John Feccarotta, who was charged with the burial and held accountable when the bodies were found, paid with his life.   Tony Spilotro was a trusted OUTFIT operative who came up as a protégé of "Mad Sam" DeStefano. His failure to remain low profile and his insistence on challenging the police in Las Vegas cost him his life. Reportedly James Marcello was a key figure in this killing after it was ordered by Joey Aiuppa. (Case cleared through Operation Family Secrets in 2005, James Marcello was held responsible at trial) **(solved)**.

Joe Ferriola

On **September 14, 1986** John A. Fecarotta 58 yrs. of 268 Gage Road in Riverside, IL. was shot to death in a doorway near a bingo hall at 6050 W. Belmont Ave. He was shot four times with a .38 cal. revolver. The victim was a business agent for John Serpico in the Laborers International Union Local #8 and a long time OUTFIT associate. It was finally revealed during Family Secrets testimony that he was killed by Frank Calabrese, John Monteleone and Nick Calabrese a government informant who was linked to the scene by blood evidence he left during the assault. Calabrese was assigned the job by Jimmy LaPietra a Boss from Chinatown. This killing was in retaliation for the botched burial of the Spilotro brothers whose bodies were found by authorities shortly after they were discarded, Fecarotta was in charge of the burial. Calabrese's blood at the scene led to his arrest by DNA comparison years later. Soon after, he began cooperating with federal authorities, allowing them to develop the Operation Family Secrets case. Calabrese plead guilty in this murder.   (Case cleared through Operation Family Secrets in 2005, Frank Calabrese Sr. was held responsible at trial) **(solved)**.

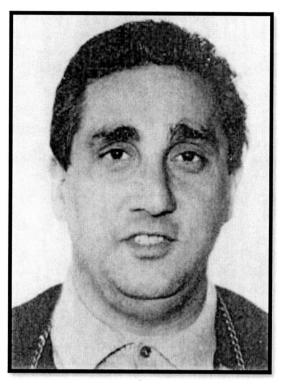

John Fecarotta

On **November 13, 1986** Thomas B. McKillip 49 yrs. was found shot and stabbed in the back of a 1977 Chevrolet Blazer in Buffalo Grove, IL. He was shot twice in the back of the head with a small caliber handgun and stabbed in the chest.

On **February 3, 1987** Don Aronow was gunned down as he walked down a Miami Street, he was a prominent speed boat manufacturer. He built cigarette boats for some of the wealthiest people in the world and the boats were also popular with drug runners. He may have been involved in money laundering for the drug trade and may have been preparing to cooperate with authorities when he was killed. Joe Lombardo and Frank Schweihs were suspected in the murder.

On **September 23, 1987** John Castaldo 28 yrs. of 10517 Essex in Westchester, IL. was found shot to death at 12:15 pm in an alley in the 100 block of Frederick in Bellwood, IL. He apparently was shot multiple times in the head and chest with a handgun where he was found. Castaldo was the owner of 2 beauty salons at 7351 W. Lake St. and 7345 Central Ave. both in River Forest, IL. He was last seen leaving one of his salons with bank deposits and was later seen entering a car with three men. A short time later his wife reported him missing and his car was located not far from the scene of the crime. Police investigations found he was a juice customer of OUTFIT loansharks. In 1993 Nick Gio a juice collector for Northside Gambling Boss Lenny Patrick was indicted for the slaying. Gio was convicted and sentenced to life in prison for the murder **(solved)**.

On **November 3, 1987** Charles Merriam an executive for a large oil company and the grandson of a respected University of Chicago Professor who was the brother of a reform Mayoral candidate in the 1950's, was gunned down in the vestibule of his Prospect Heights, IL. townhome. Chicago Police Intelligence Unit Detectives investigated this murder as a cold case in 1994. Police speculated this killing may have been related to his work with the oil company and sanctions against those he investigated and testified against. Organized Crime members were suspected of involvement in the killing. The case was eventually linked to other murders in 1982 and 1986. All three cases were tied together by local gas stations, but remain unsolved.

In **December of 1987** Gadiuso Giovanni was gunned down in a Harlem Ave. parking lot, possibly over a dispute with Local OUTFIT associates.

On January 23, 1988 Union Racketeer Dominic Senese was the victim of a botched OUTFIT hit in the exclusive Chicago suburb of Oak Brook. He survived a shotgun blast to the face and lived long enough to have the contract on his life canceled. He died of natural causes on January 29, 1992. His son Lucien would also survive an OUTFIT hit on September 6, 1990 when a bomb placed in his car ignited as he left his girlfriend's home in Little Italy. Lucien would be barred from Teamsters Local 703 involvement by a federal judge for his associations.

On **February 14, 1988** William Benham a local businessman and juice customer was shot to death in his place of business. At the time of the shooting Benham in an attempt to protect himself shot his assailant and blood was found on the scene. Years later an informant coupled with new DNA technology identified Cicero OUTFIT member and hitman James Diforti as the killer. DiForti was arrested on July 2, 1997 and died in prison on June 6, 2000 **(solved).**

James DiForti

On **February 18, 1988** Joseph J. Gehl 28 yrs. was murdered in a tavern at 2922 W. Irving Park Road in Chicago. His body was found on March 6, 1988 near Valparaiso, IN. Joe Gehl was a rigger at McCormick Place and a known Melrose Park bookmaker. He was suspected of being an informant in an Arlington Heights gambling raid. His father was Fred R. "Sonny" Gehl a Cicero gambler and contractor associated with Joe Ferriola. He was lured to the tavern by its owner James Maples 35, who did not have the $15,000 he owed Gehl. At the tavern Maples and Mathew Meierkort 26, alledgedly beat and strangled Gehl to death. The men were arrested and charged with the killing. Maples was convicted while Meierkort was acquitted in a separate trial, both presided over by Judge Earl Strayhorn **(solved).**

On **August 14, 1988** John E. Pronger 64 yrs. of 2547 Springhill Dr. Schererville, IN. was killed by two .357 magnum rounds as he stood in the doorway of his residence.

On **November 22, 1988** Phillip Goodman 73 yrs. of Las Vegas was found by a motel employee beaten to death in the Admiral Motel at 9353 Waukegan Rd. in Morton Grove, IL. The victim formerly of Chicago suffered massive head trauma. Goodman was an associate of the Spilotro crew in Las Vegas. He started a lucrative travel business which came to the attention of Lenny Patrick who made himself a partner and drove the business into the ground. As the business was on the brink of collapse Goodman was suspected of informing to investigators in Las Vegas. In 1994 this case was reviewed by the Chicago Police Intelligence Unit to no avail. At that time Patrick, one of his collectors and a former Rush Street crew member were suspected of setting up the killing which remains unsolved.

On May 2, 1989 it was reported that OUTFIT assassin Gerald Scarpelli was being held in the Metropolitan Correction Center at Clark and Van Buren. He had provided detailed information on OUTFIT activities and then covered his head with plastic bags before hanging himself in a 21st floor shower room. It has been suspected by many in law enforcement that he may have received help in this suicide.

In **September of 1989** Joseph Bova was killed when a bomb in his truck went off as he started it. He was the secretary-treasurer of a Teamster local in the area and the killing was allegedly related to OUTFIT involvement in the union.

On **November 19, 1989** Salvatore Canzoneri was found shot to death in his Highland Park, IL. home. He was a former Chicago Police Officer, an entrepreneur and allegedly an associate of the late northside Boss Joe "Caesar" DiVarco. The case was investigated by the Highland Park P.D. who were able to identify a suspect, but were unable to charge them at the time.

On **December 19, 1989** Reportedly Mike Oliver 30 yrs. and Bobby Hatridge 40s were found in what was believed to be a Mob graveyard in Downers Grove, IL. Both men had been murdered and were alledgedly associates of mobster

Gerry Scarpelli. Oliver reportedly ran shakedowns of porno bookstores in the western suburbs and was allegedly killed in 1979 during a Mob raid of a pornographer near Elk Grove. Hatridge was described by authorities as a hit man and thief from Cincinnati who would come to Chicago to carry out Mob business such as murders, home invasions and thefts.

Approx. number of Chicago TOC related murders in the 1980s: 51
Approx. number of Chicago TOC related murder cases in the 1980s solved: 18
Approx. number of Chicago TOC related murders in the 1980s of Police Officers: 0

Chapter 9. The 1990's

During the early 1990s several prominent mobsters completed prison sentences and re-joined their contemporaries in the ethnic enclaves of Chicago. None of them were more enigmatic than Joey "The Clown" Lombardo. The Clown served ten years for his part in a bribery scheme, union racketeering and the Las Vegas skimming case and was felt at the time by most TOC aficionados as a top Advisor to the Chicago OUTFIT if not THE Boss.

In 1990 the Chicago Crime Commission vehemently opposed the appointment of admitted OUTFIT associate, John Serpico, as Chairman of the Chicago Port Authority District by the Governor of Illinois. Serpico still took office and was not deposed until 1999 by a different Governor after he had been barred from a labor union for life because of the associations made public by the CCC.

In 1990 OUTFIT enforcer Frank Schweihs was convicted of extorting money from a pornography vendor in Old Town. Schweihs was sentenced to 13 years in prison and upon his release in 1994 returned to his illicit duties for the OUTFIT. Schweihs has been a suspect in several OUTFIT killings over the years and was finally indicted in 2005 (Operation Family Secrets) only to slip through the fingers of the local FBI and go on the run. After a tip he was arrested months later in Kentucky but died in federal custody before he could be tried.

In 1990 an eight year multiagency investigation by the FBI, IRS, Illinois State Police and the Chicago Police culminated with the indictment of 20 Chicago OUTFIT figures including Rocco Infelise, Harry Aleman and Sal DeLaurentis for Murder, extortion, bribery and racketeering. This case presented federal prosecutors with their first opportunity to characterize the Chicago OUTFIT as a criminal enterprise under the RICO statute.

In 1990 Federal indictments in Operation "Gambat" loosened the OUTFIT's grip on the 1st ward. Subsequent convictions removed OUTFIT operatives from office and for the first time in over 100 years, turned the ward over to its constituents. Later in 1990 an undercover investigation by federal authorities called "Operation Kaffeeklatsch" looked into 1st Ward corruption and the protection of gambling operations for the OUTFIT. The case was aided by informants Robert Cooley and B.J. Jahoda. A second phase of the investigation known as the "Commission" case focused on OUTFIT leadership in the person of: John "No Nose" DiFronzo, Sam "Wings" Carlisi, Vince Solano Sr., Joe "The Builder" Andriacci, James "Lapper" LaPietra, Dominick Palermo and Jimmy "Legs" D"Antonio.

Mob Leaders: Joe "The Builder" Andriacci, Sam "Wings" Carlisi, Anthony Centracchio, Ernest "Rocky" Infelise

Critical events of the 1990s

On **June 4, 1990** James Pellegrino 31 yrs. of 122 Thomas Court in Mokena, IL. was found murdered in the Des Plaines River around 8901 W. Lawrence Ave. He was reported missing by his wife on May 14th. The victim was found by two German tourists canoeing on the river when they spotted a tarp caught on the branch of a tree limb. They pulled it ashore and found the body. The 16th District Police responded and found the victim had been shot in the back of the head with a .25 cal. handgun. His head had a plastic bag over it, his hands and feet were tied with rope. Reportedly at the time of the killing the victim had a falling out with his associates who were burglars and drug dealers. Eventually, a former police officer was found guilty of the crime, but was released over a decade later in a reversal of his conviction **(solved)**.

On **July 1, 1990** Victor Lazarus 88 yrs. of Evanston, IL. was found dead in the trunk of his car parked in the parking lot at 2050 W. Peterson Ave. It was determined that the victim was shot in the head twice before being put in the trunk. Reportedly the victim was a reputed OUTFIT bookmaker and associate dating back to the 1940's. He was aligned with the Spilotro crew in Las Vegas and had moved back to Chicago when his wife became ill and eventually died. At the time he was living in a senior citizens residence/hotel in nearby Evanston, IL. when he was killed. Chicago Police Department Detectives from Area 6 Homicide and the Intelligence Unit investigated this case between 1990 through 1997 to no avail.

On September 6, 1990 at 1006 S. May, Teamsters Local 703 Official Lucien Senese was blown up when he went to his car and turned the ignition. He survived the blast although the motive was never verified.

On **November 6, 1991** Edward Pedote 49 yrs. was found murdered in a furniture resale store at 1823 S. Cicero in Cicero, IL. He was beaten and shot in the face with a small caliber handgun. Pedote was a fence and wholesale jeweler at 5 S. Wabash known as Jewelers Row and left his Naperville, IL. home carrying a large amount of jewelry and $50,000, his pockets were empty when he was found. He had pled guilty in 1985 to robbery, weapons and drug charges. He received probation in the case while his associates Dan Bambulas and Mike Swiatek a member of the Grand Avenue street crew went to prison. That may have had something to do with the killing. In 1992 the Cicero Police Department arrested and charged Glenn W. Devos AKA: Benes with the killing, the outcome of the court case is unknown **(solved)**.

On **December 21, 1991** Wallace Lieberman 60 yrs. of Northbrook, IL. an estate liquidator was found dead in the alley behind 6000 W. 31st Street in Cicero, IL. about 35 yards from his Mercedes Benz two days after he was reported missing. He worked as an auctioneer under contract to the U.S. Bankruptcy Courts in Chicago. He died of a single gunshot wound to the neck. His associates included mobster Robert Bellavia who was on trial at the time charged with racketeering.

On **November 5, 1992** Sam Taglia 50 yrs. of 416 Thatcher in River Forest, IL. was found murdered in the trunk of his car at 13th and Main Sts. in Melrose Park, IL. He had been shot twice in the head and his throat had been cut. Taglia had a long arrest record for Robbery, Burglary, Auto Theft and Narcotics and had done 5 years in 1967. He was reportedly killed by OUTFIT associate Albert Vena over a failed drug deal. Vena was found not guilty in 1993 for this killing **(solved)**.

On **November 5, 1994** Giuseppe Vicari was found dead is his restaurant La Casa De Caffe at 5243 N. Harlem Avenue. He had been beaten and shot in the head. He had recently moved his restaurant from Addison, IL. Reportedly he had been in the U.S. since 1989 and was involved with Mob gambling through a faction in Bari, Italy. He was out on bond from a case in DuPage County Court on gambling charges.

Herbie Blitzstein

On **January 6, 1997** Herbert "Fat Herbie" Blitzstein an OUTFIT enforcer and Tony Spilotro confidant was murdered in his Las Vegas townhouse at 3655 Mount Vernon Ave. He was discovered slumped over in a chair and was shot in the back of the head three times. Herbie was a former Rush Street hood who hung around with the likes of: Albert "Obie" Frabotta, Joe Arnold, Joe DiVarco, Ken Eto, Moe Shapiro, Sherman Goldman and Marvin Marks, he was one of the last remnants of the Spilotro crew once serving as Spilotro's top aide. Two east coast mobsters Alfred Mauriello and Joseph DeLuca were later charged and convicted of the killing that appeared to be a dispute over criminal activities in Vegas **(solved)**.

In 1997 OUTFIT collector and union racketeer James DiForti was arrested and charged with the 1988 murder of juice customer William Benham, during a shootout, DiForti was wounded and DNA technology identified him in this case.

On **December 4, 1997** Robert C. Cruz disappeared from his home where he was putting up Christmas lights. In 2007 his body was recovered from a suspected Mob burial ground in suburban Chicago. He had been shot by unknown gangsters. He was the cousin of prolific Mob killer Harry Aleman and had spent 14 years on death row for the double murder of a Phoenix, Arizona businessman, Patrick Redmond and his mother-in-law on **December 31, 1980**. After numerous trials he was acquitted in 1995 when a jury found a witness against him who was a participant in the killing was unreliable **(solved)**.

On **December 23, 1999** Ronnie Jarrett of South Lowe Ave. was shot several times as he left his Bridgeport home. He died a month later. The first Law Enforcement officer on the scene was reportedly an FBI agent which is rare in these types of street crimes. Apparently after the death of Jarrett's Outfit Boss Angelo LaPietra he lost his attraction to the gang. Family Secrets testimony revealed that John Monteleone the new Boss of the Chinatown crew after the deaths of Angelo and Jimmy LaPietra wanted Jarrett dead because he was dealing drugs against OUTFIT orders and was resisting paying street taxes for a gambling operation he controlled. It was also revealed during Family Secrets testimony that Jarrett was involved in several of the killings discussed in the trial.

Approximate number of Chicago TOC related murders in the 1990s: 11
Approx. number of Chicago TOC related murder cases in the 1990s solved: 6
Approx. number of Chicago TOC related murders in the 1990s of Police Officers: 0

Chapter 10.
Critical events of the new millennium

On **March 21, 2001** Richard Hauff was found murdered in a restaurant he owned in Greencastle, Indiana. On November 10, 1964 Frank "The German" Schweihs 34, was arrested by Cook County Sheriff's Police Sergeant John Flood. During routine patrol in suburban Schiller Park, Sgt. Flood observed Schweihs armed with a lead pipe and creeping up on a vehicle containing OUTFIT associate Richard W. Hauff 28, and an unnamed woman. The officer prevented the attack. Reportedly Hauff was involved in the OUTFIT operations of golf courses and night clubs. Two other men sitting in a getaway car believed to be driven by Joey "The Clown" Lombardo fled almost running down the Sergeant. It was believed to be a planned hit. This killing was almost 40 years after the attempt on his life. Schweihs and Lombardo were both indicted in 2005 concerning a federal investigation of 18 unsolved OUTFIT related murders in the case titled "Family Secrets". However this case was not one of them.

On **November 20, 2001** Anthony "The Hatchet" Chairamonti 67 yrs. of LaGrange, IL. was gunned down in the vestibule of a Brown's Chicken restaurant at 3850 S. Harlem in Lyons, IL. A van pulled in front of the victim and a male Hispanic got out of the car and exchanged words with Chiaramonte at which time he walked back into the restaurant where the assailant followed shooting him five times, three times in the head, once in the arm and once in the chest. The shooter then retreated to the van which fled west on 39th Street. The Hatchet died months after the natural death of his Southside Boss John Monteleone. At the time of his death the victim was driving a new BMW automobile registered to PIC Transportation at 3840 S. Laramie in Cicero, IL. He was the first of a group of hoods to be released from prison in 1998 after a 1993 conviction. He was at the time a top money maker for the OUTFIT in sports bookmaking and loansharking along with being a feared OUTFIT collector and suspected killer. Police suspect a power struggle over the operations that the Hatchet ran, albeit interim. He reported to Anthony "Little Tony" Zizzo who was released from prison himself shortly before the killing and disappeared a short time later. Reportedly this murder was arranged by Anthony C. Calabrese (no relation to Frank and Nick) and Robert Cooper, both members of a south side robbery gang, although the case remains unsolved.

On **August 31, 2006** Anthony "Little Tony" Zizzo 71 yrs. left his Westmont IL. home never to be seen again. His car was found abandon in a Melrose Park restaurant parking lot. Reportedly court documents confirm that he was feuding with Cicero OUTFIT Boss Michael Sarno. The men fought over control of the lucrative video poker business in the western suburbs. Federal authorities are convinced Zizzo was murdered, but will not elaborate.

On **January 1, 20**..

Approximate number of Chicago TOC related murders after 2000: 3
Approx. number of Chicago TOC related murder cases after 2000 solved: 0
Approx. number of Chicago TOC related murders after 2000 of Police Officers: 0

Total number of Chicago TOC related murders : 1401
Total number of Chicago TOC related murder cases solved: 278
Total number of Chicago TOC related murders of Police Officers: 38

The OUTFIT Street Crews and TOC Murder

The Chicago OUTFIT has always maintained a strong division of labor and developed into sub-groups/street crews within the ethnic enclaves and neighborhoods of the Chicagoland area. These groups were synonymous with the areas in which they operated. The **OUTFIT/TOC street crews** are known as:

Taylor Street
Grand Avenue
26Th Street-Chinatown-Levee
Northside
Rush Street
Elmwood Park
Southside/Chicago Heights
Westside/Cicero
Lake County

TOC MURDER

Murder, once a hall mark of TOC in Chicago, has now in its absence, been misinterpreted as an indicator of the demise of TOC altogether. This has been reported by the media, academics and Law Enforcement Officials themselves. I warn people regularly not to fall prey to such reports and point to other indicators such as Union, gambling activities and continuing public corruption scandals to declare the OUTFIT alive and well in the Chicago metropolitan area.

The litany of prolific MOB killers in Chicago bears the names of individuals such as: "Machine Gun" Jack McGurn AKA: James or Vincenzo Gibaldi, Lenny Patrick-Murder Inc., and Harry "The Hook" Aleman. While this list fills the pages of this entire book we must consider the level of TOC slayings that have been tracked in this book. Chicago TOC according to our tracking and research has been responsible for approx. **1,401** killings. What is most startling is the unwillingness or inability of Law Enforcement to solve such crimes. Reportedly between 1926 and 1929, over 260 TOC murders occurred in Chicago, only 2 were solved, in 1932 of the 35 TOC killings that occurred that year none were solved, between 1919 and 1964 of the 986 murders reported in Chicago only 21 offenders were tried.

However we can't discount the efforts of Federal Authorities in recent years as stated below:

In April of 2005 with great fanfare the United States Attorney for the Northern District of Illinois announced "14 DEFENDANTS INDICTED FOR ALLEGED ORGANIZED CRIME ACTIVITIES; "CHICAGO OUTFIT" NAMED AS RICO ENTERPRISE IN FOUR DECADE CONSPIRACY ALLEGING 18 MOB MURDERS AND 1 ATTEMPTED MURDER.

The case code-named Operation Family Secrets struck at the leadership of the OUTFIT and cleared 18 murders committed between 1970 and 1986 with the help of OUTFIT members turned government informants Frank Calabrese Jr. and Nicholas Calabrese. Those indicted include: James Marcello, Joseph Lombardo (captured in Elmwood Park in February of 2006 after several months as a fugitive), Frank Calabrese Sr., Nicholas Calabrese, Frank Schweihs (captured in Kentucky in December of 2005 after several months as a fugitive, succumbing to cancer in July of 2008 before he could be tried), Frank "Gumbo" Saladino (found dead of natural causes after the indictment), Paul Shiro, Michael Marcello, Nicholas Ferriola, Anthony Doyle and Michael Ricci (died of natural causes in January of 2006).

In this indictment Frank Calabrese Sr. was accused of thirteen killings to include those of: Michael Albergo, Paul Haggerty, John Fecarotta, Billy Dauber, Charlotte Dauber, Frank Ortiz, Art Morawski, Butch Petrocelli, Henry Cosentino, John Mendell, Vincent Moretti, Donald Renno and Michael Cagnoni.

While the case is the greatest attempt to clear OUTFIT murders in history, it does not clear every OUTFIT murder in that time period as this book will demonstrate. It also addressed what some refer to as the lifeblood of the OUTFIT being video gambling. The M&M Amusement Inc. in Cicero run by James and Michael Marcello played a key role in the indictment.

During research on this book Statistics were amassed from several reliable sources that included killings outside of Chicago, but attributable to the Chicago Mob or its minions. These cases were retrieved from public and private records, media reports, references found in publications and from personal experiences and knowledge from human sources. While reviewing historic documents it was revealed that the same dismal stats existed in reviewing cases solved with a total of 260 before recent prosecutions that brought the total to **276**. This shows us that many dedicated and honest officials were stifled by the rampant corruption of the past. Hopefully, we can take heart from recent progress and continue with efforts to solve every homicide, not just those that are politically correct. And lastly, a review has been conducted to record the number of police officers killed at the hands of the MOB. This resulted in the death of **38** police officers.

Since the late 1980s a dramatic decrease in murders has occurred due to internal policy changes and more level headed leadership of the OUTFIT.

Recent prosecutions by the U.S. Attorney's Office demonstrated the ability to solve these very complicated cases by solving 18 MOB/OUTFIT murders from the last 30 years with the cooperation of OUTFIT insider Nick Calabrese. This has led to the greatest closure of OUTFIT murders in Chicago history. This was a truly great day in law enforcement.

TIME LINE

While it would be decades before they would even acknowledge TOC, the FBI was formed in 1908 as the Bureau of Investigation.

In January of 1911 public opinion began to turn against vice and corruption. Heeding the call Alderman Charles E. Merriam announced his candidacy for the Republican nomination for Mayor. He was a man of unquestioned integrity and was supported by reformers and good government types, but would lose his quest to be mayor. Decades later his grandson would fall from a mobster's bullets for exhibiting the same qualities.

In Chicago, Second Deputy Superintendent M. C. Funkhouser was assigned in 1913 to investigate corruption in the newly formed Morals Squad led by Inspector W. C. Dannenberg, he released several controversial reports that indicated several police districts as "Wide Open" meaning that vice laws were not enforced and the police were taking bribes.

By 1915 Mob Boss Big Jim Colosimo entered labor racketeering, taking over several local unions and raiding their treasuries.

In 1917 Johnny Torrio continued to expand Colosimo's empire and purchased the Speedway Inn, which would later become the first roadhouse of note with the introduction of Prohibition.

While on the northside, gangsters such as Charles Dion "Deanie" O'Banion, Hymie Weiss AKA: Earl Wajciechowski, Nails Morton and Ben Jerus were interning with Charles "The Ox" Reiser one of the most notorious safe crackers of the day. He taught them how to use explosives. By 1918 O'Banion and Hymie Weiss put this knowledge to work blowing the safe at the Western Dairy Company and stealing $2,000.

On January 1, 1919 The Chicago Association of Commerce in response to crime and vice conditions in the city, established the Chicago Crime Commission. The first Director is Edwin West Simms, former U.S. Attorney and past head of the Vice Commission of Chicago in 1910. This is the same year Prohibition is signed into law as the Volstead Act.

In the Spring of 1919 the Manhattan Brewing Company at 3901 S. Emerald is purchased by the fore-thinking hood Jonny Torrio and brewer Joe Stenson. Later Northside gangsters/bootleggers Charles Dion "Deanie" O'Banion, and Hymie Weiss AKA: Earl Wajciechowski buy-in as co-owners.

In December of 1919 just before the inception of Prohibition, Charles Dion "Deanie" O'Banion hijacked the first beer shipment of the Prohibition era.

About the time that Prohibition emerged, Torrio was contacted by his dear friend Frankie Yale AKA: Uale or Ioele from New York, who asked him if he could use the services of a fellow gangster from the notorious Brooklyn Five Points gang, who worked in one of his saloons. This tough young man was eager to use his fists and was a suspect in two murders when Yale sent him to Chicago in 1919, at least until the heat died down. That young man would change the history of TOC in America and was named Al "Scarface" Capone. Capone soon emerged as Torrio's top Lt., helping him run Colosimo interests.

In February of 1920, a mere 2 weeks after the initiation of the Volstead Act, the first raid on a speakeasy occurred.

On July 20, 1921 Mob controlled Governor Len Small is indicted for embezzlement and other crimes by a Sangamon County Grand Jury shortly after being acquitted of charges filed against him when he was the State Treasurer. Small was remembered for his wholesale pardons of gangsters at the request of the Chicago Mob.

In 1921 Charles Dion "Deanie" O'Banion enters into a partnership with Samuel J. Markowitz AKA: "Nails Morton" and William Schofield to open a florist shop at 738 North State Street. Dion would later be murdered there.

In 1922 John Torrio began importing whiskey from Canada through the Purple Gang in Detroit. The gang employed several former members of the "Egan's Rats" gang from St. Louis who became known as the "American Boys" when put on the payroll by Al Capone and his mostly Italian gang in Chicago around 1928. They would gain notoriety with Chicago gangsters by carrying out the St. Valentine's Day massacre in 1929. By the end of 1922, Torrio developed a standing army of 100 men under the auspices of Al Capone to protect his operations.

On November 7, 1922 rising political star Anton Cermak is elected as President of the Cook County Board. The young Bohemian has great support among liquor interests as Secretary of United Societies, a group representing saloonkeepers, brewers and distillers that opposed prohibition laws. He used his position to develop the Cook County Democratic machine to the organization it is today. He remained in charge of the County Board until elected Mayor of Chicago on April 7, 1931, while developing close associations with certain gangsters such as Roger Touhy, Edward M. "Teddy" Newberry, Billy Skidmore and William R. "Big Bill" Johnson.

On April 3, 1923 Judge William E. Dever is elected as Mayor of Chicago in a three-way race in which the incumbent Bill Thompson withdraws due to scandals in his administration. Dever a true reformer appoints Morgan A. Collins as Chief of Police. Their efforts at reform would change Organized Crime in Chicago for decades to come and force the Torrio-Capone gang to move their headquarters to Cicero during the conflicts known by the media as the "Beer Wars".

On May 13, 1923 Samuel J. Markowitz AKA: "Nails Morton", a tough born and raised westsider, decorated Army veteran and a close associate and confidant of Dion O'Banion was felled in a most unusual way, at least for gangsters of the era. While riding his horse on his way to the lakefront bridle paths in Lincoln Park he was thrown from the horse and died of a severe head injury at the corner of Diversey and Clark Sts. Legend has it that northside gang boss Dion O'Banion hearing the news, ordered one of his gunman, Louis "Two Gun" Alterie AKA: Leland Deveraigne, Leland Varain, to put a bullet in the horse's head.

It was in 1923 that "Machine Gun" Jack McGurn AKA: James or Vincenzo Gibaldi left the Circus Gang to join the Torrio/Capone organization and would become one of their most prolific killers.

In June of 1923 Illinois Governor Len Small under the orders of John Torrio granted pardons to Jake and Alma Guzik. This continued practice put approximately 1,000 hoods on the street prematurely. This along with the theft of state funds resulted in an eventual indictment and prison term for Small.

In October of 1923 John Torrio held his first gang summit at the Sherman Hotel where he tried to incorporate many of the local rackets into one organization to capitalize on the potential of prohibition. Some of the gangs joined him while others did not.

On May 10, 1924 J. Edgar Hoover becomes acting Director of the U. S. Justice Department's Bureau of Investigation becoming the Federal Bureau of Investigation in 1935. Hoover would lead the agency for decades and repeatedly rejected Organized Crime as a Federal concern until pressured by congress in the 1950's.

On May 19, 1924 Charles Dion "Deanie" O'Banion set up John Torrio for an arrest while he was allegedly selling him his share of the Sieben brewery in Chicago, the police raided the brewery at 8:00pm that evening. The Federal raiding party found Chicago Police Officers guarding the operation. Torrio and O'Banion entered into a partnership in the brewery after prohibition agents shut it down in August of 1923. The men were also partners in the Manhattan Brewery on the Southside and in a Casino in Cicero called the Ship. This was one of several events that would escalate the war between the Northside gang and the Southsiders that would culminate in hundreds of killings and a massacre.

In 1924 Chicago Police Chief Morgan Collins ordered a raid on the twenty-five person auditing office for the Torrio-Capone syndicate led by Det. Sgt. Edward Birmingham. On April 6, 1925 at the Capone gang's business headquarters at 2146 S. Michigan Ave. the gang carried out their day to day operations with Jake Guzik, Frank Nitti, Joe Fusco, Robert McCullough and Johnny Patton in attendance. Sgt. Birmingham and his Detective Squad burst through the door on a raid that would secure books, ledgers and other records of liquor and brothel sales that exposed the gang's entire operation. After turning down a large cash bribe ($5,000) from Johnny Patton, the men were removed to headquarters, questioned and spent the night in jail before being released on bond. The newspapers blared the event in large print anticipating the demise of the gang's business interests. Prematurely, Mayor Dever proclaimed a future victory against Torrio-Capone. However, Circuit Court Judge Hayes ordered the records into the custody of the court and away from prying law enforcement eyes. While continuing the case, the Judge met with Mob attorneys the following day and turned the records over to them claiming the raiders violated search and seizure rules. What was thought to be a coup for the police fizzled out as a non-event.

On November 3, 1924 a meeting of gangsters was assembled at the notorious gambling establishment "The Ship" on Cicero Ave. and 22nd street in Cicero. Capone led the meeting that was attended by Torrio, O'Banion, Nitti, Maritote, Weiss, Rio, Mondi and Drucci. O'Banion a partner in the venture refused to forgive a $30,000 gambling debt run up by Angelo Genna. The Genna's controlled the Alky cooking operation in Little Italy and both groups were dependent upon him at this time. Capone in an effort to keep the peace between the gangs insisted on forgiving the debt, which infuriated O'Banion. Torrio told O'Banion to collect the debt himself and Dion left in a huff. This issue would drive a wedge between the groups that would cost many lives in the following years.

On November 8, 1924 Mike Merlo President of the powerful Unione Siciliana succumbed to cancer. He was succeeded by Angelo Genna one of the "Terrible" Genna brothers. Merlo's death had an adverse effect on the entire city because he was so well respected and was able to maintain peace between O'Banion's group, the Gennas and the Torrio factions. That ended immediately after his death.

In 1925 "Machine Gun" Jack McGurn AKA: James or Vincenzo Gibaldi after being ordered by Capone to find more shooters, employs the services of a young gang member as his driver, the man's name is Tony Accardo.

On January 18, 1925 John Torrio as a result of the Seiben Brewery Raid is convicted for violations of the Volstead Act. He is fined $5,000 and sentenced to nine months in jail, which he serves in the DuPage County Jail in Illinois.

On October 1, 1926 a Federal Indictment was secured for violation of Prohibition laws. Named in the indictment was Al Capone, Edward Vogel, the Mayor of Cicero, the Chief of Police in Cicero and other hoodlums. The outcome of this case is unknown specifically, but was probably dismissed.

On April 5, 1927 Chicago voters made in clear that their liquor was more important than reform and returned Bill Thompson to the Mayor's office. Capone was said to have donated more than a quarter million dollars to the campaign. Thompson replaces Police Chief Collins within days and places Capone Mob associate Dan Seritella (future congressman) as City Sealer leaving him and his associate Harry Hochstein AKA: Weisman free to corrupt the office and steal from the citizens of Chicago.

A 1927 a Chicago Crime Commission report indicates 84 racket outfits in operation in just the downtown Loop district of Chicago.

In 1927 CCC Director Frank Loesch is placed on a national crime investigating committee known as the Wickersham Committee by President Hoover. By 1929 President Hoover ordered all his federal agencies to concentrate on getting Capone, although J. Edgar Hoover had no intention of entering a fray he could not win and stayed out of it until 1957.

In 1927 a U. S. Supreme Court decision upheld in United States v. Sullivan 274 U.S. 259, that even unlawful income was subject to income tax. This statute would become very useful to federal prosecutors in their war on organized crime.

In 1927 the Capone syndicate took control of a west suburban Dog Track in Cicero, Illinois.

Back in 1927 when Monte Tennes retired from gambling in the midst of conflicts over who would control it, he sold 50 percent of his General News business, a wire service, to entrepreneur Moe Annenberg and the remainder to James Lynch. The business provided race results to bookmakers across the country and was a gold mine. James Regan was picked by Annenberg as General Manager. Regan was a tough individual whose brother established the sports club "Regan's Colts" on the Southside of Chicago. Years later when the OUTFIT was diversifying, Frank Nitti in an attempt to take over the company managed to turn the owners against each other and Annenberg wound up the sole owner while providing the OUTFIT with a fee of $100,000. However, that would not be the last time the OUTFIT would make a run at the company.

After an extremely violent primary election and prior to the 1928 general election for State's Attorney, Frank J. Loesch, newly appointed President of the Chicago Crime Commission meets privately with Al Capone asking for peace in the upcoming election. Capone, not Loesch contacted the police department and had many of his sluggers swept up by police until after the election.

On October 18, 1928 Treasury Officials allow Internal Revenue Service investigators to open a tax case against Al Capone.

On December 6, 1928 a meeting of a national organized crime "Commission" took place in Cleveland, Ohio at the Statler Hotel. Thirteen guns were found in the room by Cleveland Police. It was first thought to be a meeting of the Unione Siciliana to discuss changes in the wake of the murders of Frank Yale AKA: Uale in New York and Anthony Lombardo in Chicago. The meeting was discovered by an unassuming beat patrolman who watched several gangsters check into the hotel. He recorded the names and turned them into the detective bureau. Two dozen mobsters from around the country were soon arrested. The meeting hosted hoods from 27 cities; this Commission was the brainchild of John Torrio. In May of 1929 another "Commission meeting was held in Atlantic City, New Jersey.

By the end of 1928 Capone promoted McGurn driver Tony Accardo to his personal bodyguard.

By 1929 The Chicago Crime Commission found the cost of racketeering in Chicago to be $136 million per year for the taxpayers.

In 1929 as TOC raged on in Chicago, William Dever one of the only true reform politicians the city had ever seen died at age sixty-seven.

On May 13-15, 1929 Al Capone traveled to Atlantic City, New Jersey with his confidante Frankie Rio for a National "Commission" meeting at the President Hotel. The war in Chicago and the massacre earlier in the year were on the agenda as it was causing nationwide problems for all the crime syndicates and the other leaders wanted it stopped. After the conference Capone and bodyguard Frankie Rio traveled to Philadelphia for a pre-arranged weapons arrest that would keep them from the heat of the investigation for several months to follow, although much to their surprise the judge gave them the maximum sentence in the case.

On October 29, 1929 the stock market crashes in what becomes known as "Black Tuesday" the first major event of the great depression. These events not only had adverse effects on most Americans, but had an adverse effect on the finances of Crime Syndicates in Chicago.

On February 8, 1930 Colonel Robert Isham Randolph announces the formation of the "Secret Six" a privately funded arm of the Chicago Association of Commerce to carry out criminal investigations. The group often thought of as part of the CCC, which it was not existed for a short time until it was disbanded in disgrace for inappropriate associations and improper handling of funds by 1933.

On April 24, 1930 the CCC publishes its first Public Enemies list naming Al Capone as Public Enemy Number One. By September of this year Judge John Lyle issues vagrancy warrants against the men listed, in his bid to run for Mayor of Chicago. Assisted by Assistant State's Attorney Harry S. Ditchburne the court became very aggressive toward prosecuting gangsters on minor charges. During this period the public finally turned against the gangster world which was sparked by the murders of Assistant States Attorney William McSwiggin in 1926, the St. Valentine's Day Massacre in 1929 and the murder of Newspaperman Jake Lingle in 1930.

In 1930 Llewelyn Morris Humphreys AKA: "Murray the Camel", Curly a shrewd Mob leader of Welsh decent, taps Ralph Pierce, a twenty year old up and comer as his personnel assistant. Pierce was suspected in an armed robbery and was known to be a paid election-day slugger who eventually rose to a position as Southside Boss from the 1950's through 1976 when he died of natural causes.

In 1931 Jim Genna dies of natural causes, he is one of the infamous Genna brothers who in earlier years ruled "Little Italy".

In 1931 John Torrio working as an advisor for TOC interests in New York, was credited with helping to formalize a national crime organization known as the "Commission". This group consisted of leaders from every major crime syndicate in the country and would meet all across America to conspire in illicit partnerships that benefited all the member organizations.

On April 7, 1931 Anton Cermak is elected Mayor of Chicago. His election begins a long tenure of Democratic domination in Chicago Politics.

On May 1, 1931 federal authorities under the direction of United States District Attorney George E. Q. Johnson secured a Federal Grand Jury indictment against 23 members of the Capone organization for violations of the Volstead Act. The indictments came on the heels of numerous raids by federal law enforcement, including those at 3136 S. Wabash and 1642 S. Cicero Ave. in Cicero, IL. After the raids several of the mobsters were caught in the act of trying to remove brewing equipment from the Wabash Ave. brewery. The federal government had also experienced recent victories with prison sentences handed down to several mobsters to include: Al Capone, Jake Guzik, Ralph Capone, Frank Nitti and Sam Guzik.

On August 1, 1931 the CCC publishes a second list of Public Enemies, but omits Frank Nitti who will lead the Syndicate upon Capone's Tax conviction.

On October 18, 1931 Al Capone was convicted of Tax evasion and failure to file tax returns, he is subsequently sentenced to 11 years in federal prison fined $50,000 and $30,000 in court costs.

On March 24, 1932 Frank Nitti is released from prison after serving time for tax evasion and arrives in Chicago as the undisputed Boss of the Capone Mob.

On April 19, 1932 New York Mob leaders Lucky Luciano and Meyer Lansky are arrested with Rocco Fischetti and Paul Ricca outside the Congress Hotel in Chicago. This is one of the first solid indicators of a national organized crime "Commission" that was meeting in Chicago. It was also speculated at the time that the New York gangsters were consulted regarding Capone's replacement, as Capone was involved in leadership issues in New York. At the time the press spent a year writing about who would succeed Capone with Jack Guzik, Frank Rio, Paul Ricca and Frank Nitti at the top of the list. However, it was Nitti who had the experience, heritage and demeanor to lead the group past Prohibition.

In May of 1932 Northside defector Ted Newberry is allowed to retire from the rackets under the watchful eye of new Mob Boss Frank Nitti. It was a scheme that would cost Newberry dearly when Nitti learned he was still involved in northside gambling operations.

In 1932 it was reported that Frankie McErlane had died of pneumonia. He was one of the leaders of the Saltis-McErlane gang who were associates of the Capone gang and responsible for a protracted war with northside gangsters, the Southside O'Donnells and the Ralph Shelton gang, and was one of the most prolific killers in a violent era in Chicago. In 1930 he received several gunshot wounds in a shootout with Bugs Moran and while recovering in the German Deaconess Hospital was attacked by northside gunman Willie Marks (suspected as the killer of Red Barker) and Ted Newberry. He produced a gun from under his pillow and fired back chasing off the attackers while receiving additional gunshot wounds which he survived from.

In 1932 it was reported that Myles O'Donnell died of unknown causes. He was one of the notorious Westside O'Donnell's and a participant in the Beer Wars conflict of the time.

In December of 1932 in a daring Loop Robbery $500,000 in Government bonds and securities were stolen by a group led by Gus Winkler AKA: August "Big Mike" Winkeler the leader of the American Boys and architects of the St. Valentine's Day Massacre. The gang would be indicted by October of 1933. It was clear that Winkler and company had become a liability to Nitti and the Mob. It had also been reported that over the years Winkler had made deals with the Touhy's and the Capone organization. It was reported that he had been seen meeting with FBI Special Agent Melvin Purvis and had turned stolen bonds over to the Secret Six, a civic committee formed out of the Chicago Association of Commerce to help bring down the Capone Mobs strangle hold on the city.

In 1932 of the 35 TOC killings reported by the CCC none were solved.

In was reported on January 7, 1933 that Chief of Detectives Schoemaker was preparing a list of all gangsters in Chicago. The list was encouraged by Mayor Cermak and when finished would include approximately 750 names.

On January 27, 1933 Murray Humphries once considered as a successor to Al Capone as the head of the Chicago Mob was indicted by a Federal Grand Jury on 4 counts of violating the Tax Code.

On February 2, 1933 members of the Touhy gang led by Tommy Touhy and Red Ryan cruised the North and West sides of Chicago looking for Nitti gangsters, namely Fur Sammons who was out looking for them. At North and Harlem Aves. the groups found each other and a vicious gun battle ensued. Tommy Touhy was gravely wounded in the legs and the shooting only ceased when a River Forest Squad car appeared on the scene and the gangsters fled. Sammons left the area and wound up in prison for robbery and after terms in two prison systems was released in 1952 at 70 years of age and nearly blind. He died alone in a boarding house at 824 W. 62nd St. in 1960.

On April 13, 1933 corrupt Westside Alderman Jacob Arvey nominates Edward J. Kelly to fill the remaining term of Aton Cermak. Under Kelly the Mob would flourish in Chicago.

On April 19, 1933 Colonel Robert Isham Randolph and the crime fighting group he oversaw known as the "Secret Six" was disbanded by the Chicago Association of Commerce (CAC) after it was alleged that Randolph had pocketed some $24,000 in operational funds. The group, similar but separate from the CCC was established by Randolph and the Chicago Association of Commerce (CAC) in 1930 with corporate support. While kept secret at the time, the members were reportedly: Julius Rosenwald-Chairman of Sears Roebuck and Co., Frank Loesch-President of the CCC, Samuel Insull-Utilities magnate, Edward E. Gore, George Paddock, and Col. Randolph who was the only member not kept secret. He claimed the group actively assisted in bringing down Al Capone which was debated at the time and that they vigorously investigated over two dozen kidnappings. Back in early 1930 the group came together after nine killings were recorded in the first week of February. They shared the views of the CAC and their aim was to assist law enforcement, especially the feds by expediting the apprehension and prosecution of the hoods who were raising hell in Chicago. They went on to provide funds for undercover operations that assisted in the tax cases against Capone and Nitti. The organization lost much of its credibility when one of its top investigators was alleged to be one Shirley Kub a woman who had done time in Bridwell and was an associate of gangster Jack Zuta. In reality the group was at odds with the State's Attorneys Office and some federal authorities that did not like being upstaged by a civic organization.

On April 28, 1933 a war was raging over control of several Teamster locals know as outlaw. Six machine gunners walked into Teamster Headquarters at 637 S. Ashland led by Roger Touhy who held several union members at gun point and told them he was going to "clean the dago syndicate out of the teamsters". The men then sat in wait for the arrival of Murray Humphries, Jack White and Klondike O'Donnell who they intended on killing. When the men did not appear Fred Sass and Morris Goldberg were kidnapped. The men were released unharmed by May 2nd.

On July 1, 1933 OUTFIT confidant Jake "The Barber" Factor AKA: Iakow Factrowitz brother of Cosmetics giant Max Factor was allegedly kidnapped coming out of the Dells Roadhouse in Morton Grove, IL. by northwest side gangster and Capone adversary Roger Touhy. The Dells was a Nitti Casino franchise and an incursion of Touhy territory on the Northwest side of Cook County. Factor's son had been kidnapped in April and his release was aided by Murray Humphreys and Samuel McPherson Hunt AKA: Golf Bag Hunt, Capone operatives. A ransom demand of $75,000 was made and twelve days later Factor was released in LaGrange, IL. Because the crime occurred in Touhy territory the investigation focused on his gang. At the Criminal Courts building a short time after the kidnapping Captain James "Tubbo" Gilbert of the States Attorney's office summoned the Chiefs of 22 northwest suburban police departments to encourage them to crush the Touhy gang. It would turn out years later that Gilbert was an emissary for the Capone Mob just before his run for Sheriff. Touhy was eventually arrested and convicted of the crime and spent over twenty five years in jail only to be killed on the door step of his sister's home the same week he was released. TOC historians and law enforcement officials alike felt the kidnapping was a set up to enact revenge on Touhy for resisting the Capone takeover of the illicit liquor business and a way for Factor to avoid the deportation process that had been initiated against him. Factor would later become an OUTFIT casino representative in Las Vegas.

On July 19, 1933 Roger "The Terrible" Touhy and 3 of his men are involved in a minor traffic accident near Elkhorn, WI. At the time Touhy was wanted by federal authorities for the allegedly bogus kidnapping of Capone ally, Jake Factor AKA: Iakow Factrowitz, Jake "The Barber". Touhy was turned over to federal authorities, convicted and sent to prison.

On July 27, 1933 an indictment was passed in Cook County charging 24 gangsters with various crimes related to labor racketeering. Murray Humphries was the top name on the list that included politicians and lawyers.

On August 3, 1933 State Representative Robert Petrone of the 21st district of Illinois, appeared at the Chicago Police Detective Bureau seeking the release of one time Capone gunman and Public Enemy Tony Accardo who was being held under investigation. It did not work as Chief of Detectives Schoemaker stated "Men who are Public Enemies and hoodlums will not be released from police custody because they have political friends". It is too bad that everyone did not share that believe with the Chief.

On August 25, 1933 Chief of Detectives Schoemaker in following suit with the CCC, released an additional list of 25 Public Enemies headed by Murray Humphries, announced legislation to prosecute the men as vagabonds and incarcerate them for up to 6 months.

On December 5, 1933 the 18th Amendment is repealed ending Prohibition.

In 1933 the CCC estimated that 7,500 gambling establishments were receiving protection from corrupt officials.

On December 29, 1933 the Cook County State's Attorney issued a new Public Enemies list containing the names of 21 individuals. While the list contained the names of local gangsters such as Murray Humphries and Tommy Touhy its main focus was on the kidnapping and bank robbery gangs led by John Dillinger and George "Baby Face" Nelson.

In February of 1934 Murray Humphries a leader in the Chicago Mob went on trial as a fugitive in a racketeering trial in Chicago. The case addressed the warfare between the Mob and the Cleaners and Dyers Institute. 18 defendants were on trial and were eventually acquitted by a jury. The State's Attorney continued to pursue another racketeering case against Humphries and others regarding his role in extorting monies from the trucking business, the case was known as the TNT case. Other cases involving the Dairy Drivers Union were anticipated at the time. Humphries eventually was sent to prison on federal tax charges.

An insurance industry study in 1934, estimated the cost of OUTFIT racketeering in Chicago at 150 million dollars a year.

Reportedly 250,000 fraudulent votes were cast in the 1934 election of Mayor Ed Kelly.

In 1935 a law was passed legalizing handbooks, but was vetoed by Governor Henry Horner.

On February 23, 1935 Frank Rio died of heart disease in his sleep. The longtime Capone bodyguard, brother-in-law and loyalist carried out a multitude of tasks for the crime Boss and was known for his dedication and contributions to the Mob.

On February 9, 1936 a local newspaper printed a detailed organizational chart of the Chicago Mob. In this chart was a breakdown of the division of labor within organized crime in Chicago. In 1997 the Chicago Crime Commission published a chart with similar distinctions that may have been the last publicly released chart of this kind.

In 1937 a Southside policy wheel operated by 3 white and 12 black gangsters, generated 13 Million a year in revenue. Some of those involved were Eddie Jones (policy king), George Jones, Pat Manno AKA: Patrick J. Manning, Peter G. Tremont, James Martin, Pat Nash, Ted Roe and Walter Kelly. This operation was brought to the attention of Sam Giancana AKA: Momo Salvatore, Mooney, or Gilormo Giangono while he was incarcerated with one of its operatives during the 1940's. The OUTFIT moved in on this operation using kidnapping and murder before taking it over.

In 1939 the CCC openly criticized two judges for their lax handling of Gambling Cases. A civil defamation suit was threatened, but never materialized.

In May of 1939 Sam Giancana AKA: Momo Salvatore, Mooney, or Gilormo Giangono is arrested a second time for moonshining and sentenced to 4 years in prison. It was this term that exposed him to black policy operators and gave him the idea to take over Southside policy operations.

On November 16, 1939 a sick and frail Al Capone was released from prison. He would spend the rest of his life with his family at his Palm Island, FL. Estate until he died in January of 1947.

Early in the 1940s political heavy weights Billy Skidmore and William R. "Big Bill" Johnson were put on trial for their gambling (32 gambling places were attributed to the men) exploits using ledger sheets as evidence, this case more than any other showed large scale graft and corruption in the city.

On July 10, 1940 Fred "Killer" Burke dies in a Michigan Prison while serving a life sentence for the murder of a police officer. Burke was the only man named as one of the St. Valentine killers by a Coroner's Jury.

By 1941 it was estimated that poor blacks on public aid were pouring 7 million dollars a year into south side policy wheels, this amount would reach 10 Million dollars a year by 1942.

In 1942 an indictment was put forth under the Civil Service Commission and the Police Morals Squad listing 4 officers as being implicated in south side policy protection.

In 1942 former FBI Supervisor Virgil Peterson takes over as Director of the Chicago Crime Commission and immediately describes the Chicago OUTFIT as part of a nationwide criminal organization, targeting them in his efforts. For over a decade this assessment was denied until it could no longer be supported and the FBI established the Top Hoodlum Program (THP) in 1957 that initiated a nationwide effort against TOC. However, this effort was independent and little collaboration existed with other law enforcement agencies due to rabid corruption and distrust within law enforcement agencies and prosecutor's offices across the country.

In 1942 after serving a 3 year prison term in Indiana where he befriended Eddie Jones a black numbers operator from the south side, Sam Giancana AKA: Momo Salvatore, Mooney, or Gilormo Giangono went into a partnership with Jones in the juke box racket and other gambling ventures. Several years later Giancana would conspire against his black partner and presented a plan to the OUTFIT to take over the south side policy/gambling enterprise previously ignored by TOC.

In October of 1942 after the prison break of Roger Touhy and some of his men, Llewelyn Morris Humphreys AKA: "Murray the Camel", Curly hired former members of the 42 gang to include Sam Giancana AKA: Momo Salvatore, Mooney, or Gilormo Giangono, Marshal Ciafano and Teetz Battaglia to guard the wives of the OUTFIT's top bosses for fear of retaliation from Touhy who had been set up by them.

In December of 1942 northside gangster Roger "The Terrible" Touhy was captured by J. Edgar Hoover and a platoon of federal agents at his hideout at

5116 N. Kenmore. Touhy and several others were the subject of a massive man hunt after their October escape from Stateville Penitentiary. Touhy had already served 8 years of his sentence in the contrived kidnapping of Jake "The Barber" Factor in 1933.

On March 19, 1943 after the Hollywood Extortion indictments were announced and in response, Frank "the Enforcer" Nitti AKA: Francesco Nitto, Ralph Nitto, Frank Raddo and Frank Sasso, committed suicide along railroad tracks in North Riverside, IL. near his home. The incident was witnessed by rail workers who were nearby at the time. Reportedly, Nitti met with gangsters Paul Ricca, Louis Campagna, Phil D'Andrea and Tony Accardo after the Hollywood indictments were announced and Ricca made it clear to Nitti that he should take the rap as Capone did in the past. This mandate from Ricca who many believe was the true leader of the OUTFIT by this time left very few options for Nitti. The suicide left Paul "The Waiter" Ricca AKA: Felice DeLucia in charge of the OUTFIT's day to day operations. This role was short lived when Ricca was imprisoned for his role in the movie shakedown scheme after a guilty verdict in December, which gave Ricca and others a 10 year sentence, Tony Accardo took over as acting Boss. Accardo the most effective OUTFIT leader in Chicago history started in the bootlegging business with the Capone syndicate and was recruited from the Circus gang. His tenure as leader and advisor for the Chicago OUTFIT was continuous until his death in 1992.

In 1943 a CCC gambling investigation lead to the questioning of promotional practices within the Chicago Police Department, 14 Captain's promotions were questioned leading to an assumption that such practices were common and testing was a sham.

At the end of World War II things changed drastically for the OUTFIT. Newly elected mayor Martin Kennelly moved on OUTFIT gambling and cleaned up the police department to some extent. OUTFIT gambling was forced to go underground and to the suburbs in a big way.

In 1944 Congressman Roland V. Libonati AKA: "Libby" the OUTFIT's man in Washington is married and Al Capone acts as his best man.

In 1944 as a reward for his money making abilities Paul Ricca hands control of the Chicago Teamster Locals to Joey Glimco AKA: Guiseppe Glielmi. Within a year Glimco through his heavy handed methods doubled the union's membership.

On March 18, 1944 the hoods favorite Mayor "Big Bill" Thompson 76 yrs. died of pneumonia after a failed attempt at the Governor's Mansion. By this time he lived in his hotel suite as a recluse. Although he earned meager salaries as a public servant he lived in the plush Blackstone Hotel on Michigan Ave. and left an estate worth more than 2 million dollars.

In 1944 a CCC investigation revealed seven police captains were involved in OUTFIT gambling operations and encouraged their dismissal.

In 1945 Mob gambling impresario Billy Skidmore dies in prison.

For a few months in 1946 the FBI, launched an investigation code named CAPGA, short for regenerated Capone Gang. This effort was the federal response to determine if remnants of the Capone syndicate had begun their criminal enterprise once more. In reality it had never stopped. J. Edgar Hoover the Bureau's director felt it was a local problem and fought the theory pronounced by the CCC that TOC was a national problem and a national TOC "Commission" existed.

In February of 1946 Tony Accardo was arrested in a gambling investigation and spent his only night in jail. The following day the arresting officers Peter McGuire and Lawrence Weir released him after a brief court appearance. Accardo would never acknowledge the arrest and claimed he never spent a night in jail.

In 1946 Chicago hood Pat Manno AKA: Patrick J. Manning was sent to Dallas, Texas to try and negotiate a deal with the local Sheriff-elect Steve Guthrie to allow Chicago Gangsters to run gambling in his area, it did not work and Manno returned to Chicago while other operatives were arrested.

In 1946 it was learned that slot machines in private country clubs in the Chicago area were owned and maintained by the Chicago OUTFIT.

Around 1946 Charles "Cherry Nose" Gioe, Harry Russell and his brother Dave Russell established a gambling lay-off business at the Russell's Silver Bar 400 S. State Street that serviced bookies from Kansas City to New York. At one time Harry was a partner with Tony Accardo in a handbook at 186 N. Clark St.

In May of 1946 the OUTFIT renewed their efforts to take over black policy wheels on the Southside of Chicago. They kidnapped one of the leaders Edward Jones. His brother George negotiated his release for $100,000 and the men left Chicago for Mexico. This left Teddy Roe as the leading wheel operator on the Southside.

On October 10, 1946 it was reported that Michael "Hinky Dink" Kenna died of natural causes. He was one of the most powerful Aldermen in Chicago History and forged an alliance with Chicago Organized Crime that can still be felt today.

On December 22, 1946 the MOB's national "Commission" held a conference in Havana, Cuba. Tony Accardo, Charles Fischetti and Rocco Fischetti cousins to former Boss Al Capone attended on behalf of Chicago interests and were reportedly accompanied on the flight by entertainer Frank Sinatra who was not allowed into the meetings. Other TOC luminaries included Lansky, Luciano, Costello, Moretti, Adonis, Anastasia, Genovese, Bonanno, Lucchese, Profaci, Magliocco, Pisano, Miranda, Magaddino, Marcello, Kastel and Trafficante. This was one of the greatest gatherings of MOB influence to ever come to the attention of law enforcement authorities.

In 1947 the CCC uncovered yet another OUTFIT vice ring that involved police officers who were subsequently dismissed.

On August 13, 1947 Paul Ricca and other participants in the Hollywood Extortion case were released from prison after being paroled, they served a minimum sentence and additional charges of Mail Fraud were dropped against them by prosecutors who were confident they would serve their full sentences. What this early release did was introduce another scandal to the American Public. This political scandal smacked of TOC influence in the Truman White House. Particularly pointing a finger at Attorney General Tom Clark, who like President Truman maintained a penchant for organized crime types from Kansas City. Those who were vocal over this travesty included the prosecutor on the case Boris Kostelanetz who opposed the parole from the start. The CCC called the parole "an outrage and national disgrace". Illinois Representative Fred Busbey, the original Judge in the case, John Bright and even Chicago Police Superintendent John Prendergast suggested barring the men from Chicago although Prendergast had been suspected as an OUTFIT friendly Police Chief. The investigation resulted in the return to prison of two lower level operatives Louis "Little New York" Campagna and Charles "Cherry Nose" Gioe, but they were again released a short time later. The FBI and the House of Representatives initiated investigations that focused on individuals associated with Clark and Truman and led to the Mobbed-up political machine in Kansas City. But, in the end the paroles stood and the gangsters went back to what they do best.

In 1947 the Chicago OUTFIT took a loan from a Teamsters Pension Fund to follow NY TOC into the casino business in Las Vegas.

Around 1947 other crime figures emerged as leaders in the OUTFIT. None were more diabolical than Sam Giancana AKA: Momo Salvatore, Mooney, or Gilormo Giangono. Momo or Mooney as he was known was a former Capone gunman who was plucked from the ranks of the 42 gang in Little Italy. He gained a reputation for his driving ability and assumed that role for OUTFIT luminaries such as "Machine Gun" Jack McGurn AKA: James or Vincenzo Gibaldi and Paul "The Waiter" Ricca.

In 1947 Mayor Kennelly allowed his police to enforce gambling laws and open gambling disappeared.

On January 25, 1947 Al Capone died of a heart attack in bed at his Palm Island Estate in FL. At this time Tony Accardo is at the reigns of the OUTFIT. When Capone died, Accardo would limit the number of hoods who would attend the funeral saying "to keep the Goddamn thing from turning into a Circus". Capone was finally interred at Mount Carmel Cemetery in west suburban Hillside, IL. across the road from his enforcer Frank Nitti.

In 1947 it was reported that Frankie Lake died of natural causes. He and his partner Terry Druggan ran the Valley Gang on the southwest side now known as Bridgeport. They ushered the gang into the Capone syndicate and became very wealthy.

In 1948 Tony Accardo through the national "Commission" declares himself the arbitrator for any TOC problems west of Chicago. He is not questioned in this.

Of the 2 remaining Genna brothers, in May of 1948 Pete died of natural causes while his brother Sam died of a heart attack in his home at 865 Blue Island Avenue in December of 1951.

Between 1947 and 49 the CCC introduced five bills through the Illinois General Assembly, designed to improve the function of criminal justice. A group of legislators from the west side of the city and the western suburbs known as the "West Block" and friendly to OUTFIT interests fought the bills vigorously. In 1951 the 5 CCC Bills were fought out on the floor of the state legislature where 2 were killed and 3 were passed.

In 1949 Harness Racing legislation was passed and the CCC learned that 9 politicians had stock in this venture.

In 1949 the Chicago OUTFIT muscled its way into the S&G gambling syndicate in Miami Florida.

In 1949 the Chicago Sanitation Workers Union succumbed to OUTFIT pressures and was taken over.

In 1949 Joe Saltis once a leader of the Saltis-McErlane gang died alone and broke in a hospital charity ward after losing most of his money through divorce and paternity suits.

In 1949 the TOC problem was addressed in speeches by the Vice President of the United States and the U. S. Attorney General. CCC Director Virgil Peterson continued to campaign toward the national implications of TOC. A short time later Senator Estes Kefauver (D) Tennessee, introduced a resolution to form an investigative commission to look at TOC in interstate commerce. While some pols tried to sidetrack the resolution, 2 TOC murders in the Kansas City Democratic Headquarters office pushed through the resolution and committee appointments.

In 1951 Charles Fischetti a major player in the Chicago Outfit and a cousin of Al Capone, died of natural causes.

In 1951 Hymie "Loud Mouth" Levin died of natural causes. He was a longtime Capone gangster and worked as a collector for the Chicago Mob.

In 1951 toward the conclusion of the Kefauver Commission, the Senator declared "there are two major crime syndicates in this country, the Accardo, Guzik, Fischetti syndicate whose headquarters are in Chicago and the Costello, Adonis, Lansky syndicate based in New York" he went on to point out that the Accardo influence went beyond Chicago to Kansas City, Dallas, Miami, Las Vegas, Minneapolis, Des Moines and Los Angles. The group later stated that Paul "The Waiter" Ricca was "the national head of the crime syndicate and America's most important criminal".

In 1951 Virgil W. Peterson the well-respected Director of the Chicago Crime Commission published a book titled: Gambling-Should It Be Legalized? The book was well received and addressed issues that are pressing to this day, especially in an area like Cook County. He followed this effort with a second book titled: Barbarians In Our Midst, published in 1952 that was one of the first comprehensive histories of TOC in Chicago. It received national acclaim for Peterson and the CCC.

By 1952 it was established that the TOC racketeering element in many of America's leading cities developed into major political powers.

In 1952 a CCC investigation revealed TOC had entered the tobacco business by use of bogus tax stamps, 22 associates were ultimately charged in the scheme.

On September 18, 1952 Phil D'Andrea, Capone ally, bodyguard and Unione Siciliana President (34-41) died of natural causes.

In 1953 the CCC took to the airwaves using radio and TV to urge political parties to purge their ranks of OUTFIT associates.

In 1953 the CCC reported that 165 "Clip Joints" operated on North Clark St. one of the original turn of the century tenderloin (vice) districts.

In 1953 the Chicago City Council appointed a committee known as the "Big Nine" to investigate vice and politics in Chicago, the results known as the "Kohn Report" revealed a link between State Senator Botchie Connors and Gambling in his District.

On March 4, 1954 Terry "Machine Gun" Druggan died of natural causes. The Irish gangster along with his partner Frankie Lake ran the Valley Gang in Chicago. His association with the Torrio/Capone gang made him millions.

In 1954 before the FBI officially investigated TOC, Guy Banister was the Special Agent in Charge (SAC) of the Chicago Office, the second largest in the country. Banister would leave the Bureau this year and move to New Orleans where he would work for the New Orleans police for a short time and establish an intelligence unit. He then started a Private Detective agency. Once in private practice Banister became the detective of choice for local Mob Boss Carlos

Marcello. Over the following years he became involved with far right racist organizations, Cuban Exile Groups and with the CIA in Coup/Assassination plots against Fidel Castro. He would become a central figure in the TOC plots to assassinate President John F. Kennedy.

In 1954 the FBI is informed of a national "Commission" meeting of TOC being held in the Chicago Area. At this point the FBI is still not interested in this local problem.

On June 2, 1955 it was reported that Sam Battaglia and other gangsters attended the wake of Louis "Little New York" Campagna. Campagna who held a prominent role in Chicago TOC for decades from the planning of the St. Valentine's Day Massacre to incarceration in the Hollywood Extortion scandal managed to out maneuver the government on more than one occasion. In the end he was living a good life when he suffered a fatal heart attack while deep-sea fishing off the Miami coast in May of 1955.

On July 8, 1955 it was reported that Anthony "Tough Tony" Capezio longtime OUTFIT muscle died of a heart attack shortly after being kidnapped by a group of young Turks praying on old hoods and making a great deal of money in the process. It was later reported that Chuckie Nicoletti fingered three of the kidnappers who were later found dead in various suburban areas.

On February 21, 1956 OUTFIT financial wizard for close to 30 years, Jake "Greasy Thumb" Guzik dies of a heart attack at St. Hubert's Old English Grill at 316 S. Federal at the age of Seventy. Murray Humphreys secretly owned the place and had Guzik's body taken to his home where authorities were called.

By 1956 Tony Accardo having total control over the Chicago OUTFIT and Las Vegas interests, stepped down again into an advisory position and elevated Sam Giancana AKA: Momo Salvatore, Mooney, or Gilormo Giangono to the head of the Chicago OUTFIT at a Coronation at the Tam O'Shanter Country Club in suburban Niles, IL. With Frank "Strongy" Ferraro acting as his Underboss, Giancana lived a very public life and spent a great deal of time in Hollywood and Las Vegas with friends such as Frank Sinatra. He established political connections and claimed to have helped elect John Kennedy as president.

On August 19, 1956 it was reported that Samuel McPherson Hunt AKA: Golf Bag Hunt died of natural causes. He was an old Capone associate and gained his moniker by carrying a shotgun in a golf bag.

In the mid-1950s the public learned for the first time through the Chicago Crime Commission that OUTFIT members that rose to prominence during prohibition were still deeply involved in the liquor business. Capone associate Joe Fusco, was part owner of 5 liquor distributors and 1 brewery in the Chicago area.

After the St. Valentine's Day Massacre Northside Gang Boss George "Bugs" Moran took the hint and left TOC in Chicago to the Capone Syndicate. He spent time as part of a gang that robbed handbooks. He then stooped to burglaries and robberies that landed him in the Ohio State Prison in 1946. His bank robbery business sent him directly to Leavenworth Penitentiary where he died of lung cancer on February 25, 1957. Soon afterward John Torrio died in a barber's chair in a New York City Hotel on April 16, 1957. Despite his prior wealth, the "Fox" left an estate only worth about $200.000.

In April of 1957 the deportation and tax case brought against OUTFIT leader Paul Ricca begins and resulted with a four year prison term that stripped him of his citizenship with a deportation order. However, through the skillful efforts of his attorneys Ricca was never deported.

On May 16, 1957 famous crime fighter Elliot Ness dies of natural causes after a brief career as Police Chief in Cleveland and a failed run at the Mayor's office.

After the November 14, 1957 Appalachian Crime Conclave in New York State, the FBI finally recognized the national ramifications of TOC in America. This meeting was held to discuss the assassination of New York Mafia Boss Albert Anastasia and the joint operations that would be effected. A conclave was also held shortly after the St. Valentine's Day Massacre in 1929 to discuss the implications of that crime on a national basis. Under intense pressure Hoover declared war on TOC in America, just imagine what would have occurred if all law enforcement agencies could have been trusted enough to partake in this effort.

In 1958 former OUTFIT Boss of the Loop, Gus Alex assumes the role of political fixer, after Paul Ricca stepped down to deal with immigration problems.

On June 21, 1958 OUTFIT powerhouse Claude "Screwy" Maddox AKA: John E. Moore dies peacefully in his sleep at his home at 3536 S. Harlem in Riverside, IL. Maddox ran the Circus Café that was the staging point of the St. Valentine's Day Massacre. However, as one of the American Boys he was spared the fate of the others that were purged at the hand of Frank Nitti in the 1930s. Through his effective union racketeering activities on behalf of the OUTFIT, coupled with his partnership in a gambling equipment business he lived a long and lucrative life.

In July of 1958 the Senate Rackets Committee held hearings that reinforced the problem of TOC on a national level.

In 1959 a Senate Crime Investigating Committee known as the McClellan Committee focused on Chicago OUTFIT Boss Sam Giancana. The Committee's chief counsel at the time was future U. S. Attorney General Robert F. Kennedy. Kennedy's grilling of Giancana was legendary and started a feud with TOC across the country that many believed resulted in the assassination of Kennedy's brother President John F. Kennedy on November 22, 1963 and eventually Robert himself.

In 1959 popular Cuban entertainer Desi Arnaz produced the television show "The Untouchables". The show tended to exaggerate the escapades of Federal Prohibition Agent Elliot Ness and his men while disparaging the Chicago Mob as a bunch of illiterate Italian immigrants. Chicago OUTFIT bosses were not happy and even considered having Arnaz killed. Even after visits from a high school friend of Arnaz by the name of Sonny Capone (Al's son) and entertainer Frank Sinatra, Arnaz would not back down. Mea Capone (Al's widow) intervened at the end to make sure nothing would happen to Arnaz.

In July of 1959 the FBI completed its' first successful installation of a bug in a North Michigan Avenue haberdasher that was used as the meeting place for top OUTFIT political fixers. The first of close to twenty such installations led to a great deal of intelligence regarding the operations of the Chicago OUTFIT until President Lyndon Johnson stopped the practice in 1965. It was later revealed that Johnson did not have any intention to target TOC as his predecessor had. This work predated federal statutes allowing for the Title III overhears that would be the basis of many successful wires and prosecutions in later years. However, this intelligence was never shared with other law enforcement agencies grappling with TOC in Chicago due to concerns with corruption in the ranks of those agencies.

In 1959 the Chicago OUTFIT and other TOC entities begin using the Teamsters Central States Pension Fund as their personal piggy bank for TOC ventures such as Casino construction in Las Vegas. This would continue until federal indictments ended the practice some 20 years later.

In 1959 Paul Ricca is arrested and convicted for income tax evasion, he is sentenced to nine years in prison.

On January 12, 1960 it was reported that James Mondi died of natural causes. He was an accountant and gambling expert for the Capone Mob.

In January of 1960 OUTFIT Boss Tony Accardo was tried, convicted and sentenced to 6 years in prison along with a $15,000 dollar fine on tax charges levied by the federal government after his subordinates went through great lengths to corrupt jurors on the case. In June of that year the Court of Appeals overturned the conviction on the tax charges.

On February 22, 1960 after the Summerdale police corruption scandal that rocked the Chicago Police Department, the CCC assists in selecting a new superintendent O.W.Wilson and supports his reform program that establishes the Internal Affairs Division and an Intelligence Unit to fight the OUTFIT in Chicago. The CCC also helped establish Chicago's first fully functional crime lab and helped build a new and adequate criminal court house at 26th and California earlier in the century.

In May of 1960 OUTFIT political fixer Llewelyn Morris Humphreys AKA: "Murray the Camel", Curly is monitored visiting the residence of Congressman Roland Libonati in Washington D.C. Libonati was also a regular visitor of Paul Ricca during his incarceration and was present for the celebration upon his release. This is the same congressman who accompanied Al Capone to a baseball game at Wrigley Field and was caught on film with Scarface. In 1961 another visit was memorialized when the "Camel" visited Congressman Tom O'Brien former Sheriff of Cook County.

In the early 1960's gambling impresario Frank "Lefty" Rosenthal was sent by the OUTFIT to Miami to run a sports gambling operation. He later gained notoriety in Las Vegas when he feuded with Tony Spilotro, after Spilotro put a murder contract on him as depicted in the movie Casino.

In the early 1960's fight promoter Bernie Glickman was beaten by OUTFIT enforcer Felix "Milwaukee Phil" Alderisio over a dispute. This presented an opportunity to the FBI and he became a federal informant despite his personal friendship with Tony Accardo. During the following weeks the word got out that he was working with the government and a contract was put on Glickman's life and he backed out of his statements in front of a federal grand jury. An angry U.S. Attorney decided to throw Glickman to the wolves, but allegedly the FBI intervened and was able to stop the contract on his life.

On May 20, 1960 long time hood James "Fur" Sammons was found dead of a heart attack at the Englewood Arms Hotel at 824 West 62nd Street.

In 1962 Edward "Spike" O'Donnell died of natural causes. He was the oldest brother and leader of the notorious Southside O'Donnells who waged war against other Southside gangs during the infamous "Beer Wars" during Prohibition.

In 1962 at the Villa Venice Restaurant in the northwest suburb of Wheeling, Frank Sinatra and his Rat Pack counterparts played a command performance at the behest of Sam Giancana. While the shows were sold out the OUTFIT ran a nearby gambling hut/casino. This appearance/demand was in retribution for the failure of Sinatra to get the Kennedy Administration to back off of their anti-TOC investigations. Front row at the show were OUTFIT luminaries such as: Sam Giancana, Felix "Milwaukee Phil" Alderisio, James Policheri AKA: "Monk" Allegretti, Joe Fischetti cousin of Al Capone and Marshall Caifano.

In the early 1960's the federal government provided an effective tool to Law Enforcement in the form of the "Hobbs Act", this was an anti-racketeering law that carried a 20 year sentence, it was first used in the Chicago area in 1963.

In December of 1962 Mob operative and Roger Touhy nemesis Jake "The Barber" Factor while fighting a deportation order was granted a Presidential Pardon.

In January of 1963 it was learned by Wisconsin Officials that Milwaukee Gang Boss Frank Balestrere allied himself with Chicago OUTFIT member Sam Battaglia and others to bring Chicago hoodlums to Milwaukee to run loan sharking and juke box operations.

In 1963, Momo Giancana took on the FBI and won an injunction against them that minimized their surveillance on his home. This highly publicized court battle was not looked upon with favor by OUTFIT advisor Tony Accardo.

In 1964 Rocco Fischetti a major player in the Chicago OUTFIT and a cousin of Al Capone, died of natural causes.

On August 24, 1964 Frank "Strongy" Ferraro Underboss and OUTFIT Treasurer to Sam Giancana and close ally of Murray Humphreys died of cancer at Wesley Memorial Hospital in Chicago, leaving yet another void for the OUTFIT to fill.

By the mid-1960's Giancana associate Chuckie English led an OUTFIT effort to control Chicago's garbage industry. This was an association that would have national implications in later years.

In a 1965 session of the Illinois Legislature, lawmakers were presented with "The Twelve-Point Legislative Program of the Chicago Crime Commission". This type of program a staple of the CCC for over forty years at the time, included a series of Bills that addressed issues such as: Syndicated Gambling, Criminal Usury/Loan Shark Rackets, Witness Immunity Law, Liquor Establishment Record Keeping, Vehicle Seizures/Gambling Devises and Proceeds, Criminally Operated Businesses, Possession of Bombs and Molotov Cocktails, Possession of Gambling Records, Wiretapping for Law Enforcement, Suppression of Evidence Law, Extending the Life of the Grand Jury and Convictions for Gambling Based on Circumstantial Evidence. All were passed while the Witness Immunity Law was vetoed.

Sam Giancana was jailed from July 1965 to May 1966 for contempt, in his refusal to testify in front of a federal grand jury after being granted immunity. Upon his release he fled to Mexico and remained in self-imposed exile until 1974 when he was evicted by the Mexican authorities. Just before he left Chicago his night club in Wheeling, IL. known as the Villa Venice mysteriously burned. It was the site of a command performance in 1962 by his friend Frank Sinatra and other members of the Rat Pack.

In the fall of 1965 President Lyndon Johnson issued an executive order declaring hidden microphones (known as BUGS) to be a violation of civil rights. This stopped the activity across the entire country and stifled the intelligence gathering efforts of the FBI and benefited TOC greatly.

On November 23, 1965 OUTFIT counselor, political fixer and former public enemy number 1, Llewelyn Morris Humphreys AKA: "Murray the Camel", Curly is found dead of a heart attack by his brother in his Marina City apartment, hours after being arrested by FBI agents for contempt of the Grand Jury. His absence would create a void in the power structure of the Chicago OUTFIT.

In 1966 the CCC crafts another seven point program to bolster police and prosecutors in their attack on TOC.

In 1967 mobster Louie "Cock Eyed Louie" Fratto died of natural causes.

On January 3, 1967 Jack Ruby dies of cancer while incarcerated in Texas. His attorneys filed yet another appeal on his behalf attempting to win a new trial in the murder of Lee Harvey Oswald for which Ruby was jailed. He was diagnosed only a month before his death. The tough Chicago westsider continued to front for the OUTFIT until the day he died never providing information to investigators about the murder conspiracy he was part of.

On March 25, 1967 the Sante Fe Saddle and Gun Club sponsored a party at the Edgewater Beach Hotel that included over 200 mobsters and 1000 guests in total. The event was to pay homage to Fifi Buccieri a top Westside Mob Boss who was climbing the ranks of the Chicago OUTFIT. Some 65 Chicago Police Detectives were staged nearby at Foster Beach for a possible raid if any gambling activities were detected.

In 1967 recognizing the dangerous level of TOC in suburban communities, the CCC develops a plan to provide a better balance of law enforcement for the entire metropolitan area to combat TOC.

On July 20, 1967 an FBI raid of the prestigious Friars Club in Los Angeles found electronic devises placed by minions of Chicago mobster Francesco Sacco AKA: Fillipo, Johnny Rosselli. He used these devises for years to cheat his celebrity friends out of hundreds of thousands of dollars while playing cards.

A presidential commission in 1967 through the "Task Force Report: The Police" further stressed the problem and national implications of TOC and in response formed the federal strike force to combat TOC, it expanded to 13 cities and was fully operational by 1970.

On December 15, 1969 James Policheri AKA: "Monk" Allegretti died of natural causes.

In 1969, a "Bingo Bill" is opposed by the CCC because of the ready access to another form of gambling by OUTFIT operatives.

In a rare occurrence for the Chicago OUTFIT no gangland slayings were reported for the year 1968.

In 1968 the Omnibus Safe Streets Act was passed and included statutes authorizing certain electronic monitoring both telephonic and oral (Title III) that became the greatest tool ever given to Law Enforcement (along with immunity) in their fight against TOC.

In 1969 Tony Accardo selects his new operations director, Fiore "Fifi" "The Nose" Buccieri who takes the helm. Fifi considered by law enforcement as the top enforcer for the OUTFIT assumes control, but dies in 1973 of natural causes.

In 1969 the FBI estimated the Chicago OUTFIT had 350 Made Members while a distinction was also made that clarified that Chicago was not a true Mafia organization as New York was. Pointing out that members; Colosimo, Torrio and Capone were not Mafia while Nitti, Ricca, Accardo, and Giancana were, it continues to obscure the true essence of TOC in Chicago that separates them as the OUTFIT.

In 1970 "Jackie the Lackey" Cerone was sentenced to five years in federal prison for interstate syndicated gambling. At the time he held a unique position of Assistant to the Chairman and was considered the successor to Accardo.

In 1971 Tony "The Ant" Spilotro is sent to Las Vegas to oversee the Chicago OUTFIT's interests there replacing the likes of Johnny Roselli and Marshal Caifano who held the positions for a short period of time and were not very effective in the eyes of their superiors back in Chicago. During the next fifteen years Spilotro's flamboyant behavior and reckless attitude continually aggravated his superiors in Chicago.

On March 13, 1971 it was reported that Red Dorfman, OUTFIT labor racketeer and close associate of Tony Accardo died of natural causes. His son Allan an OUTFIT Associate would die at the hands of the OUTFIT some 12 years later.

On August 11, 1971 Mario Dispensa died of injuries suffered from an attempted arson of the Hut Restaurant at 5301 W.159th, Oak Forest, IL. His co-defendant Anthony Rocco an ex Chicago Police officer was injured. Dispensa of 3218 S. Lowe was a sometime collector for Frank Calabrese.

On September 25, 1971 Felix "Milwaukee Phil" Alderisio died. He was a killer of renown for the OUTFIT and died while in federal prison of natural causes.

On December 12, 1971 Joseph "Joe Gags" Gagliano died of natural causes. He was a juice lender for the mob and employed heavy handed collectors such as Willie Messino.

On October 2, 1972 Ross Priola AKA: Prio the Northside operations Boss and the man credited with introducing narcotics to the OUTFIT, passed away of a heart attack, leaving yet another void to fill for OUTFIT leadership.

On October 11, 1972 Paul "The Waiter" Ricca dies of a Heart Attack at 74 in Presbyterian St. Luke's Hospital. At the time he was living comfortably in his west suburban apartment fighting health problems.

On October 30, 1972 Frank LaPorte died of a heart attack in his Flossmor home. He was semi-retired for the last several years and spent much of his time in California. He was a Southside boss for the OUTFIT and ran several establishments on their behalf. He was also suspected in numerous killings. Eventually a driver of his named Alfred Pilotto would take over his territory in the Southland.

FiFi Buccieri led the OUTFIT into the 70s and is replaced by James "Turk" Torello in 1973 after Fifi's death on August 17, 1973 of natural causes. Torello was overseer of the west area until this appointment. He was thought to have been a killer of renown and served as Boss until his death from cancer reported on April 16, 1979.

On June 1, 1973 it was revealed that Cook County Circuit Court Judge Daniel J. Covelli and Chief Judge Joseph A. Power had used their official positions in writing letters for imprisoned OUTFIT Associate Allan Dorfman. They wrote to Federal Judge Murray I. Gurfein of the District of New York singing the praises of Dorfman and trying to win a reduced sentence for him. This clearly demonstrates the level of corruption in Cook County.

On September 7, 1973 former OUTFIT leader Sam "Teetz" Battaglia died of natural causes.

In 1974 Tony Spilotro, Joey "The Clown" Lombardo, Allen Dorfman and others were indicted by a Federal Grand Jury in Chicago for defrauding the Teamster's Central States Pension Fund of $1.4 Million Dollars

On July 23, 1974 former OUTFIT Boss Sam Giancana was scheduled to testify in front of a Federal Grand Jury in Chicago just days after his expulsion from Mexico. His last grand jury subpoena resulted in a year in jail for contempt. This time around the OUTFIT leaders are worried if Sam can take the heat one more time.

On November 24, 1974 it was reported that Ralph "Bottles" Capone the 81 year old brother of Al Capone died in obscurity of natural causes.

On August 12, 1975 it was reported that Mario DeStefano died of a heart attack. He was the brother and partner of Mad Sam DeStefano the OUTFIT's juice loan kingpin. He was a mobster for over 40 years starting his career in 1934. At the time of his death he was awaiting a retrial for the murder of Leo Foreman and was a suspect in the murder of his brother Michael on September 27, 1955 who was a drug addict. He was also suspected in the murder of Mad Sam on April 14, 1973.

On September 8, 1975 William "Willie Potatoes" Daddano Sr. died while incarcerated. He was an OUTFIT luminary who started his career in the 42 Gang with the likes of Sam Giancana. He was incarcerated for conspiracy to rob a bank in Franklin Park, IL.

On July 2, 1976 it was reported that Ralph Pierce died of natural causes. In 1930 he was recruited by OUTFIT luminary Murray Humphries as his assistant and rose to be the longtime Southside gambling Boss along with being a suspect in numerous killings.

On July 27, 1976 it was reported that long time OUTFIT member Dominic "Bells" DiBella died of natural causes, he was one of the infamous three Dom's consisting of Dominic "Nags" Brancato, DiBella and Dominic "Libby" Nuccio. The 3 close friends were long time Chicago Gangsters and very close friends and collaborators.

In August of 1976 political fixer and Lake County Boss Les "Killer Kane" Kruse of 2437 Greenleaf Ave., dies of natural causes.

On December 6, 1976 it was reported that Joseph Fusco died of natural causes. He was a business partner and close associate of Al Capone. He was also a suspect in the murder of Alex Louis Greenberg in 1955.

On June 16, 1977 it was reported that OUTFIT Vending Co. impresario Eddie Vogel died of Leukemia at Columbus Hospital. At the time of his death he resided in the Ambassador East Hotel. He was semi-retired over the last 15 years and handed control of the company over to Gus "Slim" Alex. For years Vogel ran OUTFIT interest in the vending business from Apex Amusement Corp. in Niles, IL. This venture was the brainchild of OUTFIT Bosses Willie "Potatoes" Daddano and gambling Boss Lenny Patrick in the early 1950's.

In 1977 voters in New Jersey passed a referendum legalizing Gambling in their state. A Mob "Commission" meeting that year led to the Chicago OUTFIT claiming exclusive rights to Las Vegas while the east coast TOC would control gambling in New Jersey.

On January 9, 1978 OUTFIT Boss Tony Accardo was on vacation in Palm Springs when he was notified by his house keeper, Michael Volpe that he had been burglarized. He returned to Chicago immediately and the search for the burglars began without police involvement. Reportedly, Underboss Jackie Cerone brought Tony Spilotro back from Las Vegas to handle this situation. When apprised of the circumstances Spilotro stated that only John Mendell could defeat that alarm. The hunt was on..........

In 1978 a federal court in Kansas City authorized an overhear warrant that initiated Federal Cases: Strawman I and eventually Strawman II. During the next several years this investigation did more damage to the Chicago OUTFIT than any case in the past. TOC leaders from Chicago and other major cities were imprisoned for skimming millions of dollars from several Las Vegas casinos. Unfortunately this case caused Federal authorities to prematurely claim victory over the OUTFIT in Chicago after two 1986 convictions.

In late February of 1978 OUTFIT Boss James "Turk" Torello of Cicero was admitted to the Hospital where it was discovered that he had inoperable Cancer. Several months later he surrendered his position as Boss of the Chicago OUTFIT.

In 1978 Frank "Lefty" Rosenthal was forced to leave his position at the Stardust (the Chicago OUTFIT's flagship casino) in Las Vegas by the Nevada Gaming Control Commission, this hurt the OUTFIT's ability to protect its interest there.

On June 19, 1978 FBI agents in Las Vegas served over 80 search warrants pursuant to their long term investigation of Tony Spilotro, the OUTFIT's man in Vegas. It was revealed during this investigation that Spilotro was a hidden owner in several Las Vegas Casinos that provided a great amount of income to the Chicago OUTFIT. This was the beginning of the end for the vicious killer. His open war with law enforcement angered his bosses back in Chicago and would eventually cost him his life.

In 1978 the CCC addresses the lenient treatment Cartage Thieves (stealing from trucks) were receiving in the courts; this activity remained a low risk hallmark of TOC.

In 1979, Accardo confidant Joey Aiuppa is put at the reigns of the Chicago OUTFIT. Aiuppa a Capone era gangster began his career in Cicero where he kept a tight reign over TOC holdings in the Town. He established a bartender's union local (450) out of Cicero and was deeply involved in TOC skimming activities in Las Vegas. He was eventually charged and convicted in the Vegas case along with several other TOC bosses. His reign ended in 1986 when he was sentenced to prison where he died in 1997.

In 1979 Joe Corngold AKA: Fifke died of natural. He was the bodyguard of Louis B. Cowan AKA: "Diamond Louis" who was shotgunned to death in his car at 5935 W. Roosevelt in Cicero in 1933. Corngold was also wounded in the attack from a passing car.

Throughout the 70s the Chicago OUTFIT stayed true to form and continued to kill those resistant to street tax and those who betrayed the code of silence. However, they crossed the line when murdering two victims in full view of their families, something that was never considered in the past, a new low even for the OUTFIT.

In September of 1980 OUTFIT operatives Jerry Scalise AKA: One-Armed Jerry and Arthur Rachel AKA: The Brain pulled off a brazen daylight robbery of Graff

Jewelers in London England. The men were quickly captured, convicted and sent to prison, although the famous Marlborough diamond they made off with was never recovered. Scalise was paroled in 1992 and Rachel in 1993. The men returned to Chicago at that time.

During the reign of Joey Aiuppa (79-86) many TOC watchers felt that Jackie "The Lackey" Cerone was a trusted advisor and held a higher position than he was credited with. He was a close confidant to Accardo since the 1940s.

In June of 1981 Al Pilotto a onetime driver for Mob Boss Frank LaPorte was shot twice on a golf course in Crete, IL. The hit was reportedly approved by OUTFIT Boss Anthony Accardo and involved a takeover of his territory by Joey Lombardo. Later that year Albert Tocco would take over the operation in Chicago Heights and the south suburbs. Daniel Bounds would later confess to being the shooter to FBI agents and was put in Witness Protection.

A number of individuals and organizations brought suit under 42 U.S.C. sec. 1983 against the United States and the City of Chicago, claiming that the FBI's Chicago office and the Chicago Police Department's intelligence division were violating the plaintiffs' First Amendment rights by overly intrusive and improperly motivated investigations of alleged subversive activities. In 1981, before a trial could be held, the defendants agreed to a consent decree, which was approved by then District Judge Getzendanner the following year, imposing detailed and onerous restrictions on the defendants' powers of investigation. This action restricted the ability of the Chicago Police Department to monitor and share information on the Chicago OUTFIT and other organized crime entities.

In 1982 several Florida and Chicago OUTFIT associates were convicted in Miami of a scheme to swindle the Laborers International Union of North America (LIUNA). One of those convicted was Al Pilotto a Southside Boss and President of LIUNA Local 5, who was shot and wounded on a local golf course in September of 1981, but survived. OUTFIT Boss Tony Accardo was acquitted in this Union case.

On November 20, 1982 Albert "Obie" Frabotta died of natural causes. He was a longtime OUTFIT member, close associate of Felix "Milwaukee Phil" Alderisio and suspect in numerous OUTFIT murders.

In 1982 Grand Ave. Crew Boss Joey "The Clown" Lombardo was convicted along with Teamster President Roy Williams for attempting to bribe a U. S. Senator, conspiracy and mail fraud. In 1986 Lombardo was convicted in his part in the Las Vegas Skimming case. During his ten year incarceration he left his duties to James Vincent "Jimmy" Cozzo, his top lieutenant. The crew survived in the absence of Lombardo, he was released in 1992 and resumed control of his crew and was then said to be a top advisor for the OUTFIT.

In 1982 the Chicago suburb of Forest Park attempted to institute Casino Gambling under home rule. The CCC spoke out strenuously against this effort feeling the OUTFIT would be deeply involved and it was stopped.

On March 4, 1983 the CCC presented testimony in front of the U. S. Senate Permanent Subcommittee on Investigations, who were in Chicago to conduct a hearing on Organized Crime. This hearing reiterated the continuing problems TOC presents to the Chicago area, current trends in TOC activities and a set of proposals to equip Law Enforcement to continue the fight against the OUTFIT in Chicago.

On October 9, 1983 Nick Calabrese and several other OUTFIT soldiers were ordered to a west suburban restaurant on Roosevelt Road where they appeared in front of the current Outfit Boss Joey "Doves" Aiuppa. At this time Aiuppa and most of the leadership of the Chicago OUTFIT carried out a ceremony that would give the men "Made" status in the OUTFIT. While this was a common process in the east coast Mafia, it was rare in Chicago. This information was presented in Family secrets testimony and the following men were "Made" that day: Albert Tocco, Jimmy Marcello, Anthony Zizzo, John Matassa, Frank Belmonte and of course the Calabrese brothers Frank and Nick.

In 1983 OUTFIT Killer and Juice operator Frank Calabrese learned that one of his collectors Phillip Tolomeo, a former Chicago Police Officer and one of his most productive collectors was skimming from his collections. Calabrese helped to beat Tolomeo and took title to a house belonging to Tolomeo's mother as retribution.

On November 3, 1983 it was reported that Frank Caruso Sr. former boss of the Chinatown Crew of the OUTFIT died of natural causes.

In 1984 OUTFIT member Peter "The Greek" Dounias was convicted of shaking down owners of "Gay Bars" for street tax. Other OUTFIT associates were acquitted.

Also in 1984 long time OUTFIT operative and California real estate speculator Jake Factor AKA: Iakow Factrowitz, Jake "The Barber" died at the age of 91 after a long illness.

In July of 1985 it was reported that seven top members of the Chicago OUTFIT were to be entered into Nevada's Black Book that would ban their presence from any gambling establishment in the state of Nevada. Those to be entered were Tony Accardo, Joey Aiuppa, John Cerone, Angelo LaPietra, Gus Alex, Vince Solano and Albert Tocco.

In April of 1985 a Presidential Commission on Organized Crime that was initiated in 1983 came to Chicago. It was the 19 member commission's first visit to Chicago and 55 witnesses were scheduled to appear. It was also anticipated that most would claim 5th Amendment protections. The Commission had on its agenda two Chicago Companies with ties to the OUTFIT and two well-known witnesses: Ken Eto former OUTFIT Gambling Boss who survived an assassination attempt and former Teamster President Jackie Presser. This Commission eventually produced a report that estimated national losses due to TOC at over 100 billion dollars representing 1.1 percent of the GNP.

In 1985 an OUTFIT chop shop operation was brought down by the FBI and CPD and 16 associates were found guilty and sent to prison.

In August of 1985 it was reported that 3 informants were to testify at the trial of several Mob Bosses in Kansas City for skimming money from Las Vegas Casinos. Two of the informants listed are from Chicago: Ken Eto and Frank Cullotta. The Chicago Mobsters on Trial are: Joey Aiuppa, Jack Cerone, Angelo LaPietra, Joey Lombardo, and Tony Spilotro. After several weeks of testimony all of the hoods were convicted and sentenced to substantial prison sentences.

On January 5, 1986 OUTFIT Lieutenant Joseph "Little Caesar" DiVarco died of natural causes in prison. He ran the day to day operations in the Rush Street area and was overseer of OUTFIT interests in the nightclub district; in 1985 he was charged with gambling and tax evasion for which he was convicted.

In 1986 several TOC leaders from Chicago (Joe Aiuppa, Jackie Cerone, Angelo LaPietra, Joe Lombardo), Kansas City and Cleveland were convicted of skimming money from Las Vegas casinos and manipulating union pension funds. This sent several leaders of the Chicago OUTFIT to prison for years and changed the face of TOC leadership.

After Joe Aiuppa was sentenced in 1986, Joe Ferriola was tapped for the leadership role. He previously ran the Taylor St. crew, was an uncle to Mob assassin Harry Aleman and was known to deal drugs. He was innovative in developing new ventures in drug sales and gambling, but he too became ill and died after a short three year term.

On June 20, 1986 it was reported that Anthony Ortenzi of Melrose Park had died of natural causes. His role for the OUTFIT was that of Bookkeeper for Joey Aiuppa.

In 1987 Louie Eboli died of natural causes. He was a longtime gangster and part of a group of killers responsible for the death of the Spilotro brothers that included: Nick Calabrese, Louis Marino, John Fecarotta, Jimmy LaPietra, Sam Carlisi and Joe Ferriola.

In 1988 Michael Glitta died of natural causes, he was a mobster involved in juice, gambling and vice activities since 1951.

In 1988 "Operation Safe bet" saw several OUTFIT associates convicted for running vice and gambling in Chicago suburbs.

In 1988 the Chicago Police Department used electronic wiretaps to conduct "Operation Colossus" that resulted in the arrest of 21 OUTFIT associates for a criminal drug conspiracy and indicated a link to immigrant OUTFIT recruits from Italy and Sicily known as Zips.

In 1989 former OUTFIT bookmaker and Cicero Assessor Frank Maltese along with 3 associates, 2 of them police officers, were prosecuted by the State Attorney General's Office for their involvement in illicit Bingo games run at a Cicero Banquet Hall. The case was adjudicated with only a $10,000 fine for the men who allegedly made between $400,000 and $800,000 in unaccounted income and untaxed funds from the scheme. Maltese would be indicted on federal charges in 1990.

In 1989 OUTFIT lieutenants Dominick "Big Dom" Cortina, Donald "Wizard of Odds" Angelini and Joe Spadavecchio were convicted of running a multi-million dollar gambling operation for the OUTFIT, all received prison terms.

In 1989 Southside Boss Albert Tocco was convicted of 23 counts of racketeering, conspiracy, extortion and tax evasion after his arrest on a tip from Tocco's wife when he returned from Greece. Herbert Panice Sr. was a significant informer in this case. At the time Tocco's wife implicated him in the murder of Tony and Michael Spilotro. Tocco died in the Terre Haute Federal prison on September 21, 2005 of a stroke. He was a major player in the OUTFIT's struggle to control auto theft and chop shop operations known as "Car Wars" between 1969 and 1983 that left 30 to 40 dead. Dominick "Tootsie" Palermo briefly took over the southland operation until his indictment in 1992. After that time the area was consolidated and controlled by the reigning Southside boss starting with John Monteleone.

On March 12, 1989 it was reported that OUTFIT Boss Joe Ferriola succumbed to cancer. After the death of Ferriola, Sam Carlisi was next in line for the top job in the Chicago OUTFIT. Carlisi for years prior to this appointment was one of the top leaders in Chicago TOC. He gained his nickname of "Wings" from his work as a courier for the OUTFIT in past years and his frequent travel by air.

While Carlisi ran the OUTFIT, Ferriola's top man Rocco Infelise maintained control over the Taylor Street crew and the lucrative gambling and extortion business of the OUTFIT until his demise at the hands of Federal prosecutors in 1992. At his side during his years running this crew were some of the most dangerous and brightest mobsters Chicago had ever seen to include: Frank "Baldy" Maltese, Harry "The Hook" Aleman, William "Butch" Petrocelli, Gerald Scarpelli, Michael "Big Mike" Sarno, Carmen "Bobby" Salerno, Jimmy "Duke" Basile, Robert Bellavia, Sal "Solly D" DeLaurentis, Louie Marino and Marco D'Amico to mention a few.

In 1989 the CCC provided written and oral testimony, urging the U. S. Congress to retain the Federal Organized Crime Strike Forces, to the U. S. House of Representatives Sub-Committee on Criminal Justice in Washington D.C.

On August 13, 1989 it was reported that Vincent "The Saint" Inserro died of natural causes. He was a longtime OUTFIT member and suspected in numerous murders.

In 1989 a bill was proposed to legalize Riverboat Gambling in Illinois, the CCC through a letter to the Governor opposed such legislation for the criminal effects it would have on the state along with TOC concerns, the bill was defeated.

In 1990, the OUTFIT's man in California, Chris Petti was convicted of money laundering in San Diego by the use of wiretaps.

On May 1, 1991 it was reported that Guiseppe Glielmi AKA: Joey Glimco died of natural causes. He was a killer of renown and a top labor racketeer for the OUTFIT.

In 1991 the Mayor of Chicago Heights and his Finance Commissioner plead guilty to extortion, conspiracy and tax fraud for receiving kickbacks from contractors that included the OUTFIT's Southside Boss Albert Tocco. This case continued into 1992 to include city council members for activities that spanned 15 years.

In 1991 the conviction of OUTFIT members Dominic "Tootsie" Palermo, Nicky Guzzino, and Bernard "Snooky" Morgano sent the three to prison for extorting protection money from bookmakers in northwest Indiana.

On January 29, 1992 Dominic Senese 75, died at his Oak Brook home. He was said to have had cancer. In 1988 while President of the 2,500 member Teamsters Local 703, Produce Drivers and Warehousemen Union he was opening a security gate outside his home when he was wounded by shotgun pellets, but survived.

In 1992 OUTFIT muscle Mario Rainone was sentence to prison for 17 years on an extortion conviction after his 1989 deal to turn state's evidence collapsed. Before 1989, Rainone was involved in an ill advised shylock scam with Phil Tolomeo and owed big money to OUTFIT Boss Sam Carlisi when he was assigned to murder Anthony "Jeep" Daddino, who the Boss feared as an informant. While tracking the target he noticed he was being followed and felt he was the subject of a contract hit himself. He turned himself in and began to cooperate, but did not follow through and was charged accordingly. He was a collector for OUTFIT shylocks.

On April 22, 1992 it was reported that Frank "Babe" DeMonte died of natural causes. He was a longtime OUTFIT figure and representative in the Laborers International Union Local 1.

On May 27, 1992 Tony "Joe Batters" Accardo died of natural causes. He was considered the most successful OUTFIT Boss of all time, spending only one night in jail, which he vehemently denied later in life. He ran Chicago's preeminent Crime Syndicate in some sense for 50 years.

In 1992 James F. Lavalley was sentenced to prison for extortion and gambling as a collector for Lenny Patrick's street crew, he turned state's evidence and entered witness protection (WITSEC). Statements made by Lavalley provided investigators in Chicago with information to solve at least one TOC murder while he was suspected in an additional killing. However, the federal government would not allow access to him and the cases both went unsolved.

In 1992 a proposed land based casino was made public by the Mayor of Chicago and a local OUTFIT connected labor leader. The CCC went through great lengths and in response published the booklet "Analysis of Key Issues Involved in the Proposed Chicago Casino Gambling Project" to fight this proposal. The plan was eventually shelved.

Upon the imprisonment of Sam Carlisi in 1992, OUTFIT investigators placed John "No Nose" DiFronzo in the top position as Boss of the Chicago OUTFIT.

On November 16, 1992 Vincent Solano 72 yrs. died of prostate cancer in his Lisle home. He was the head of Local 1 of Laborers International Union of North America (LIUNA) and Boss of the Rush Street crew. He was previously a bodyguard and driver for the late northside Boss Ross Priola AKA: Prio.

On January 13, 1993 it was reported that Gus Sam Zapas AKA: Zapantis had died. Zapas 74, a longtime official with the Laundry, Cleaning and Dye House Workers International Union Local 46, died in Northwestern Memorial Hospital. He was a longtime labor racketeer for the OUTFIT and a subordinate to Westside leadership. In 1954 he was questioned in the kidnapping and murder of Robert Greenlease by Senator John McClellan in front of a special senate investigation committee, but never charged.

In 1993 OUTFIT fixer Gus Alex and Nick Gio were sentenced to prison for their extortion activities with Lenny Patrick that preyed on successful business owners as Patrick had done in the past as far away as Las Vegas. James LaValley and Lenny Patrick who wore a wire in the process testified against their contemporaries receiving reduced sentences. Alex the long time OUTFIT fixture died in prison in July of 1998.

In 1993 OUTFIT Boss John DiFronzo and gambling impresario Don Angelini were convicted of extortion in their bid to take over a native Indian Casino in San Diego.

In 1993 a large OUTFIT gambling ring from Cicero, IL. was sent to prison for Murder, racketeering and Gambling. The crew was led by Ernest "Rocco" Infelise and included members such as Louis Marino, Sal DeLaurentis, Robert Salerno and Robert Bellavia. The conviction was facilitated by cooperation from gambling overseer William "BJ" Jahoda who would spend the rest of his life in hiding and speaking out against gambling for the CCC. Jahoda died in 2004 of natural causes.

On March 13, 1993 it was reported that Pat Marcy died of natural causes. Marcy was born as Pasqualino Marchone. He was a legendary political boss and a trusted and valued associate of the OUTFIT. His official title was, "Secretary of the First Ward." Marcy ran Chicago's old 1st Ward which encompassed Chicago's Downtown. The "Secretary" regularly held court and dispensed favors from the "First Ward table" at the "Counselor's Row" restaurant. He was indicted in 1991 and died during his trial.

On April 3, 1993 it was reported that Dominic "Butch" Blasi died of natural causes. He was a close associate of Sam Giancana and a suspect in the laters murder.

In 1993 the CCC continued to oppose land based casino gambling in Illinois and in response a CCC Board Member was appointed to the Illinois House Speakers Task Force on Gambling.

In 1993 an OUTFIT betting/extortion ring aligned with the On Leong Chinese Merchants Association caused OUTFIT members of Chicago's 26th Street crew under Angelo LaPietra, to be indicted. The members included Joe "Shorty" LaMantia, Aldo Piscitelli, Joe Wing, Ken Hom, Dominic Scalfaro, Phil Bertucci, Joe Cutrano, Gino Levato, Joe Coco and Joe Gallo. The case was thrown out due to improprieties by a grand juror. The case was reinstated and tried in 1996 and LaMantia and his step son Aldo Piscitelli were fined and sent to prison. A Grand Juror, Robert Girardi was convicted in 1994 of leaking information in the case that caused the escape of Joe DiFronzo brother of OUTFIT Boss John DiFronzo. Joe DiFronzo was sentenced to 8 years in prison in abstentia.

On September 9, 1993 it was reported that James "Lapper" LaPietra died of natural causes. He was the brother of crew Boss Angelo "The Hook" LaPietra and both were known killers for the OUTFIT.

In August of 1993 Frank Maltese the Assessor in Cicero, Illinois was sentenced to prison for his role in the gambling operations of Rocco Infelise's crew. He died a short time later on October 21, 1993.

On December 12, 1993 it was reported that James D'Antonio succumbed to injuries he sustained in a car accident. He was a long time luminary of the OUTFIT and rose to be a top lieutenant for OUTFIT Boss Joey "The Clown" Lombardo. He was also a skilled burglar and thief involved with corrupt police officers during his decade's long career.

In December of 1993 Sam Carlisi was found guilty with several of his minions on racketeering, gambling, loan-sharking, extortion, arson and tax charges. He served as OUTFIT Boss until his indictment in 1992. Along with Carlisi the others convicted were: James Marcello, Anthony Zizzo, Anthony Chairamonti, Brett O'Dell, Joseph Bonavolante, Richard Gervasio, and Gill Valerio. It was this case that long time mobster and Northside gambling Boss, Lenny Patrick turned on Carlisi and testified under a federal immunity agreement. Patrick would take the stand and admit to six murders in order to gain credibility. Prior to his testimony and in an attempt to intimidate Patrick against testifying a car belonging to Patrick's daughter was blown up in the driveway of her Rogers Park home. Patrick would later be indicted in 1995 for 3 of the murders by the Cook County State's Attorneys Office who made no such immunity deal regarding Patrick's testimony. He was later released before trial without explanation. Carlisi as Boss was sentenced to 13 years in prison while Marcello was sentenced to 12 ½. The men were sent to prison where Carlisi died on January 1, 1997.

In 1993 the street crew of Rocco Infelise that included Mike Sarno, Louis Marino, Robert Bellavia, Sal DeLaurentis and Bobby Salerno was decimated by a conviction after an 8 year investigation led by the Internal Revenue Service, CID. They were charged with crimes ranging from horse and sports gambling, racketeering and murder conspiracy. A large part of the case was based on the testimony and undercover video compiled by a former member of the crew, William "BJ" Jahoda.

In 1994 Wilson Moy the unofficial Mayor of China Town and other operators of the On Leong Chinese Merchants Association of Chicago were convicted of conspiracy and racketeering for running a casino for more than 20 years.

In 1994 the weapons arrest of Vic Arrigo a federal informant and former enforcer for the northside crew of late OUTFIT Underboss Joe DiVarco, launched an investigation by the CPD Intelligence unit to re-visit several unsolved OUTFIT murders that included 3 killings between 82 and 87 related to several gas stations. The investigation was expanded to include the 88 and 90 murders of 2 former Las Vegas OUTFIT associates. The cases were dropped due to a lack of interest from prosecutors and a lack of inter-agency cooperation.

On October 29, 1994 John D'Arco Sr., 82, the former longtime Democratic committeeman of the old 1st Ward, who federal authorities say served as a link between organized crime and politics, died after a long illness.

In 1994 an OUTFIT sponsored pot growing operation in Inverness, IL. sent Joe DiFronzo, Joseph Duenser, Mike Fusco, Theodore Kotsovos, Anthony Sanello, Bruce Ventura, and David Wutzen to prison for conspiracy and distribution of narcotics. Michael Coffey, whose home was used for the growing, provided a great deal of intelligence to the authorities in his federal profer.

In 1994 Marco D'Amico, head of the Elmwood Park Street crew, Tony & Carl Dote, Robert Abbinanti, Roland Borelli, Frank Catapano, Frank Marnato, Robert Scutkowski and William Tanuta were sent to prison for operating a gambling and extortion ring.

On December 19, 1995 Chicago Police and State's Attorneys Investigators arrested Lenny Patrick charging him with three of the six murders he admitted to in federal court after he was indicted by the Cook County State's Attorneys Office. At the time Patrick was said to have been the highest ranking Chicago Mobster ever to cooperate. Patrick was released several months later when the local charges were dropped without explanation.

In 1995 Frank Calabrese and 8 members of his loansharking crew were indicted after a 9 year investigation by the FBI. The men were charged with racketeering, mail fraud, witness tampering, extortion and tax violations. This case ultimately sent Calabrese, his brother Nick, a son Frank Jr., Phillip Fiore, Phillip Tolomeo, Terry Scalise, Lou Bombacino, and Robert Dinella to prison in 1997. This case resulted in cooperation from Calabrese's brother Nick and his son Frank Jr. and ultimately lead to a sweeping indictment in 2005 known as Family Secrets.

In 1996 Frank "One Ear Frankie" Fratto died of natural causes. Over the years he had been a suspect in numerous Outfit killings.

On January 20, 1996 long time OUTFIT mouthpiece and legal advisor Sydney Korshak dies at his palatial home in California. His brother Marshall was a long time Chicago alderman and died on January 19, 1996.

On July 26, 1996 John "Jackie the Lackey" Cerone 82 yrs. probably the most underrated OUTFIT Boss in history died in Good Sheppard Hospital in Barrington after being released from prison and after serving more than a decade behind bars. He was convicted with other mobsters for the scheme that skimmed 2 million dollars from Las Vegas Casinos as portrayed in the movie Casino. He got his start as a driver and bodyguard for the late OUTFIT Boss Joey Aiuppa

In 1996 an indictment was passed down on OUTFIT associate Bernard Prestigiacomo, James J. Yaros, John J. Capodice, Michael A. Alvarez, Donald R. Cusak, Michael J. Grieco, Ronald E. Kadlubowski, John C. Lamonica, John Lanno, William S. Lesniak, Thomas E. Malloy, Steven J. Nolfe, John Sciaccotta Jr., Samuel G. Ventura and Ronald Antos for the operation of a sports gambling business that existed for over 6 years.

On January 4, 1997 it was reported that Sam "Wings" Carlisi former OUTFIT Boss died of natural causes while in prison.

On February 24, 1997 it was reported that OUTFIT boss Joseph "Doves" Aiuppa died of natural causes while incarcerated.

In 1997 the CCC filed an Amicus Curiae brief supporting the City's request of the federal court to minimize provisions of the 1983 consent decree that limits the Chicago Police Department's ability to investigate TOC, gangs and terrorism. A second brief was submitted by the CCC in 1999.

In 1997 the CCC published "The New Faces of Organized Crime", in this book Organized Crime is newly defined as both Traditional Organized Crime (TOC) (Mafia, Mob, OUTFIT, Syndicate) and Non-Traditional Organized Crime (NTOC) (Street Gangs, Drug Cartels, Motorcycle Gangs, etc. and additional ethnic groups). Included in this publication was a new Organizational Chart for Chicago's OUTFIT, the most current chart available to the public and maybe the last to be released to the public. Upon this release the CCC called for a re-commitment of resources by Chicago Area Law Enforcement to fight TOC that went unheard.

In 1997 the CCC assisted the Office of the GEB Attorney for the Laborers International Union of North America in preparing local hearings to oust OUTFIT associates from its ranks, a complaint for trusteeship was filed and the Chicago Crime Commission provided testimony at the hearings. 23 past and current OUTFIT associates were listed, 18 were ultimately ousted.

In 1997 when a casino in Curacao, (a Caribbean resort) went bankrupt, officials initiated an investigation into the way it was run under a ranking Chicago mobster. He was the former acting boss of the Grand Ave. crew during the incarceration of Joey "The Clown" Lombardo and he was also implicated in a 1998 probe of a west suburban bingo parlor.

In 1997 in suburban Northlake, IL. Police Chief Seymour Sapoznik pleads guilty to racketeering for his part in gambling operations in Northlake taverns. He was videotaped meeting with Westside Underboss Anthony Centracchio and accepted bribes to ignore gambling in his town. Tom Tucker the former Chief of Detectives in nearby Stone Park was also implicated in the investigation. Several mayors of other nearby towns were implicated, but Centracchio died before he could be taken to trial.

In 1998 the CCC provided investigators in Arizona with links to the Chicago OUTFIT by a group behind the Arizona State University point shaving scandal. In response to this case and a similar scandal at Northwestern University, the CCC constructed the areas first Campus Gambling Conference in cooperation with DePaul University and the Illinois Attorney General's Office at the State of Illinois building. A second Conference was held in 1999 at Northern Illinois University in DeKalb and a third at the University of Illinois at Champaign-Urbana in 2000.

In 1998 an OUTFIT thief under indictment in Tampa turned state's evidence and revealed the existence of a Jewelry Theft ring operating out of Chicago and run by former police Deputy Superintendent William Handhart, and other criminals with OUTFIT connections. The case mandated a wiretap of Handhart's home and led to a conviction and incarceration. Handhart was suspected of having OUTFIT connections throughout his career. He would claim that these connections allowed him to be more effective. Apparently this case proved otherwise and put a spotlight on the continued TOC influence in the Chicago Police Department. Handhart was released to a halfway house in 2011.

In 1998 after a politically charged trial of OUTFIT crew Boss Frank M. Caruso Jr.'s son, in a brutal hate crime attack, the CCC supported the retention of the judge handling the case, who was later allegedly the subject of an OUTFIT murder contract that was never carried out.

In 1998 a federal investigation revealed subjects associated with Russian Organized Crime (NTOC) were involved a white slavery ring and were providing dancers for local OUTFIT associated strip clubs, this is a hallmark of TOC in Chicago.

On July 24, 1998 it was reported that Gus "Slim" Alex the OUTFIT's political fixer for decades died of natural causes while in prison.

In 1998 Ed Hanley the president of the Hotel and Restaurant Employees Union was forced into retirement. Hanley a bartender was first brought into the union in 1961 by Joey Auippa the future OUTFIT Boss. By the time he was forced to retire he was making over a quarter million dollars a year and was allowed to retain that salary as his pension.

In December of 1998 law enforcement raided the home of OUTFIT Bookmaker Emmitt "Greg" Paloian 47 yrs., they found $6,090 in his pocket and $150,000 in cash in the house. It was stashed in safes in a secret room behind a false wall in a basement closet. After more than 20 years of running what federal prosecutors call "a hugely successful" mob-connected bookmaking operation, raking in millions of dollars, he was nabbed. In March, he pleaded guilty to charges of bookmaking, and in July, he was sentenced to 41 months in prison.

On March 28, 1999 it was reported that Angelo "The Hook" LaPietra died of natural causes. He was a longtime OUTFIT Boss of the Chinatown Crew and an OUTFIT killer.

On June 25, 1999, Governor George Ryan signed into law a dramatic expansion of gambling in Illinois. The law allowed a new casino, based in densely-populated Cook County. The state's existing riverboat casinos could drop anchor and offer dockside gambling day and night. And finally, the Illinois government will hand over $56.9 million yearly, in tax breaks and subsidies, to the state's ailing horse-racing industry. The Illinois Economic and Fiscal Commission estimated that taxpayers could lose as much as $14 million yearly thanks to the new law.

On July 20. 1999 it was reported that Alfred Pilotto died. He was a prominent Southside Boss for the OUTFIT, former President of LIUNA Local 5 and survived an assassination attempt when shot on a golf course in September of 1981.

In 1999 the CCC calls to task a USA Today reporter for a story marking the demise of TOC in America. This was viewed as misinformation and a great disservice to the public and law enforcement.

In 1999 the CCC is lauded for its organized crime work and it's assistance in naming a local charted OUTFIT figure to the Nevada Blacklist which precluded him from entering any gaming establishment in the state. He was also blacklisted by the state of Vermont sometime later.

On November 24, 1999 it was reported that Dominic "Big Dom" Cortina OUTFIT gambling overseer died of natural causes.

In 1999 several OUTFIT associates under the direction of Westside OUTFIT Boss Anthony Centracchio were indicted in a case that highlighted 20 years of sanctioned OUTFIT gambling in at least 5 suburban towns west of Chicago. This case, an expansion of a 1997 investigation in Northlake, IL. discovered gambling in 73 locations involving approx. 500 video poker machines capable of generating $100,000 a year each. This case indicated classic TOC influence in government and law enforcement and may only be the tip of the iceberg in OUTFIT gambling activities. Political leaders from the respective towns and state liquor officials claimed ignorance when queried as to why the taverns mentioned were allowed to remain licensed and some even maintained video poker machines. All those charged were convicted in 2000.

On December 23, 1999 Ronald "Ronnie" Jarrett 55 yrs. AKA: Ronald Garnett, Anthony Forzato was shot as he walked to his car in front of his Bridgeport home. He died one month after the shooting. Ronnie was a longtime OUTFIT member who spent 13 years in prison for masterminding a $40,000 jewelry store robbery in 1980. He was considered a top lieutenant for Southside Boss John "Johnny Apes" Monteleone when he was killed. In the past he was the former driver for the late south Area Boss Angelo LaPietra, was suspected of involvement in OUTFIT killings and coordinated the activities of all OUTFIT sanctioned burglars and thieves in Chicago. The lone shooter escaped in a rented van that was found burning blocks away. The case remains unsolved.

On January 7, 2000 Edward Hanley Sr. died in a car accident in Wadsworth, Illinois. He was the former General President of the Hotel Employees and Restaurant Employees International Union (HEREIU). He was handpicked for this position by OUTFIT Boss Joey Aiuppa. He was forced into retirement by Federal Authorities and was the brother-in-law of Frank Calabrese a convicted OUTFIT killer.

In 2000 the son of imprisoned mobster Louis Marino, Dino Marino was sentenced for his part in a ghost pay-rolling scheme in Cicero IL. Marino provided no work as a highly paid health inspector in the town.

In 2000 the son of OUTFIT Lt. Bill Galioto, Sal, pleaded guilty in St. Louis to his part in a Medicare scheme designed to defraud the agency of 1.5 million dollars.

In 2000 NY MOB associate Vincent Amarante was arrested during a raid of a suburban Chicago strip club. The CCC assisted in identifying Amarante as a member of the Bonanno crime family.

On December 8, 2000 it was reported that Donald "the Wizard of Odds" Angelini dies of natural causes. He was a gambling impresario and odds maker who helped orchestrate OUTFIT gambling operations for decades.

In 2001 John "Johnny Apes" Monteleone died of natural causes. He was a Mob Boss from the Southside and was suspected for his involvement in several killings.

On July 26, 2001 an explosion occurred in front of a Bridgeport residence belonging to the mother of slain mobster Ronnie Jarrett. Jarrett who was shot leaving his Bridgeport home in December of 1999 succumbed to his wounds in January of 2000. The van that was damaged belonged to Jarrett's oldest son who believed the incident was related to his father's death.

On August 9, 2001 it was reported that Anthony Centracchio an OUTFIT area boss died of natural causes.

In 2002 "Big" Joe Arnold a former OUTFIT overseer of operations in the Rush Street area for Joe "Cesar" DiVarco died of natural causes.

In 2002 Joe "Shorty" LaMantia died of natural causes. He was a member of the Chinatown crew involved in gambling and was indicted in 1993.

In August of 2002 after a twelve year investigation and indictment, Cicero OUTFIT Boss Michael B. Spano Sr. along with Town President Betty Loren Maltese (wife of the late Town Assessor Frank "Baldy" Maltese), noted OUTFIT bookmaker and conduit were indicted and eventually convicted of an insurance scheme that bilked the town out of twelve million dollars. Former police Chief Emil Schullo was also indicted and later convicted along with several associates.

In November of 2002 Willie "the Beast" "Wee Willie" Messino a noted juice collector and west suburban operative dies of natural causes.

On September 6, 2003 it was reported that Marshall Caifano AKA: John Marshall former OUTFIT muscle and Vegas overseer died of natural causes.

In 2004 Ken Eto AKA: Tokyo Joe died of natural causes while living in Witness Protection. On February 10, 1983 the OUTFIT gambling overseer survived 3 GSWs to the back of his head at 7129 W. Grand. The men who bungled the hit were killed and Eto lived to testify in numerous Mob trials from Witness Protection sending many of his former colleagues to prison.

In 2005 Dominic "Nags" Brancato and Dominic "Libby" Nuccio both died of natural causes, they were two of the infamous 3 DOMS consisting of Dominic "Bells" DiBella, Brancato and Nuccio. The 3 close friends were long time Chicago Gangsters and very close friends and collaborators.

On July 18, 2005 it was reported that a suburban mayor trying to secure a casino license for his municipality met in 1999 with 5 top OUTFIT members and 2 OUTFIT associates. The information was provided by an FBI Supervisory Special Agent citing details provided by a Mob informant who has had statistical accomplishments for the Bureau. The informant went on to say the meeting took place on May 29, 1999 at Armands restaurant in suburban Elmwood Park. Mob control of various contracts regarding construction and operations were discussed. Those attending were John DiFronzo, Peter DiFronzo, Joey Lombardo, Joseph Andriachi, Rudy Fratto, William Messino and Rick Rizzoulo.

In July of 2005 the federal investigation of the HIRED TRUCK scandal was rocking city hall to its foundations with allegations of trucking firms hired while posing as minority subcontractors and trucks being paid to sit at work sites and produce no work. Politically OUTFIT connected individuals had hidden interests in trucking firms to cash in on these lucrative contracts. Well, when money is to be found one cannot count the OUTFIT out as Emmitt E. "Greg" Paloian will attest to. Greg is a convicted OUTFIT gambling impresario and bookmaker and had an interest in one of the trucking firms associated with the Hired Truck scandal despite his recent gambling conviction.

On July 21, 2005 Ernest Rocco Infelise 82, died of natural causes in a federal medical facility 40 miles west of Boston. He was serving a 63 year sentence at El Reno, Oklahoma that he received in 1993 for murder, bookmaking and tax violations. At one time the former military paratrooper rose to the number 3 position in the Chicago OUTFIT

On September 21, 2005 south suburban OUTFIT Boss Albert "Caesar" Tocco 76, died at the Federal penitentiary in Terre Haute, IN. The cause of death was reported to be complications from high blood pressure. In his criminal career Tocco collected money from gambling and prostitution rackets and was suspected in at least nine killings. He gained a great deal of notoriety in 1990 when his wife revealed his participation in the burial of Tony and Michael Spilotro in 1986. He was serving a 200 year prison term when he died.

In January of 2006 former Cicero Mayor Betty Loren-Maltese lost an appeal in front of U.S. District Judge John Grady to reduce her sentence. It remained at 97 months. However, at this time a reduced sentence was given to Michael Spano Jr. the son of OUTFIT Boss Michael Spano Sr. and former attorney Charles Schneider both of whom were convicted in the same case. In front of a different Judge Former Cicero Public Safety Director Emil Schullo along with mobsters Michael Spano Sr. and James Inendino had their sentences reaffirmed by U.S. District Judge Ruben Castillo.

In 2007 James Vincent "Jimmy" Cozzo, a top lieutenant to Joe Lombardo and his Grand Ave. street crew died of natural causes.

On June 2, 2007 a disturbing report was published in a Chicago newspaper citing the failures of law enforcement agencies to trust, share information or collaborate with other agencies during critical investigations. This report came on the heels of a U.S. Justice Department Office of Inspector General's investigation. Several federal agencies were queried and mentioned a lack of communication and outright refusal of some agencies to share information. This was exemplified in 2005 when Chicago Police and FBI agents unwittingly arrested an undercover ATF agent. Some leading agency figures claim that any problems may stem from personal conflicts not agency partnerships.

On March 4, 2008 John "Jack" Duff Jr. 82, died of natural causes. He was a convicted labor racketeer and close associate of OUTFIT Boss Tony Accardo. He had testified on Accardo's behalf in a 1960 tax-fraud trial. Mr. Duff headed the Liquor and Wine Sales Representatives Local 3 and owned several companies accused of defrauding the City of Chicago out of millions of dollars in set aside contracts for minority owned businesses. He was also close friends with powerful politicians and had complete access to city Hall.

On July 23, 2008 Frank "The German" Schweihs 78, died in Thorak Hospital on the northside of Chicago where he was taken from the Metropolitan Correctional Center downtown. The German was awaiting trial in the infamous Family Secrets investigation that alleged mobsters had killed at least 18 people among other crimes. He had been in custody for two years awaiting this landmark prosecution that sent several OUTFIT Bosses to prison for the rest of their lives. News coverage following his death mentioned a plethora of Notable Mob killings he was suspected of or complaisant in to include: Riccardo Scalzetti AKA: Richard Cain, Jimmy Catuara, Allan Dorfman, Joe Testa, Sam DeStefano, Patsy Riccardi, Chuckie Nicoletti, Francesco Sacco AKA: Fillipo, Johnny Rosselli, Angelo Boscarino and Gerald Scarpelli. While he was never convicted of any of these murders, authorities felt at different times that he was a strong suspect.

In February of 2009 a suburban task force led by the Addison Police Department arrested mobsters Mario J. Rainone and Vincent T. Forliano for a number of high end residential burglaries and thefts. The men were followed by police for several weeks through two dozen prominent suburbs where they would target affluent residences. Proceeds and burglary tools were recovered. Reportedly in the past the men have worked as juice collectors and were suspected in OUTFIT killings.

On March 24, 2009 it was reported that mobster Michael Marcello would testify against a former Deputy U.S. Marshall for allegedly passing information about federal investigations to Mob associates. Marcello is the half-brother of Outfit Boss Jimmy "The Man" Marcello who was sentenced to life in prison after the "Family Secrets" trial.

On May 17, 2009 Alfonso Tornabene AKA: Al, Pizza Man, died in a Berwyn Hospital of natural causes. It was reported that he was an OUTFIT Boss for many years helping to run Southside operations. He opened his first Pizza restaurant in 1955 and expanded it to three other locations.

On April 2, 2010 it was reported that a high level political candidate from Illinois and a local banker had been engaged in banking activities with convicted felon Tony Rezko an insider to convicted Governor Rod Blagojevich. Additional reports cite other banking activities with Mob associates Michael Giorango and Demitri Stavropoulos. Goirango was alleged to promote a nationwide prostitution ring while Stavropuolos ran a bookmaking ring across several states.

On April 9, 2010 it was reported that OUTFIT members Jerry Scalise 73, Bobby Pullia 69, and Art "The Genius" Rachel 71, were arrested by federal authorities outside the fortress like home of deceased OUTFIT Boss Angelo "The Hook" LaPietra at 250 W. 30th St. in Chicago. The men were under surveillance for a previous bank robbery and were casing a second bank in Lagrange, IL. Apparently they suspected valuables were being kept in the LaPietra home. Two of the men Scalise and Rachel were arrested in London in 1980 for the theft of the famous Marlborough diamond from Graff Jewelers. They were incarcerated and served 13 year prison terms in England, but the diamond was never recovered. In January of 2012 Scalise and Pullia plead guilty. Reportedly the men will serve 6 to 9 years in prison.

On December 22, 2010 Cicero OUTFIT Boss Michael Sarno 52 yrs., Samuel Volpendesto 86 yrs. an elderly gangster and bomb maker and Mark Polchan 41 yrs., a long time OUTFIT associate and member of the Outlaw motorcycle gang along with others were convicted of racketeering, witness intimidation, a string of burglaries and robberies and orchestrating the February 2003 bombing of a Berwyn video gaming business that competed with a OUTFIT controlled company. The crew enlisted the help of several law enforcement officials from Cicero and Berwyn in their criminal enterprise. The men were convicted and sentenced: Polchan 60 yrs., Volpendestro 35 yrs. and Sarno was sentenced to 25 years in prison the maximum allowed by law.

On March 8, 2011 it was reported by the press based on unsealed federal documents that the two men now leading the Chicago OUTFIT are Michael Sarno and Salvatore Cataudella. Sarno is in custody from a 2010 federal conviction and was sentenced to 25 years in prison which leaves Cataudella as the last man standing. OUTFIT leadership has always been hard to establish as this report is refuted by some Mob watchers

On December 25, 2012 renown OUTFIT killer Frank Calabrese Sr. died peacefully in a Federal Prison in South Carolina.

In 2013 "The Chicago Way" was published by Mob expert Don Herion. In the book he cited sources that revealed the Chicago Police Department disbanded the Gambling Unit of the Organized Crime Division. This information matches other reports that the department has removed all its investigators in the Intelligence Unit from working on the Chicago Outfit. This has to cause great celebration within the OUTFIT as they continue to run lucrative gambling operations with little police interference.

On June 6, 2013 it was reported that several relatives of those killed by the Chicago OUTFIT would share $1.7 Million dollars restitution from the estate of mobster Frank Calabrese Sr.

The Story continues....................

PHOTO INDEX

From the Collection of W. Johnson & S. Simon

Murray Humphreys 127
Joe Aiuppa 182
Lenny Patrick at 95 Arrest 183
Lenny Patrick arrest report 184
Marshall Caifano 188
Tony Accardo & Jackie Cerone 218
Richard Cain 230
Harry Aleman 239
Joe Amato 242
Angelo LaPietra 243
Willie Messino 249
Frank Calabrese Sr. 252
Ronnie Jarret 255
Frank Saladino 259
John Monteleone 260
James Inendino 262
Billy Dauber 266
Butch Petrocelli dead 267
Albert Tocco 269
Albert Piloto 270
Lenny Yaras dead 275
Chuckie English dead 276
Joe Ferriola 279
John Fecarotta 280
James DiForti 281
Mob Leaders 285
Herbie Blitzstein 286

From the collection of J. W. Touhy

Joey Lombardo 12
Tammany Hall 16
Mike McDonald 17
Monte Tennes 21
Bill Thompson 23
Jim Colisimo 24
Chas. Fischetti 27
Johnny Powers 29
Frank McErlane 30
Gov. Len Small 40
Joey Glimco 46
Big Tim Murphy 50
Chief Morgan Collins 56
Danny Stanton 59
DeGrazia, Campagna, Maddox 64
Scalise&Anselmi 65
Teddy Newberry 66
Genna Family 69
Hymie Weiss 70
Schemer Drucci 71
Tony Genna dead 72
Samoots Amatuna 74
Atty Bill McSeiggin dead 82
John "Mitters" Foley 85
Joe Aiello 89
Theodore Anton dead 90
"Pollack Joe" Saltis 91
Officer Dan Healy 94
Jones, Winkler & Burke 95
Frank Gusenberg 101
Big Tim Murphy home 107
Frankie Yale dead 108
George "Red" Barker 111
Tony Lombardo dead 112
Pasqualino Lolordo dead 115
Joseph "Hop Toad" Guinta 116
Joseph "Hop Toad" Guinta dead 122
Mayor Anton Cermak shot 128
Terry Druggan/ Frankie Lake 135
Jack Zuta dead 138
Teetz Battaglia 141
August Battaglia 142
Mike "The Pike" Heitler 144
Lenny Patrick 150
Sgt. Harry Lang 154
Joe Corngold 159
William "Three Finger Jack" White 161
Louis Alterie dead 165
Prignano & Capone 167
Jack Ruby 169
Louis Canpagna 174
George Brown 175
Frank Loesch 175
Red Dorfman 176
DiVarco-Cerone-Prio 181
Tony Capezio 189
Mayor Kennelly & Sen. Kefauver 196
Lt. William Drury 198
Brancato-Trambino dead 199
Nicolletti & Alderisio 201
Cherry Nose Gioe dead 204
Willie Bioff explosion 206
Lou Greenberg murder scene 207
Martin Accardo 210
Gus Alex 211
Roger Touhy shot 215
Joe DiVarco 217
Wm. Action Jackson 222
Fifi Buccieri 224
Tony Spilotro 226
Frank Schweihs 228
"Mad Sam" DeStefano 229
Frank LaPorte & Al Capone 233
Monk Allegretti 235
Ralph Pierce 239
Joey Glimco 250
Campise death car 273

Newspapers/Publications

Kenna & Coughlin Library of Congress 22
Frankie Yale NYC Public Libabry 26
Al Capone Trib 33
Bootleg Map-Gem of the Prarie 35
Mayor Wm. Dever Library of Congress 37
Dion O'Bannion National Archives 38
Jim Colisimo Trib dead 42
George Meegan 55
Spike O'Donnell Trib 62
Bubbs Quinlan Trib 68
Tony Aiello Brooklyn Lib. 86
Sam Giancana Trib 87
Frank Koncil 93
Jack McGurn 97
Green Mill Gardens 100
Dominick Aiello dead
Getty image 109
St. Valentine's Day Massacre Herald Examiner 120
Frank Nitti dead Trib 129
Paul Ricca, AP wire photo 130
John "Dingbat" O'Berta 132
Jake Lingle dead 136
Willie Marks 156
Joe Genero 166
Mario DeStefano Trib 205
Larry Nuemann Trib 208
OUTFIT Leadership Chgo. Today 237
Mad Sam DeStefano dead Trib 241
The Last Supper: Accardo et. al. 246
Giancana dead & gun ued Trib 248
Park Ridge Murders 257
Michael Cagnoni's car Trib 268
Ken Eto testifies Trib 272

Art Work by Harper College Art Student Daniella Boyd

Giancana Toe Tag Cover, 1

Bibliography

Abadinsky, H. (2000) Organized Crime, Sixth Edition. Belmont, CA: Wadsworth.
Abadinsky, H. (2003) Organized Crime, Seventh Edition. Belmont, CA: Wadsworth.

Bilek, A. (2008) The First Vice Lord, Big Jim Colisimo and the Ladies of the Levee, Cumberland House Publishing, Nashville, TN.

Binder, J.J. (2003) Images of America, The Chicago Outfit, Chicago, IL: Arcadia.

Burke, E. M. & O'Gorman, T. J. (2007) End of Watch, Chicago, IL. Chicago's Book Press.

Chicago Crime Commission (1919-2011) Archives, Chicago, IL.
Chicago Crime Commission (1990) Organized Crime in Chicago 1990, Chicago, IL.
Chicago Crime Commission (1997) New Faces of Organized Crime, Chicago, IL.

Churney, D. (2003) Capone's Cornfields, The Mob in the Illinois Valley. USA: BookSurge LLC.

Coen, J. (2009) Family Secrets, Chicago, IL. Chicago Review Press.

Cooley, R. & Levin, H. (2004) When Corruption was King, How I helped the Mob rule Chicago, Then brought the Outfit down. New York: Carroll & Graf.

Cullota, F. & Griffin D. (2007) Cullotta: The Life of a Chicago Criminal, Las Vegas Mobster and Government Witness Huntington Press, Las Vegas Nevada

Eghigian, M. Jr. (2006) After Capone, The Life and World of Chicago MOB Boss Frank "the Enforcer" Nitti. Nashville, Tennessee: Cumberland House.

Fischer, S. (2005) When The Mob Ran Vegas, Stories of Money, Mayhem and Murder. New York: MJF Books

Frost, T.M. & Seng, M. (1984) Organized Crime in Chicago, Myth and Reality. Chicago: Center for Urban Policy, Loyola University of Chicago.

Griffin, D. (2006) The Battle for Las Vegas: The Law vs The Mob Huntington Press, Las Vegas Nevada

Heimel, P.W. (1997) Eliot Ness, The Real Story. Coudersport, PA: Knox Books.

Helmer, W.J. & Bilek, A. J. (2004) The St. Valentine's Day Massacre, The Untold Story of the Gangland Bloodbath That Brought Down Al Capone. Nashville, Tennessee: Cumberland House.

Herion, D. (2008) Pay, Quit, or Die, Xlibris Corporation Publishing,

Herion, D. (2013) The Chicago Way, Xlibris Corporation Publishing,

Johnson, W. A., Petrenko, J., Lindberg, K., & Gladden, J. (1998) TOC in Chicago. International Review of Law Computers & Technology, 12(1), 47-73.

Kurson, R. (2002) Best American Crime Writing, The Chicago Crime Commission. New York: Vintage Books.

Lindberg, R.C. (1991) To Serve and Collect, Chicago Politics and Police Corruption from the Lager Beer Riot to the Summerdale Scandal. New York: Praeger.

Lindberg, R.C. (1999) Return to the Scene of the Crime, A Guide to infamous places in Chicago. Nashville, TN: Cumberland House.

Lindberg, R.C. (2001) Return Again to the Scene of the Crime, A Guide to even more infamous places in Chicago. Nashville, TN: Cumberland House.

McLaughlin, J.B. (1975) A Comparative Analysis of the Development of the Sicilian and American Mafia, Champaign-Urbana, IL: Police Training Institute, University of Illinois.

Napoli, A. (2004) The Mob's Guys, Virtualbbikworm.com Publishing Inc. College Station, TX.

Osterburg, J. W. & R. H. Ward (1992) Criminal Investigation, 2nd ed. Cincinnati, OH: Anderson.

Peterson, V.W. (1952) Barbarians in Our Midst, The story of the alliance of politics with crime and vice in Chicago with tentacles that reach far across the country. Boston, MA: Little, Brown and Company.

Pileggi, N. (1996) Casino, Love and Honor in Las Vegas. New York: Pocket Books.

Reppetto, T. (2004) American Mafia, A history of its rise to power. New York: Henry Holt and Company.

Roemer, W. F. Jr. (1989) Man Against the Mob, New York: Donald Fine Inc.

Roemer, W. F. Jr. (1994) The Enforcer, Spilotro: The Chicago Mob's Man Over Las Vegas, New York: Ballantine Books.

Roemer, W. F. Jr. (1995) Accardo: The Genuine Godfather, New York: Ballantine Books.

Russo, G. (2001) The Outfit, New York: Bloomsbury USA.

Russo, G. (2006) SUPERMOB, How Sidney Korshak and His Criminal Associates Became America's Hidden Power Brokers, New York: Bloomsbury USA.

Spiering, F., (1976) The Man Who Got Capone, Indianapolis/New York: The Bobbs-Merrill Company, Inc.

Touhy, J. W., (2011) WHACKED, ONE HUNDRED YEARS, MURDER AND MAYHEM IN THE CHICAGO OUTFIT, Made in the USA, Lexington, KY.

Waldron, L. & Hartmann, T., (2005) Ultimate Sacrifice, John and Robert Kennedy, the Plan for a Coup in Cuba, and the Murder of JFK, New York: Carroll & Graf Publishers, An Imprint of Avalon Publishing Group Inc.

Waldron, L. & Hartmann, T., (2009) Legacy of Secrecy, The Long Shadow of the JFK Assassination, Counter Point Press, Distributed by Publishers Group West, Berkeley, CA.

Internet Sources:

American Mafia.com
http://www.americanmafia.com/

Yahoo-Organized Crime
http://dir.yahoo.com/Society_and_Culture/crime/organized_crime/

WMOB.com
http://www.wmob.com/

The Sinatra Files
http://www.amazon.com/exec/obidos/ASIN/0812932765/rickporrellosame/104-1248193-2838338

The Center for Public Integrity
http://www.publicintegrity.org/default.aspx

FDLE Public Corruption Study
http://www.fdle.state.fl.us/publications/corruption_study/corruption_comission_final_report.html

Dan E. Moldea-Moldea.com
http://www.moldea.com/

Crime Magazine.com
http://www.crimemagazine.com/

Combined Counties-IPSN.org
http://www.ipsn.org/#.TOP

BGA-bettergov.org
http://www.bettergov.org/

The New Criminoligist
http://www.newcriminologist.co.uk/article.asp?aid=1161295533

Chicago Crime Commission.org
http://www.chicagocrimecommission.org/

Northwestern University: Homicides in Chicago 1870 to 1930
http://homicide.northwestern.edu/

CPSIA information can be obtained at www.ICGtesting.com
Printed in the USA
LVOW09s1634210514

386773LV00014B/652/P